Women and madness in the early Romantic novel

Manchester University Press

Women and madness in the early Romantic novel

Manchester University Press

Women and madness in the early Romantic novel

Injured minds, ruined lives

Deborah Weiss

MANCHESTER UNIVERSITY PRESS

Copyright © Deborah Weiss 2024

The right of Deborah Weiss to be identified as the author
of this work has been asserted in accordance with the
Copyright, Designs and Patents Act 1988.

Published by Manchester University Press
Oxford Road, Manchester, M13 9PL

www.manchesteruniversitypress.co.uk

British Library Cataloguing-in-Publication Data
A catalogue record for this book is available from the British
Library

ISBN 978 1 5261 7571 7 hardback

First published 2024

The publisher has no responsibility for the persistence or
accuracy of URLs for any external or third-party internet
websites referred to in this book, and does not guarantee that
any content on such websites is, or will remain, accurate or
appropriate.

Typeset
by Cheshire Typesetting Ltd, Cuddington, Cheshire

To Francis and Owen, the best boys that ever were, who snored and twitched in their beds by my side for two years while I worked on this book. And to my husband Fred and my daughter Louise, who keep me endlessly entertained.

Contents

Acknowledgements	viii
Introduction: women and madness in the early Romantic novel	1
1. Madness and Maria: *The Wrongs of Woman* and patriarchal control	41
2. Of madness and monitors: *Secresy; or, the Ruin on the Rock*	73
3. Death by despair: fatal melancholia in *The Victim of Prejudice*	101
4. Misplaced passions, erroneous associations, and remorse: madness reconsidered in *Belinda*	134
5. The impossibility of love-madness: *The Father and Daughter*	173
Coda: *Wide Sargasso Sea* – the erasure of love-madness and the mad woman's revenge	203
Select bibliography	214
Index	227

Acknowledgements

I explored ideas for this book over two years with three classes of students at the University of Alabama. These years corresponded exactly to the emergence and worsening of the COVID-19 crisis, which makes my students' consistent enthusiasm for unfamiliar texts and their ability to generate insights all the more remarkable. I am grateful to the undergraduates in 'Jane Austen and the Injured Body' (EN 433 Spring 2020) and 'Mad Women of Romanticism' (EN 433 Spring 2022) and to the graduate students in 'From Defiance to Despair: Madness and the Post-Revolutionary Feminist Novel' (EN 674 Spring 2021) who did extraordinary work in class that semester entirely via Zoom. All these students contributed to the development of my ideas about the topic and to interpretations of the novels that ended up in this book. I'd also like to thank the circulation and Interlibrary Loan staff at the University of Alabama's Gorgas Library for ensuring the prompt and consistent flow of research materials that made this book possible.

I am particularly grateful to several very generous friends and colleagues who read parts of this book in manuscript along the way. My thanks to Steve Arata of the University of Virginia for his enthusiasm about the project in its early stages and for his willingness to read more than his share of proposal drafts and chapters – and of course, as always, for his love of *Belinda*. I'd also like to thank my colleagues at the University of Alabama – Steve Tedeschi, Albert Pionke, and Jolene Hubbs – for their useful comments and suggestions and for their remarkable promptness in reading drafts of chapters. And last but certainly not least, my thanks to my husband, Fred Whiting, for his decades-long service as reader of drafts and baker of delicious things.

Introduction: women and madness in the early Romantic novel

Bertha Rochester is certainly one of the most recognizable mad women in British literary history. But well before Charlotte Brontë wrote *Jane Eyre*, women authors of an earlier generation used their novels to expose the causal relationship between male power and female madness. This study focuses on Mary Wollstonecraft, Eliza Fenwick, Mary Hays, Maria Edgeworth, and Amelia Opie, women authors who, as the eighteenth century ended and the nineteenth began, wrote novels in which the protagonist or another important female character experiences a prolonged bout of madness caused entirely or in part by privileged men. Each of these authors recognized that a cluster of related avenues of male control – namely, guardianship, libertinism, marriage, and gendered Rousseauvian educational ideas – inflicted sufficient damage on women to result in psychological harm and even madness.[1] Moreover, they understood that these avenues of control were aided and abetted by two seemingly unrelated, even antithetical, discourses dedicated to explaining human sickness and health: the scientific and the imaginative; or, more precisely, medicine and literature. These five authors saw that medical models for mental disease and the popular literary figure of the love-mad maid provided rationales for male domination that explained women's madness through inherent physical and mental weakness, thereby making it possible for male guardians, seducers, lovers, and husbands to hide their culpability for injuring women. All these authors recognized that the novel, through its ability to locate psychologized characters within a complex socio-cultural environment, could be used to expose the practices of a society in which men were allowed free rein to abuse women. And they realized that by telling stories about psychologically complex women, they could critique the gender-based power dynamics rooted in medical and sentimental discourses that facilitated male power by circulating models of inherent female frailty. Mary Wollstonecraft is the best known of the five authors, and her *The Wrongs of Woman; or, Maria*, with its setting in a madhouse, is most obviously about mental illness. But Fenwick in *Secresy*, Hays in *Victim of Prejudice*, Edgeworth in

2   *Women and madness in the early Romantic novel*

Belinda, and Opie in *The Father and Daughter*, at exactly the same historical moment, also challenged the prevailing models for female madness by directing causality away from female weakness and toward, with varying degrees of emphasis, structures of male privilege and male power.

Mary Wollstonecraft was, of course, the most prominent advocate for women's rights during the early Romantic period. She and her close associates Mary Hays and Eliza Fenwick were among those who had hoped that the Revolution in France would usher in dramatic reforms in Britain, including improvements to the lives of women. In a rush of enthusiasm for change, Wollstonecraft wrote *A Vindication of the Rights of Woman* (1792), which argued for reforming societal structures that subjugated women by keeping them uneducated, overly sexualized, and dependent on male attention and financial support. Wollstonecraft and her circle were optimistic that the time had finally come for England to break away from traditional social practices and legal structures that oppressed women. The tide turned very quickly, however, against those who anticipated radical social change when the French Revolution veered into violence and France declared war on Britain in 1793. Wollstonecraft and Hays, as well-known female intellectuals and advocates for women's rights, were vilified in the conservative press during this 'anti-Jacobin' period. The disappointments and harassments of the early Romantic period are evident in late-century novels by Wollstonecraft, Fenwick, and Hays, in which female madness can be understood as reflecting the failure of the authors' revolutionary ambitions. Rather than present protagonists who successfully strive for independence and happiness, these novels tell stories about intelligent, admirable women so injured by male guardians, lovers, libertines, and husbands as to fall into debilitating, often fatal, states of mental disease. In these stories, the characters struggle unsuccessfully against hysteria and melancholia because men and male-controlled institutions deny them legal rights, fill their minds with romantic expectations, and school them into dependence. These novels of political disillusion conclude in tragedy when the protagonists' minds are injured to the point of madness and their lives are destroyed by the avenues of male control their authors thought the Revolution would abolish.

In contrast, Edgeworth and Opie were not disappointed revolutionaries, but rather political moderates hoping for reform.[2] While they agreed with Wollstonecraft, Fenwick, and Hays that medical and sentimental models of female madness perpetuated fallacious ideas about women's inherent debility, they did not agree that systemic male privilege was the primary cause of women's mental afflictions. Indeed, they disagreed so extensively with Wollstonecraft, Fenwick, and Hays about gendered power dynamics and male-inflicted injury that their novels can be seen to constitute a revision of their contemporaries' narratives of harm. While Edgeworth and Opie recognized the harm men could do to women, their novels express a far less totalizing and pessimistic account of male power, and they present women as moral agents who can help one another, rather than as isolated victims of male control. In their narratives, avenues of male power – Rousseauvian education in Edgeworth's novel and libertinism in Opie's – contribute to female madness but are not its only cause. Instead, women's madness in their novels comes from erroneous associations, misplaced passions, and remorse. Edgeworth and Opie offer alternative causalities and possible remedies for madness that stem from a less victimized perspective and, in Edgeworth's case, a greater knowledge of psychologized medical thinking.

Although Edgeworth and Opie did not believe women were trapped in a web of male control, they did, like Wollstonecraft, Fenwick, and Hays, revise both medical and literary models that presented women's mental afflictions as the result of inherent, physical weakness. They, like the other three, rejected the dominant medical understanding of women's madness that still, at the turn of the nineteenth century, held that the weak, aberrant female body explained such conditions as hysteria, mania, and melancholia. Instead, they presented female madness as a psychological condition caused by emotional responses to circumstances and events. Moreover, all five authors rejected the traditional literary model of female mental affliction by revising the figure of the love-mad maid – the woman who loses her mind when she loses her man. By using complex plots and psychologized characterizations, Wollstonecraft, Fenwick, and Hays, as well as Edgeworth and Opie, showed that women's mental afflictions were not caused by the impact of disappointed love on feminine sensibility, nor by the influence of an inflamed imagination on a dysfunctional reproductive system, but rather by cumulative, male-inflicted injuries, the shock of traumatic experience on the human psyche, or remorse stemming from deeds that could not be undone. In their stories, the love-mad maid is no longer a figure driven mad by the loss of her lover but is instead a woman either debilitated by socially sanctioned male abuse or tormented by the consequences of her own actions. In either case, her multi-faceted, psychologically complex story exposes the standard versions of female madness to be lies perpetuated by male medical authors and sentimental literary traditions.

The special case of Rousseau's *Émile; or, On Education*

Perhaps surprisingly, given the authors' focus on madness, it is not a medical, but rather a literary, writer who is shown to consistently cause women's mental afflictions. Four of the five authors in *Injured Minds* view Jean-Jacques Rousseau as a primary factor in perpetuating men's control over women through inflicting psychological damage on them.[3] Although Wollstonecraft focuses on the erotic trap of *Julie: ou, La Nouvelle Héloïse* (1761), Fenwick, Hays, and Edgeworth all see *Émile* (1762) and its gendered educational programme as a source of considerable harm to women.[4] *Émile* does not feature in *Wrongs of Woman*, but Wollstonecraft had identified Rousseau's educational novel in *A Vindication of the Rights of Woman* as the purveyor of a dangerous and fundamentally erroneous educational plan for girls.[5] In Chapter V, entitled 'Animadversions on Some of the Writers who have Rendered Women Objects of Pity, Bordering on Contempt,' she began with Rousseau and offered an extended critique of his ideas about gender, most notably his claims that women should be weak and passive, that they were formed to please and be subject to men, and that women's education should always be focused on caring for and serving men.[6] Wollstonecraft clearly saw a connection between Rousseau and influential English programmes for women's education, as she placed critiques of the popular conduct books *Sermons to Young Women* (1766) by James Fordyce and *A Father's Legacy to his Daughters* (1774) by John Gregory within the same chapter on 'Animadversions.'[7] In *Secresy*, *Belinda*, and to a lesser extent *Victim of Prejudice*, Fenwick, Edgeworth, and Hays all identify Rousseau's gendered educational ideas as particularly injurious to women. Each of the three finds fault with Rousseau's belief that education – for boys or girls – should be carried out away from society, opposing Rousseau's methods in part because they believe such isolation would breed vice rather than virtue in boys and ignorance in girls. Fenwick and Edgeworth expose Rousseauvian education as a fantasy of male control designed, as Wollstonecraft noted in the second *Vindication*, to make grown women into passive, sexually desirable children. Wollstonecraft's critique of *Émile* in the *Vindication* was more sociological than psychological; in contrast, both Fenwick and Edgeworth demonstrate through their novels that Rousseauvian educational ideas are among the most psychologically injurious of all patriarchal avenues of control.

Definitions and terminology

My approach to the mental afflictions and emotional disturbances within these novels relies on terminology that would have been recognizable in the last decade of the eighteenth century. Thus, to a great extent, I have adopted the language of the times in an attempt to convey how the authors and their readers might have understood conditions that compromised rational thought, disrupted emotional balance, and/or prompted a physiological response that impacted motor control. Although the term 'madness' is perhaps offensive to readers who might prefer the language of disability, it is a word with a rich history evoking the blend of the literary and the medical that forms the contextual background for this study.[8] 'Madness' as it was employed during my authors' lifetimes was a broad and loose term covering conditions that compromised the individual's mental or emotional functioning or both.[9] That madness could be either cognitive or affective is evident in Samuel Johnson's *Dictionary*. His first definition for 'madness' is 'distraction; loss of understanding; perturbation of the faculties,' which explains madness as a severely altered cognitive state. His second is 'fury; wildness; rage,' to which he adds for 'mad,' 'over-run with any violent or unreasonable desire.'[10] This second definition indicates a condition of emotional disorder or the complete loss of emotional control. My choice of the term 'mental affliction,' which I use as well as 'madness,' is an attempt to refine the idea of madness into a condition that falls short of a cognitive state in which the individual cannot differentiate between what is real and what is not, or an affective state so debilitating as to interfere with all daily functioning. The commonly used eighteenth-century term 'affliction' – a disease or condition causing ill health or pain, or an illness or ailment – captures the distress experienced by the novels' characters without sounding too anachronistic or necessitating a particular diagnosis.[11] Some characters appear mad because they cannot differentiate the real from the imaginary or are temporarily unable, because of emotional shock, to process information. Some faint, convulse, or experience paralysis due to an emotional injury that has compromised their physical control. And some are so overcome by melancholy that their lives are prematurely ended by despair. These episodes of madness are all afflictions, not diseases or medical conditions, because – as I make clear in the course of my argument – they are caused by social rather than somatic disorders. If there is a chronic disease in these novels, it lies deep within the structure of patriarchal power, with its symptomology being the array of mental and emotional afflictions suffered by women as victims of that power.

One of the difficulties of a study like this is that the mental and emotional afflictions of today are not the same as in the past; but neither are they so alien as to be unintelligible. Our medical diagnoses and popular terms are the descendants of the medical diagnoses and popular terms of the late eighteenth century, which creates opportunities for understanding, as well as the potential for confusion. The key eighteenth-century terms of mania, hysteria, melancholia, and hypochondria are still used today, but their meanings are no longer as capacious or as central to models of mental affliction as they once were. Broadly speaking, the narrowly medical elements of these conditions have over time been redistributed into new clinical profiles, while the popular meanings have remained in a reduced form from which metaphorical suggestion and historical reach has been drained. For example, hysteria is no longer an ancient medical diagnosis with a wide and protean symptomology. The term now is used colloquially only to describe a state of extreme emotional excitement in which rational thinking is compromised, although it maintains its historical connection to exaggerated female feeling and lack of emotional self-control. The somatic elements that once were central to hysteria's profile have been separated into a variety of other conditions including anxiety disorder, post-traumatic-stress disorder, and functional or conversion disorder.[12] Melancholy has also lost its broad meaning, with the term itself now used primarily as an adjective to label a mood or landscape rather than to describe either a temperament or a chronic condition inclusive of fear and sadness. An ancient affliction, melancholia has been reduced in scope and changed to depression, which is a term that in its psychological meaning can be traced to the middle of the eighteenth century, when it was used to describe just one aspect of the melancholic condition. Hypochondria, which in the eighteenth century overlapped with hysteria and melancholia and was considered a physical ailment originating in the abdomen, lost its medical significance by the early nineteenth century and acquired its current meaning as a condition of psychosomatic or imagined illness.

It is the case that the words we now use colloquially to describe compromised mental or emotional states are descended from and related to the same or similar words of the past. But because the terms in the past were so broad and overlapping, and because they were used medically to explain conditions largely understood as somatic in origin, we cannot assume a direct correlation between the hysteria, hypochondria, and melancholy of yesterday and today. As G. S. Rousseau says of depression, 'to remove the lexical boundaries, anachronistically impose the newer psychological depression back on to the eighteenth century, violates history, linguistic usage, and the context of unfolding grief and the guilt usually accompanying it.'[13] With Rousseau's injunction against linguistic presentism in mind, I have for the most part avoided anachronistically applying current psychiatric terms and colloquial usages backwards and have tried not to treat conditions of the past as if they were equivalent to modern mental illnesses. That said, there are times when the current colloquial language of mental health as well as modern psychiatric terminology can help readers comprehend the experiences and sufferings of the characters. So I do, from time to time, use such phrases as 'mental illness,' 'trauma,' and 'depression' to help my readers better understand the manifestations of mental and emotional distress they might otherwise find melodramatic, unrealistic, or even absurd.

Women and madness in the early Romantic novel 7

A term I use frequently that was not common in the late eighteenth century is 'psychological' (or 'psychology'). However, my use of the word is intentional in that it conveys a new conceptualization of the mind that was central to how the authors covered in *Injured Minds* understood madness. In effect, 'psychology' as we conceive of it today was under construction in the latter eighteenth century with the result that, according to Neil Vickers, the term became 'associated with the study of mental experience of all kinds' in the Romantic period.[14] The first definition the *OED* offers for 'psychology' is the 'study or consideration of the soul or spirit,' from 1654. The second definition registers the impact of the Scientific Revolution and its shift to material investigations and explanations: 'The scientific study of the nature, functioning, and development of the human mind, including the faculties of reason, emotion, perception, communication, etc.' One of the examples illustrating this definition is from David Hartley's *Observations on Man* (1749), which states that 'psychology' is the 'Theory of the human Mind, with that of the intellectual Principles of Brute Animals.'[15] The shifting definition over a century reflects the way, as G. S. Rousseau puts it, that psychology seemed to 'blend into' and 'emerge from philosophy.'[16] The development of a psychological perception of mind led to what Akihito Suzuki describes as a '"psychologized" understanding of madness,' one that 'compelled medical theorists and practitioners to employ language of the contemporary philosophy of mind' and to reject a medical approach reliant on ideas of nervous predispositions and physical sickness.[17] A case in point is Alexander Crichton's *An Inquiry Into the Nature And Origin of Mental Derangement* (1798), in which Crichton uses the term 'psychologists' to describe those who study the workings of the human mind.[18] Each of the five authors in this study, to varying degrees, conceptualized the mind as consisting of the faculties of reason and emotion in interaction with one another and with the environment. Their belief that madness and mental afflictions came from emotional distress rather than from the inherently weak female body stems from this emergent, modern, 'psychologized' understanding of the mind.

Feminist criticism and female madness: a short history

Madness was once central to how feminist critics understood women's writing. As Helen Small has observed, 'the attraction of the madwoman as a deconstructive key to all texts produced under patriarchy is evident.'[19] In the late 1970s, Sandra Gilbert and Susan Gubar famously identified the madwoman as the embodiment of female authorial rage and claimed that before the twentieth century all women writers were debilitated by illness, madness, and paralysis.[20] In assessing women authors, they used the language of their times to name female afflictions – anxiety, anorexia, agoraphobia, claustrophobia, neurosis, schizophrenia – and made mental illness a pre-condition of writing for women. The argument of *The Madwoman in the Attic* – that women authors projected passivity while creating figures who found power through their madness – was widely replicated in subsequent feminist criticism. As Elaine Showalter observed a few years after *Madwoman* was published, 'for many feminist theorists, the madwoman is a heroine, a powerful figure who rebels against the family and the social order; and the hysteric who refuses to speak the language of the patriarchal order, who speaks otherwise, is a sister.'[21] Indeed, feminist critics in the wake of Gilbert and Gubar viewed women's madness in general, and hysteria more specifically, as a form of female protest tied to the common, fundamental experience of living as a woman in patriarchal society. For example, Juliet Mitchell wrote that 'hysteria is the woman's simultaneous acceptance and refusal of the organisation of sexuality under patriarchal capitalism. It is simultaneously what a woman can do both to be feminine and to refuse femininity, within patriarchal discourse.'[22] In this vein, Mary Jacobus asked, 'Can women's writing ever be anything other than hysterical?'; and she quoted Julia Kristeva's assertion that 'women's writing is "the discourse of the hysteric"' and Mitchell's claim that "'the woman novelist must be an hysteric.'"[23] Even after the majority of feminist critics abandoned such positions, the idea of hysteria as a protest language has persisted. In a recent article on motherhood and hysteria, Heather Meek has written, 'More than mere bodily excess and passion, hysteria becomes in some of the literature produced by women a form of potential resistance – a revolt against the constraints and limitations of motherhood.'[24] Such a comment, almost 40 years after the publication of *Madwoman in the Attic*, suggests the ongoing attraction of madness for feminist critics.

Elaine Showalter and Helen Small were among the feminist critics who early on objected to seeing women's madness as a form of power and resistance. Showalter insisted on looking at hysteria not as a cause for celebration, but rather as an ancient vehicle used for the oppression of women. Noting how long hysteria had served as a biologically based catch-all for women's afflictions, she observed that one of the most surprising turns in the long history of hysteria was the 'modern marriage of hysteria and feminism, the fascination [with hysteria] among feminist intellectuals [and] literary critics.' She criticized scholars influenced by semiotics and discourse theory for seeing hysteria as a 'specifically feminine protolanguage, communicating through the body messages that cannot be verbalized.'[25] And in a separate article, Showalter maintained that 'to label women's writing "hysterical" is to denigrate it as art ... Feminist critics should be especially aware that

Women and madness in the early Romantic novel

labelling women's texts, and especially feminist texts, as "hysterical" has long been a device of ridicule and trivialization.'[26] With a position similar to Showalter's, Small took feminist critics to task for universalizing and celebrating a condition that 'risks culpably reinscribing women in precisely the debilitating gender constructions feminism might hope to free them from, equating them once again with irrationality, silence, nature, and body.'[27] Small added that the celebration of literary madness 'ignores the medical history of women's relationship to madness – hysteria and depression have been far from liberating.'[28]

Although Small's *Love's Madness* is now over 25 years old and Showalter's *The Female Malady* is more than a decade older than that, both offer important insights and useful models for returning to the topic of female madness. Showalter and Small found fault with the feminist understanding of madness of the 1980s and 1990s, not only because it echoed historically misogynistic attitudes, but also because it was divorced from the specificity of the past. In their own work, they stressed the importance of careful attention to medical and social history and to the use of generic representations. Their approach understands female madness as it was represented in literature to be an articulation of gender ideologies that were constructed in tandem with the development of medical ideas. In the hands of women authors, Small and Showalter believed, madness could function as a critique of patriarchal power; but it was also deeply intertwined with the society's understanding of female frailty and could be mobilized for repressive political purposes.[29] Showalter's *The Female Malady* begins in 1830 and is directly concerned with the Victorian period, while Small's *Love's Madness* touches briefly on the 1790s before moving on to the later Romantic period and the nineteenth century. *Injured Minds* is inspired by these two historicist works, most particularly by Small's *Love's Madness* in which one of the most important insights is to see that literary convention functions as a vehicle through which writers – in this case women writers – might interpret, critique, and reformulate ideas. Small encourages those who understand literature as a place of female expression where the meaning of femininity is 'constantly being reinvented' to pay attention to 'the nature of literary convention and the degree to which it can be resisted, reformed, or, for that matter, rejected.'[30] Although such attention to the ideologies conveyed by convention is by now commonplace, scholars have, in the more than two decades since Small's book was published, paid little attention to the convention of love-madness.

Despite the role women's madness once played in feminist histories of British literature, it has received only limited attention in recent years. There is room, I would argue, for considerably more research into this topic, both from a strictly historicist angle like my own and from other

10   *Women and madness in the early Romantic novel*

frameworks, such as disabilities studies, that might offer different perspectives. Female madness in literature has a very long history, and whether it appears in texts by male or female authors, it offers fertile ground for scholars interested in uncovering more about how women's health was both understood and deployed in the past. *Injured Minds* isolates from the lengthy literary history of female madness one very short period – 1795 to 1801 – years in which the rapid collapse of radical political ambitions led to a hardening of restrictions on women. In looking at the early Romantic period, *Injured Minds* stands as the first monograph on female madness dedicated entirely to pre-Victorian literature.[31] While there is a pressing need for a full-length account of female mental affliction in the long eighteenth century, my reason for choosing a short period is primarily this: long overviews are invaluable, but what they offer in breadth, they must inevitably sacrifice in depth. There are important cultural, legal, and ideological continuities across the long eighteenth century that are relevant to a study of female literary madness, such as restrictions on employment, property rights, education, and political representation, as well as expectations for gender expression, marriage and motherhood, and the experience of sexual abuse. But while a broad survey can link particular texts to particular restrictions, expectations, and experiences, it cannot reveal the nuances of difference in how women authors living at the same time understood their lives, their sufferings, and their options; nor can a long survey discuss in any detail how authors used similar literary resources to express this understanding. And a long survey cannot uncover the ways that women, living at the same historical moment, could be in dialogue with one another about the most important topics of the day. The turbulent late 1790s deserves close attention, as it was a time when new forms of narrative developed, alternative ways of understanding mental disease emerged, and feminism was forced into an accommodation with increasingly restrictive ideas about gender identity and female agency outside the home. It is therefore a period full of potential for scholars seeking to better understand the role of women's health in the development of women's literature, the novel, and feminist thought.

Madness in the eighteenth century and early Romantic period

The eighteenth century was a time of considerable change in the way British society understood madness. Prior to the last third or so of the eighteenth century, physiological and theological models dominated explanations of insanity, which was generally held to be a physical ailment that caused the soul to lose its way.[32] Anatomical developments of the Scientific Revolution

Women and madness in the early Romantic novel

led to the nervous system becoming the primary locus of disease responsible for mental afflictions for most of the eighteenth century.[33] Toward the end of the century, however, empirical philosophy intersected with anatomical science to occasion a shift toward more psychologized explanations of madness and other mental ailments. At the same time, the belief that madness was primarily a deficit in reason was slowly being replaced by a model more reliant on disorders of the passions.

Johnson's *Dictionary*, which describes madness as both cognitive and affective, provides a revealing mid-century snapshot of madness in transition. On the one hand, madness was, as Michel Foucault explains, a kind of self-deception arising from the individual's inability to reason correctly.[34] The madness Foucault describes – the madness of cognitive affliction – was constituted, in Andrew Scull's words, by the 'preternatural force with which certain irrational ideas dominated the mind, heedless of the ordinary corrective processes proved by experience and persuasion.'[35] This sort of madness was thus a disconnection from, or misinterpretation of, the reality of the empirical world as observed and understood by others. In the early part of the eighteenth century, medical and popular writers emphasized the force of the deluded imagination that sent the wrong messages to the mind. Locke, for example, believed the madness of cognitive error arose from wrong reasoning based on people taking the workings of their imaginations for reality: 'For they do not appear to me to have lost the faculty of Reasoning: But having joined together some Ideas very wrongly, they mistake them for Truths; and they err as Men do that argue right from wrong Principles. For by the violence of their Imaginations, having taken their Fancies for Realities, they make right deductions from them.'[36] Later in the century, more emphasis was placed on how the passions could darken or overpower reason. According to Kathleen Grange, while passions were understood to consist of all emotional states of mind, those most important to medical and moral writers were the 'predominant and neurotic obsessions toward hate, grief, wealth, and power.'[37] The shift in emphasis toward the passions and away from error and the deluded imagination marks an important milestone in the development of more modern ways of understanding mental afflictions. At the century's end, influential physicians and medical writers came to believe that madness could be caused by the impact of experience on the emotions, which then produced mental derangement, either partial or complete. In terms of the relative weight put on a psychological versus a somatic model, the psychogenic approach reached its peak in the very early nineteenth century with the work of Philippe Pinel. Thereafter, as Stanley Jackson explains, the psychogenic model, while still in play, gradually retreated as new physiological frameworks emphasizing the brain came to the fore.[38]

For most of the eighteenth century, medical writers and practitioners believed that the underlying cause of madness could be found in the nervous system. Well before the celebrated Edinburgh professor William Cullen identified nerve theory as the primary cause of mental afflictions in 1772, the nervous system dominated medical and popular thinking about what we would now understand as mental illness. As G. S. Rousseau observes, 'No topic in physiology between the Restoration and the turn of the nineteenth century was more important than the precise workings of the nerves, their intricate morphology and histological arrangement, their anatomic function.'[39] As early as 1730, a whole host of afflictions – including melancholia, hysteria, hypochondria, dementia, spleen, and vapours – were all considered nervous conditions.[40] And by the middle of the eighteenth century, the nervous system was well established in diagnostic as well as theoretical medicine.[41] In the second half of the century, all major medical writers adhered to nerve theory as the basis for their understanding of mental afflictions.

Although everyone of course had nerves, the makeup of the nervous system was believed to vary considerably according to gender and status. In explaining these differences, leading physician and medical professor Robert Whytt, for example, wrote that 'All diseases may, in some sense, be called affections of the nervous system ... However, those disorders may, peculiarly, deserve the name of nervous, which, on account of an unusual delicacy, or unnatural state of the nerves, are produced by causes, which, in people of a sound constitution, would either have no such effects, or at least in a much less degree.'[42] William Battie, physician to St Luke's Hospital and author of *A Treatise on Madness* (1758), offered slightly more clarity when he explained that the '"ill conditioned state of the nerve" derives from a defect in the fibres enveloping the nerves. Poorly constituted fibres simply will not shield the nerves from trauma and excitement.'[43] Thus, according to accepted medical thought, those with tight, well-constituted nerves were better able to withstand the impact of disturbing events compared to those whose nerves were loosely put together or made of delicate materials. For much of the period, elite men and all women above the labouring classes were believed to have delicate nerves and therefore be prone to nervous disorders. There was some sense that lifestyle could play a role, as evidenced by George Cheyne's popular *The English Malady* (1733), which argued that nervous ailments located in the body were exacerbated by inactivity and luxurious living. As Roy Porter explains, 'the nerves of fine-spirited people needed to be highly elastic and vibrant ... Among the fine-spirited, however, the danger was that high living would clog the nerves.'[44]

Women, however, did not need to indulge in high-living to be prone to nervous conditions, given that medical professionals understood the female body to be inherently weak. Whytt, for example, thought women's distinctive physiology made them susceptible to nervous conditions caused by emotional experiences. He wrote that for this reason, 'doleful or moving stories, horrible or unexpected sights, great grief, anger, terror, and other passions, frequently occasion the most sudden and violent nervous sympathies. The strong impressions made in such cases on the brain and nerves often throw the person into hysteric fits, either of the convulsive or fainting kind.'[45] The somatic origin of these afflictions has to do with the internal sympathies of the body, sympathies strongly connected to both gender and class. As Foucault explains, 'softer, more penetrable bodies are more prone to hysteria and to a disease more various in its forms. In firm bodies, where there is little available space, hysteria is rare.'[46] Female bodies, it goes without saying, were conceived of as internally soft and penetrable; but the belief in the internal delicacy of women was limited to those who did not have to labour.[47] For example, Robert James wrote in his mid-century *Medicinal Dictionary* that women 'brought up in idleness' or who were of a 'soft texture, and delicate constitution' were particularly susceptible to hysteria.[48]

Toward the end of the century, as psychologized explanations of the mind moved from moral philosophy into medicine, a small group of medical writers developed new models to explain mental affliction based on the individual's emotional response to experience. This psychologized understanding can be traced to John Locke's late-century influence, despite the fact that he is generally believed to have cast madness as a cognitive disorder. Louis Charland argues that Locke provided an innovative and ultimately influential understanding of the role of emotion in madness by showing that, while madness is a disorder in the association of ideas, 'those derangements are often the result of disordered affective states and processes.'[49] It is emotion, Charland argues, that cements ideas together incorrectly, rendering associations impervious to change and resistant to reason.[50] Although Locke laid out his affective and experiential account of madness in 1700, in the fourth edition of his *Essay Concerning Human Understanding*, it took more than half a century for medical writers to shift their focus from the body to the mind and to the mind's affective experiences and associationist tendencies. According to Akihito Suzuki, this 'drastic change in the language of psychiatry' began around 1760.[51] He writes that 'earlier medical writers conceptualized madness exclusively as a bodily disease ... With the shift of emphasis from what the mind received to what the mind did, madness became the disease of the mind *per se*, its deviation in judgement and passion.'[52] The necessary element of this shift was the melding of 'psychology,' at the time a branch of philosophy, into medical thinking through such figures

14 *Women and madness in the early Romantic novel*

of the Scottish Enlightenment as the medical writers John Gregory, William Cullen, Thomas Arnold, and Alexander Crichton. The eighteenth century thus witnessed, as Suzuki explains, 'not only the growth of a new pattern of psychiatric practice ... but also the transformation of the conceptual model of madness' to one that was considerably more 'psychologized,' thanks to the incorporation of philosophies of mind.[53] In Roy Porter's words, late eighteenth-century medicine began to understand that madness did not come from the body – be it from brain, blood, or nerves – but was an 'an authentic mental disorder, requiring treatment with "moral" or as we would say, psychological means.'[54] These new ideas were exemplified through the work of American physician Benjamin Rush and French physician Philippe Pinel, who believed some of their patients' mental diseases resulted from the traumatic emotional experience of living through a Revolution.[55]

Before the shift to psychogenic models late in the century, there was little consideration in Britain or France that madness could be cured.[56] Inmates at mental institutions were often subjected to physical deprivation, restraint, and harsh treatments based on the belief that madness was a bodily affliction that needed to be addressed by bodily control.[57] The 1790s, however, saw the development of a new treatment termed 'moral management,' epitomized by the founding of William Tuke's Quaker Retreat at York in 1792 and Philippe Pinel's release of the shackled inmates at Salpêtrière and Bicêtre in 1796.[58] Moral management rejected bodily causes of madness in favour of new psychological models, and it aimed to restore the mad to reason through humanity and kindness.[59] This 'custodial process,' as Roy Porter calls it, motivated patients to deploy their self-control in order to gain certain benefits, including the approval of the practitioner. The aim of such treatment was, according to Porter, to 'build up the self-esteem of the patients, and thus co-opt them to be motivated to act for their own improvement.'[60] The most important aspect of moral management, according to Vieda Skultans, was 'the restoration of the attributes of humanity to the insane and with it the possibility of encouraging self-control and self-discipline.'[61] Precisely because the understanding of madness had shifted to the emotions, Skultans explains, 'afflicted individuals could be helped to recover through cultivating the will, or, to be more precise, habits of self-control.'[62] Although Foucault was highly critical of moral management, seeing it as an internalization of confinement, most historians acknowledge that the movement brought about humane improvements for the insane.[63] It is the case, however, that the period in which moral management provided a relatively compassionate alternative was short-lived. Within a few decades, the medical establishment once again emphasized the body, and at this point, in Andrew Scull's

Women and madness in the early Romantic novel

words, moral management became a 'mechanism for inducing conformity' and a 'veil' that provided legitimacy for treatment programmes that were far from humane.[64]

Mania and melancholia

Most historians of psychiatry and mental illness agree that madness was not in the least a clearly defined or stable concept in the eighteenth century. Rather, different descriptions and classifications competed with one another in a kind of moving flow of symptom and affliction.[65] That said, mania and melancholia emerge out of the chaos and competing nosologies of the period to be literally written in stone as forms of madness.[66] Two statues, one personifying 'raving' (or maniacal) madness and the other 'melancholy' madness, sat atop the gates of Bethlehem Hospital in London highlighting their status as the two dominant types of eighteenth-century mental derangement.[67] The characteristics of mania and melancholia are laid out by Foucault, who draws on Thomas Willis (1621–1675), one of the great British figures in the history of medicine.

> Willis opposes mania to melancholia. The mind of the melancholic is entirely occupied by reflection, so that his imagination remains at leisure and in repose; the maniac's imagination, on the contrary, is occupied by a perpetual flux of impetuous thoughts. While the melancholic's mind is fixed on a single object, imposing unreasonable proportions upon it, but upon it alone, mania deforms all concepts and ideas ... the totality of thought is disturbed in its essential relation to truth. Melancholia, finally, is always accompanied by sadness and fear; on the contrary, in the maniac we find audacity and fury.[68]

Foucault's interpretation of mania and melancholia in what he terms the 'Classical Period' conforms to what other historians and literary authors of the period also observe: that the melancholic is preoccupied by fear and sadness and fixated on a single object, while the maniac is highly energized and lacks mental lucidity as his or her mind is flooded with a rush of uncontrollable thoughts and images.[69]

Mania, a form of wild, uncontrolled delusion, was much less interesting to medical writers and the culture at large in the eighteenth century than was melancholia, a depressive condition believed to be endemic to the English. Skultans notes that when melancholy as a medical diagnosis became increasingly common in the eighteenth century, 'it acquired many new names' which included 'the spleen, vapours, hypochondriasis, hysteric fits, the hyp and finally and most aptly the "English malady."'[70]

But despite melancholia's nebulous blending into spleen and other nervous disorders, historians studying the condition have been able to locate significant consistencies in its description over a considerable length of time. At its core, eighteenth-century melancholy retained its connection to its etymological roots: melancholia is a Latin transliteration of a Greek word, which meant a 'mental disorder involving prolonged fear and depression.'[71] In the eighteenth century, the condition was usually described as a 'form of madness and as a chronic illness without fever' which often involved 'a state of dejection and fearfulness without an apparent cause, and some particular circumscribed delusion.'[72] That melancholy could meld into madness can be seen in Bernard Mandeville's *A Treatise of the Hypochondriack and Hysterick Diseases* (1730). Allan Ingram and Stuart Sim explain that, according to Mandeville, 'among the features of a melancholy mind is the tendency to imagine the worst in any given situation, to build, perhaps upon trifles – fancies, the merest suggestions ... and to become so obsessed that only an "utmost" exertion of the "Soul" can return the mind to "things as they really are."'[73] According to eighteenth-century medical beliefs, the madness of melancholy came not so much from an individual's pervasive sadness as it did from his or her anxiety and obsessive thoughts.

As the eighteenth century progressed, melancholy's fear and fixation did not disappear; however, the condition's historically attractive and even prestigious qualities came more to the fore with a renewed emphasis on depression, or 'depressed spirits.'[74] Melancholia's prestige came from its ancient connection to genius and from the emergence of new associations with sympathy and taste within the culture of sensibility. Although melancholy's link to genius had faded after the Renaissance, it re-emerged at the end of the eighteenth century to once more become a noble feature of the soul. As Jennifer Radden observes, 'again the suffering of melancholy was associated with greatness; again it was idealized, as inherently valuable and even pleasurable, although dark and painful. The melancholy man was one who felt more deeply, saw more clearly, and came closer to the sublime than ordinary mortals.'[75] As the culture of sensibility developed, melancholia became linked to the idea that superior individuals possessed finer nerves which made them more virtuous through sensitivity to their own suffering and to that of others.[76] Melancholy also became associated with the superior individual's ability to experience a more profound sense of beauty and to appreciate the aesthetics of mood within an environment.[77] By the end of the century, melancholia as an affliction contained more of depression, combined with genius and sensibility, than it did anxiety and mental fixation.

Hypochondriasis and hysteria

Among the most commonly diagnosed illnesses of the eighteenth century, hypochondriasis and hysteria – according to Foucault – 'slowly joined the domain of mental diseases.'[78] Both were ancient afflictions long associated with abdominal causation (the spleen for men and women, the uterus for women alone), and both covered an array of symptoms that eventually came under the rubric of 'nervous' disorders. Hypochondriasis, with a messy and imprecise set of symptoms, was often understood as the male, and thus less severe, form of hysteria; at the same time, it overlapped considerably with melancholia.[79] The blending of hypochondriasis into melancholia can been seen in James Boswell's column 'The Hypochondriack' in which he describes and discusses a condition similar to today's blend of depression and anxiety. By the late eighteenth century, however, hypochondria had taken on a meaning similar to how it is understood today. According to the provincial physician and author Thomas Arnold, writing in 1782, an hypochondriacal patient is 'forever in distress about his own state of health, has a variety of disagreeable, and sometimes painful feelings, to which he is ever anxiously attentive, and from which he can rarely divert his thoughts.'[80] Hypochondria's history in the eighteenth century, then, is that it originates as an ancient, multi-faceted disease rooted in abdominal disorder, becomes indistinguishable from spleen or the vapours, overlaps with melancholia, is classified as a nervous disorder of men, and ends as a condition of excessive preoccupation with, and fancies about, one's own health. No condition better represents the shifting of eighteenth-century mental afflictions from somatic to psychogenic causes than hypochondriasis, which begins in the body and ends in the mind.

Hysteria also demonstrates the shiftiness of eighteenth-century mental illnesses and the importance of gender to how such afflictions were conceptualized. However, unlike hypochondriasis, its sometime male corollary, hysteria does not become a psychologized affliction at the end of the century. On the contrary, it remains tethered to somatic causes, although those causes move from the uterus to the nerves and back to the uterus. A woman's disease, hysteria has been linked for its entire history to the belief that the female body is inherently disordered.[81] Texts from the fifth century BC school of Hippocrates explain that the uterus, as Mark Micale puts it, 'rampages destructively through the female body cavity [causing] dizziness, motor paralyses, sensory losses, and respiratory distress as well as extravagant emotional behaviours.'[82] Hysteria's cure, when it was understood to be exclusively a physical disorder of the womb, was long believed to be marriage, which offered the womb the sexual intercourse and resulting pregnancy it supposedly craved.[83] Over time, hysteria exhibited an abundance of physical symptoms, thanks to the womb's malign capacity (as was generally believed) to move throughout the body. Hysteria had, in G. S. Rousseau's words, a 'protean ability' to be sustained 'without a stable set of causes and effects or, more glaringly, a category identifiable by commonly agreed upon characteristics.'[84] Hysteria as a diagnosis for much of the eighteenth century was complicated by an unstable and messy set of other afflictions, including hypochondria, melancholia, spleen, vapours, and nerves – all of which constituted, as Heather Meek puts it, 'indistinguishable conditions with a plethora of overlapping physical and mental symptoms.'[85] Hysteria's open-endedness as a diagnosis comes in part from the historical misogyny of doctors and medical authors who used the term, according to Micale, to describe 'everything that men found irritating or irascible, mysterious or unmanageable, in the opposite sex,' and who considered the unstable symptomology to 'mirror the irrational, capricious, and unpredictable nature of Woman.'[86] Leading eighteenth-century medical writers perpetually showcased hysteria's wide-ranging and imprecise symptomology. Robert Whytt, for example, observed that 'many hysteric women are liable to be seized with faintings,' as well as with 'catchings and strong convulsions.' The fits could be accompanied by coldness, stiffness in limbs or body, low spirits, a feeling of oppression in the precordia, wind in the stomach or gas, the feeling of a ball in the throat, shortness of breath, a fluttering heart, giddiness, loss of sight, and a noise in the ears.[87] Although hysteria was protean and open-ended in medical descriptions and diagnosed for a range of ills, it did display a degree of symptomatic consistency, namely a globule in the throat (called 'suffocation of the mother'), fainting, palpitations, difficulty breathing, and convulsions.[88]

After more than a millennium of blaming the womb directly for its chaotic movements through the body, medical authorities accepted seventeenth-century anatomical studies that revealed the uterus could not roam. But doctors and medical writers and the culture at large still considered women's bodies to be responsible for the hysterical affliction. Authors of influential medical texts determined that the female nervous system was weaker than the male and that women's bodies were internally softer and more susceptible to the injuries of emotional shock.[89] For example, although the anatomist Thomas Willis is often given credit for insisting that the uterus could not rise, he still maintained that women, by virtue of their weaker physical constitutions, were much more susceptible than men to hysteria.[90] And Robert Whytt, at a time when the wandering womb had long been disproven, wrote: 'Women, in whom the nervous system is generally more moveable than in men, are more subject to nervous complaints, and have them in a higher degree,' and he connected this sensitivity directly to the reproductive capacities.[91] With the rise of nervous disorders as an explanatory model for mental afflictions, the connection between the womb and hysteria became less direct; nonetheless, medical writers were still able to figure out how its influence persisted. In his mid-century *Medicinal Dictionary*, Robert James explained that the uterus, with its corrupt 'seminal juices' and the 'peccant state' of its menstrual blood could exert a malign influence on women's bodies and minds: 'I am fully persuaded, that it [hysteria] arises from the womb, and its membranes and vessels … and that the spasmodic structure of these parts communicates itself to the adjacent nerves.'[92] According to this model, although the uterus itself cannot move, it can transfer its influence to other parts of the body via the brain and nervous system and thereby cause hysterical symptoms, such as pains in the back, limpid urine, troubled breathing, seizures, convulsions, and emotions that 'know no moderation and are constant only in inconstancy.'[93] As Foucault explains the period's gendered understanding of physiology, the female body 'from one extremity of its organic space to the other … encloses a perpetual possibility of hysteria.'[94] Foucault's description gets at the diffuseness of the womb's connection to hysteria throughout most of the eighteenth century. Medical writers persisted in imagining the female body as place of weakness and susceptibility based on the womb's influence, but because of the dominance of nerve theory, they believed the womb had to enact its influence on the body and mind through sympathies and secondary channels.

In the late eighteenth century, at the exact time progressive physicians and medical writers began to use more psychologized models to explain mental afflictions, medical authorities were insisting on an even more precise connection between the womb and hysteria.[95] After more than a century in which the influence of the womb on women's hysterical symptoms had been thought to arise more diffusely, via the nerves, a more immediate connection was re-established. The definition of the 'hysteric affection' in the *Encyclopaedia Britannica*, 1797–1801 edition, clearly roots the disease in the uterus: '"It is a spasmodico-convulsive affection of the nervous system, proceeding from the womb.'"[96] As the century came to a close, hysteria began to blend with a new, more directly sexual affliction called 'nymphomania' or by its older name, 'furor uterinus,' which was a condition in which women craved sex and could not be satisfied by marital relations. Hysteria was, of course, always considered a sexual pathology; but the late eighteenth century turned it into an affliction that could not, as in the past, be solved by marriage.[97] William Cullen, in his *Synopsis Methodicae* (1769) considered 'furor uterinus' or 'mania of the uterus' to be relatively common.[98] In the 1780s, he continued his discussion of the pathological category called 'libidinal hysteria' which, as Mark Micale explains, 'he likened to the new diagnosis of nymphomania, and which he proposed was caused by a turgescence of blood in the female genitalia.'[99] Nymphomania itself attracted attention in 1775 when an English translation of M. D. T. de Bienville's *Nymphomanie, ou Traité de la fureur uterine*, titled *Nymphomania, or, a Dissertation concerning the Furor Uterinus*, brought the term into circulation as a particular type of hysteria.[100] Despite the clear movement toward more psyche and less soma at the end of the eighteenth century, the medical understanding of hysteria remained rooted in women's aberrant and distinctive physiology, with the diseased sexual imagination, thanks to de Bienville's account of nymphomania, now added in.[101] Thus, the nineteenth century began with the medical establishment once again believing that women, by virtue of their bodies, were always, perpetually, on the verge of mental affliction.[102]

Love-madness and the love-mad maid

Women's madness in literature before the nineteenth century was almost always caused by a man – by his death, his betrayal, his indifference, or his unsuitability as a spouse.[103] Such love-madness would manifest itself in one of two ways: in hysteria, a condition marked by frustration, violence, and fury; or in melancholia, a state of passive, often mentally vacant, sorrow. The maniacal version of the love-mad woman was popular early in the eighteenth century and re-emerged in the nineteenth, as later Romantic preferences for emotional intensity took hold.[104] For the last third or so of the eighteenth century, the dominant form of the love-mad woman was the passive, victimized version, a figure so widespread as to appear in sophisticated literary texts, poems, ballads, paintings, prints, and operas.[105] The most influential literary incarnations of this version were Maria from Lawrence Sterne's *A Sentimental Journey* (1768); the unnamed mad woman in Bethlehem Hospital from Henry Mackenzie's *The Man of Feeling* (1771); and William Cowper's Crazy Kate. *The Task* (1785), which prompted, as Helen Small notes, a flood of imitative poetic and prose narratives in the magazines and miscellanies of the 1790s.[106] This version of the love-mad maid is quiet and subdued and has a great deal in common with another popular figure of the time: the seduced maiden. Like the seduced maiden, the love-mad maid has deeply loved one man. And, as Susan Staves says of seduced maidens, 'having once loved, though they may discover that the seducer was unworthy and did not return their love, they can never love another.'[107] However, whereas the seduced maiden generally transgresses, repents, suffers, and dies in a story that takes her from seduction to redemption and death, the love-mad maid is static, lacks a detailed history, and experiences cognitive as well as emotional disturbances. Although she is

Women and madness in the early Romantic novel   21

clearly melancholic, the most remarkable aspect of her characterization is that her cognitive function has been compromised by the emotional shock of losing her lover. Quite often she is unable to understand who or where she is or to fully process what has happened to her lost lover.[108] In Philip Martin's description, 'her mind is vulnerable to the disturbances caused by an obsession with past happiness or promises, perhaps an excessive desire for the lost object of her love. In some cases this disturbance leads to insanity and eventually even death.'[109] The love-mad maid's presentation is relatively uniform: she is mentally distracted because she has been abandoned or bereaved; she is young; she is beautiful; and she is alone. That is, she is alone until a male visitor, the protagonist of the novel or the poet himself, stops by to appreciate her beauty and weep for her loss. As Melina Esse describes the figure, the 'distracted heroine' appears to 'abandon her body,' which leaves her prey to 'the voracious and voyeuristic gaze of spectators who partake gleefully in [her] grief.'[110]

By looking at the reasons for the love-mad maid's loss, we can see how the figure permits society to divert its attention away from the systemic injustices that allow women to be mentally and emotionally injured by men. When the love-mad maid loses her mind, it is usually because her lover dies or betrays her, or because her father forbids her to marry her lover – after which her lover generally goes away and does not come back. If the lover dies from drowning in a shipwreck or from fever in the West Indies, the lovely woman who loses her mind seems to be just a victim of fate. We pity her because she wanted to be happy, but fortune has swept her lover away. However, upon closer examination, when the lover drowns or succumbs to fever, he generally has been forced to leave because of either poverty or his social status. But the vignette's focus on the pathos of the beautiful woman's loss allows the reader to overlook how issues of social inequity, ideas about women only loving once, and female financial dependency impact women's mental health. If, in a different scenario, the lover is lost because he has betrayed the woman, she seems to be yet another victim of the inevitable in a story that naturalizes libertinage. After all, the reader might think, loving women and then leaving them is something men have always done. In such cases, the reader might pity the abandoned woman without considering that society permits and even encourages such sexual predation. And in cases in which the lover dies after the father forbids the marriage, the reader might pity the woman because she is a victim of her father's tyranny. In such instances, readers may feel animosity toward this specific cruel father who, instead of caring for his daughter, has sacrificed her health and happiness for mercenary reasons. With their pity directed toward the daughter and their anger focused on the father, readers might not acknowledge the fact that male guardianship gives men a legal right to oppress women. In each of

22   *Women and madness in the early Romantic novel*

these scenarios, the reader might feel pity for the woman's loss rather than rage at the injuries she has suffered. Pity makes readers feel virtuous but does not help them recognize or condemn the systemic societal problems that have caused the love-mad maid to lose her mind.

The most famous sentimental vignettes of the love-mad maid – those featuring 'Mad Maria' in *A Sentimental Journey* and the woman in Bethlehem Hospital in *The Man of Feeling* – focus on the response of the male visitor while obscuring any vision of the larger societal problems that adversely impact women. The *Man of Feeling*'s sentimental vignette occurs when Harley, the protagonist, is touring Bethlehem Hospital. After viewing and speaking with some madmen, he notices a young woman who retains traces of gentility and beauty and whose face shows a 'dejection of that decent kind, which moves our pity unmixed with horror.'[111] The keeper tells her story to the assembled visitors: she was once affluent and fell in love with a man her father forbade her to marry, who then travelled to the West Indies where he fell ill with fever and died. The young man, while not sufficiently wealthy for the father, was a socially acceptable match. After her lover's departure, the young woman's father pressed her to marry a much older man and, as the keeper says, 'between her despair at the death of the one, and her aversion to the other, the poor young lady was reduced to the condition you see her in.'[112] The young woman notices Harley, who is weeping, says she loves him for resembling her Billy, and gives him a ring she made from gold thread. Harley pays the keeper, urging him to be kind to the woman, and leaves in tears.[113] Although the attendant gives two causes for the woman's madness – despair and aversion – the woman herself is only fixated on the loss of her lover, Billy, and on Harley's resemblance to him.[114] In this popular version of the love-mad maid vignette, the primary cause of the woman's madness – patriarchal control – is covered over by the secondary cause, the death of the worthy lover. The woman's suffering from being forced to marry an older man for money and to endure the death of her lover is made into a sentimental amusement, complete with an affecting song, for Harley's enjoyment. Indeed, he pays for his pleasure by giving the keeper (but not the woman herself) a large tip. But Harley does not only get pleasure from entering into the scene and being mistaken for Billy, he also receives moral credit for being sufficiently sensitive to attract the woman's attention and to weep for her. Since the woman herself is relatively emotionally composed, all the affective focus of the scene is on Harley, which makes the reader connect emotionally to him, rather than to her. He is not called upon to do anything, however, to assist this woman he pities, as her madness is incurable. It is enough that he weeps for her and gives her the illusion that her Billy has returned, making it possible for her to demonstrate that even in madness, she is faithful to her lost lover. In the

Women and madness in the early Romantic novel 23

end, because the reader is intended to weep along with Harley, it becomes clear that the vignette is not about the mad woman at all, but rather about Harley's and the reader's own sensibility.[115]

In another classic example of female love-madness, *A Sentimental Journey*, Yorick is also a visiting actor in the drama of female madness, but he is an actor whose erotic ambitions are much more evident than are Harley's and thus his similarity to libertines is more pronounced. Yorick's entire journey is marked by erotic conversations with beautiful women, and his visit to 'Mad Maria' is no exception. As with the scene in Bethlehem Hospital, the man of feeling weeps for the mad woman, but unlike in the *Man of Feeling*, the madwoman in *A Sentimental Journey* weeps as well. One cannot tell, however, what she is weeping for, as she has lost her lover, her goat, and her father. 'Her goat had been as faithless as her lover; and she had got a little dog in lieu of him, which she kept tied by a string to her girdle ... "Thou shalt not leave me, Sylvio," said she. I looked in her eyes and saw she was thinking more of her father than of her lover, or her little goat; for as she uttered them, the tears trickled down her cheeks.'[116] It is not clear by what mystical process Yorick determines that Maria is weeping for her father. He has learned from Maria's mother that her father died a month earlier because of anguish over Maria having lost her mind when she lost her lover. The father's death did not make Maria more mad, as her mother feared, but rather somewhat restored her to herself. Although paternal tyranny is an important contributor to female love-madness in general, Yorick has determined, with no evidence, that Maria's tears are for her father rather than for her lover, dog, or goat – a determination that eliminates patriarchal control as the cause of the woman's injury. Patriarchy in this vignette appears devoted and supportive, and far from causing young women injury, patriarchy itself is injured by the young woman's earlier, stubborn refusal to return to sanity and emotional equilibrium. Moreover, Maria's return to herself, somewhat, after her father's death seems to suggest that the father has sacrificed himself for her welfare.

Having determined that the father is the source of Maria's woe, Yorick – himself old enough to be her father – inserts himself into her story as a sympathetic actor in order to facilitate an erotic encounter with her. After Maria tells Sylvio the dog that he shall not leave her, Yorick sits next to her, weeps with her, and through a shared handkerchief the two intermingle their tears: 'I sat down close by her; and Maria let me wipe them away as they fell, with my handkerchief. I then steeped it in my own, and then in hers, and then in mine, and then I wiped hers again; and as I did it, I felt such undescribable emotions within me, as I am sure could not be accounted for from any combination of matter and motion.'[117] At this point, it is clear that the cause of Maria's sorrow does not matter because the scene's purpose is

24 *Women and madness in the early Romantic novel*

the erotic gratification and anti-materialist confirmation Yorick gets from weeping along with Maria. When Maria proposes that she wash Yorick's tear-soaked handkerchief in the stream and dry it in her bosom, she offers a clue to the true cause of her weeping.[118] Maria is not weeping for her father as Yorick supposes, but rather for her lost lover – a sentiment expressed through her comment that it would do her good to dry the handkerchief in her bosom. Doing so would be beneficial to her for the same reason the woman in Bethlehem Hospital is relieved by giving Harley the gold ring: the male visitor fills the void of the lost lover and gives the love-mad woman the sense of emotional and erotic fulfilment. Importantly, however, this feeling is only temporary because the love-mad woman cannot be cured. She exists to reinforce the idea that women are physically, emotionally, and intellectually dependent on men; and her ability to draw forth pity works to obscure the structures of male power that have injured her in the first place. In this case, the vignette transforms the male guardian and the libertine into men of feeling – into soft and sensitive men who pity, rather than injure, beautiful young women.

The love-mad maid, as she was popularized in sentimental literature of the late eighteenth and early nineteenth centuries, is not a character as much as she is an icon.[119] That is, she is a fixed, static image whose whole story could be taken in with a glance. Her presence courts no interpretation other than the simple fact that she deserves pity for having lost her mind when she lost her man. She has no detailed past, no psychological complexity, and no possibility of change. She can never be cured and so she will never develop, and thus her injuries appear to be inevitable, even perpetual. Her frequent placement outdoors reinforces the message that her condition is natural and therefore unchangeable. As an icon who expresses woman's eternal fragility and the abandoned, betrayed, or bereaved woman's lack of personhood, she has no interiority, no ability for reflection, no history beyond the tale of loss, and no psyche to be explored. And while she may be the subject of a poem or ballad, she is never the protagonist of a novel. She confirms for the reader or viewer that women are inherently frail and need to be completed by men.[120] And all that the visitor, reader, or viewer can do is offer her pity and enjoy the exquisite sorrow of her situation and the beauty that will never fade.

In their novels, the five authors featured in *Injured Minds* critique, augment, and revise love-madness to uncover the misogynistic medical models that support it and the systems of male control that it hides. Each of the five authors, in presenting a mentally afflicted character, is responding to the love-mad maid and the messages about women that she conveyed, whether or not that character is injured by a lover's betrayal. When characters in the novels are driven to madness or despair by the loss of a lover, the authors offer an extensive backstory that exposes other causal factors, such as sentimental literature, marriage, or male guardianship, making the characters' afflictions considerably more complex than simply losing their minds when they lose their man. And when the authors present characters not afflicted by the loss of a lover, the absence of erotic betrayal opens up more causal possibilities for women's afflictions. And with these possibilities, the authors offer a more complex, more psychologized, and less gendered understanding of the mind. Whereas the typical love-mad woman is intended to make readers pity what they cannot change, the mentally and emotionally afflicted figures in these novels prompt social criticism and expose the way men use their privileges and their power to injure women. In these novels, a woman never loses her mind just because she loses her man; and women's madness is never a picturesque form of camouflage for the wider abuses of men. Instead, women's madness emerges as a vehicle that exposes what the typical figures and vignettes seek to disguise: that women's mental afflictions are not caused by fate or female fragility, but rather by specific forms of patriarchal control or by the complex and ungendered workings of the human mind.

Chapter synopses

The first three chapters focus on madness as an injury inflicted by patriarchal power, with Chapter 1 covering Mary Wollstonecraft's final, unfinished novel *The Wrongs of Woman; or, Maria* (1798). The chapter argues that Wollstonecraft reworks the inter-connected medical and sentimental models for women's madness in order to expose the systems of male power that defined both health and disorder for women and that produced the states they pathologized. Although Wollstonecraft subscribed to the commonly held eighteenth-century belief that women of refinement were more susceptible than men and other women to mental afflictions, her novel demonstrates that husbands, with their legal rights and social privileges, inflict on women the injuries that cause melancholia and other nervous disorders. Wollstonecraft also identifies sentimental literature as a potent avenue of male power that, by offering itself as an antidote to the repressions of marriage, entraps women in destructive romantic fantasies. Wollstonecraft's protagonist, Maria, is ensnared by her romantic imagination while imprisoned in a madhouse by her husband, which suggests that sentimental literature is as harmful to women as the power the law gives to husbands. Wollstonecraft includes in her critique a restaging of the vignette of the love-mad maid that exposes how sentimental literature, in addition to producing distracting, destructive fantasies for women, also allows men to benefit morally from the harm they inflict. Wollstonecraft offers women some strategies for resistance in the form of life-writing and female friendship, but the novel's lack of a conclusion makes it impossible to determine if Wollstonecraft believed women could escape from the linked, psychologically destructive experiences of marriage and the romantic imagination.

The second chapter looks at the little discussed, anonymously published *Secresy; or, The Ruin on the Rock* (1795), the only novel by Wollstonecraft's friend Eliza Fenwick. The chapter argues that through writing a novel that features two mad characters – a man and a woman – Fenwick revises the narrative of love-madness to identify the nexus of male guardianship, libertinism, and gendered Rousseauvian educational ideas, rather than women's inherent weakness, as the cause of female mental affliction. In a clear rejection of medical models of female frailty, Fenwick casts Sibella Valmont as inherently both mentally and physically strong as she battles her guardian's attempt to inflict Rousseauvian ideas about women's natural passivity and docility upon her through an isolated education. She succumbs, however, to a romantic imagination, the product of social isolation and limited intellectual opportunities that make her idealize her libertine lover. Fenwick contrasts Sibella's madness with that of the young Arthur Murden, who falls more quickly and more easily into love-madness than does Sibella, which further undermines sentimental and medical models of inherent female frailty. Fenwick's novel is more pessimistic than Wollstonecraft's in that there is no ambiguity about her character's fate: she dies from melancholia and the physical effects of hysteria. Moreover, Fenwick actively destroys female friendship as a way for women to maintain their mental health, showing that women's relationships are battered by the web of male power. In the place of female friendship, Fenwick presents an option that Wollstonecraft never considered in *Wrongs of Woman* – that men might be persuaded through moral instruction and tragic fiction to change their libertine ways.

Chapter 3 looks at Mary Hays' *The Victim of Prejudice* (1799), a novel that, like *Secresy*, tells the story of an admirable heroine who is psychologically destroyed by inter-connected avenues of male power. As in *Secresy*, the channels of power are guardianship, libertinage, and Rousseauvian educational ideas. However, male guardianship in *Victim* is inadvertently injurious and the Rousseauvian educational ideas are more subtly presented. In Hays' hands, the guardian is enlightened and well-meaning, not retrograde and tyrannical; nonetheless, he injures the heroine, Mary Raymond, by following Rousseauvian ideas about isolating children to preserve them from social contamination. In an attempt to keep Mary's mind 'pure,' he hides from her the important information that she is the

Women and madness in the early Romantic novel 27

daughter of a prostitute executed as an accomplice to murder and therefore cannot be accepted into society. The novel follows Mary's struggles with melancholia from the moment her Edenic childhood isolation is broken and she is introduced to male power in the form of the father of her future lover. Mary battles with melancholia as she struggles to recover from her privileged lover's abandonment and her sexual assault by a powerful man. Through Mary's story, Hays makes the point that women's mental disease comes directly from their disadvantaged position in relation to men, and most particularly from libertinage in its most destructive form – as a social practice that controls women through sexual assault. In contrast to both *Wrongs of Woman* and *Secresy*, *Victim of Prejudice* never considers the role of sentimental literature or the romantic imagination in women's plight, which makes the line of causality from men's actions to women's victimization more direct and the novel more didactic. Although it focuses much more than the other two novels on just one avenue of male control, *Victim* concludes, like *Secresy*, with the tragic death of its heroine from mental illness and with the failure of female friendship to provide shelter from male abuse. And like *Secresy*, *Victim* ends by suggesting that the only salvation for women is to write tragic novels that might occasion the reformation of men.

Chapter 4 initiates *Injured Minds'* transition from novels that present female madness as the product of patriarchal structures to those that revise these narratives. The first part of this chapter, on Maria Edgeworth's *Belinda* (1801), argues that Edgeworth uses Lady Delacour's madness – consisting of hysteria, hypochondriasis, mania, melancholia, and Methodism – for a multi-faceted revision of both the standard causes of women's mental afflictions and of her contemporaries' narratives of female victimization. Like Wollstonecraft, Fenwick, and Hays, Edgeworth rejects physiological models for women's madness. But unlike the other three, Edgeworth counters the sentimental portrayal of love-madness by refusing to engage with it in the Lady Delacour plot. At the same time, she rejects her more radical contemporaries' accounts of female madness by removing men from responsibility for Lady Delacour's many afflictions. In the Lady Delacour section of the novel, Edgeworth replaces female frailty and male avenues of power with a new, gender-neutral psychological model for madness that draws on false associations, misplaced passions, and remorse. Although Lady Delacour is in part responsible for her own mental afflictions, Edgeworth's new psychological model makes recovery possible in a way that neither medical authors' physiological explanations nor her contemporaries' anti-patriarchal frameworks could. By incorporating the new treatment techniques of moral management, Edgeworth positions Belinda as a mental-health practitioner who guides Lady Delacour back to rational control and emotional balance.

28   *Women and madness in the early Romantic novel*

Edgeworth's focus on recovery and on ungendered models of madness severs the association Wollstonecraft, Fenwick, and Hays made between women's mental afflictions and male abuse. In this way, Edgeworth's Lady Delacour plot functions as a repudiation of her contemporaries' conviction that women were trapped by structures of male control. In Lady Delacour's story, men not only do not cause women's madness, they are able to help women recover. And importantly, in contrast to Wollstonecraft, Fenwick, and Hays, Edgeworth makes female friendship central to women's ability to live happy, emotionally balanced lives.

Although Edgeworth repudiates her contemporaries' exposés of male avenues of power in the Lady Delacour plot, she replicates and augments their critiques of gendered Rousseauvian education in her section on Virginia, Belinda's rival for Clarence Harvey's affections. Chapter 4, in addressing Virginia, argues that Edgeworth presents Rousseau's *Émile* as a text that conveys an educational ideology based on a male sexual fantasy that is harmful to women. Edgeworth offers considerable insight into how a Rousseauvian education damages women's minds by attempting to make them into passive, childlike sexual objects. Like Fenwick, Edgeworth shows that an isolated, male-controlled education stifles independent, adult thought, stimulates the romantic imagination in women, and produces melancholia. Edgeworth, however, diffuses the threat of the gendered Rousseauvian education by refusing to take it seriously. Instead of following Fenwick's lead and causing her character to die from terminal love-madness stemming from her education, she lets her character live to be reunited with the man she loves. This happy ending, however, is undercut by Edgeworth's use of romance tropes and by her highlighting the fictionality of her tale. The point is not to make readers suspect the overall happy outcome of her novel, but rather to make them see Rousseau's educational programme as fantastical, fictitious, and absurd. The gendered Rousseauvian education that harms women through breeding passivity and the romantic imagination is the only avenue of male control Edgeworth is willing to entertain. But Edgeworth shows this form of control to be a romance itself – that is, she shows it to be an improbable work of the imagination. In this way, she easily dispatches both the threat of gendered educational models and her contemporaries' narratives of victimization.

The final chapter argues that Amelia Opie's popular *The Father and Daughter* (1801) is similar to Edgeworth's *Belinda* in that it rejects physiological models for women's madness and revises victimization plots written by Wollstonecraft, Fenwick, and Hays. Opie does so through turning the story of the love-mad maid into a tale about a father who loses his mind when his daughter, Agnes, runs away with an officer. The daughter, too, experiences bouts of madness, but these are caused entirely by her own actions – by her remorse over the mental injury she has inflicted on her father. Although the novel seems to reinforce structures of male control by blaming the daughter for her own and her father's illnesses, Opie demonstrates a considerably more diverse set of ideas about mental disease and male avenues of power than one might assume. In reversing the narrative of the love-mad maid, Opie shifts gendered power dynamics to make the daughter the guardian of the father after he goes mad. The novel thus criticizes patriarchal structures not for abusiveness, but rather for weakness. Moreover, when Agnes does lose her mind, it is not because she has lost her lover, but rather because she has lost her father. In this way, Opie downgrades the importance of romantic love for women and gives them greater self-determination. Although the novel ends with Agnes' death, Opie, like Edgeworth, resists seeing women as psychologically damaged victims of male control. Instead, women in her novel demonstrate considerable moral and mental strength in that they are capable of great acts of courage and sacrifice in the service of those they love.

Women's madness and innovation

Helen Small has written that nineteenth-century women writers were 'spurred ... into remarkable innovation' in their uses of female madness.[121] Late eighteenth-century women authors, too, innovated when they challenged established medical and literary models of women's mental afflictions. This innovation took place across several arenas. All authors covered in *Injured Minds*, without being medical professionals, were working in the vanguard of the period's understanding of the human mind. At a time when physicians and medical writers still located women's mental afflictions in what was considered to be the aberrant female body, these authors, by focusing on women's emotional experiences, used a model that was more modern than that of most psychologically oriented medical writers, teachers, and practitioners of the day. At a time in which the static, beautiful love-mad maid was popular and widely circulated, these authors challenged what was a uniform and exploitive staple of sentimental culture. For those who identified avenues of patriarchal control as the cause of female madness, the innovation was to use an expanded understanding of human psychology to identify the precise ways in which male power caused women to go mad or lose themselves in despair. For those who rejected or modified the avenues of patriarchal control, the innovation was to use ungendered explanatory models for madness that allowed women to recover their agency, autonomy, and sanity. All the authors were 'spurred' into formal innovation through their challenges to medical and sentimental literary models of female madness. They made their primary formal innovation at the level of character when they replaced the static icon of the love-mad maid with characters whose psyches were worth exploring. Whereas before their novels were published, there were just two kinds of female love-mad madness – the violent and the passive – the novelists covered in *Injured Minds* created the conditions for variety and differentiation. In their five novels, there are six women suffering from mental and emotional afflictions, each different, each with her own story, each with her own uniquely psychologized mind. In individualizing women's psyches, these five authors contributed substantially to the establishment of complexly psychologized female characters in the nineteenth-century novel. And in so doing, they anticipated the development of modern psychological models in which the emotional experience of systemic abuse and injustice is understood to shape individuals' minds and to impact their happiness and their health.

Notes

1 A more expansive time frame might include Frances Burney's *Cecilia* (1782), in which the protagonist experiences temporary madness.

2 In the mid-1790s, Opie was closely associated with Mary Wollstonecraft and her future husband, the philosopher William Godwin, but her politics moderated considerably in the latter years of the decade. Edgeworth's politics have been much debated, and she has often been described as 'conservative.' Within the context of the Revolutionary and post-Revolutionary period, however, I think the best label would be a 'moderate' reformer.

3 *Émile* was frequently reprinted and was widely discussed in the later eighteenth century. See Shane Greentree, 'Writing against Sophie: Mary Hays' *Female Biography* as Enlightenment Feminist Critique of Jean-Jacques Rousseau's *Émile*,' *Eighteenth-Century Life* 41, no. 2 (April 2017): 74, https://doi.org/10.1215/00982601–3841384.

4 Scholars frequently mention Wollstonecraft's quarrel with Rousseau in the second *Vindication*, but discussions of other British women writers' engagements with his ideas are much less common. Exceptions include Nicola Watson, *Revolution and the Form of the British Novel, 1790–1825: Intercepted Letters, Interrupted Seductions* (Oxford: Oxford University Press, 1994); Annette Wheeler Cafarelli, 'Rousseau and British Romanticism: Women and the Legacy of Male Radicalism' in *Cultural Interactions in the Romantic Age: Critical Essays in Comparative Literature*, ed. Gregory Maertz (Albany: SUNY Press, 1998); Stephen Behrendt, 'Rousseau and British Women Writers' and Frances Ferguson, 'Jean-Jacques Rousseau, *Émile* and Britain,' both in *Jean-Jacques Rousseau and British Romanticism: Gender and Selfhood, Politics and Nation*, eds Russell Goulbourne and David Higgins (London: Bloomsbury, 2017),

ebook; and Melissa A. Butler, 'Eighteenth-Century Critics of Rousseau's Views on Women' in *Rousseau et la Critique/Rousseau and Criticism*, eds Lorraine Clark and Guy LaFrance (Ottawa: North American Association for the Study of Jean-Jacques Rousseau, Pensee libre No. 5, 1995), http://rousseauassocia tion.org/wp-content/uploads/2020/07/PL5–Butler.pdf. Mary Trouille's *Sexual Politics in the Enlightenment: Women Writers Read Rousseau* (Albany: SUNY Press, 1997) includes Wollstonecraft but focuses primarily on French authors. As I show in the following chapters, Rousseau is a strong presence in the novels of British women authors of this period, even when he is not mentioned by name, or only mentioned in passing.

5 To quote Laura Kirkley, 'it is difficult to overstate the influence of Jean-Jacques Rousseau on the works of Mary Wollstonecraft.' Here, and in Chapter 1, I can only address a small sampling of her 'Rousseauism,' which Kirkley describes as 'delineating a complex pattern of enthrallment, identification, and antagonism which not only shapes her political, pedagogical, and philosophical convictions but also her literary self-construction.' Laura Kirkley, 'Jean-Jacques Rousseau' in *Mary Wollstonecraft in Context*, eds Nancy E. Johnson and Paul Keen (Cambridge: Cambridge University Press, 2020), 155, ebook.

6 Mary Wollstonecraft, *The Vindications: The Rights of Men and The Rights of Woman*, eds D. L. Macdonald and Kathleen Scherf (1792; Peterborough: Broadview Press, 1997).

7 Cafarelli notes that John Gregory and James Fordyce were among the 'many male writers of books of female guidance who advocated the highly gendered Rousseauvian education in which middleclass and aristocratic women were encouraged to direct their training to please men' ('Rousseau and British Romanticism,' 134).

8 Other scholars who have chosen to retain period language include Jane Darcy, *Melancholy and Literary Biography, 1640–1816* (Basingstoke: Palgrave Macmillan 2013); Neil Vickers, 'Coleridge and the Idea of "Psychological Criticism,"' *British Journal for Eighteenth-Century Studies* 30 (2007), https://doi.org/10.1111/j.1754–0208.2007.tb00336.x; James Whitehead, *Madness and the Romantic Poet: A Critical History* (Oxford: Oxford University Press, 2017); and Anne Digby, *Madness, Morality, and Medicine: A Study of the York Retreat 1796–1914* (Cambridge: Cambridge University Press, 1985).

9 Roy Porter stresses the broadness of the term 'mad' in the period and refers to eighteenth-century madness as 'protean.' *Madmen: A Social History of Madhouses, Mad-Doctors, and Lunatics* (Rpt *Mind-Forg'd Manacles*, 1987; Stroud, Gloucestershire: Tempus Publishing, 2004), 27.

10 Samuel Johnson, *A Dictionary of the English Language*, vol. 2 (London: W. Strahan, for J. and P. Knaptor & etc., 1755), ECCO. The *OED* definitions are: Mad: 1. 'Disordered in the mind; broken in the understanding; distracted.' 2. 'Over-run with any violent or unreasonable desire.' 3. 'Enraged, furious.' Madness: 1. 'Distraction; loss of understanding; perturbation of the faculties.' 2. 'Fury; wildness; rage.'

11 The *OED* definition is: 3.b. 'A disease or other condition causing ill health, pain, etc.; an illness, an ailment.' This is an Anglo-Norman word having to do with misery, distress, tribulation, and illness.

12 Functional disorder, previously known as conversion disorder, is a condition in which impediments in motor or sensory function cannot be explained through physical models. Common examples include blindness, paralysis, non-epileptic seizures, difficulty swallowing or walking, and involuntary muscle contractions. Symptoms 'typically begin with some stressor, trauma, or psychological distress that manifests itself as a physical deficit' and there is 'no underlying physical cause for the symptom (s).' Shahid Ali, Shagufta Jabeen, Rebecca J. Pate, Marwah Shahid, Sandhya Chinala, Milankumar Nathani, and Rida Shah, 'Conversion Disorder – Mind versus Body: A Review,' *Innovations in Clinical Neuroscience* 12, nos 5–6 (May-June 2015): 27, bit.ly/3OX1lba.

13 G. S. Rousseau, 'Depression's Forgotten Genealogy: Notes Toward a History of Depression,' *History of Psychology* xi (2000): 73–4, https://doi.org/10.117 7/0957154X0001104104. See Rousseau's discussion in this article of the difficulty of using modern mental health terminology to discuss afflictions of the past.

14 Neil Vickers, 'Coleridge and the Idea of "Psychological Criticism,"' 275.

15 *OED*, 'Psychology.'

16 G. S. Rousseau, 'Psychology' in *The Ferment of Knowledge: Studies in the Historiography of Eighteenth-Century Science*, eds George Rousseau and Roy Porter (Cambridge: Cambridge University Press, 2010), 165–6.

17 Akihito Suzuki, 'Dualism and the Transformation of Psychiatric Language in the Seventeenth and Eighteenth Centuries,' *History of Science* xxxiii (1995): 418, https://doi.org/10.1177/0073275395033004.

18 Alexander Crichton, *An Inquiry Into the Nature And Origin of Mental Derangement: Comprehending a Concise System of the Physiology and Pathology of the Human Mind. And a History of the Passions And Their Effects* (London: T. Cadell, junior and W. Davies, 1798), preface, v and xxvii, HathiTrust.

19 Helen Small, *Love's Madness: Medicine, the Novel, and Female Insanity, 1800–1865* (Oxford: Clarendon Press, 1998), 26.

20 Sandra Gilbert and Susan Gubar, *The Madwoman in the Attic: The Woman Writer and the Nineteenth-Century Literary Imagination* (New Haven: Yale University Press, 1979), 51.

21 Elaine Showalter, 'Representing Ophelia: Women, Madness, and the Responsibilities of Feminist Criticism' in *Shakespeare and the Question of Theory*, eds Patricia Parker and Geoffrey Hartman (New York and London: Methuen, 1985), 91.

22 Juliet Mitchell, *Women, the Longest Revolution: Essays on Feminism, Literature, and Psychoanalysis* (London: Virago, 1984), 136–7.

23 Mary Jacobus, *Reading Woman: Essays in Feminist Criticism* (New York: Columbia University Press, 1986), 201.

Women and madness in the early Romantic novel   33

24 Heather Meek, 'Motherhood, Hysteria, and the Eighteenth-Century Woman Writer' in *The Secrets of Generation: Reproduction in the Long Eighteenth Century*, eds Raymond Stephanson and Darren N. Wagner (Toronto: University of Toronto Press, 2015), 248.

25 Elaine Showalter, 'Hysteria, Feminism, and Gender' in *Hysteria Beyond Freud*, eds Sander Gilman, Helen King, Roy Porter, G. S. Rousseau, and Elaine Showalter (Berkeley: University of California Press, 1993), 286, ebook.

26 Elaine Showalter, 'On Hysterical Narrative,' *Narrative* 1 (1993): 33, www.jstor.org/stable/20106990.

27 Small, *Love's Madness*, 27.

28 Small, *Love's Madness*, 27

29 See Small's discussion of the use of insanity in political writing during and after the French Revolution in Chapter 4 of *Love's Madness*.

30 Small, *Love's Madness*, 28.

31 That is, it is the first monograph of which I am aware dedicated to pre-Victorian madness. There are a handful of books that discuss Romantic-period female madness, but none for which it is the exclusive topic, and none that are devoted to female madness in woman-authored texts. In terms of its coverage and focus, *Injured Minds* builds on Small's *Love's Madness* and, to a lesser extent, Philip Martin's *Mad Women in Romantic Writing* (New York: St Martin's Press, 1987). Another monograph, Adriana Craciun's *Fatal Women of Romanticism* (Cambridge: Cambridge University Press, 2002), includes some overlapping interests, although her book focuses on the resurgence of maniacal women in later Romantic-period fiction. Other books that include at least one chapter on mad women in the Romantic period include Darcy, *Melancholy and Literary Biography* and Peter Melville Logan, *Nerves and Narratives: A Cultural History of Hysteria in 19th-Century British Prose* (Berkeley: The University of California Press, 1997). A few articles and chapters covering female mental afflictions in the long eighteenth century can be found in 'Depression in the Enlightenment,' special edition, *Studies in the Literary Imagination* vol. 44, nos 1 & 2 (Spring/Fall 2011), ed. Richard Terry and in *Melancholy Experience in Literature of the Long Eighteenth Century: Before Depression, 1660–1800*, eds Allan Ingram and Stuart Sim (London: Palgrave, 2011). The latter includes Stuart Sim's 'Despair, Melancholy and the Novel.' Jane Kromm's freestanding article on the topic is 'Olivia Furiosa: Maniacal Women from Richardson to Wollstonecraft,' *Eighteenth-Century Fiction* 16, no. 3 (2004), https://doi.org/10.1353/ecf.2004.0020. The articles in the special issue of *Studies in the Literary Imagination*, 'Suicidal Romanticism: Origins and Influences,' ed. Michelle Faubert, vol. 51, no. 1 (Spring 2018), https://doi.org/10.1353/sli.2018.0000 do not focus on madness.

32 Suzuki explains that 'the crux of orthodox physicians' argument was that the essence of the soul remains absolutely intact during the most violent fit of madness, and the disorder takes place only in the body' (Suzuki, 'Dualism,' 419).

33 G. E. Berrios explains that the nervous system replaced the circulatory system as the 'ontological principle around which the bodily economy was organized.'

34   *Women and madness in the early Romantic novel*

See 'Dementia during the Seventeenth and Eighteenth Centuries: A Conceptual History,' *Psychological Medicine* 17 (1987): 834.

34 Michel Foucault, *Madness and Civilization: A History of Insanity in the Age of Reason*, trans. Richard Howard (1965; New York: Vintage Books, 1988), 108.

35 Andrew Scull, *The Most Solitary of Afflictions: Madness and Society in Britain 1700–1900* (New Haven: Yale University Press, 1993), 72.

36 John Locke, *An Essay Concerning Human Understanding*, 5th edn (London: Awnsham and John Churchill, 1706), 93, ECCO.

37 Kathleen Grange, 'Pinel and Eighteenth-Century Psychiatry,' *Bulletin of the History of Medicine* 34, no. 5 (1961): 445–6, www.jstor.org/stable/444 46818.

38 Jennifer Radden represents the psychogenic model as relatively short-lived. See Jennifer Radden, *The Nature of Melancholy: From Aristotle to Kristeva* (Oxford: Oxford University Press, 2000), 19–28. In contrast, Stanley Jackson traces the ongoing relationship between psychogenic, somatic, and pre-dispositional models during the early decades of the nineteenth century. See Stanley Jackson, *Melancholia and Depression: From Hippocratic Times to Modern Times* (New Haven: Yale University Press, 1986), 147–66. Jackson notes that despite the growing influence of hereditary and somatic models after mid-century, there was a 'psychological explanatory tradition that came and went throughout the century' (157).

39 G. S. Rousseau, 'Nerves, Spirits, and Fibres: Towards Defining the Origins of Sensibility' in *Studies in the Eighteenth Century III: Papers Presented at the Third David Nichol Smith Memorial Seminar, Canberra 1973*, eds R. F. Brissenden and J. C. Eade (Toronto: University of Toronto Press, 1976), 145, ebook.

40 By 1730, according to Rousseau, these afflictions were 'seen by leading nerve doctors as entirely somatic in origin.' See G. S. Rousseau, "'A Strange Pathology": Hysteria in the Early Modern World, 1500–1800' in *Hysteria Beyond Freud*, 153.

41 Rousseau, '"Strange Pathology,"' 206, note 184.

42 Robert Whytt, *Observations On the Nature, Causes, And Cure of Those Disorders Which Have Been Commonly Called Nervous, Hypochondriac, Or Hysteric: to Which Are Prefixed Some Remarks On the Sympathy of the Nerves* (Edinburgh: T. Becket, and P. Du Hondt, London, and J. Balfour, Edinburgh, 1765), 94–5, HathiTrust.

43 Rousseau, 'Psychology,' 173, note 46. Rousseau observes that Battie's explanation of madness is 'almost entirely, if not entirely, anatomic.' Battie's discussion can be found in *A Treatise on Madness* (London: J. Whiston, and B. White, in Fleet-Street, 1758), 35–6, ECCO.

44 Porter, *Madmen*, 92.

45 Whytt, *Observations*, 212.

46 Foucault, *Madness and Civilization*, 149.

47 The idea that women had a delicate nervous texture lasted well beyond the end of the eighteenth century. This idea, as G. S. Rousseau says, was the 'fulcrum

on which the theory of nervous diseases, including hysteria, was to be pegged for the next century' ('"A Strange Pathology,' 212, note 238).

48 Robert James, *A medicinal dictionary; including physic, surgery, anatomy, chymistry, and botany. In all their branches relative to medicine. Together with a history of drugs; ... With copper plates.* Vol. 2 (London: T. Osborne, 1743–1745), 'HYS' (no page numbers), ECCO.

49 Louis Charland, 'John Locke on Madness: Redressing the Intellectualist Bias,' *History of Psychiatry* 25, no. 2 (2014): 138, https://doi.org/10.1177/09571 54X13518719.

50 Charland, 'Locke,' 145.

51 Suzuki, 'Dualism,' 426.

52 Suzuki, 'Dualism,' 437.

53 Suzuki, 'Dualism,' 418.

54 Roy Porter, 'Psychosomatic Disorders: Historical Perspectives' in *Treatment of Functional Somatic Symptoms*, eds Richard Mayou, Christopher Bass, and Michael Sharpe (Oxford: Oxford University Press,1995), 17.

55 George Rosen, *Madness in Society: Chapters in the Historical Sociology of Mental Illness* (Chicago: University of Chicago Press, 1968), 170.

56 As Porter explains, 'Madhouses grew up largely as places of safe-keeping or as living space. Their rules were principally about diet and duties, not applications of institutional psychiatry' (*Madmen*, 163).

57 See Porter's *Madmen* for a detailed description of and explanation for such treatments.

58 These were the asylums in Paris for the female and male sufferers from insanity.

59 Dora Weiner emphasizes that in French, '"Moral" does not mean "moral" but "psychologic.'" See Dora Weiner, 'Mind and Body in the Clinic: Philippe Pinel, Alexander Crichton, Dominique Esquirol, and the Birth of Psychiatry' in *The Languages of Psyche: Mind and Body in Enlightenment Thought*, ed. G. S. Rousseau (Berkeley: University of California Press, 1990), 346–7, ebook.

60 Roy Porter, 'Was There a Moral Therapy in Eighteenth-Century Psychiatry?' *Annual of the Swedish History of Science Society* 81 (1981): 15.

61 Vieda Skultans, *English Madness: Ideas on Insanity, 1580–1890* (London: Routledge & Kegan Paul, 1979), 62.

62 Skultans, *English Madness*, 11.

63 Foucault writes that with moral management, the madman becomes 'morally responsible for everything within him that may disturb morality and society, and must hold no one but himself responsible for the punishment he receives' (*Madness and Civilization*, 246). Andrew Scull offers a balanced assessment of moral management, one that appreciates the improvements in treatment, but that also recognizes the more coercive aspects that developed in the nineteenth century. See *Madness and Society in Britain*, 8.

64 Scull, *Madness and Society in Britain*, 8. See Radden for a discussion of the re-emergence of physical models for understanding mental afflictions in the nineteenth century. She observes that in the mid to late nineteenth century 'somatism'

36   *Women and madness in the early Romantic novel*

replaced the 'moralism' of the early nineteenth century, and 'psychological disease' came to be understood as brain disease (*The Nature of Melancholy*, 25).

65 Roy Porter has observed that 'during the seventeenth and eighteenth centuries madness was an extremely broad sociocultural category, with many manifestations and meanings' (*Madmen*, 9).

66 William Cullen considered the 'different states of insanity' largely 'under the two heads of Mania and Melancholia.' William Cullen, *First lines of the practice of physic*, vol. 4 (Edinburgh and London: C. Elliot, 1788), 143, ECCO.

67 Bethlehem Hospital, or 'Bedlam,' was founded in the thirteenth century and became an institution housing the mentally ill during the Tudor period.

68 Foucault, *Madness and Civilization*, 125.

69 Stanley Jackson explains that 'mania came to be thought of as a state of mental derangement associated with severe excitement and often wild behaviour' while 'melancholia came to mean fear and despondency, usually associated with aversion to food, sleeplessness, irritability, and restlessness; often associated with one or another particular delusion, with being misanthropic and tired of life.' (Stanley Jackson, *Melancholia and Depression*, 250).

70 Skultans, *English Madness*, 26. Skultans' list illustrates the difficulty even of attempting to pin down melancholy. She notes that the spleen is 'heir to melancholy, taking over as a catch-all for many vague nervous and physical discomforts. It is thought to affect the English in particular' (*English Madness*, 15). Specific descriptions of spleen, however, such as the one by William Stukeley in *Of the Spleen* (1723), quoted in Skultans' book, add symptoms that come to overlap considerably with hysteria (*English Madness*, 30).

71 Jackson, *Melancholia and Depression*, 4.

72 Jackson, *Melancholia and Depression*, 129–30. As Jennifer Radden observes, the phrase 'without cause' is ambiguous in that it begs the question, 'without any cause, or without sufficient cause?' (*The Nature of Melancholy*, 337).

73 Allan Ingram and Stuart Sim, 'Introduction: Depression Before Depression' in *Melancholy Experience*, eds Ingram and Sim, 9.

74 As James Whitehead notes, melancholy 'became more visible over the eighteenth century, and accrued cultural prestige that returned it almost to its Renaissance standing' (Whitehead, *Madness and the Romantic Poet*, 57).

75 Radden, *The Nature of Melancholy*, 16.

76 Jane Darcy writes that the melancholy of sensibility is 'good' in that the 'trembling sensitivity of sufferers, which leaves them vulnerable to melancholy, can also give them the capacity for exquisite sympathy—the virtue which binds society together' (*Melancholy and Literary Biography*, 73).

77 See Stephen Bending, 'Melancholy Amusements: Women, Gardens, and the Depression of Spirits,' *Studies in the Literary Imagination* 44, no. 2 (2011): 42, https://doi-org.libdata.lib.ua.edu/10.1353/sli.2011.0013 and Radden, *The Nature of Melancholy*, 30.

78 Foucault, *Madness and Civilization*, 137.

79 Clark Lawlor observes that hypochondria in the eighteenth century, as seen in Boswell's relations of Dr Johnson's conversations, meant depression.

Women and madness in the early Romantic novel   37

Clark Lawlor, 'Fashionable Melancholy' in *Melancholy Experience*, eds Ingram and Sim, 41. Jane Darcy clarifies, explaining that 'Hypochondria, crucially, was seen as a distinct disease, although the pejorative meaning we have today was gradually building up' (*Melancholy and Literary Biography*, 70).

80 Late eighteenth-century hypochondriasis, however, could be an alarming condition. Thomas Arnold observes that the hypochondriac's fears 'often lead him to fancy himself threatened, or wasting, with dreadful diseases, which exist only in his distressed imagination.' Thomas Arnold, *Observations on the nature, kinds, causes and prevention of insanity, lunacy or madness*, vol. 1 (Leicester: G. Ireland for G. Robinson and T. Cadwell, 1782), 220–1, ECCO.

81 Hysteria as a medical diagnosis was used quite far into the twentieth century and was only removed from the *Diagnostic and Statistical Manual of Mental Disorders* (DSM) in 1980.

82 Mark Micale, *Approaching Hysteria: Disease and Its Interpretations* (Princeton: Princeton University Press, 1995), 19. Over three centuries of medical interest in hysterical disease, Micale charts three major shifts in medical understanding: at the end of the seventeenth century, both Thomas Willis and Thomas Sydenham rejected uterine theories going back to Ancient Greek medical texts when they developed a 'fundamentally new neurological model of the disorder.' In the late eighteenth century, Micale explains, 'Bossier de Sauvages, Cullen, and Pinel re-eroticized the diagnosis as part of a far-ranging reorientation of attitudes toward the psyche and the body.' And then at the end of the nineteenth century, Freud used hysteria as a founding diagnosis for psychoanalytical theory and treatment (*Approaching Hysteria*, 293).

83 See Ilza Veith, *Hysteria: The History of a Disease* (Chicago: University of Chicago Press, 1965), Chapter 1.

84 Rousseau, '"A Strange Pathology,"' 92.

85 Heather Meek, 'Medical Discourse, Women's Writing, and the "perplexing Form" of Eighteenth-Century Hysteria,' *Early Modern Women: An Interdisciplinary Journal* 11, no. 1 (2016): 177, www.jstor.org/stable/26431447.

86 Micale, *Approaching Hysteria*, 68.

87 Whytt, *Observations*, 231–2.

88 Rousseau, '"A Strange Pathology,"' 100.

89 Rousseau writes that after 1700, 'all versions of feminine hysteria and melancholy were represented in the language and images of weakness: weak spirits, weak nerves, weak fibres, frail and passive physiology wrapped into one flawed female creature no matter how lovely and beautiful' ('Depression's Forgotten Genealogy,' 100).

90 Veith, *Hysteria*, 131.

91 Whytt, *Observations*, 118. In John Mullan's words, 'A putative feminine "sensibility" exists on the edge of an abyss which is "the too great sensibility of the nervous system," the excess which is dangerous affliction. The woman's body, collapsing or beyond control, is the very register of disorder.' John Mullan, 'Hypochondria and Hysteria: Sensibility and the Physicians,'

38   *Women and madness in the early Romantic novel*

The Eighteenth Century 25, no. 2 (1984): 153, www-jstor-org.libdata.lib. ua.edu/stable/41467321.

92 James, *Medicinal Dictionary*, 'HYS.'

93 James, *Medicinal Dictionary*, 'HYS.' James' description of hysterical symptoms covers an astonishingly wide variety of parts of the body and emotional responses. James writes: 'Nor is it their only misery that the body is so severely disorder'd and shaken, and is become like a house every-where threatening to fall into ruins; for the mind still suffers more grievous afflictions than the body. For it is the nature of this disease to be accompanied with an incurable despair … Upon little or no occasion they indulge terror, anger, jealousy, distrust, and other grievous passions; and are enemies to joy and hopes.'

94 Foucault, *Madness and Civilization*, 154.

95 I refer to those medical writers and practitioners using a psychogenic model as 'progressive' because an approach emphasizing external causality—or the interaction between the environment and the emotions—opened up a greater possibility for treatment and recovery than older approaches that focused on physical causes.

96 Quoted in Small, *Love's Madness*, 16.

97 Micale observes that 'no one has adequately explained the sudden reversion to genital theories of hysteria during the late eighteenth and early nineteenth centuries after the accomplishments of the English "neurological" school of the seventeenth century.' Mark Micale, 'Hysteria and its Historiography: A Review of Past and Present Writings (I),' *History of Science* 27 (1989): 244, https://doi.org/10.1177/007327538902700301.

98 G. S. Rousseau, 'The Invention of Nymphomania' in *Perilous Enlightenment: Pre-and Postmodern Discourses; Sexual, Historical*, ed. G. S. Rousseau (Manchester: Manchester University Press, 1991), 45.

99 Micale, *Approaching Hysteria*, 23.

100 Rousseau, 'Nymphomania,' 44–5.

101 Bienville emphasizes the role of the '*matrix*' which he describes as having 'impressions and affections' and considers to be the 'chief seat of those disorders, the dreadful picture of which I shall attempt to paint.' He then later explains that the ignorance in which young women are educated inflames the imagination when they feel the natural attraction of one sex to another. M. D. T. De Bienville, M.D. *Nymphomania, or, a dissertation concerning the furor uterinus*, trans. Edward Sloane Wilmot, M.D. (London: J. Bew, 1775), 18 and 162, ECCO.

102 Elaine Showalter maintains that in the nineteenth century, mental illness came to be seen as a female affliction. See *The Female Malady: Women, Madness, and English Culture, 1830–1980* (London: Virago, 1985). This argument, however, has been contested. See, for example, Joan Busfield, 'The Female Malady? Men, Women and Madness in Nineteenth-Century Britain,' *Sociology* 28, vol. 1 (1994), www.jstor.org/stable/42855327.

103 An exception would be a novel such as Charlotte Lennox's *The Female Quixote* (1752) in which the protagonist, Arabella, is considered to be mad because she attempts to live as the heroine of a romance.

Women and madness in the early Romantic novel   39

104 Early eighteenth-century examples include Alovisa and Ciamara in Eliza Haywood's *Love in Excess* (1719). More antecedents to violent love-mad women can be found in seventeenth-century French drama, such as the heroine of Racine's *Andromache*. See G. S. Rousseau, 'Depression's Forgotten Genealogy,' 85. Romantic-period versions of the maniacal love-mad woman include Charlotte Dacre's Appollonia in *The Passions* (1811) and Victoria from *Zofloya* (1806). Donizetti's *Lucia di Lammermoor* (1835), an adaptation of Sir Walter Scott's novel *The Bride of Lammermoor* (1819), has a famous 'mad scene' in the third act that exaggerates what was, in fact, a small section in the original. See Showalter, *The Female Malady*, 14 and 17.

105 According to Helen Small, 'between about 1770 and about 1810, stories about bereaved or deserted women fallen into insanity were the subject of an extraordinary vogue in sentimental prose, poetry, drama, and painting' (*Love's Madness*, 11–12).

106 Small, *Love's Madness*, 3. Robert Mayo, in his research into popular magazines published in 1798, found that 'bereaved mothers and deserted females were almost a rage in the poetry departments of the 1790's.' Robert Mayo, 'The Contemporaneity of the *Lyrical Ballads*,' *PMLA* 69, no. 3 (June 1954): 496, https://doi.org/10.2307/460070.

107 Susan Staves, 'British Seduced Maidens,' *Eighteenth-Century Studies* 14, no. 2 (1980–81): 119–20, www.jstor.org/stable/2738330.

108 Elaine Showalter traces the origins of the love-mad maid to Ophelia and stage presentations that reflected an influential duality centred on female sexuality. According to Showalter, the Restoration took up the subversive or violent possibilities of the Ophelia figure, but on the eighteenth-century stage, the force of female sexuality represented by Restoration mad scenes was muted, with the preference being for sentimental versions of the figure. See 'Ophelia,' 80–2.

109 Martin, *Mad Women*, 1.

110 Melina Esse, 'Performing Sentiment; or, How to Do Things with Tears,' *Women and Music: A Journal of Gender and Culture* 14 (2010): 7, https://doi.org/10.1353/wam.2010.0002.

111 Henry Mackenzie, *The Man of Feeling* (1771; London: J.M. Dent, 1893), 36, HathiTrust. Michael DePorte writes that 'throughout the seventeenth and most of the eighteenth century, until its doors were shut to the public in 1770, Bethlehem Hospital was a favourite London tourist attraction.' Michael De Porte, *Nightmares and Hobbyhorses: Swift, Sterne, and Augustan Ideas of Madness* (San Marino: Huntington Library, 1974), 3.

112 Mackenzie, *Man of Feeling*, 36.

113 Mackenzie, *Man of Feeling*, 38.

114 Philip Martin notes that the scene in Bedlam enacts a 'potent and deeply engrained ritual wherein the woman is momentarily made whole again by the presence of the man' (*Mad Women*, 19).

115 In her discussion of sentimental operas featuring fallen or mad women, Melina Esse writes that 'male spectators were just as prone to tears as women; indeed, by showing their susceptibility they demonstrated the nobility of heart so

40 *Women and madness in the early Romantic novel*

valued by the bourgeois' ('Performing Sentiment,' 5–6). The exchange of sympathy is central to the sentimental dynamic, regardless of artistic form.

116 Laurence Sterne, *A Sentimental Journey* (1768; Oxford: Oxford University Press, 2008), 95.

117 Sterne, *Sentimental Journey*, 95.

118 Sterne, *Sentimental Journey*, 96. That is, if Sterne could be pinned down to a true cause.

119 Philip Martin refers to the love-mad maid as both a 'myth' and an 'archetype' in his Introduction.

120 Elaine Showalter sees the figure as a 'touching image of feminine vulnerability and a flattering reminder of female dependence on male affection' (*The Female Malady*, 13). Describing the Ophelia figure, Michelle Faubert observes that 'women were so dependent upon their relationships with men that with the destruction of their bonds with the opposite sex would surely come the destruction of their mental health and of their very beings.' See 'A Gendered Affliction: Women, Writing, Madness' in *Cultural Constructions of Madness in Eighteenth Century Writing: Representing the Insane*, by Allan Ingram (Houndsmills, Basingstoke: Palgrave, 2005), 154.

121 Small, *Love's Madness*, 31–2.

1

Madness and Maria: *The Wrongs of Woman* and patriarchal control

Mary Wollstonecraft's unfinished *The Wrongs of Woman; or, Maria* begins in madness and ends in despair, with the protagonist Maria's mental condition at beginning and end caused by male abuse. In addition to permitting her to allegorize women's experiences, the setting in the madhouse allows Wollstonecraft to explore her own fears of mental breakdown and to rework the trope of love-madness by offering an extended examination of how marriage combines with other elements to bring about Maria's struggles with melancholia. Trapped in misery, in a situation reinforced by the legal system, Maria allows her romantic imagination to attach itself to a handsome fellow inmate, Mr Darnford, through the medium of Rousseau's *Julie; ou La Nouvelle Héloïse.* Although Maria appears to be in a healthy mental state in the last fully structured scene, in which she defends Darnford in court from a charge of criminal conversation, in several of the fragmentary endings she suffers from suicidal melancholia as a result of Darnford's desertion.[1] Far from fashioning her into an object for picturesque titillation and superficial pity, Maria's love-madness makes her a tragic, shocking figure in that she attempts suicide while pregnant. In contrast to the stereotypical love-mad woman, who still needs a man to heal her mind, in the most developed ending, Maria appears to be saved by a woman, her former jailor Jemima, who arrives with the lost daughter just in time to save Maria's life. However, this is just one of several possible endings to a story that makes marriage, sentimental literature, and libertinage into a web that entraps and psychologically destroys women.

Wollstonecraft sets this novel, her last written work, in a madhouse in order to detail how women's mental and emotional wellbeing is compromised by unequal power relations between the sexes.[2] In *Wrongs*, she demonstrates that the patriarchal social system defines both health and disorder for women and also produces the states it pathologizes. At the time Wollstonecraft was writing, the male-dominated medical profession still located women's mental afflictions exclusively within the body, thus providing cover for the harm patriarchal society inflicted on women

42   *Women and madness in the early Romantic novel*

through systems of domination. Marriage, aided and abetted by men's control of the law and the economy, is the most obvious avenue of male power in this novel. But sentimental literature also acts as an instrument of male control in that it teaches women to invest emotionally in romantic fantasies in order to distract them from their unhappiness and their subordinate status.[3] These channels of male domination work together, forming a web of power that restricts women's autonomy and deprives them of rights. Wollstonecraft uses the story of Maria's unjust incarceration not only to expose systems of male domination, but also to revise the medical models and literary forms that upheld those systems. Through her novel, she shows that female madness is not caused by inherent physical weakness or women's natural need to depend on men, but rather by women's entrapment in systems of domination that create pathologies. More specifically, she shows how legal, domestic, and economic institutions and practices damage women's psychological resilience by preventing them from living independently. Wollstonecraft thus sees women as trapped in a prison of male control from which there is little chance of escape. By placing her character within a madhouse, Wollstonecraft not only constructs an effective metaphor for women's oppression, she also explores and revises medical and literary models for female madness, demonstrates how these models further male control, and tests strategies that might alleviate mental duress and possibly free women from patriarchal domination. Above all, she shows love-madness to be a horrific, potentially fatal emotional affliction caused by deep-rooted patriarchal structures that destroy women's desire for autonomy.

Wollstonecraft's mental health and writing *The Wrongs of Woman*

Wollstonecraft's letters show that she suffered from emotional swings and various nervous disorders, the symptoms of which resemble the eighteenth-century afflictions of hypochondriasis, hysteria, and, most notably, melancholia. Long before she wrote her second *Vindication* or laid eyes on Gilbert Imlay, the lover who left her, she complained to friends and family about melancholy and nervous ailments and repeatedly wrote that she wished she were dead.[4] G. J. Barker-Benfield writes that 'among the physical symptoms Wollstonecraft attributed to her nerves were: headache, a pain in the side, exhaustion, weakness, declining health, fits of trembling, a rising in the throat, nervous fever (an especially persistent factor), spasms, giddiness.'[5] Through much of the eighteenth century, such symptoms were associated with hypochondriasis and hysteria, although Wollstonecraft, in keeping with the times, refers to her afflictions as 'nervous.'

The Wrongs of Woman *and patriarchal control*   43

Jane Darcy argues that 'melancholic' is the most appropriate term to describe Wollstonecraft's self-description in her correspondence, although today we might recognize her complaints as depression with anxiety.[6] It is well known that Wollstonecraft tried twice to end her own life at the end of her relationship with Imlay, the father of her first child, whose affection and interest waned soon after the baby's birth. At the time of her greatest distress, when she travelled to Scandinavia as Imlay's agent between her two attempts at suicide, Wollstonecraft wrote letter after letter describing her melancholy and imagining casting herself into the sea.[7] Although Wollstonecraft's struggles with mental illness were at their most acute during the protracted period of abandonment by Imlay, she had suffered from persistent nervous disorders and melancholia earlier, throughout her time as a governess in Ireland.[8] Even later, during her relationship with the philosopher William Godwin, when she finally found romantic stability and happiness, she continued to be plagued by inexplicable bouts of melancholia, complaining to Godwin about torpor, lowness of spirits, and painful memories.[9] These struggles with nervous disorders make the topic of mental affliction in *Wrongs* particularly personal, and her presentation of madness is no doubt informed by her own experiences and fears.

Wollstonecraft was most likely aware that her personal history and her status as a female author could be used against her by readers, and she feared that she might be dismissed as a love-mad woman telling a personal story of disappointment, rather than be seen as a political writer offering an important critique of systemic male abuse. In the 'Author's Preface,' Wollstonecraft writes: 'There are a few, who will dare to advance before the improvement of the age, and grant that my sketches are not the abortion of a distempered fancy, or the strong delineations of a wounded heart'.[10] In saying that only the enlightened minority will read her novel correctly, Wollstonecraft expresses the fear that the unenlightened majority might read it incorrectly. To read the novel incorrectly would be to read it as a mental 'abortion' – as a narrative expelled before its completion from a deranged, disordered imagination.[11] Wollstonecraft thus, in defending her novel, expresses the anxiety that readers could see it as the failed product of personal, emotional injury – as a mere narrative sketch of a woman's broken heart. If she were seen as a woman writing from the personal experience of a broken heart and her novel were to be therefore dismissed, then readers would have failed to understand one of her primary points: that female feeling must be taken seriously, not only because women's suffering needs to be recognized in order to be alleviated, but also because emotional experience leads to interpretive insights.[12]

The insights Wollstonecraft offers have to do with her ability to tell a story that is both personal and widely politically applicable. One of

Wollstonecraft's primary contributions to feminist thought is that she viewed women as a body, collectively injured by men, a perspective that is fundamental to her critique in *Wrongs of Woman*.[13] In the preface, Wollstonecraft explains how the specific, emotional suffering of one woman stands in for the mental abuse of women as a group. Her heroine, she explains, is to be both an individual in her own right and the representative of womankind. The 'main object,' she says, is to exhibit the 'misery and oppression, peculiar to women, that arise out of the partial laws and customs of society' (67). This character she has created, then, does not mirror the mental and emotional turmoil of Wollstonecraft's own experience, but rather conveys a story about the injuries women as a body suffer from prejudicial laws and customs in a male-dominated society. 'The history ought rather to be considered, as of woman, than of an individual. The sentiments I have embodied' (67). Wollstonecraft thus seeks to give concrete form – a fictional body – to the idea that all women are rendered miserable as the victims of male tyranny. In this way, she creates a novel that functions at once as an illustration of directly experienced injury and as an exposé of broader, generalized wrongs. The wrongs Maria suffers are wrongs suffered by all women in a male-dominated society; and her struggle with the melancholic disorder that stems from the web of male control is the struggle of all women in a patriarchal society.

The madhouse where Maria's husband imprisons her is a political metaphor, an experiential arena for psychological exploration, and a literal place. That is, in addition to representing women's entrapment in patriarchal systems of control and providing a space for Wollstonecraft to ruminate about women's mental afflictions, madhouses were real places where women could be legally confined by their husbands or fathers. As in Wollstonecraft's novel, confinement in eighteenth-century England was useful to men who sought control over women's fortunes. Jonathan Andrews and Andrew Scull have found evidence demonstrating that: 'women with fortunes … were genuinely vulnerable to incarceration as mad … all the more so, given the hazy boundaries of those disorders of mind and body being constituted by doctors and owned by sufferers as vapours, spleen, and nerves.'[14] Thus the medical profession, through its ample and imprecise descriptions of female mental disorders, assisted men who used the law to incarcerate their wives for their own gain. The kind of asylum where Maria is imprisoned, a private facility, was particularly useful for the discipline and control of women. Roy Porter writes that 'throughout the century, private asylums remained tainted with accusations of neglect and corruption. Early on, the prime grievance was wrongful confinement.'[15] Doctors and lawyers colluded with husbands wishing to confine their wives, women who, according to Elizabeth Foyster, often faced 'difficulty proving their sanity and their innocence.'[16] The phenomenon would have been of considerable interest to Wollstonecraft since, as Foyster writes, 'the subject of confinement raised issues about women's rights over their bodies, personal liberties and identity within the law.'[17] Confinement also brought together all the avenues of injury Wollstonecraft identified in *Wrongs* as the most detrimental to women's mental and emotional wellbeing: the law, medicine, marriage, and the sentimental literary tradition.

The mansion of despair: Maria's melancholia

Through her character Maria Venables, Wollstonecraft explores the mental affliction she herself was the most familiar with – melancholia – and casts it an as ambiguous condition that gives her protagonist sensibility and genius, but that also puts her at risk of profound depression.[18] Wollstonecraft's deployment of melancholy to build a character of intellect, inspired feeling, and refined taste is in keeping with its use by male authors in the early Romantic period, when, in Jennifer Radden's words, melancholy's ancient association with 'brilliance, intellectual refinement, genius, [and] creative energy' came back into vogue.[19] As Elizabeth Dolan observes, 'male poets of the period were able to move easily between the medical definition and the literary tradition of melancholia because both were symptomatic of rationality and intelligence for men.'[20] In contrast, she continues, 'women poets who invoked the literary tradition of melancholia ran the risk of being culturally disempowered by medical definitions of women's nervous illnesses or by an association with unfeminine reason.'[21] Wollstonecraft makes her concern for this sort of interpretation clear in the preface, and she tries to fend off being dismissed as a mentally unfit female author through explaining the connection between her protagonist's feelings and the general, oppressed situation of women. In her *Letters Written During a Short Residence* (1796), Wollstonecraft had successfully used the literary tradition of male melancholy to convey the distinctive genius and emotional depth of her writerly persona, whom she cast as a woman of feeling with great intellectual acumen. Wollstonecraft employs the same tactic in *Wrongs* when she makes her autobiographical protagonist's melancholic sensibility the catalyst for trenchant political commentary. However, in *Wrongs*, Wollstonecraft investigates the destructive, as well as the constructive, tendencies of the condition.

Wrongs of Woman opens *in media res*, with Maria traumatized, inert, and unable to collect her thoughts. Wollstonecraft uses Maria's temporary mental impairment to explore in personal terms how it feels to know one is the victim of patriarchal structures of mental imprisonment.

The narrator refers to the asylum where Maria has been unjustly imprisoned as a 'mansion of despair' and claims that no Gothic setting could compare to the place where Maria sits, 'endeavouring to recall her scattered thoughts' (69). The Gothic reference reinforces the idea that women's madness stems from male oppression, and it conveys the horror and fear that the thought of madness provokes. Wollstonecraft describes Maria's mind as 'almost shattered,' and she puts her in a state in which 'surprise, astonishment, that bordered on distraction, seemed to have suspended her faculties, till, waking by degrees to a keen sense of anguish, a whirlwind of rage and indignation roused her torpid pulse' (69). It is as if Maria has just realized the full force of her state of legal and medical victimization, and the result is bewilderment, then bereavement, and then rage. Maria's initial state is that of temporary insanity, as shock and agony have unseated her reason: 'One recollection with frightful velocity following another, threatened to fire her brain, and make her a fit companion for the terrific inhabitants, whose groans and shrieks were not unsubstantial sounds' (69). Maria shifts quickly from an inert emotional and mental state to one in which her thoughts and feelings move so rapidly she seems to have transitioned instantly from melancholia to mania. As past events become clarified, the narrator gives Maria a specific reason to be mad: the emotional trauma of the loss of her child.[22] Given that there is nothing illegal about either her husband taking the baby or his committing her to an asylum, the novel suggests that a mother could be driven mad from the pure horror of having no rights to her child or her liberty. The horror and fear Maria feels when she returns to consciousness, and her shifting between melancholia and mania, point to the extensive power her husband has over her as the cause of her temporary madness.

As Maria comes back to cognitive clarity and emotional control, Wollstonecraft continues to draw on the multiple meanings of the madhouse. Metaphorically, all women are trapped in a prison of male control in which they may go mad or, at the very least, suffer from mental and emotional afflictions. As Diane Long Hoeveler has observed about this novel, 'patriarchy is one large holding tank for women – a madhouse from which none escape.'[23] Through Maria's attempts to regain her equilibrium and maintain her sanity in the madhouse where she is confined, Wollstonecraft offers readers strategies for coping with the mental and emotional duress of the metaphorical prison that is patriarchal society. 'Indulged sorrow,' the narrator says, 'must blunt or sharpen the faculties to the two opposite extremes, producing stupidity, the moping melancholy of indolence; or the restless activity of a disturbed imagination' (72–3). Maria recognizes that indulging in sorrow will have an impact on her mental functioning, producing one of two outcomes – either melancholy or mania. She therefore

The Wrongs of Woman *and patriarchal control*   47

exerts herself in an attempt to maintain her sanity. The narrator writes: 'Now she endeavoured to brace her mind to fortitude, and to ask herself what was to be her employment in her dreary cell? Was it not to effect her escape, to fly to the succour of her child, and baffle the selfish schemes of her tyrant – her husband?' (70). The advice here is to exercise mental strength, find employment, perform one's maternal duty, and defy the husband's power. Maria demonstrates for readers how one might resist encroaching mental disease by pulling herself out of her two days of insanity through an intentional resistance to victimization. Anger, contempt, outrage at her husband's injustice help to direct her thoughts, and once she has done so, she thinks about employment – about what she will do while she is imprisoned and how she will escape to be reunited with her child. In having her character determine on an 'employment,' Wollstonecraft follows conventional wisdom about mental afflictions, particularly melancholia. James Boswell, for example, in his anonymous column 'The Hypochondriack,' used his writing to combat his own melancholy and recommended to his readers that they find something productive to do.[24] In Maria's case, the employment of thinking about how to escape functions as a way to combat melancholia and to resist male tyranny.

Although the confinement of marriage brings with it the horrible prospect of mental affliction, Wollstonecraft shows women how they might combat the 'lack of occupation' and 'unvaried prospect' that lies before them by using the rational mind to transform emotional pain into sociological critique (73). Maria jumps from contemplating her own depressed spirits to an awareness of the representative nature of her own experience, saying to herself, 'was not the world a vast prison, and women born slaves?' (73). Wollstonecraft uses Maria's musings to create a create a feedback loop between female emotional injury and political critique. Maria understands that the unjust exercise of male power has put her into a miserable situation; yet she also realizes that her misery allows her to perceive that she suffers because she is a woman. Maria's powerful political metaphor of confinement, then, of being 'bastilled' for life develops out of her own suffering (137). All married women are trapped by patriarchal legal and social structures, and so all women are at risk of feeling the same sense of depression and futility. Even more, all women are metaphorically trapped, as Maria is literally in the asylum, because they lack meaningful occupation and because they cannot exercise their autonomy. But the madness that results from such victimization can be resisted by following Maria's model. Although a woman may experience psychological duress when she realizes that patriarchal society deprives her of rights, freedom, and moral purpose, this awareness can itself be an act of political resistance and a bulwark against madness.

48   *Women and madness in the early Romantic novel*

Wollstonecraft uses Maria to explore two other avenues for coping with and trying to prevent the melancholia that comes from entrapment in male systems of power: reading and writing. Wollstonecraft perhaps draws on Samuel Johnson, whose well-known precepts were 'be not solitary, be not idle,' and 'employ yourself in little things' when she has Maria at first seek to 'find employment' which was to 'find variety, the animating principle of nature' (74).[25] She tries conversing with Jemima, and as a result, obtains books, paper, pens, and ink in response to her complaints of listlessness. She first attempts reading as her main employment, but she cannot concentrate, and her mind is led astray by her imagination. The narrator explains that 'earnestly as Maria endeavoured to soothe, by reading, the anguish of her wounded mind, her thoughts would often wander from the subject she was led to discuss, and tears of maternal tenderness obscured the reasoning page' (74). Traumatized, isolated, and in a state of profound emotional pain, Maria is not able to concentrate on books that demand rational thought. But at the same time, she is made worse by books of fiction because they trigger, in the narrator's words, 'feverish dreams of ideal wretchedness or felicity, which equally weaken the intoxicated sensibility' (75). As Alan Richardson observes, such reading provokes 'a morose daydreaming that only aggravates her depression.'[26] In representing reading as detrimental because it encourages fantasies, Wollstonecraft replicates a familiar eighteenth-century concern about the imagination. Wollstonecraft's readers would have been familiar with Samuel Johnson's warnings about the link between the imagination and madness, as illustrated through the astronomer in *Rasselas*, who imagines he can control the natural processes he observes.[27] Wollstonecraft is here perhaps also concerned that because women are less educated than men in general, have less to do (when they are of means), and are not trained to concentrate or exercise their reason, they are more susceptible to the uncontrolled imagination.

Writing, on the other hand, is active, not passive, and unlike reading, it produces mental acts that are more deliberate, controllable, and therapeutic. Maria's reasons for writing her memoir are thus similar to Boswell's for writing his column: writing functions as a form of therapy to combat melancholy.[28] However, Maria's therapy comes not from ruminating on melancholy itself, but rather from writing with a political intention. Her aim in writing the memoir is to 'instruct her daughter, and shield her from the misery, the tyranny, her mother knew not how to avoid' (75). Maria's purpose, then, which acts as a model for the reader, is to teach girls how to avoid the injuries of living under patriarchal control. Such writing also works to combat the mental ravages of being subject to male power by giving women a meaningful task that combines memory, feeling, and analysis. And writing is a form of resistance to male power,

The Wrongs of Woman *and patriarchal control* 49

whether it is read or not. Heather Meek extends the purpose of Maria's memoir to *Wrongs* as a whole, writing that 'the text operates as counsel for Wollstonecraft's female readers, specifically mothers ... it becomes a manifesto of sorts, warning both Wollstonecraft's contemporaries and subsequent generations of mothers of the "wrongs of woman."'[29] The memoir itself, as a part of the overall novel, is a document that makes women's life-writing into a form of political resistance and into an educational genre for future generations.

Although Wollstonecraft presents Maria's memoir as a form of resistance to the generational injuries of male power, she seems ambivalent about writing's effectiveness when women are faced with the intoxication of romantic love that arrives via sentimental literature. Writing at first seems to be a therapeutic cure for the enticements of the literature of sensibility.[30] However, as soon as Maria becomes aware of the handsome stranger who walks in the yard outside her window, her attention is diverted from her memoir. Soon, she is devouring Rousseau's *La Nouvelle Héloïse*, indulging in romantic fantasies, and meeting with Darnford in her cell, rather than writing her memoir and plotting her escape. At one point, Maria wakes from a dream about her child to look for Darnford walking in the early morning, which suggests that her romantic interest in the stranger has taken her mind away from both her maternal bond and her educational project. Moreover, the memoir itself, intended for the daughter, goes instead to Darnford, who reads it as an erotic provocation and uses it to make sexual advances. The memoir, which seems to offer a powerful avenue of escape from the injuries of male power, is not only sacrificed to the romantic imagination; it also becomes a tool of libertine control.

The injuries of marriage

In her understanding of women's mental afflictions, Wollstonecraft combines a mainstream socio-medical perspective on women's fragility with a searing critique of marriage as an engine of emotional harm. Wollstonecraft stands out among the authors in *Injured Minds* in that she adheres, at least in part, to the standard eighteenth-century belief that genteel women were more susceptible than men and women of a lower class to nervous afflictions. As early as 1733, George Cheyne, in his influential treatise *The English Malady*, established links between sensibility, status, and nervous disorders and, in John Mullan's words, 'firmly [disposed] of the notion that those involved in such an activity as labour [could] aspire to the delicacy and refinement which [revealed] themselves in nervous disorder.'[31] Wollstonecraft uses these ideas to establish both the class identification

50 *Women and madness in the early Romantic novel*

and the femininity of her protagonist. This class-and-gender-based model is evident in how she depicts the differing impact of injuries experienced by Maria and Jemima. The illegitimate daughter of two servants, Jemima suffers considerable gender-based harm from the moment of her birth; however, as she survives injury after injury, it is clear she does not have the soft and delicate internal makeup that would register experiences in terms of cumulative impressions on the nerves. In contrast, Maria comes to suffer from nervous diseases that were, as Elizabeth Foyster explains, 'very much in vogue in this period, especially amongst these social groups, who believed that a greater susceptibility to nervous illness was a sign of refinement and class superiority.'[32] This correlation between genteel women and nervous susceptibility evident in *Wrongs* was, then, well-established in the medical literature and exhibited in the lived experiences of women.

Wollstonecraft blends the standard understanding of refined women's psychological delicacy with a more radical, sociologically based critique of the damage inflicted through marriage. Maria has the delicacy of a refined woman of sensibility, and so she is particularly at risk emotionally from the injustices and abuses of marriage. Because Maria as a refined woman has a nervous temperament, her daily experiences of ill-treatment within marriage take their toll as they constitute a series of injuries that make repeated impressions on her mind. Whereas in her second *Vindication*, Wollstonecraft attacked privileged women for their false delicacy and sexual manipulations, in *Wrongs* she sees them as particularly at risk from the injuries of marriage, as long as their sensibility is true and not affected. As she shows through her protagonist's experiences, a run-of-the-mill bad match to an unscrupulous man can impress itself on the nervous system of a woman of true sensibility and result in emotional harm.

Although Maria, as a refined woman of true sensibility, is susceptible to nervous ailments, Wollstonecraft makes it clear that her husband – a man who victimizes his wife in her own home – is responsible for the low spirits she experiences during her marriage.[33] In blaming the husband for the wife's emotional disturbances, Wollstonecraft identifies a key causal factor that was largely absent from mainstream medical assessments of women's afflictions. Women of Wollstonecraft's own time, however, would have recognized that a husband who abuses a wife could be responsible for her nervous disorders. Foyster discusses court documents from mid-century indicating that women were conscious of the way mistreatment by their husbands could cause hysteria and other afflictions.

> Women in these cases may have been using the language of hysteria and nervous illness in an attempt to extend the boundaries of what was permissible in the courts as evidence of marital cruelty. Rather than using what had

become the almost formulaic language of black and blue bruising to describe marital cruelty, they were providing evidence of emotional distress expressed through nervous illness. But by so doing they laid themselves open to accusations of insanity, and to their stories of cruelty being seen as the products of mad fancy.[34]

As Foyster's passage indicates, women who attempted to defend themselves by establishing a connection between marital abuse and their nervous disorders were not likely to be taken seriously by either the courts or the male members of their families. Foyster gives the example of Mary, Viscountess Coke, who was confined at home by her husband for six months. The Viscountess 'complained in 1750 to the London consistory court that her husband's cruel behaviour had meant she had become "afflicted with hysteric fits."' According to Foyster, she described a catalogue of nervous disorders, including a 'frequent nervous cough, a weak pulse and reduced appetite.' Her father-in-law, however, Foyster notes, 'believed it was all "affectation."'[35] The Viscountess' attempt to hold her husband to account for his abuse was, of course, met with scepticism by the courts. Although Maria does not use the law to seek damages for her unjust confinement, in the crim. con. case she does attempt to demonstrate to a judge that she is an autonomous individual able to make decisions about sexual relationships. Before she gets to court, however, Maria, like the Viscountess, suffers from nervous afflictions caused by her husband's mistreatment of her – including his attempt to confine her within the house. Maria's experiences as a wife seem less metaphorical when considered in the context of historical women's experiences, such as those Foyster discusses. If marital strife was, as Foyster says, 'understood as a common trigger for both female nervous illness and insanity' then some of Wollstonecraft's readers would have recognized that the mental harassment and depressed spirits Maria experiences during her marriage are, like her unjust incarceration, caused by her husband's cruelty.[36]

It is essential for Wollstonecraft's exposure of marriage as the primary avenue of injurious male control that George is neither monstrous nor interesting, but rather a regular man – perhaps a bit more desperate than most and more immoral than some – but decidedly unexceptional. This unexceptionality allows him to play the role of an everyman, embodying the wrongs perpetuated by men much as Maria embodies the wrongs experienced by women at the hands of men. Maria writes the story of her marriage after she fights melancholia in the asylum, but her narrative makes it clear that this idealistic, intelligent young woman has already been emotionally injured by her entrapment in an unhappy marriage. Maria's detailing the miseries of her domestic life moves the novel directly into its critique of

52   *Women and madness in the early Romantic novel*

marriage as an institution designed by men to control women. She begins by complaining that a woman is chained to her husband, regardless of how unkempt, unfaithful, or intoxicated he might be. But, she observes, if the situation were reversed, the man would be excused for seeking out a mistress. Condemning the injustice, Maria writes: 'Woman, weak in reason, impotent in will, is required to moralize, sentimentalize herself to stone, and pine her life away, labouring to reform her embruted mate' (136). The male-controlled institution of marriage requires a woman with a brutish husband to engage in a false system of compensation that deadens her true emotions ('sentimentalize herself to stone') or subjects her to long-term depression ('pine her life away'). And women are already at a disadvantage ('weak in reason' and 'impotent in will') – because their minds are impaired by the education they receive in an unjust, patriarchal society. Their only recourse when married to brutes such as George is to turn to moralizing and sentiment, neither of which provide for emotional satisfaction. On the contrary, the hopeless work to reform the brutish husband through moralizing and sentiment causes either emotional hardening or prolonged, lingering dissatisfaction and depression.

Maria knows of what she speaks. In her account of her life with George, she emphasizes the emotional consequences of her ill-matched marriage – consequences Wollstonecraft presents to the reader as significant. Maria explains that she attempted to sympathize with George, but when she realized she was 'bound to live with such a being forever' she lapsed into what we would understand as depression: 'My heart died within me; my desire of improvement became languid and baleful, corroding melancholy took possession of my soul. Marriage had bastilled me for life. I discovered in myself a capacity for the enjoyment of the various pleasures existence affords; yet, fettered by the partial laws of society, this fair globe was to me an universal blank' (137). Maria here delineates the mental and emotional impact on a woman of realizing she is yoked to an immoral, disgusting man for life. That her heart dies indicates the extinction of all hope for love, and that her desire to improve becomes languid suggests the listlessness and hopelessness of depression. And that the same desire becomes 'baleful' high-lights her miserable distressed state, with the suggestion of something evil or malignant. She is prisoner to a depression that 'corrodes,' or gradually eats away at her being. Despite her excitement about life, about the possibilities of being alive, the whole world becomes a blank because she cannot escape from her marriage. In this way, Wollstonecraft conveys to readers accus-tomed to considering only physical harm as cause for separation, the lasting impact of the psychological injuries of marriage.

One of Wollstonecraft's principal targets in this novel is that way that the law functions as the most important avenue for male control of

The Wrongs of Woman *and patriarchal control*   53

women within marriage. Indeed, the law not only supports male control, it is designed to inflict and pathologize mental anguish but never to acknowledge women's psychological injuries. Wollstonecraft's critique of the harmful structure of marital law runs through her narrative before it culminates in the courtroom scene. Of a husband, Maria complains: 'He can rob [his wife] with impunity, even to waste publicly on a courtesan; and the laws of her country – if women have a country – afford her no protection or redress from the oppressor, unless she have the plea of bodily fear; yet how many ways are there of goading the soul almost to madness, equally unmanly, though not so mean' (140). Here, Wollstonecraft makes the point that men design laws to facilitate male abuse of women and to ensure that women have no protection under the law from that abuse. Because women are not considered to be citizens, they have no redress and are subject to psychological duress at the hands of their legally sanctioned tyrants. Maria, in frustration, says that when such laws were made, lawgivers should have first decreed 'that the husband should always be wiser and more virtuous than his wife, in order to entitle him, with a show of justice, to keep this idiot, or perpetual minor, for ever in bondage' (141). In the medical literature of the time and within asylums, individuals deemed 'idiots' or 'naturals' – those with congenital intellectual impairments – were often grouped in with people suffering from various forms of madness or dementia. Maria thus resorts to the language of cognitive disability to describe the legal situation of women. In the eyes of the law, a woman is considered an 'idiot' or 'perpetual minor'; that is, she is considered a person who cannot be held responsible for her own actions because her mind is undeveloped, underdeveloped, or 'defective.' Wollstonecraft thus suggests that because such people – children, 'idiots,' and women – have no rights as autonomous individuals under the law, they can be subject to psychological abuse by those who make the laws.

The romantic imagination and 'fancy, treacherous fancy'

Wollstonecraft is aware that women learn to compensate for their suffering and lack of power within male-controlled society through indulging in the romantic imagination, but the romantic imagination, too, is an avenue of male control. Maria's romantic imagination originates with her education from her uncle, a man disappointed in love who shaped her character.

This uncle, who 'received a liberal education,' was betrayed in his youth by his beloved and his best friend and afterwards was attacked by a 'raging fever, followed by a derangement of mind, which … gave place to a habitual melancholy' (113). A fever brought on by disappointment in love is a classic literary response, and the uncle's condition draws on longstanding connections between a scholarly disposition, disappointment in love, and male melancholia.[37] The uncle instils in Maria his way of thinking and feeling, as she explains in the memoir she writes for her daughter: 'I drew dear to him in proportion as I imbibed his sentiments' (113–14). Maria's explanation of her education has a sinister undertone, although she expresses no resentment about the relationship. But it is as if the deeply bitter and melancholic older man finds new life in transferring his beliefs and feelings to an impressionable female child. As he educates Maria, he shifts his 'sentiments' – his deep, destabilizing feeling and disappointed idealism – to her. She observes that he 'drew such animated pictures of his own feelings, rendered permanent by disappointment, as imprinted the sentiments strongly on my heart, and animated my imagination' (114). Maria's feelings and imagination are thus permanently marked by her uncle's depression.[38] She sums up her account of her uncle by explaining, 'these remarks are necessary to elucidate some peculiarities in my character, which by the world are indefinitely termed romantic' (114). Maria has been taught to be melancholy and idealistic and to have a romantic imagination by an older man who, it seems, found relief from his own misery in forming her in his own image. In casting the uncle as the man who moulds Maria's psyche, who shapes her imagination and her emotions, and who feeds her a poisonous brew of failed idealism and melancholia, Wollstonecraft suggests that male-controlled education is responsible for her character's melancholic sensibility.

The romantic traits Maria absorbs from her uncle are highly ambiguous in this novel. On the one hand, Maria's melancholy, idealism, and imagination give her a sensibility that makes her both appealing to the reader and superior to her philistine family. On the other, Maria inflicts considerable damage on herself by romanticizing men, and she indulges in the erotic imagination to distract herself from the painful trap of her situation. Maria originally married George because she enhanced him through her imagination, filling him with a host of imagined virtues, and fancying herself 'in love with [the] disinterestedness, fortitude, generosity, dignity, and humanity' with which she invested her 'hero' (116). This romanticization, in tandem with her father's tyranny and her uncle's secret offer of a dowry, ensnares her in a miserable marriage that allows George to take away her freedom.[39] Inside the asylum, when Maria encounters Darnford, she pours all her romantic imagination into a man who, as far as the fragmentary endings suggest, will abandon her without remorse. It is this romanticization of Darnford that has led some scholars to conflate character with author and suggest that Wollstonecraft was trapped within her own sensibility.[40] However, it is not Wollstonecraft who is trapped in her own sensibility, but rather the character she has created to show that the romantic imagination,

The Wrongs of Woman *and patriarchal control* 55

while offering certain advantages, causes women to idealize men and to gloss over their entrapment in unequal relationships of power.

Wrongs shows that few avenues of male power entrap women in dependence and degrade their psychological resilience more than the romantic imagination. Wollstonecraft dwells on how Maria's fancy comes to dominate her perception of Darnford. No longer able to distract herself through writing and feeling no closer to a plan for escape, she is at a point of despondency when Jemima arrives with a new parcel of books from a mysterious man. She is saved from sinking more deeply into melancholy, not by the arrival of the books, but by imagining the books' owner when told they belong to a gentleman confined in another part of the asylum (78). But even before she reads his notes and 'fancy, treacherous fancy' prompts her to 'sketch a character, congenial with her own,' Maria responds with emotion: 'her heart throbbed with sympathetic alarm' and she 'turned over the leaves with awe' (78). She sketches his character from his marginal notes, adds a shape and requisite masculinity from Jemima's description of his 'vehemence of eye' and his ability, were his hands free, to 'manage both his guards' (79). And, after reading the stranger's copy of Rousseau's *Julie; ou, la Nouvelle Héloïse* all night, Maria obsesses about him, thinking she has seen him before, waiting for the sound of his voice, and attempting to colour the 'picture she was delineating on her heart' (82). Maria is particularly impacted by *Julie* because it offers her the fantasy of erotic choice as an alternative to her husband George.[41] When Maria selected George, she endowed him with more appealing traits than he possessed. With Darnford, she does the same; but this time, the traits are considerably more erotic and are drawn from sentimental fiction.[42] And this time, her romantic imagination causes her to divert her thoughts from her daughter to Darnford. She either thinks only of him; or if she thinks of her daughter, it is 'to wish that she had a father whom her mother could respect and love' (82). Romantic love emerges in this novel as a powerful force disseminated through sentimental fiction that encourages women to invent the characteristics of their lovers and to neglect a truer love, which is maternal.

Maria's love for a man she does not know, whose character she invents, leads to an unhealthy obsession that is at once individualized in Maria's experience and applicable to the generality of women. Through Maria's affair with Darnford, Wollstonecraft makes the argument that women's investment in the romantic imagination is closely connected to their mental afflictions, and she suggests that they make this investment for various reasons. One reason is the inability to choose their own romantic partners. Indeed, as Jane Kromm argues, Wollstonecraft insists that 'mental disorders in women are socially determined and caused primarily by a lack of freedom in relationships for which "romantic notions" are

56   *Women and madness in the early Romantic novel*

paltry substitutes with their own debilitating consequences.'[43] Women are prevented from directing their energies and imaginations into any creative venture, and so they focus on the one thing patriarchal society allows: love. But because they are sheltered and allowed limited exposure to ideas and broad experience, they invest in the romantic imagination and exaggerate traits that seem to correspond to their desires. Women are doubly trapped because, while they are limited by their environment to focusing all their energies on love, their ambition is supposed to be marriage. Thus, they are easily misled by imagining qualities in a man they would like to marry. And, they are not afforded the opportunity to meet more men or allowed time to determine if any given man might live up to their expectations. Moreover, they lack the ability to engage in meaningful labour that might occupy their minds or allow them to establish independence. As the narrator observes, it is difficult for 'women to avoid growing romantic, who have no active duties or pursuits' (80). Romance gives the illusion of freedom, choice, and a higher meaning, all the while providing a form of pleasure that diverts women from their misery and distracts them from their entrapment.

Romance, which seems so fulfilling, in fact acts as a narcotic, providing pleasure that takes away pain, producing dangerous side-effects. Maria's experience suggests that the more a woman depends on a man as a replacement for her own self-determination, the more subject she could be to a melancholic disorder because of that dependency. The narrator writes that as a result of her prison romance, Maria felt 'beloved, and every emotion was rapturous' (90). The intoxication of romantic love dulls Maria's pain and delights her with pleasure; but it causes her harm in that it makes her disregard her own freedom and neglect her emotional ties to other women – to Jemima and her own daughter. Although Wollstonecraft wishes to validate women's feelings as the only real and valuable aspect of the romantic fantasy, she also highlights the way Maria's emotional dependence on Darnford leads her to abandon her daughter, her friend, her desire for freedom, and eventually her wish to live.

The romantic imagination that Wollstonecraft identifies as so intoxicating and perilous for women is inextricably connected to sentimental literature as an avenue of male power. Rousseau's *Nouvelle Héloïse*, a 'classic of sensibility' that Darnford lends Maria, epitomizes in Marilyn Butler's words, 'a mode which functions to trap women in sexual daydreaming.'[44] Maria has read *Nouvelle Héloïse* before, but this time, with its connection to the handsome stranger whose annotations entice and seduce her, she devours it in one night. At this point, as Annette Wheeler Cafarelli notes, Maria 'succumbs, like many women, to the pitfall of relying for distraction and escape on the misleading fictions of Rousseau.'[45] The *Nouvelle Héloïse* offers women the fantasy of sexual autonomy and fulfilment, only

The Wrongs of Woman *and patriarchal control*   57

to reinscribe them within the patriarchal order of marriage. This 'classic of sensibility,' then, anesthetizes women through the romantic imagination, blunting their awareness of their real incarceration within marriage. In the end, Rousseau's novel represents women's erotic freedom as something that must be sacrificed for a woman's traditional duties, which is the identical message conveyed by the judge at the end of *Wrongs of Woman*. In effect, Rousseau's story fosters Maria's romantic imagination, and at the same time mirrors the patriarchal juridical position that refuses to sanction Maria's having acted on her erotic desires. Given that Maria's romantic investment in a man she has largely invented brings on a deadly melancholy in the end, the literature of sensibility, as represented by Rousseau's novel, emerges as a particularly potent vehicle of injurious male control. Like a dangerous drug, it alleviates symptoms and dulls pain, but it entraps women through creating dangerous, life-threatening dependencies.

Sentimental literature: viewing the mad

La Nouvelle Héloïse is not the only version of sentimental literature that Wollstonecraft incorporates into *Wrongs of Woman*. She also includes a vignette drawn from the sentimental encounter between Harley and the madwoman in *The Man of Feeling*. Wollstonecraft revises this literary trope to expose the passive love-mad woman as a figure whose victimization by men cannot be papered over by pity or erotic appeal.[46] Helen Small writes that 'Wollstonecraft makes immediate and crucial changes in the way Mackenzie, Cowper, and their imitators … represented the mental distress of women disappointed in love' by making Maria's 'supposedly deranged consciousness the novel's focus.'[47] And Small makes the point that, 'although the name immediately evokes Laurence Sterne's madwoman, this Maria is no picturesque object for the reader's gratified contemplation but an angry and articulate woman.'[48] Wollstonecraft exposes sentimental portrayals of the love-mad woman as a form of trafficking in female suffering, and through Maria, she replaces the woman who loses her mind when she loses her lover with a woman who is, as Small observes, articulate, angry, and capable of critique. But Wollstonecraft does more with the love-mad trope than Small has space to discuss in her short discussion of *Wrongs of Woman*. When Wollstonecraft puts her own Maria Venables in place of Sterne's 'Mad Maria,' she effects a multi-faceted critique of the way patriarchal society uses the love-mad woman. She replaces a narrative about inherent female fragility and dependence with a story showing how male power first creates fragile women and then causes them to become psychologically damaged. And she shows how male power uses the women who have been psychologically damaged as erotic stimulants that serve as vehicles to showcase male moral superiority. In making her revisions to the sentimental trope, Wollstonecraft rejects the idea that emotional injuries impede women's ability to use their reason. On the contrary, she shows that such feelings strengthen the reasoning faculty, giving women a greater understanding of male systems of control and serving as a bulwark against madness.

Wollstonecraft gives Maria what no sentimental love-mad maid ever had: rational self-awareness and the ability to observe and evaluate madness through a mind that is at once empathetic and sharply analytical. Maria's incarceration gives her a perspective that is personal and emotional, as well as clinical and objective, which allows Wollstonecraft to offer a multi-dimensional account of madness. From her more objective perspective, Maria perceives that the asylum's residents are divided into categories of affliction: melancholia, 'imbecility' (in our terms, a congenital mental disability), and mania.[49] Although medical writers in the latter eighteenth century consistently developed new classificatory systems, mania and melancholia remained the two primary types of disorder in the period.[50] Drawing on Maria's observations, the narrator explains that melancholics and those suffering from 'imbecility' are allowed physical freedom within the asylum because they are calm, quiet, and manageable, whereas the frantic, because of their violence, must be kept confined.[51] Their condition, according to the narrator's description, is caused by ungovernable, excessive imagination and passion, which was a standard framework through which maniacal madness was understood in the period.

Maria is not only an objective viewer of the mad – she too is confined in the asylum, which allows Wollstonecraft to look more deeply than the standard sentimental vignette generally permits into the fear that the threat of madness evokes. Although love-mad maidens in sentimental literature are presented as having cause for distress in their abandonment, their emotions when they interact with the male visitor are rather muted. The love-mad maidens provoke pity, but their outstanding feature is not emotional distress, but rather cognitive dislocation – they do not quite know where they are or whom they are with. As Philip Martin observes, 'the confusion of past and present' functions as the 'prime means of indicating derangement.'[52] The loss of the beloved has fractured the love-mad maid's ability to understand herself in relation to time, space, and other people. Such cognitive deficiency and affective blankness leave the emotional realm open for appropriation by the man of feeling who comes to hear her story and demonstrate his virtues by weeping for a woman whose very sense of self has been lost along with her lover. In contrast, if Maria is the love-mad maid's replacement as Small suggests, then she is a love-mad maid whose

The Wrongs of Woman *and patriarchal control*   59

intellect has not been impacted by her loss. And she is a love-mad maid who understands that insanity is fearful and terrible, and not at all picturesque or alluring.

Maria is not in a new, treatment-oriented institution like the Retreat at York, or even in a place where private owners attempted to implement humane methods. Rather, she is in a corrupt, antiquated institution, most likely based on Bethlehem Hospital, the primary asylum for the insane in London.[53] By placing Maria in such a place, Wollstonecraft emphasizes the point that madness is horrific, not touching or aesthetically pleasing. In her first few days in the asylum, Maria is terrorized by her fellow inmates when their incessant, incoherent sounds, particularly during the night, express the appalling condition of overpowering feeling combined with the loss of reason and linguistic expression. Like figures in a Gothic drama, they infiltrate her imagination and disrupt her sleep, uttering shrieks of rage and despair 'as proved the total absence of reason, and roused phantoms of horror in her mind, more terrific than all that dreaming superstition ever drew' (83). In her depiction of the horror of madness, Wollstonecraft reflects what Foucault described as the 'animality that haunted the hospitals of the period.'[54] But this animality could feel close to the viewer – as Roy Porter has observed, 'passions of all kinds could mushroom into madness.'[55] Drawing on the period's anxiety about the passions, Maria contemplates the wild energy of the insane, as their 'enthusiasm turned adrift, like some rich stream overflowing its banks, rushes forward with destructive velocity, inspiring a sublime concentration of thought' (76).[56] Maria's contemplation of the inmates produces a set of personal ruminations that disclose the true horror of madness. Wollstonecraft here follows Locke who, as Louis Charland explains, placed madness on a 'continuum from normal to abnormal,' seeing all humans as 'mad to some degree.'[57] When she contemplates the mad, Maria feels a sensation of terrifying intellectual vertigo that threatens to destabilize her own sense of sanity (76). For her, reason is fragile and unstable; passions are unwholesome, wild, and profuse. To see a mad person is to see one whose passions have become toxic to his reason. Thus, the horror lies in the fact that sanity is tenuous, particularly for women, for whom 'mental convulsion' – some sort of violent emotional agitation coming from male abuse – could happen at any time.

Although, as Small says, Wollstonecraft replaces Sterne's 'Mad Maria' with her own Maria Venables, Wollstonecraft also puts Maria into the position of the male viewer to revise the actual vignette of the love-mad maid. The woman referred to by Jemima as the 'lovely maniac' is the only inmate (other than Darnford) who is individualized in *Wrongs*, and so she stands out as an important part of Wollstonecraft's exposure of how patriarchal avenues of control drive women mad.[58] In this case, the avenues are

60   *Women and madness in the early Romantic novel*

guardianship, marriage, and the sentimental literary tradition. Through her presentation of this woman, Wollstonecraft depicts the love-mad maid as a formulaic vehicle of male control that hides its power through pity; and she insists that the proper attitude toward such madness is not pity or sexual arousal, as is generally the case in sentimental literature, but rather shock and horror.

> And Jemima gave her a new subject for contemplation, by describing the person of a lovely maniac, just brought into an adjoining chamber. She was singing the pathetic ballad of old Robin Gray, with the most heart-melting falls and pauses ... She began with sympathy to pourtray to herself another victim, when the lovely warbler flew, as it were, from the spray, and a torrent of unconnected exclamations and questions burst from her, interrupted by fits of laughter, so horrid, that Maria shut the door, and turning her eyes up to heaven, exclaimed, 'Gracious God!' (80)

When introduced, the 'lovely maniac' resembles the woman Harley encounters in Bethlehem Hospital, in that she is attractive and young and sings a beautiful song. Her story about having been married against her will to a rich old man further replicates that of the madwoman in *The Man of Feeling*. But whereas Harley has a tender moment with the madwoman, who responds to his pity and seems to confuse him with her lost 'Billy,' Maria is horrified, not only by the madwoman's insane laughter and nonsensical speech, by also by the shocking disparity between the loveliness of her ballad and the dreadfulness of her insanity.

Wollstonecraft's casting of the 'lovely maniac' as a figure not of pity, but rather of horror, also ruptures the aesthetic and sexual pleasure the male visitor and the reader get from the conventional love-mad maid. Maria is enjoying the woman's lovely song, much as a reader might enjoy Sterne's or Mackenzie's prose and expressions of feeling, only to have that pleasure turn to shock and dismay when the 'lovely warbler' turns into a raving lunatic. Given that she is not melancholic and passive, but rather maniacal and threatening, the woman's expression of madness is in stark contrast to that of the love-mad women in the sentimental tradition. The mental distraction of Sterne's 'Mad Maria' or of the lovely maniac Harley encounters in Bedlam is never threatening, violent, or unfeminine. On the contrary, the passivity of their suffering augments their feminine allure. In response, Wollstonecraft shatters the scene with horrid, insane laughter, making it impossible for a viewer to enjoy feeling pity for the woman's pain or to take aesthetic pleasure from female madness.

In the sentimental tradition, the love-mad maid loses her mind when she loses her lover because the culture believes that beautiful, genteel women are inherently fragile and dependent on male affection and care. In her

The Wrongs of Woman *and patriarchal control*   61

portrayal of the 'lovely maniac,' Wollstonecraft combines established ideas about female fragility with political points about the abuse of women, much as she does through Maria's own story. The scant details of the woman's background conveyed by Jemima suggest a connection between feminine delicacy and madness and between madness and childbirth. According to Jemima, 'she had been married, against her inclination, to a rich old man, extremely jealous (no wonder, for she was a charming creature); and that, in consequence of his treatment, or something which hung on her mind, she had, during her first lying-in, lost her senses' (80). The 'lovely maniac' has thus been pushed into madness not only by the loss of her lover, but more directly by being forced to marry an older man and to give birth to his child. Just like the influential medical writers believed, a series of emotional shocks created impressions that led to madness. Indeed, as John Mullan has observed describing literary sensibility more generally, the very traits that make women feminine also make them susceptible to psychological injury.[59] Childbirth, as well, was considered by medical authorities as a potential cause of hysteria.[60] Maria's conclusion that woman is a 'fragile flower' corresponds to theories that locate the cause of madness in the delicate nervous makeup of women, particularly when they are genteel and beautiful. However, Wollstonecraft links a series of wrongs of woman to this character's madness, wrongs inflicted by her father and husband, rather than merely her inherent weakness.[61] This woman may be a 'fragile flower,' but she has been forced to give up her lover and marry for gain; she has been abused by her spouse; and she has given birth to the child of her abusive husband, rather than of her lover.

In the account of the woman's past and through the song she sings, Wollstonecraft emphasizes that multiple external injuries – all the result of patriarchal avenues of control – have precipitated the 'lovely maniac's' madness. The song gives the reader additional insight into the cause of her insanity. According to Gary Kelly's notes, 'Auld Robin Gray' tells of a young woman whose true love went to sea, and in his absence, because her parents fall on hard times, she agrees to marry an elderly man. Her lover Jamie then returns, only to take his 'final farewell.'[62] There is another version, however, published in Edinburgh in 1825, that tells a different story, one that better fits the details Jemima offers and the backstory of the mad woman in *The Man of Feeling*, whom Wollstonecraft's 'lovely maniac' resembles. In this alternate version Jamie also goes to sea, but the marriage comes about through Auld Robin Gray's abusive machinations, rather than Jenny's desire to help her parents. Not only does Auld Robin know she is in love with Jamie when he marries her, he steals her parents' cow to render them so destitute Jenny must marry him to save her family from starvation.[63] The 'lovely maniac's' backstory, limited as it is, combined with

62   *Women and madness in the early Romantic novel*

the variations on the ballad, suggest that her madness originates in linked patriarchal abuses.

Defending female feeling

The end of the novel is, of course, unfinished, with only fragments for a conclusion. But before the novel dissolves into mostly tragic bits and pieces, Wollstonecraft gives Maria the task of defending the absent Darnford from charges of adultery and seduction.[64] For the most part, the court scene reinforces how the structures of power Wollstonecraft has been critiquing all along collude to control women. It is not an irony of the scene that George, as the husband in a crim. con. case, is the injured party, while his abuse of his wife is never brought to court – it is, instead, evidence of the foundational structure of patriarchal society. Men have the power to define women as sane or mad; the male-dominated medical profession sees all women as always on the verge of hysteria; and husbands have the legal right to incarcerate wives who seek to escape from their control. As the novel suggests, both the law and medical definitions are made by men to perpetuate male control. George's version of events conforms to a standard medical understanding of women's mental illness, as his counsel makes him out to be the victim of his wife's 'defects of temper' (170) rather than the cause of her need to escape. According to George's side of the story, 'after the birth of her child, her conduct was so strange, and a melancholy malady having afflicted one of the family, which delicacy forbade the dwelling on, it was necessary to confine her' (170). If she has 'defects of temper' she is, as it were, primed for further mental disturbance by her already delicate constitution and by the assumption, because of her uncle's condition, that madness runs in the family. Her inherent propensity to mental instability is assumed to have been activated by the birth of her child, which, according to physiologically oriented medical writing, is to be expected.[65] George's lawyers represent Maria's flight from her abusive husband as strange behaviour that points to a madness they believe is confirmed by her delicate mental condition after childbirth and by heredity. George's ability to commit Maria demonstrates the power men have over their wives, the complicity of a legal system that accepts such logic as solid grounds for incarceration, and the responsibility of a medical establishment that views women as always potentially mentally unstable.

The court scene is ostensibly a crim. con. case in which Maria tries unsuccessfully to defend her lover against the charge of seduction. But its real focus is on whether a woman has the right to act according to her own feelings. In her written statement, Maria uses powerful logical reasoning

The Wrongs of Woman *and patriarchal control* 63

..gue for her rights, claiming sexual autonomy, legal personhood, the right to regulate her own conduct, control her own inheritance, and leave her husband. She refuses gendered virtues when she insists that it is a 'false morality' that makes 'all the virtue of women consist in chastity, submission, and the forgiveness of injuries' (172). She condemns marriage for making 'women the property of their husbands' (172). She argues for women's sexual freedom when she says, 'I deemed, and ever shall deem, myself free' and insists that a woman must be allowed to 'consult her conscience, and regulate her conduct, in some degree, by her own sense of right' (172). After listening to her statement, the judge says that she is definitely immoral, certainly dangerous, and possibly mad. And he adds, 'we do not want French principles in public or private life,' because 'if women were allowed to plead their feelings, as an excuse or palliation of infidelity, it was opening a flood-gate for immorality' (174).[66] From the position of the law, women must be controlled and not allowed to act on their feelings because, if they did, it would be the end of morality as we know it. It would invite a dangerous French precedent into both private and public life, and so women's feelings are not to be accepted as a reason to give them any rights at all. Marriage, the judge determines, is about stability and control, not about how women feel. Thus, it would seem that Maria's attempt to establish autonomy has hit a dead-end and that Maria's story – despite exposing the way medicine, marriage, sentimental literature, and law all collude to control and injure women – will end in defeat.

The judge rejects Maria's entire defence of Darnford (and herself) and rules in George's favour in the crim. con. case.[67] However, in a statement that generally goes unnoticed by scholars, he is less certain after hearing her statement that she is mad. 'The proofs of an insanity in the family might render [confinement] however a prudent measure; and indeed, the conduct of the lady did not appear that of a person of sane mind,' he comments. But he qualifies his assessment, saying: 'Still such a mode of proceeding could not be justified, and might perhaps entitle the lady ... to a sentence of separation from bed and board' (174). The judge here seems to think that Maria's mental state is quite anomalous and somewhat insane, but he does not believe her behaviour justifies her being committed to an asylum. Importantly, despite his ruling in George's favour and his rejection of any argument for divorce or women's sexual autonomy, he treats Maria both as a rational individual and as a person who has been wronged. When he rules for George, the judge is ruling against Darnford – not against Maria – finding him guilty of seduction and determining he must pay damages. In a trial that is not about Maria's guilt or innocence, but rather about whether her lover seduced her and owes her husband compensation, Maria is unable to prove her lover's innocence through establishing her right, based on her

64   *Women and madness in the early Romantic novel*

feelings, to control her own sexual acts. But the judge listens to and responds to Maria's arguments. Moreover, he recommends bed and board – that is, a legal separation – based on George's treatment of her.[68] Kathryn Temple notes how much progress Maria has made from the novel's opening in the madhouse to its not-quite-concluding courtroom scene: 'At the beginning of the novella, she is all object: objectified by her family, then by her husband, then by the law when she is incarcerated in a madhouse, the object of legal action. By the end, she is a legal subject, a person in a legal sense, with a person's right to present a case and be heard.'[69] Temple is right about these important victories that accompany the judge's actions. Despite George's lawyer's efforts to portray Maria as mad, the judge treats her as sane, listens to her reasoned opinions, responds with a rational argument, tilts in her favour as to her sanity, and recommends she be allowed to legally separate from her husband. The trial scene, then, could be considered as not a complete failure; rather, it could be seen to present a model for women to gain some control of their lives and an illustration of how they might resist being considered both medically and legally mad. If the novel had ended with the courtroom scene, Wollstonecraft would have left her readers with the idea that women, by using reason to validate the importance of their feelings, might one day be able to change enough men's minds to remake the structures that oppress and control them.

Conclusion: inconclusion

The novel, however, does not end with the courtroom scene; and instead of a clear conclusion, Wollstonecraft left several fragments, most of which suggest Maria succumbs to mental disease. In the most pessimistic fragment, a pregnant Maria commits suicide after having been abandoned by Darnford. If this were, in fact, the end, the reader would have to conclude that Maria – with all her intelligence, passion, and energy – has been psychologically destroyed by a man she believed offered her an alternative to the imprisonment of marriage. Through this fragment, Wollstonecraft seems to be saying that it is the romantic imagination – more than the medical establishment, the law, or even marriage – that restricts, mentally confines, and drives women to madness. An episode prior to the courtroom scene, in which Maria refuses to leave the asylum when the keeper flees and the inmates have the chance to escape, illustrates how the romantic imagination confines women and leads them to destruction. Jemima says to Maria, '"I am prepared ... to accompany you in your flight." "But Darnford!" exclaimed Maria, mournfully, sitting down again, and crossing her arms – "I have no child to go to, and liberty has lost its sweets"' (166). It is only by

The Wrongs of Woman *and patriarchal control*   65

telling Maria that Darnford, too, will go free, and that Maria will be able to see him in London, that Jemima can motivate Maria to escape while she has the chance. When she sits down in her cell, refusing to leave, Maria shows that she would rather remain imprisoned within her romantic fantasy, with the 'magic lamp' (90) of erotic love her only light, than seek freedom, independence, and solidarity in friendship with Jemima. Wollstonecraft's concluding fragments suggest that this internalized prison of the romantic imagination is the most dangerous of all the male structures of control. Even when compared to the legal restrictions of marriage, the absence of political rights, the lack of economic opportunity, and medical definitions of hysteria, the romantic imagination is most deadly because it takes over a woman's mind by promising her pleasure rather than independence.

In the end, the only way Wollstonecraft suggests that women might evade the structures of male control that lead to madness and despair is for them to live apart from men as much as possible and to seek the society of other women. In the most extensive conclusion Wollstonecraft left, Maria is saved by Jemima who arrives just in time with the original lost daughter in tow. This sequence begins with the particularly horrific image of Maria's body as the tomb for an unborn child, which makes her, in attempting suicide, the potential murderer of her baby. However, when Jemima arrives, Maria vomits sufficiently to recover from the toxic substance she has swallowed.[70] Embracing the daughter she thought she had lost, she exclaims, 'The conflict is over! – I will live for my child!' (177). As Wollstonecraft has conceived of this potential ending, Jemima knows that Maria's survival is dependent on the child, and so she tells Maria she suspected deception about the child's death and went in search of her. 'I snatched her from misery – and (now she is alive again) would you leave her alone in the world, to endure what I have endured?' (177). This rescue suggests that the only escape from the relentless psychological injuries inflicted by men is female solidarity of a particular type: a new domestic partnership in a shared home with a shared child.[71]

Maria had, earlier in the novel, offered Jemima the opportunity to be a co-mother to the child in exchange for helping her escape from the asylum: 'In the name of God, assist me to snatch her from destruction! Let me but give her an education – let me but prepare her body and mind to encounter the ills which await her sex, and I will teach her to consider you as her second mother, and herself as the prop of your age' (108). It is this proposition that makes Jemima the agent of Maria's liberation, and later, in the most developed ending, the one who delivers her from the near deadly effects of mental disease. Female community is thus, as many scholars have noted, the only remedy this bleak novel offers for the 'wrongs of woman' – wrongs shown to be caused by a network of inter-related channels of male

66 · Women and madness in the early Romantic novel

power. Wollstonecraft conveys a fair degree of ambivalence about this solution, however, given that the majority of the other fragments suggest tragedy. The *deus ex machina* of Jemima's appearance with a child who was determined to be dead earlier in the novel should not, then, overwrite the horror of Maria's attempted suicide with a foetus in embryo, an act that represents extreme psychological distress.[72]

That said, Jemima, it seems, is the hero of the novel, while Darnford competes with George to be the villain. Symbolically, female friendship appears to save the day as the only force that can combat the intertwined systems of marital control and the romantic imagination. As the hero, Jemima shows a strength of mind and a determination not to be defeated that allows her to resist the stigma of illegitimacy, the abuse of men, and all the harmful elements of male control. Despite this victimization – indeed, as a method of overcoming her victimization – Jemima shows an extraordinary ability to care for Maria. It is significant that the solidarity that develops between the two women is based on Jemima's tenacity in refusing to allow Maria's child to suffer as she has suffered. The novel thus offers a glimpse of a way to break the chain of injury: women must resist the temptations of a romantic imagination, which is a deadly drug; they must be financially independent of men; they must not compete with, but rather help one another; and they must form new, all female families and live together in mutually supporting societies. This is perhaps not the feminotopia some readers have imagined, but it certainly suggests that avoiding men altogether is the best way for women to save themselves from debilitating and potentially deadly psychological injuries.

Notes

1 A criminal conversation case, often shorted to crim. con., was a suit for damages by the husband against his wife's lover.
2 The madhouse in *Wrongs of Woman* has long been recognized as an allegory for patriarchal control; although scholars have, perhaps surprisingly, spent little time discussing madness in the novel. The primary exception is Patricia Cove, '"The Walls of Her Prison": Madness, Gender, and Discursive Agency in Eliza Fenwick's *Secrecy* and Mary Wollstonecraft's *The Wrongs of Woman*,' *European Romantic Review* 23, no. 6 (December 2012), https://doi.org/10.1080/105095 85.2012.728828. Cove approaches the topic through Foucault. For discussions of the madhouse as an allegory, see Anne K. Mellor, 'Righting the Wrongs of Woman: Mary Wollstonecraft's *Maria*,' *Nineteenth-Century Contexts* 19, no. 4 (1996), https://doi.org/10.1080/08905499608583434; Diane Long Hoeveler, 'Reading the Wound: Wollstonecraft's *Wrongs of Woman, or Maria* and Trauma Theory,' *Studies in the Novel* 31, no. 4 (1999); www.jstor.org/stable/29533355;

The Wrongs of Woman *and patriarchal control*   67

and Eleanor Ty, *Unsex'd Revolutionaries: Five Women Novelists of the 1790s* (Toronto: University of Toronto Press, 1993).

3 There is an older tradition of Wollstonecraft scholarship that sees her as an author trapped by her own sensibility. See Syndy Conger, *Mary Wollstonecraft and the Language of Sensibility* (Rutherford, NJ and London: Fairleigh Dickinson University Press, 1994): xii; Mary Poovey, 'Mary Wollstonecraft: The Gender of Genres in Late Eighteenth-Century England,' *NOVEL: A Forum on Fiction* 15, no. 2 (1982): 119, https://doi.org/10.2307/1345219; and Nicola Watson, *Revolution and the Form of the British Novel, 1790–1825: Intercepted Letters, Interrupted Seductions* (Oxford: Oxford University Press, 1994), 57.

4 To George Blood on 3 July 1785: 'I have been very ill … My harassed mind will in time wear out my body … my spirits are quite deprest [*sic*]—I have lost all relish for life—and my almost broken heart is only cheered by the prospect of dearth [*sic*].' *The Collected Letters of Mary Wollstonecraft*, ed. Janet Todd (London: Penguin, 2003), 52.

5 G. J. Barker-Benfield, 'Mary Wollstonecraft's Depression and Diagnosis,' *The Psychohistory Review* 13, no. 4 (1985): 16.

6 Jane Darcy, *Melancholy and Literary Biography, 1640–1816* (Basingstoke: Palgrave Macmillan 2013), 123. Darcy counts over 50 examples under the index heading 'melancholy' in Janet Todd's *Collected Letters* to support her claim.

7 To Imlay from Hull on 12 June 1795: 'I have looked at the sea, and at my child, hardly daring to own to myself the secret wish, that it might become our tomb' (Todd, *Collected Letters*, 297). To Imlay from Copenhagen on 6 September 1795: 'I am strangely cast off.—How often, passing through the rocks, I have thought, "But for this child, I would lay my head on one of them, and never open my eyes again!"' (Todd, *Collected Letters*, 320).

8 She wrote to George Blood on 1 May 1786: 'My spirits are very low, and am so opprest [*sic*] by continual anxiety 'tis a labour to me to [do] anything—my former employments are quite irksome to me' (Todd, *Collected Letters*, 67). To her sister Fanny on 17 November 1786: 'I long for my eternal rest—My nerves are so impaired I suffer much more than I supposed I should do' (Todd, *Collected Letters*, 90).

9 6 December 1796: 'I am not well, to day, yet I scarcely know what to complain of, excepting extreme lowness of spirits … I hate this torpor of mind and senses' (Todd, *Collected Letters*, 382). 28 December 1796: 'Lowness of spirits, which I cannot conquer, leave me at the mercy of my imagination, and only painful recollections and expectations assail me' (Todd, *Collected Letters*, 387).

10 Godwin compiled the 'Author's Preface' out of notes Wollstonecraft left and parts of a letter. See Gary Kelly's note from *Mary and the Wrongs of Woman*, ed. Gary Kelly, (Oxford: Oxford World's Classics, 2009), 66 and 67. All references will be to this edition.

11 See Christine Cooper's discussion of this passage. 'Reading the Politics of Abortion: Mary Wollstonecraft Revisited,' *Eighteenth-Century Fiction* 14, no. 4 (2000): 736, https://doi.org/10.1353/ecf.2004.0057.

12 For a discussion of how Wollstonecraft uses this approach in her *Letters Written during a Short Residence in Sweden, Norway, and Denmark* (1796), her last publication before her death, see my 'Suffering, Sentiment, and Civilization: Pain and Politics in Mary Wollstonecraft's *Short Residence*,' *Studies in Romanticism* 45, no. 2 (Summer 2006), https://doi.org/10.2307/25602044.

13 Marilyn Butler calls this perspective Wollstonecraft's 'special contribution' in that she applies gender to her 'contemporaries' insights into cultural politics,' seeing women 'as a class exploited in all cultures and all ages.' Marilyn Butler, 'Introduction' in *The Works of Mary Wollstonecraft*, eds Janet Todd and Marilyn Butler (London: Pickering and Chatto, 1989), 17 and 25.

14 Jonathan Andrews and Andrew Scull, *Undertaker of the Mind: John Monro and Mad-Doctoring in Eighteenth-Century England* (Berkeley: University of California Press, 2001), 152.

15 Roy Porter, *Madmen: A Social History of Madhouses, Mad-Doctors, and Lunatics* (Rpt *Mind Forg'd Manacles*, 1987; Stroud, Gloucestershire: Tempus Publishing, 2004), 153.

16 Elizabeth Foyster, 'At the Limits of Liberty: Married Women and Confinement in Eighteenth-Century England,' *Continuity and Change* 17, no. 1 (January 2002), 40, https://doi.org/10.1017/S0268416002004058.

17 Foyster, 'Limits of Liberty,' 40.

18 This is the sort of sensibility Wollstonecraft saw as part of her own character. Jane Darcy writes that 'throughout her letters Wollstonecraft maintains that the core of her identity is her sensibility—her ability to feel deeply and to suffer. She equates an elevated form of sensibility as the quintessence of humane, refined moral feeling' (*Melancholy and Literary Biography*, 125).

19 Jennifer Radden, *The Nature of Melancholy: From Aristotle to Kristeva* (Oxford: Oxford University Press, 2000), 15. Radden traces this link to Aristotle's *Problems* in which he asks: "'Why is it that all men who have become outstanding in philosophy, statesmanship, poetry or the arts are melancholic, or are infected by the diseases arising from black bile?'" (*The Nature of Melancholy*, 12).

20 Elizabeth Dolan, 'British Romantic Melancholia: Charlotte Smith's *Elegiac Sonnets*, Medical Discourse and the Problem of Sensibility,' *Journal of European Studies* 33, no. 3/4 (January 2003): 238, https://doi.org/10.1177/0047244103040416.

21 Dolan, 'British Romantic Melancholia,' 238.

22 Readers will remember that Maria believes her husband, George Venables, has paid her maid to drug her and steal the baby.

23 Hoeveler, 'Reading the Wound,' 392.

24 James Boswell, *Boswell's Column. Being his Seventy Contributions to The London Magazine under the Pseudonym The Hypochondriack from 1777 to 1783*, ed. Margery Bailey (London: William Kimber, 1951), 50.

25 These are Margery Bailey's comments on Johnson. See her 'Introduction,' in Boswell, *Boswell's Column*, xiii.

The Wrongs of Woman *and patriarchal control*   69

26 Alan Richardson, *British Romanticism and the Science of the Mind* (Cambridge: Cambridge University Press, 2001), 395.

27 Samuel Johnson, *The History of Rasselas, Prince of Abissinia* (1759; Oxford: Oxford World's Classics, 2009), Chapters XLI–XLIII.

28 Boswell says as much through his epigraph from Horace: 'Words will avail the wretched mind to ease,/And much abate the dismal black disease' (Boswell, *Boswell's Column*, 21).

29 Heather Meek, 'Motherhood, Hysteria, and the Eighteenth-Century Woman Writer' in *The Secrets of Generation: Reproduction in the Long Eighteenth Century*, eds Raymond Stephanson and Darren N. Wagner (Toronto: University of Toronto Press, 2015), 253.

30 For a discussion of the memoir as therapeutic cure, see Shawn Lisa Maurer, 'The Female (As) Reader: Sex, Sensibility, and the Maternal in Wollstonecraft's Fictions,' *Essays in Literature* 19, no. 1 (1992): 37.

31 John Mullan, 'Hypochondria and Hysteria: Sensibility and the Physicians,' *The Eighteenth Century* 25, no. 2 (1984): 157, https://www-jstororg.libdata.lib.ua.edu/stable/41467321.

32 Foyster, 'Limits of Liberty,' 55.

33 Meek rightly identifies the abusive husband as the cause of Maria's afflictions, but she views Maria's condition as hysteria rather than melancholia. See 'Motherhood, Hysteria.'

34 Foyster, 'Limits of Liberty,' 56.

35 Foyster, 'Limits of Liberty,' 56.

36 Foyster, 'Limits of Liberty,' 56.

37 For the association of male melancholia with literary genius, see Radden, *The Nature of Melancholy,* 15.

38 Daniel O'Quinn is one of the few scholars to note the harm the uncle does to Maria. See Daniel O'Quinn, 'Trembling: Wollstonecraft, Godwin, and the Resistance to Literature,' *ELH* 64, no. 3 (Fall 1997): 769, www.jstor.org/stable/30030239.

39 Maria finds out only after she has married George that her uncle offered him an enticing dowry.

40 See, for example, Mary Poovey, *The Proper Lady and the Woman Writer: Ideology as Style in the Works of Mary Wollstonecraft, Mary Shelley, and Jane Austen* (Chicago, University of Chicago Press, 1984), 97.

41 Julie, the heroine of Rousseau's novel, has a sexual relationship with her tutor St Preux, who, because of his status, is not an acceptable spouse for her. She later marries an older man of her father's selection. Jean-Jacques Rousseau, *Julie; or, The New Heloise*, trans. Philip Stewart and Jean Vaché (1761; Lebanon, NH: Dartmouth College Press, 1997).

42 Maria's invention of Darnford is frequently mentioned by scholars. For just one example, see Adam Komisaruk, 'The Privatization of Pleasure: "Crim. Con." in Wollstonecraft's Maria,' *Law and Literature* 16, no. 1 (March 2004): 48, https://doi.org/10.1525/lal.2004.16.1.33.

70   *Women and madness in the early Romantic novel*

43 Jane Kromm, 'Olivia Furiosa: Maniacal Women from Richardson to Wollstonecraft,' *Eighteenth-Century Fiction* 16, no. 3 (April 2004): 370, https://doi.org/10.1353/ecf.2004.0020.

44 Butler, 'Introduction' to *Works*, 25.

45 Annette Wheeler Cafarelli, 'Rousseau and British Romanticism: Women and the Legacy of Male Radicalism' in *Cultural Interactions in the Romantic Age: Critical Essays in Comparative Literature*, ed. Gregory Maertz (Albany: SUNY Press, 1998), 132. Cafarelli is just one of many scholars to observe that Wollstonecraft criticizes Rousseau through the impact of *Julie* on Maria. Gary Kelly is an outlier in describing Wollstonecraft's use of Rousseau as 'emancipatory' ('Introduction' to *Mary and the Wrongs of Woman*, xxvii).

46 See the section on 'Love-madness and the love-mad maid' in this book's Introduction.

47 Helen Small, *Love's Madness: Medicine, the Novel, and Female Insanity, 1800–1865* (Oxford: Clarendon Press, 1998), 21.

48 Small, *Love's Madness*, 21.

49 Wollstonecraft's descriptions of the mad are most likely based both on her reading and on her visit to Bethlehem Hospital on 6 February 1797 with Godwin and the publisher Joseph Johnson. William Brewer references Godwin's diary for the information. See William Brewer, *The Mental Anatomies of William Godwin and Mary Shelley* (Cranbury: Associated University Presses, 2001), 129.

50 Porter, *Madmen*, 55.

51 Frantic meant 'affected with mental disease; 'lunatic', insane; (in later use) violently or ragingly mad' (*OED*).

52 Philip Martin, *Mad Women in Romantic Writing* (New York: St Martin's Press, 1987), 22.

53 Bethlehem Hospital, or 'Bedlam,' was investigated by the House of Commons in 1815–1816 and found to be a place of 'gross negligence in the care and management of patients.' Jonathan Andrews and Andrew Scull, *Undertaker of the Mind: John Monro and Mad-Doctoring in Eighteenth-Century England* (Berkeley: University of California Press, 2001), 40.

54 Michel Foucault, *Madness and Civilization: A History of Insanity in the Age of Reason*, trans. Richard Howard (1965; New York: Vintage Books, 1988), 72.

55 Porter, *Madmen*, 35.

56 Michael DePorte observes that, whatever their theory, all doctors in the last half of the eighteenth century agreed that 'the passions were a primary threat.' *Nightmares and Hobbyhorses: Swift, Sterne, and Augustan Ideas of Madness* (San Marino: Huntington Library, 1974), 12.

57 Louis Charland, 'John Locke on Madness: Redressing the Intellectualist Bias,' *History of Psychiatry* 25, no. 2 (2014): 142, https://doi.org/10.1177/0957154X13518719.

58 S. Leigh Matthews also calls attention to the inter-textuality of this scene; however, she reads it as a way to give 'voice' to silenced women. '(Un)Confinements: The Madness of Motherhood in *Wrongs of Woman*' in *Mary Wollstonecraft and Mary Shelley: Writing Lives*, eds Helen M. Buss, D. L.

The Wrongs of Woman *and patriarchal control* 71

Macdonald, and Anne McWhir (Waterloo: Wilfrid Laurier University Press, 2001), 87–8.

59 Mullan, 'Hypochondria and Hysteria,' 153–4.

60 See Meek, 'Motherhood, Hysteria,' 240.

61 Kromm makes a similar observation when she writes that the young woman's condition is 'drawn from social causal factors in male/female relationships rather than inherent natural flaws' ('Olivia Furiosa,' 369).

62 Kelly references *The Oxford Book of Eighteenth-Century Verse*, ed. David Nichol Smith (Oxford, Clarendon Press, 1926). See Kelly, 'Introduction' to *Mary and Maria*, 541–2.

63 This version of the ballad concludes with Auld Robin Gray dying and bequeathing to Jamie his property and his young wife. See Verse IX. 'Auld Robin Gray.' National Library of Scotland. https://digital.nls.uk/publications-by-scottish-clubs/archive/78395475 (accessed 4 September 2021).

64 As Adam Komisaruk observes, 'Wollstonecraft's audience would have known that a man could sue his wife's lover for the offense known as "criminal conversation" or "crim. con"' ('The Privatization of Pleasure,' 34).

65 Heather Meek notes that 'the association of mental illness with pregnancy and childbirth was often articulated in medical texts' at the time, and she adds that 'woman's propensity towards hysteria and illness was, in the accepted medical view, only aggravated by pregnancy and motherhood' ('Motherhood, Hysteria,' 240 and 239).

66 The political aspects of Wollstonecraft's novel as a post-Revolutionary text, evident elsewhere, come to the foreground here with the judge's reference to French principles.

67 Most readings view the trial as a failure because the judge is unconvinced by Maria's argument about her sexual liberation. See, for example, Hoeveler, 'Reading the Wound,' 402 and Poovey, *Proper Lady*, 108. However, in the real world of the 1790s it would have been unthinkable for the judge to determine in Darnford's favour on the basis of Maria's declaration.

68 Marilyn Butler explains that this would be the business of a different court. 'Ecclesiastical courts could grant divorce from bed and board, a legal separation which provided the wife with alimony, but prohibited remarriage' ('Introduction' to *Works*, 181, note a).

69 Kathryn Temple, 'Heart of Agitation: Mary Wollstonecraft, Emotion, and Legal Subjectivity,' *The Eighteenth Century* 58, no. 3 (October 2017): 379, https://doi.org/10.1353/ecy.2017.0031.

70 The fragments suggest Wollstonecraft was thinking particularly autobiographically in her attempt to conclude the novel. She had attempted suicide by laudanum overdose in May 1795 after discovering Imlay had another lover.

71 Some readers see considerable optimism in the fragmentary conclusion—an optimism based on the idea of co-mothering and all-female communities. See Conger, *Mary Wollstonecraft and the Language of Sensibility* and Maurer, 'Sex, Sensibility, and the Maternal in Wollstonecraft's Fictions' on the regenerative potential of bonding through motherhood. For optimism

about avoiding heterosexual plots and building same-sex communities, see Claudia Johnson, *Equivocal Beings: Politics, Gender, and Sentimentality in the 1790s: Wollstonecraft, Radcliffe, Burney, Austen* (Chicago: University of Chicago Press, 1995), 65–6; Vivien Jones, '"The Tyranny of the Passions": Feminism and Heterosexuality in the Fiction of Wollstonecraft and Hays,' in *Political Gender: Texts and Contexts*, eds Sally Ledger, Joesphine Mcdonagh, and Jane Spencer (London: Routledge, 1994): 181; and Susan Lanser, *Fictions of Authority: Women Writers and Narrative Voice* (Ithaca: Cornell University Press, 1992), 237.

72 I disagree with both Christine Cooper, who argues that the novel endorses abortion as a form of female autonomy, and with Michelle Faubert, who sees the suicide attempts as liberational political protest. See Cooper, 'Politics of Abortion,' 776 and Michelle Faubert, 'The Fictional Suicides of Mary Wollstonecraft,' *Literature Compass* 12, no. 12 (December 2015): 657, https://doi.org/10.1111/lic3.12282. Neither Cooper's endorsement of abortion nor Faubert's valorisation of suicide takes into account the ambiguity of the concluding fragments and the deep despair embedded in most of the potential conclusions.

2

Of madness and monitors: *Secresy; or, The Ruin on the Rock*

In Eliza Fenwick's anonymously published, epistolary novel *Secresy*, two characters – a woman and a man – die of mental illnesses which are the result of disappointment in love.[1] In the case of the young woman, Sibella Valmont, love-madness and the eventual melancholic and hysteric conditions that ensue are unconnected to any inherent weakness or proclivity. In a clear rejection of late eighteenth-century medical ideas about hysteria and established literary conventions of the love-mad maid, Fenwick creates a character whose madness results from an onslaught of male abuse. Sibella is imprisoned on her uncle's estate and raised in isolation according to Rousseau's educational ideas as expressed through the character Sophie in *Émile*.[2] Although Fenwick never mentions Rousseau by name, she carries out an extensive argument with him in the first half of the novel, in which she contests, as Isobel Grundy puts it, his 'gendered system of education' and ties it to both patriarchal and libertine abuses.[3] When the Rousseauvian-educated Sibella dies, it is because the confinement and restricted education inflicted on her by her villainous uncle, Mr Valmont, has led her to develop an idealized version of Clement Montgomery, her lover, whose betrayal causes her fatal hysterical attack. In contrast, Arthur Murden, the young man who dies from love-madness, shows all the signs of inherent mental and emotional instability associated at the time with female sensibility. Fenwick uses Murden's madness to transfer traditional ideas about women's inherent mental and emotional weakness onto a man, which facilitates her multi-faceted exposé of injurious male actions as the real cause of women's mental disease.[4]

Although from the novel's start Sibella suffers from a light form of love-madness, Fenwick eschews tracing her condition to native sensibility, inherent feminine weakness, or a physiological propensity to hysteria. Instead, Fenwick blames men for the pernicious ways they think about and try to shape women. The desire for women to be docile, subservient wives or idealized, erotic mistresses motivates the men in this novel to attempt to control and influence Sibella. Rousseau's influential *Émile* offers a plan to

74 *Women and madness in the early Romantic novel*

do both, which makes it the target of Fenwick's critique as the unnamed inspiration for Valmont's 'system,' as Sibella's friend and correspondent Caroline calls it (39). In Sue Chaplin's words, Valmont's Rousseauvian project requires 'that a woman be kept in ignorance of virtually everything except the best way to please her future husband.'[5] Fenwick's novel shows that the desire to create docile wives who double as desirable mistresses – an ambition shared by the novel's patriarchs and libertines – denies women their natural intellectual abilities and forces them into psychologically destructive ways of thinking. Whether she is wanted by the patriarch as an obedient wife or by the libertine as an alluring mistress (or both at once), Sibella is subject to the plots, plans, and fixations of men who disregard her desires and whose cumulative abuses drive her mad. Although Sibella's death is understandable within the context of late eighteenth-century medical ideas, and although she appears to be a love-mad maid, the novel's broad political critique places the blame for Sibella's mental deterioration on abuses inflicted by patriarchal control, libertinism, and a Rousseauvian education.[6]

'You are a glorious girl': the madness of Sibella Valmont

The novel's insistence on female reason, which is seen in the opening letters, is central to Fenwick's revision of love-madness.[7] Valmont believes women incapable of reason, and Caroline skilfully manipulates his disparaging opinions into permission to allow a correspondence with Sibella, whom she has met during a visit with her mother to Valmont Castle. Several minor characters in the novel make scornful remarks linking Sibella to the 'unreason' of madness, but Caroline emphasizes her intellectual strength and high-minded sense of independence.[8] She writes to Sibella: 'You are a glorious girl … You awaken my mind to more and more love of those fervid qualities that shine so eminent in you' (89). Sibella shows her reasoning power early in the novel when she recounts an argument with Valmont about the capacities of the female mind. She tells Caroline about Valmont's complaint that, despite his 'pondering on [her] welfare,' somehow she is not the 'docile and grateful creature' he expects (42). Sibella explains how she responded with logic and self-assertion: 'Am I to be unhappy, because I and not you have discovered how I might be very, very happy?' (42). Fenwick makes the conversation deliberately cryptic because it is not until later that she allows Sibella to reveal she is in love with Clement, Valmont's adopted son, and that Valmont has forbidden the relationship and sent Clement away. The opacity of Valmont's motivations aside, the conversation points to Sibella's reasoning power and her awareness of her guardian's cruel and tyrannical use of power. The conversation Sibella reports to Caroline shifts quickly to her use of her mind, which Valmont deplores. Frowning, he says, 'Always reasoning ... I tell you, child, you cannot, you shall not reason.' To which Sibella replies, 'I do not think as you think,' and he answers, 'you are not born to think; you were not made to think.' Valmont then silences her by raising his voice and asserting his power: 'Silence, Sibella!' (43). Sibella explains to Caroline how she reasoned through her fear, asking herself what more he could do to her and discovering that this sort of internal dialogue helps her manage her fright.

Sibella's articulation of free and independent thought through her letters to Caroline represents a challenge to both Valmont's power over her and to the conception of women as inherently susceptible to love-madness. Despite her uncle's anger and denigration of her intelligence, Sibella understands her mind to be free, and she exercises intellectual defiance, which she bases on her capacity for reason. Expressing herself through a Cartesian exercise in autonomy and self-respect, Sibella writes to Caroline: 'But I know, and he knows too if he would but own it, that I do think; that I was born to think: – and I will think' (43), and she refers to thought as 'the soul of existence!'(44). Sibella understands that thought – comprising reason, feeling, and imagination – frees her from Valmont's control. As Nicola Watson observes, 'Sibella demonstrates that "natural" (uneducated, insulated, unsocialized) womanhood is in fact independent and active – the exact opposite of her uncle Valmont's ideal woman.'[9] As long as she uses her naturally, highly capable mind and exercises her desire for independent thought, he cannot make her conform to his version of what a woman should be – an inherently intellectually feeble being, incapable of reason.

Not only is Sibella naturally rational and desirous to learn, she also possesses an extraordinary integrity – an ethical steadfastness and a sense of wholeness in her sincerity – that is central to her character. Sibella first shows her integrity when Arthur Murden sneaks into the Valmont estate and masquerades as a hermit to gain access to her. Pretending to be a seer, he attempts to engage her in conversation, but she resists him and refuses to speak with a supposed supernatural entity. 'I do not deem you worthy of enquiry,' she says, 'for you came with pretences of falsehood and guile, and those are coverings that virtue ever scorns' (103). The enigmatic figure entreats her to secrecy, which makes Sibella suspicious. She tells Caroline: 'I warned him to depart. I told him ... that I had ever scorned to separate my wishes from my acts, or my actions from my words' (105–6). Later, when accused by her uncle of lying about what Clement has told her upon his return from two years spent in the outside world, Sibella responds: 'Falsehoods! ... Sir, I have nothing to do with falsehoods' (121). At this point in the novel, Sibella draws strength for resistance from her sincerity and sense of self-respect. However, the integrity she displays in these instances deteriorates later in the novel after she is convinced by Clement to lie to her uncle about their sexual relationship. This coerced self-betrayal contributes to the onset of mental disease later in the novel. She is, early in the novel, independent, clear-thinking, sincere, and incorruptible; but later, with her mind fettered by her misguided love for Clement, she will be the fuzzy-minded keeper of a debilitating secret that destroys her sense of self.

Although Sibella is rational, sincere, and valiant when the novel begins, she is already suffering from a form of love-madness. In the novel's first letter, Caroline describes her impression of Sibella as being unhappy: 'Yet it is only by her sudden wanderings in conversation, and that apparent restlessness of dissatisfaction in her, which seeks change of place because all places alike are irksome, that I ground my opinion' (40). The description shows an absence of mind and an unsettledness associated with both love-madness and melancholia. In addition to seeing that Sibella is pensive and distracted, Caroline notices she frequently gazes on a portrait of herself and weeps while caressing her pet fawn, whose collar bears the initials 'C. M.' Philip Martin notes that the 'myth' of the love-mad woman centres on the 'woman's madness being a consequence of her private and sometimes her secret emotional life.'[10] This is certainly the case for Sibella, whose mysterious sadness prompts Caroline's sympathy and curiosity, although she does not consider Sibella to be mad.

At first glance, Sibella seems to resemble the more stereotypical love-mad maids, such as Sterne's 'Mad Maria' and the woman Harley encounters in Bethlehem Hospital – characters whose primary role is draw forth the morally valuable sympathy of the reader and the male protagonist while offering mild titillation and reinforcing feminine codes of behaviour and dependency.[11] In Elaine Showalter's words, these figures offered a 'touching image of feminine vulnerability and a flattering reminder of female dependence on male affection' while posing no threat to 'domineering parents and false-hearted men.'[12] Although Sibella's melancholy highlights her feminine attractiveness and, as Caroline and the reader come to discover, stems from sorrow over an absent lover, Sibella's situation and characterization diverge considerably from the more standard models of female love-madness. In the first place, she is not observed by a male protagonist seeking erotic stimulation and moral validation, but is rather befriended by a woman who wishes to set her free. Second, she is not a vacant, passive figure, but is rather a strong-minded young woman with a complex psychological makeup and a past that cannot be reduced to abandonment by a lover. And third, rather than reinforce female dependency on men, Sibella resists her domineering guardian and poses a threat to her false-hearted lover who has reason to fear her sincerity.

Of madness and monitors: Secresy 77

Sibella's resemblance to and divergence from more standard representations of female love-madness constitutes a set of revisions, on Fenwick's part, to the love-mad maid. In her revisions, Fenwick carefully orchestrates Sibella's emotional displays at the beginning of the novel to add a sense of sublimity, rather than either a comforting pathos or an inherent fragility, to her character. There is a solemn mystery to Sibella that tips the balance away from love-madness and toward melancholy, as there seems at first to be no cause for Sibella's sadness.[13] Sibella is further differentiated from the standard love-mad maiden by her association with mysterious, otherworldly, mythological powers. As Sue Chaplin observes, Caroline is the 'first to suggest to the reader the sublime spiritual qualities possessed by Sibella.'[14] Sibella walks the grounds at night, unafraid, and she is constantly seated beneath a great oak, which implies Druidical powers.[15] Moreover, Caroline describes her as a 'Wood Nymph, Dryad, and Hymadriad' [*sic*] (54), which gives her a mythological connection to nature. Sibella's moonlit wanderings and her association with natural mythology hint at the ancient connection of madness with divine inspiration – a connection furthered by her name's etymological link to the ancient Greek prophetesses, the sibyls. Her characterization here calls to mind what Max Byrd terms the 'ambiguity of madness,' or its ability offer a 'compensatory magical power.'[16]

Sibella is further distanced from the standard love-mad maid in that the melancholy she displays when first introduced was more often claimed by men than women in the early Romantic period. After melancholy had been disparaged for much of the eighteenth century, it was revived at century's end as a mark of genius, as it had been in the Renaissance and before. As Jennifer Radden notes, the melancholy man was one who 'felt more deeply, saw more clearly, and came closer to the sublime than ordinary mortals.'[17] Sibella's initial melancholy exemplifies what Anne Digby describes as an 'early romantic sensibility' that saw the 'perceptions of the mad as authentic experience similar in its validity to that of the poet.'[18] Sibella's melancholy, then, as described by Caroline, is the mark of the noblest faculties of mind and soul, faculties at the time associated not with the love-mad maid, but with the inspired male genius.

Not only does Fenwick alter the profile of the love-mad maid to connect her melancholia to genius and the sublime, rather than to the mere absence of her lover, she also gives her an extended backstory to explain her bereavement. This backstory shows that women are susceptible to emotional injury, not through inherent fragility, but through their male-controlled psychological formation. One of the most important aspects of Sibella's incipient love-madness is that Valmont has been successful in following Rousseau's dictate that 'the whole education of women ought to relate to men.'[19] Although Valmont failed to make Sibella docile, he

78 *Women and madness in the early Romantic novel*

succeeded in making her emotionally dependent on Clement by bringing him to the castle as his 'adopted' son after starving the young Sibella of love. Because Sibella is intellectually, emotionally, and socially isolated, she idealizes love. And because she has been exposed to only one person she can love, she loves him in an idealized way. Sibella is convinced that Clement shares and reflects her feelings to the extent that there is little individuation between them. She writes to Caroline: 'Our minds, our principles, our affections are the same; and, while I trace his never to be forgotten image within my breast, I know how fondly he cherishes the remembrance of mine' (59). The fact that it is not Clement's portrait she dotes on, but rather a portrait of herself painted by Clement, suggests that the love she feels for him erases her sense of herself as a separate being. This erasure of self that lies behind the more typical love-mad maid's vacant bereavement is here shown to be the product of Sibella's Rousseauvian education.

Although Caroline cannot figure out what game Valmont is playing in ordering Clement to think of Sibella only as a sister, she recognizes that he has set Sibella up to dedicate herself to love and to fall in love with Clement. 'With such an education as he has given you,' she writes to Sibella, 'it was impossible you should not have become a romantic enthusiast in whatever species of passion first engaged your feelings: and Valmont took care to make that first passion *Love*' (140). Although a woman of reason, Caroline is not opposed to love and sexuality. Rather, she objects to Sibella's choice being the only man she has ever known. Caroline understands that Sibella's limited education and lack of exposure to the outside world ensured that she would pour herself with no sense of pragmatism into the first thing to excite her emotions, which Valmont made sure was Clement. The problem Caroline identifies (and one that is applicable far beyond this novel) is that, isolated from society, Sibella is unable to reflect upon the man she loves and evaluate his moral character. Caroline is convinced that an upbringing within society would have changed Sibella's love by giving her the capacity to accurately judge Clement's qualities. Sibella's love for Clement – which will become debilitating – is thus, according to Caroline, entirely the product of Valmont's experiment in emotional engineering.

The turning point in Sibella's life – when she moves from being a highly rational, albeit melancholic, romantic and begins her slide into mental disease – comes when she determines that she and Clement must unite sexually and commit to a 'marriage' of the heart. As a woman who will eventually die from love-madness, she begins the journey to her death by an act of sexual agency, which is in stark contrast to the sexual passivity conveyed by the typical love-mad maid. The event occurs while Clement is suffering from Mr Valmont's displeasure after his two-year absence has failed to make him despise society as his (adoptive) father wishes.

Of madness and monitors: Secresy 79

Sibella sees he lacks spirit and believes he is anxious about Mr Valmont's vague references to another suitor, and so she proposes a 'union' with Clement to restore him to himself (129). As Mercy Cannon observes, Sibella 'sees romantic commitment as an antidote to Clement's infirmities.'[20] However, Sibella mistakes Clement's character, thinking her act will bring back the 'animated noble Clement' of the past (129) when in fact, he has always been insincere and cowardly. Sibella explains in the 'billet' she gives Clement that she wants to put his mind at ease by proving that he cannot lose her, and so she invites him to her room to assure him of her fidelity: 'With pure hearts and hands, we will plight our fervent unspotted faith. Say I am your's [sic], and you are mine, and sorrow and jealousy will vanish as a mist. You shall go the transported confiding husband' (131). Sibella believes this commitment, this contract, will dispel the injuries of his mind – his sorrow, jealousy, and despair – and send him back into the 'world' full of confidence in her fidelity and love. However, in tending to Clement's wellbeing, Sibella harms herself in that the contract very quickly takes a toll on her mental health – but not because she has violated the rules of female propriety. Rather, Sibella becomes anxious and ill at ease because she has been persuaded by Clement to hide the relationship from her guardian. In making this agreement, Sibella violates her sense of integrity, a violation that, along with Clement's equivocal behaviour, sets her on a path toward madness.

Sibella's invitation to Clement to become her 'husband' can be understood as an act that is in keeping with Rousseau's ideas about women. In rebelling against Valmont and acting according to her feelings, Sibella behaves like a 'Jacobin' heroine – like Mary Hays' Emma Courtney, for example, who, mirroring Rousseau's Julie, believes in the purity of erotic love outside of marriage. As Nicola Watson observes, Sibella is both Julie-like in her revolutionary union of the heart outside of marriage and Sophie-like in seeking to serve her male partner.[21] However, although Watson argues that the conflict between the 'Julie' and the 'Sophie' versions of Sibella is central to the novel's struggle against male authoritarian control, the two Rousseauvian ideas of women are not opposed but are rather closely linked. Stephen Behrendt explains that Rousseau makes the point in both texts that 'woman's primary duty is to attend to the comforts of her male partner, submitting entirely and willingly to his inclinations and desires (in part by anticipating them) while nurturing a humbly subordinate but infinitely supportive behaviour that is grounded in her own innate physical and imaginative beauty and sensitivity.'[22] In their 'union,' Sibella does just that: she anticipates Clement's desires, nurturing him through supportive behaviour, and dedicating her beauty and sensibility to his service. In this way, Sibella's seeming act of sexual autonomy can be

80   *Women and madness in the early Romantic novel*

understood as an act of self-injury resulting from having been trained to be both Julie and Sophie.

Sibella's mistaken devotion to Clement, a mistake stemming from the Rousseauvian education Valmont has inflicted on her, leads her to willingly abandon her chastity. But more serious in the world of this novel than Sibella's loss of 'virtue' is her abandonment of a different kind of virtue: her high-minded sense of integrity. As Mercy Cannon observes, Sibella's secrets are fatal 'not because they flout social customs or parental authority, but because the diseased nature of secrecy exists in opposition to the integrity of the individual.'[23] Having compromised her integrity through hiding the 'marriage,' and suffering from her vow of secrecy, Sibella experiences a deterioration in her mental condition soon after Clement's return to London. At this point her earlier mysterious and sublime melancholy turns into a melancholic disease exemplified by the complaint: 'Clement – my Clement is gone! All is silence around me' (156). Previously content with her woods and her fawn, Sibella was able to find solace in nature and her own thoughts; now she finds her mind is 'disgusted with its own conceptions,' and she senses herself sinking into 'languor and dissatisfaction' (156). By intentionally hiding the nature of her relationship with Clement from Valmont, Sibella has sacrificed her integrity, a core aspect of her sense of self, and becomes susceptible to the ravages of a melancholic disease.

With Clement's absence after their 'union,' Sibella's mental condition deteriorates rapidly. She notes that 'every fond affection of [her] soul revolts' against the secrecy, and she is plagued by doubts and anxieties about Clement. Although Sibella wilfully disregards what Caroline has told her about Clement's behaviour in London, his failure to contact her causes afflictions of both body and mind. She notes 'one hour heavily creeps after its fellowed hour' and complains that 'broken sleep and appalling visions create debility of mind and body for the ensuing dawn' (249). Sibella's inability to sleep is a sign of mental duress, and that sleeplessness creates further mental and physical weakness. When she does sleep, she has nightmares – 'appalling visions' – that wake her and exhaust her physically and mentally. With a condition corresponding to Stanley Jackson's description of melancholia – 'fear and despondency, usually associated with aversion to food, sleeplessness, irritability, and restlessness'[24] – Sibella's affliction differs considerably from the incipient love-madness and sublime melancholy she exhibited at the beginning of the novel.

Sibella's mental disease worsens after she admits to her 'union' with Clement and is faced with a letter from Clement to Valmont denying the relationship. Caroline hears that Sibella now 'droops under her uncle's cruelty' and learns that she 'eats little, sighs deeply, but weeps seldom' and can been heard talking of a letter that she holds between her hands as she 'traverses her apartment in extreme agitation,' saying '*He never never wrote it!*' (306). When Valmont discovers Sibella's pregnancy, he imprisons her in her room, denying her freedom of movement. From this point, the various descriptions of Sibella – from Lord Filmar and Arthur Murden, who have both surreptitiously gained access to her – point to the rapid deterioration of her mind. She paces, talks to herself, fasts, weeps, is distracted, and lacks awareness of her surroundings. Her imprisonment augments the injury of Clement's equivocal behaviour and further damages her mind and her emotional wellbeing. Anxiety, sleeplessness, fixation, lack of interest in her previous occupations, weeping, pacing, and absence of appetite – these are all indications that Sibella's melancholy is turning into a dangerous disease.

The novel moves towards its tragic close in a chaotic scene narrated by the libertine Lord Filmar who, discovering Sibella is pregnant after he has abducted her, takes her to Caroline's house in London where Clement has just married Caroline's mother for her money.[25] Clement's exit from the room, which confirms his faithlessness, acts as the final blow to Sibella's already damaged psyche, and she collapses in a faint. When she stirs after having fainted from shock, Sibella finally, although only temporarily, conforms to the pattern of the love-mad woman. She becomes distracted and confused, unsure of her own and of Caroline's and Clement's identities, and is unaware of her role in Caroline's weeping.[26] Gazing intently at Caroline's face, 'as if in search of something,' she finally exclaims, in Filmar's description, '"It is Caroline!"' And, 'spreading her arms wide, she looked down upon herself: "Sibella!" – then, every muscle of her face convulsed with anguish, she bent her eyes upon the door – "and that was Clement! – Oh!"' (347). With the self-recognition and the understanding that the man who rejected her was, in fact, her beloved Clement, Sibella's mind settles into a blank, despairing acceptance. Sibella at this moment succumbs to love-madness and conforms to the sentimental model of losing her mind when she loses her man. But she is an atypical love-mad maid in that Fenwick gives her a subjective voice, an heroic personality, a complex psyche, and a detailed backstory filled with cumulative male-inflicted injuries.

From a late eighteenth-century medical perspective, Sibella's affliction at the end is hysteria – she collapses in a faint because of an emotional excess, and later she experiences convulsions. Medical professionals, as we have seen, still believed in the nervous-system theory of hysteria in which women were understood to have weaker and more sensitive internal organs and systems than men.[27] Even though Fenwick rejects gendered explanations of hysteria, Sibella's illness and death can still be understood through the period's medical science. When Sibella collapses at the discovery of

82 *Women and madness in the early Romantic novel*

Clement's betrayal, she is experiencing the mental and physical impact of an emotional shock. Drawing on the influential physician and medical writer Robert Whytt, Foucault offers an assessment of medical thinking that explains how Sibella could be killed by such a blow. Whytt, he writes, 'admits that an intense emotion can provoke madness exactly as impact can provoke movement, for the sole reason that emotion is both impact in the soul and agitation of the nervous fibre.'[28] Sibella's emotional shock at realizing Clement's betrayal causes both convulsions and paralysis, in addition to the mental dislocation of distraction. The shock of his betrayal travels through the nerves, permeating a body already weakened by melancholia, creating a violent internal agitation that causes her death. Her condition is an example of Enlightenment thinking about what Roy Porter calls 'sympathetic symbioses' and what Whytt referred to as the 'laws of union between the soul and the body.'[29] Although Sibella dies from an emotional shock that travels through the nerves and disrupts bodily functioning, this is not because she is, as a refined woman, predisposed to nervous disorders. Rather, at the beginning of the novel, Fenwick makes it clear that she is both mentally and physically robust. The long plotline shows that her disease is of external, rather than internal, origin and that her mind has been injured by the selfish actions of both patriarchs and libertines, making her unable to survive her lover's betrayal.

The injurious patriarchs

Through Sibella's tyrannical guardian Mr Valmont, Fenwick bundles together libertinage, misogyny, repression, and Rousseau under the sign of the patriarch.[30] Within the long history leading up to Sibella's fatal love-madness, blame for the tragedy falls clearly on Mr Valmont, the man in charge of her education who is an incarnation of repressive patriarchal power. 'Valmont' is, of course, the name of the libertine anti-hero of Choderlos de Laclos' *Liaisons Dangereuses* (1782), and through the use of this name Fenwick links injurious patriarchs to injurious libertines. Fenwick's Valmont, disgusted by an increasingly meritocratic society that lacks reverence for his ancient name, has retreated to his remote country estate to raise his niece and supposed adopted son according to unnamed Rousseauvian educational principles. Mrs Ashburn's friends tell Caroline that Valmont's father was obsessed with the 'great deeds of his ancestors' (61) and they note that this Valmont, the eldest son, is 'not a whit behind his father in his veneration for high birth' (62). Valmont was disappointed, however, when he went out into the world as a young man and discovered that his birth and ancestry meant very little to anyone else. Fenwick makes

Of madness and monitors: Secresy 83

it clear that Valmont's ideas about women match the medieval timbre of his upbringing. As Isobel Grundy observes, 'Valmont's experimental views on educating or mis-educating women are shown to be reactionary, not merely as a contemporary reaction against the French Revolution, but in interdependence with the feudal character of his physical setting and his concept of family.'[31] And the castle itself is associated with a masculine obsession for a glorious militaristic past. Miriam Wallace points out that the novel 'situates the gothic within 1790s Britain itself rather than abroad in Catholic Europe or in the pre-Enlightenment past,' an observation suggesting that the oppressive male power Fenwick critiques was deeply rooted in English traditions and still present in English society at the time of publication.[32]

What patriarchs want, Fenwick shows, are docile women through whom they can reproduce themselves. And although the patriarchs are in the position of guardians, they have no regard for the emotional and mental welfare of the young women for whom they are responsible. In two letters written by Valmont to Lord Elsings, who shares guardianship of Sibella, Valmont exposes the selfishness of his plans for his ward. Here, he reveals not only that Clement is his own son, but also that Sibella is an heiress (which he has hidden from her) and that he plans to marry her to Clement before she comes into her inheritance. Although Sibella certainly wants to marry Clement (whether formally or not), Valmont's reasoning and motivations are both self-serving and psychologically terrifying. In his first note, he claims to know what will make Sibella happy, based on her education: 'It is only with a man who is prepared by such opinions as I have laid down to keep his wife in seclusion, that Sibella Valmont can be happy. I have purposely educated her to be the tractable and obedient companion of a husband, who from early disappointment and a just detestation of the miserable state of society is willing to abandon the world entirely' (182). Showing the patriarch's dedication to Rousseau, Valmont expects Sibella always to defer to her husband. As Rousseau writes in *Émile*: 'As she is made to obey a being who is so imperfect, often so full of vices and always so full of defects as man, she ought to learn early to endure even injustice and to bear a husband's wrongs without complaining.'[33] Valmont's matter-of-fact explanation reveals the scope of his plan to engineer the perfect wife for his son, and it shows a disregard for Sibella's feelings and her subjective experience that is inseparable from a Rousseauvian approach to educating women.

In the second letter, Valmont exposes even more of his selfish, chilling plan. Not only does he seek to control Sibella and make her into the ideal wife for Clement, he also plans to use her to repair the errors of his own past and to perpetuate the Valmont race. Valmont informs Lord Elsings that at age 21 Sibella will inherit her fortune and become independent of her guardians. Valmont has been plotting to make sure that never happens, although he represents himself as acting in her interest when he says 'You know, my Lord, I could have no sinister design in teaching Miss Valmont to believe herself dependent upon me. My well-known integrity forbids the possibility of such a surmise' (277). The truth, however, is that Valmont does not want Sibella to achieve independence or exercise autonomy. Rather, by steering her into marriage to Clement before she reaches the age of maturity, he can make her a dependent for life. Not only does the abusive patriarch see his ward as a pawn in a game in which money and 'blood' stay in the family, he also seeks to use her to purify his family line by joining his bastard to his brother's legal heir. The marriage will allow his illegitimate son to keep the Valmont land and the Valmont legacy within the family, making his own lack of a legitimate son a forgettable blip in family history. Valmont's ambition goes beyond the usual aristocratic desire for familial longevity in that his intention is to live again and remake his life through his son. In educating Sibella and Clement in isolation according to his 'system,' he plots to use Clement as a proxy for himself and to make Sibella into the wife he wishes he could have had. Clement is thus to be the new him, the next Valmont – a carbon copy with an ideal wife created just for him. The key to the plan is a woman engineered through a Rousseauvian education to obediently produce new Valmonts just like the old ones.

The tyranny of Valmont's project and its harmful impact on the chosen woman is not observed by either Lord Elsings or his son, Lord Filmar – an omittance suggesting wider male approval of the misogynistic ideas Valmont promotes. Lord Elsings, named co-guardian by Sibella's father, has never questioned Valmont, never checked on Sibella's welfare, and never shown concern for her desires. Complicit in his silence, he is an old patriarch supporting another old patriarch through inaction. And his son Lord Filmar, determined to abduct Sibella, is enchanted by the idea of a wealthy wife who will stay quiet, do as he bids, and generally stay out of his way. This acceptance of Valmont's plan serves as a wider critique of how men expect their wives to behave. A traditional approach that demands wives 'love, honour, and obey' is attractive to such men as appear in this novel, as it gives them license to disregard, belittle, and subjugate Sibella. The outcome of the old-style patriarchal marriage is thus the destruction of the wife's autonomy, happiness, and psychological health. If the husband believes the wife must be isolated in order to be happy, and insists that she is most content in submission and obedience, then he will cause her to lose connection with the outside world and set her up for illness both of body and mind. The prime example in *Secresy* is Valmont's own wife. Isolated against her will in Valmont castle and married to a man who maintains

Of *madness and monitors:* Secresy 85

absolute control, her endless hypochondriacal complaints and nervous illnesses testify to her suffering.

Valmont's response to Sibella's 'union' with Clement and to her pregnancy reveals both the patriarch's need for control over women and his emotional fragility. Even though Valmont has been secretly manoeuvring Sibella and Clement toward a formal union, Sibella's pregnancy 'wound[s] him almost to madness' because it represents a failure of patriarchal control over the female body (306). Valmont's maniacal, and then melancholic, response invites no sympathy and instead stimulates the reader's concern for Sibella as the victim of his tyranny. Valmont effectively extends his control and imprisonment of her, denying her freedom to roam the woods and epistolary access to Caroline because of the 'atrocity of her conduct' (294). He expresses his anger in typically patriarchal terms, with attention to family honour and female frailty, referring to the female mind as a 'mere compound of mischief' (294). Valmont takes no responsibility for his role in her education; and without expressing the slightest interest in her feelings or desires, resorts to his usual misogyny in chastising Sibella. The fear of female sexual independence is, of course, the very foundation of patriarchal anxiety, and it is the precise reason for the control of young women. Sibella's value to Valmont rests on her ability to transfer the family money and family name legally from one generation to the next. Anything else, including her desires, thoughts, and values, are not only irrelevant, they are an impediment to the patriarch's goal of controlling women for his own self-perpetuation – a goal the novel shows to be both tyrannical and a primary contributor to female madness.

The injurious libertines

In this novel, Sibella is beset by both patriarchs and libertines – and the two are linked through names (Valmont and Filmar), misogynistic ideas about women, and harmful actions.[34] In a letter that comes immediately after Caroline has made a mistakenly enthusiastic claim to a group of society friends, including Arthur Murden, that Sibella already has a lover worthy of her (95), Fenwick shows clearly that Clement, Sibella's lover, is a thorough libertine. In this, his first letter, Clement instantly demonstrates he is a rake through writing in the style of Samuel Richardson's Lovelace, and he makes it clear to the reader that he is far from worthy of Sibella.[35] Weakly imitating Rousseau's educational programme in *Émile*, Valmont has attempted to make Clement into his version of a virtuous man by isolating him on the estate and by giving him short lectures on the evils of society. He has sent Clement out into the world, expecting him to

86 *Women and madness in the early Romantic novel*

be revolted by his experiences and prepared upon his return to enjoy the 'pleasant solitude of Valmont castle' (116). Valmont's system, however, has backfired in that rather than be repelled by society's superficialities and immoralities, Clement has embraced them with gusto. Fenwick, the future teacher and writer for children, makes her anti-Rousseauvian point clearly: isolating a child from society to inculcate independent attitudes and stoic values will leave him unable to resist the pleasures and enticements of the social world. And chief among those pleasures and enticements for Clement are the ever-various bodies of women. For the young libertines, women are 'goddesses' – their primary purpose being to provide sexual pleasure. Like the patriarchs, the libertines are misogynists, but their misogyny is hidden by gallantry and professions of love for women. Their habits, however, are dissolute; and through their sexual pursuits and veneration of the female body, they inflict considerable psychological harm on women.

Apart from Valmont, Clement is the character who does the most damage to Sibella, which begins when, returning to the castle after a two-year absence, he is overwhelmed by his newly reactivated sexual desire for her. In the letter he writes to Murden after his 'marriage' to Sibella, Clement describes the sensual intoxication he felt at his return. Because he sees women as sexual objects designed for his own pleasure, he has no interest in the union of souls Sibella believes has taken place. He writes fresh from the 'transports' that have 'wrap[ped] [his] senses in delirium' after Sibella appeared in his chamber with a paper for him to read (130). 'Did you think I had not dared to follow? O, Yes! It was not to face the stern Valmont; no, it was in secret to receive Sibella to my arms, whom I love more than life. It was to out plot Valmont. To enjoy a glorious though secret triumph over this rival, this chosen, this elected of Mr Valmont's favour' (130). Sibella had written to Caroline that if Clement's heart were not 'in unison' with hers, then he would 'refuse the offer' (129) – meaning, she was confident that if Clement did not feel the same for her as she felt for him, then he would decline the sexual union. But Clement, as a true libertine, is motivated primarily by sexual opportunity. And in the aftermath, he locates his enjoyment not only in the physical delight he experienced, but also in his victory over Valmont and an (imagined) competitor for possession of Sibella's body. He is as thrilled to have out-plotted and defeated Valmont as he is to have experienced such sublime sexual pleasure.

Although Clement feels inspired to renounce his libertine ways after his 'union' with Sibella, he quickly reverts to his old behaviour. In the novel's conclusion, it is through his callous abandonment that he afflicts Sibella with the love-madness that ultimately kills her and their baby, which is delivered stillborn after Sibella's hysterical collapse. Already greatly weakened by injuries previously inflicted on her by Clement and Mr Valmont, when

Sibella attempts to embrace Clement, he rebuffs her and looks away. Lord Filmar narrates this moment: 'Never shall I cease to remember the changes of her countenance – from rapture to astonishment from dumb astonishment to doubt: – and from doubt, the quick transition, to despair!' (345). Sibella moves rapidly through emotional states as she comes to realize that Clement is rejecting her. When Clement can no longer bear her gaze, he pulls away from her and leaves the room, at which point she says, 'Clement, lover, husband, all!' (346). When the door closes, she shrieks and sinks upon the floor. 'She crossed her arms upon her bosom, with a violent pressure, as if to bind the agony; her teeth grated against each other; and every limb shuddered' (346). The fit signals a mental breakdown, after which Sibella is distracted and unable to recognize Caroline or understand why she is weeping. Although Caroline blames Valmont for the injuries of his educational scheme, the scene places the immediate blame for Sibella's tragedy on Clement. Already weakened by her doubts and anxieties about him, Sibella receives a fatal shock when she finally understands that he has betrayed her. When she calls him 'lover, husband, all,' she conveys the totalizing force of her love, the words expressing the fact that he is all she lives for. But a libertine – at least in this case – is beyond reform.

'My mind is my disease': the madness of Arthur Murden

In a novel that tells the long backstory behind the beautiful young woman's death from love-madness, the most deranged character is a privileged young man. Clement's friend Arthur Murden begins the story in an unstable condition – Caroline's observations show he vacillates between acting like a libertine and being a man of feeling – and he manifests his disorder through frenzy, obsession, and delusions. Murden's symptoms seem to be those of mania, which Stanley Jackson explains 'came to be thought of as a state of mental derangement associated with severe excitement and often wild behaviour.'[36] Mania was, according to G. E. Berrios, understood to be a 'chronic collapse of reason and thinking leading to confusion, generalized delusions, fits of fury, jolliness, excitation or aggression.'[37] As these descriptions indicate, mania's wild behaviour and excessive excitement was inseparable from a failure of the reasoning faculty. Drawing on a longstanding eighteenth-century distrust of 'fancy,' Fenwick shows that Murden's mania comes from an uncontrolled imagination that leads to his reason being compromised by excessive passion.

Murden's maniacal condition blurs the boundaries between hypochondriasis and hysteria at a time in which those boundaries were defined more by gender than by any particular set of symptoms. In a description

88   *Women and madness in the early Romantic novel*

easily applicable to Murden, Robert Whytt in his book on nervous disorders wrote:

> a delicate or easily irritable nervous system, must expose a person to various ailments, from causes, affecting either the body or mind, too slight to make any remarkable impression upon those of firmer and less sensible nerves. Thus, any accident occasioning sudden surprise, will, in many delicate people, produce strong palpitations of the heart, and sometimes fainting with convulsions.[38]

Whytt followed this description by noting that he knew men with just such 'delicate and moveable' nervous systems. Given Murden's gender, hypochondriasis – a 'disorder of heightened sensibility and unrestrained imagination' – seems an appropriate diagnosis.[39] However, rather than suffering from hypochondriasis, the nervous disorder of men, Murden appears to be afflicted by hysteria, the disease of women. Murden displays what Mark Micale describes as 'extravagant emotional behaviours' and falls into fits from sights that make a strong impression on his emotions.[40] Hysteria was the diagnosis of choice for medical professionals treating afflicted women, but G. S. Rousseau observes that 'virtually every serious medical author who wrote about hysteria after [Thomas] Sydenham's death in 1689 … included men among their lists of those naturally afflicted.'[41]

In contrast to Sibella, Murden seems predisposed to nervous disorders, a predisposition that could be explained by internal and external factors. As a man of feeling, his natural sensibility suggests an inherently delicate nervous system that is highly susceptible to emotional shocks or outside impressions that might trigger excitability.[42] But this sensibility comes with a cost. As John Mullan notes, 'in both the novel and the "medical" text, sensibility can be a special and desirable capacity, but it can also usher in the possibilities of melancholy, delirium and defeat.'[43] G. J. Barker-Benfield describes the man of feeling's tendency to suffer from mental and physical afflictions: 'They were to love exclusively and extravagantly. Their love was like sickness; its symptoms were ill-humour, listlessness, exhaustion, anxiety, and the destruction of [intellect].'[44] Murden's madness tracks closely to both medical and conventional literary ideas about sensibility, as his susceptibility to mental affliction is built into his nature as a man of feeling. Indeed, as Patricia Cove observes, Murden is constructed as a 'model of madness' due to how feeling motivates his insanity.[45]

Fenwick adds environmental and educational elements and a decidedly 'Jacobin' flavour to the reasons for Murden's tendency toward nervous disorders. Having been raised outside of both his father's more simple, rural origins and his uncle's mercantile class, Murden finds himself socializing with privileged young men whose money comes from inherited wealth.

The pressure to fit in with the young libertines works against his natural impulses as a sensitive man of feeling, but he lacks the strength to resist the socialization demanded by his new status. At one point he writes to Clement that he struggled to 'wear a character opposite to [his] inclinations' in company (243). He notes that in public he pretends to 'seduce the attentions of women' from whose 'hours of private yielding' he flees 'in disgust' (243). Murden clearly feels compelled to behave in public like other rich young men – that is, to behave as a libertine. But in private, he cannot stand that version of himself. Thus, he pursues the standard pleasures of a young gentleman in a state of alienation and distress. Calling himself 'the mere automaton of habit' (243), Murden is a man without a stable identity, a man who has nowhere to turn for an alternative, and no one to help him escape from the emptiness of his life.

Through Murden's self-critique, Fenwick hints that a better education and more morally oriented company might have saved him from the psychic instability that leads to his demise. In expressing his distress at living as a libertine, Murden observes that his licentious lifestyle removed him from any society that would have 'taught [him] the importance of mental pursuits' (243). Lifted at some unspecified point in the past to wealth, Murden is aware that his education has been neglected. As he flails about, filling his days with empty flirtations, he feels that somewhere there must be a society that could teach him the value and the pleasure of using his mind. For this reason, he is attracted by what Caroline has to offer him. However, by the time he meets her, the damage of his miseducation has been done, and she is unable to serve as a successful mentor, or 'monitor.' At the point in the novel when he masquerades as a hermit to gain access to Sibella, he tells her, 'I am unstable in wise resolutions; and yielding, as childhood, to temptation. I wanted a guide, a monitor. I sought one in the world, and found only tempters' (105). The need for education, better company, and moral guidance come together in Murden's comments about his observations while travelling in Europe with Clement and a tutor. While Clement, also a victim of a bad education, 'perpetually [hunts] after variety,' Murden is bothered by the individual suffering and systemic oppression he witnesses on the Continent. Recalling his thoughts in a letter to Caroline, Murden notes that he recognized 'oppression, priestcraft, and blindness,' but says he dismissed these as without remedy because neither his tutor nor his companions were 'capable of stimulating' him to inquire into the 'moral and physical causes' of these evils (244). A better education and companions attuned to political discourse might have allowed him to turn his moral sympathy into philosophical analysis and philanthropic or political action. Instead, he looks elsewhere for an emotional outlet and a sense of purpose and becomes increasingly mentally and emotionally unstable.

90   *Women and madness in the early Romantic novel*

When Murden gives up on political critique – on engaging his mind in an attempt to understand political injustice – he instantly becomes a romantic enthusiast. This is an example, in Isobel Grundy's words, of how 'male virtue [is] squandered on being romantic instead of revolutionary.'[46] Murden explains to Caroline that, because he could not determine the cause of the social evils he witnessed, he turned to love instead and 'quixoted [his] fancy into the wildest hopes' (244). Looking back, Murden recognizes that his expectation was delusory, that he imagined a woman who could never be real. However, once he determines to quest after a romantic ideal, he stays in this state of quixotic expectation until he hears Caroline describe Sibella. At this point, he fixes his romantic illusions onto her – a woman he believes satisfies all his requirements. It does not matter to him that Sibella is in love with Clement, that Clement is his friend, or that he has never laid eyes on her. It is immediately after he realizes the woman Caroline has described is Clement Montgomery's beloved that Murden exclaims to Caroline, 'My mind is my disease' (96). He is struck at this moment, it would seem, with the love-madness that will prompt him to hide, sneak, and don a disguise, ruin his health, run into frenzy, lapse into melancholy, and die, still seeking Sibella's acknowledgement of his love.

In being victims of love-madness, Sibella and Murden share the mental disease of the romantic imagination, and they share the disappointment of rejection by their love object. Fenwick positions the diseased imagination as an important factor in their madness, although Murden's madness comes more from his sensibility, while Sibella's originates in the abuses of her education. The similarity of their afflictions is highlighted in a brief conversation that occurs when Murden has snuck back into the Valmont estate to see Sibella, he thinks for the last time. The scene's tragic poignancy is augmented by the fact that it is narrated by Sibella, who has no idea that Murden has pursued a romantic fantasy of her and that he is now physically and mentally ill because of her. Sibella describes to Caroline her meeting with Murden, in which he identifies himself. He says to her that he is 'already the victim of unsuccessful love,' to which she replies, 'Whose victim are you?' (255). Because he is her victim and she has no idea, he repeats the question 'loudly and wildly' and then declares that 'death is of icy coldness!' Sibella does not understand that he feels she has injured him by not loving him; moreover, she expresses little sympathy for his suffering. In her mind, there is only one thing to do when one's beloved is gone, and that is to die. They agree that when the beloved's 'eye beams no tidings' and 'heart feels no warmth' it is time to 'Alas! Die also!' (256).[47] In the end, these are the two characters who do die, and they die at almost the same time. Murden dies because Sibella, in love with Clement and pregnant with his child, can never be his. And Sibella dies because Clement, having married Mrs Ashburn, has betrayed her. Both, then, die of love-madness when their love is no more.

While both Sibella and Arthur expose the way the unchecked romantic imagination is psychologically harmful, there are key differences in their conditions. Most importantly, Sibella is not responsible for her emotional investment in Clement, as she has been engineered by Valmont to love only Clement, to think only about Clement, and to look only to Clement to satisfy all her desires. Clement and Murden have also been formed by their educations, but as men they have had the opportunity to go out into the world and seek out improving associations and experiences. Further, because of her isolation, Sibella is not aware that she is idealizing Clement or that fixating on a romanticized version of another person is a form of madness. Murden, in contrast, understands quite well that he is, in his words, pursing a 'dream, a phantasy!' As he explains to Caroline without mentioning Sibella, he is fully conscious of the fact that his will 'acts in opposition to acknowledged reason,' and that he feels a 'despair [that] casts its length of shade around [him]' (160). He cannot, however, help himself; and rather than combat his dangerous fixation, he pursues Sibella further. Even after he is aware of her 'union' with Clement he cannot give up the fantasy. He is, as he says, 'lunatic-like' galloping after his fantasy 'over hedge, bog, and briar' (160), his mental state a compound of frenzy, delusion, irrational persistence, and despair. Thus, the most irrational and psychologically fragile character in the novel is not the woman who eventually succumbs to love madness, as one might expect, but rather a young man of feeling whose madness comes from his failure to strengthen his mind, school his reason, and become his own moral monitor.

Murden's mental instability becomes a debilitating disease in the process of his attempt, with his farmer friend Mr Richardson, to carry out Caroline's plan of rescuing Sibella.[48] Murden has already displayed symptoms of madness – frenzy, excessive passion, physical disarray, unaccountable fury, and self-harm – after receiving notice from Clement about his 'union' with Sibella (151). His mental disease becomes terminal when, in executing the rescue, he sees the visual evidence of Sibella's sexual bond with Clement in the form of her pregnant body, which he experiences as a psychic blow from which he can never recover. Meghan Burke suggests that the pregnancy creates 'visual, and therefore undeniable, evidence that she is not the ethereal idol of his creation but an active being who possesses a sexual, corporeal body with its creative power.'[49] His idealization challenged by corporeal evidence, Murden's mind cannot stand the truth. Not only does he almost faint when he sees Sibella is pregnant, he almost faints into her arms, reversing the gender codes for male strength and female weakness. His friend Richardson is not impacted by Sibella's

92   *Women and madness in the early Romantic novel*

pregnancy, but he is shocked by the feminine weakness Murden displays, whispering 'shame' and 'you are unmanned!" (322). Although Murden is a man, he seems to have been struck by an hysterical fit at the sight of Sibella and by imagining (or remembering) that Clement is the father.[50] By telling Murden he is 'unmanned,' Richardson calls attention to Murden's feminized response of fainting at a disturbing sight. Indeed, Richardson is right, according to the medical and literary formulas of the day. Not only did women of sensibility faint frequently in sentimental literature, medical writing conceived of women as highly likely to respond physically in the form of an hysterical response to emotionally shocking sights. In the chain of events that leads to Sibella's tragic death, Murden's emotional weakness at this moment is key. Although he gets her safely away from the castle with Richardson's help, Murden is so disturbed by the horror of Sibella's pregnancy, so preoccupied with his own suffering, and so depleted by his unbalanced mental state that he gives Lord Filmar an easy opening to abduct Sibella, which prevents her from being protected and assisted by Caroline. This loss of Sibella strikes a fatal mental blow to Murden, who becomes so incapacitated by his hysteric disease that Caroline must come to collect him from the inn where he loses Sibella and have him carried back to London.

When Murden dies, he dies of love-madness – a diagnosis confirmed by the fact that he expires forcing an embrace by Sibella, who is near death herself. In contrast to both Sibella and the conventional love-mad maid, Murden is in a selfish state, suffering from a condition that is harmful to others. In the first place, as much as he fixates on Sibella, it does not matter to him that she does not love him. And not only does she not love him, she has no interest in him and never expresses anything other than a cool response to his eccentricities until she articulates her gratitude when he and Richardson come to her rescue. His self-indulgent plunge into melancholy at the shock of her pregnancy – despite Caroline's warnings and his own knowledge of her sexual relationship with Clement – allows her to be abducted by Lord Filmar. And his neglect of his own health in pursuit of a woman he knows to be a fantasy leads to the bereavement of an uncle who dotes on him. Finally, he injures Sibella directly through his insistence on seeing her before he dies. In trying to force her to recognize his pain and in pushing a physical connection that she is too weak and depleted to resist, Murden causes Sibella to become dangerously agitated. Moreover, in addition to making her feel reproached for surviving the loss of Clement, Murden's words also make Sibella realize that she is the woman he has loved. At this point, Murden bends forward, embraces her by locking her in his arms, puts his head on her pillow, and says 'Then, let the same grave receive us!' before dying (356). Murden here makes a

Of madness and monitors: *Secresy* 93

last-ditch effort to possess Sibella in death when he was unable to make her love him in life. Caroline reports that the 'event' caused Sibella a series of convulsions that 'became each hour more and more rapid and exhausting' (356). In these last hours before her death, Sibella is forced to endure the presence of a man she does not love or even know, to be reminded of her pain, to be blamed for his disease, and to have him die beside her, with his arms around her. Although Caroline, infatuated with Murden to the end, appreciates that he was able to die with a smile 'so dearly purchased' (357), the harm he inflicts on Sibella in her last hours is considerable. She hastens toward her demise as a result of a series of convulsions caused by the additional emotional pain he inflicts upon her; and it is only at the very end that the fits cease, and she is able to die in peace. Both end up dying of love-madness. But the male character dies because of inherent weakness and a tendency toward hysteria, while the female character expires from a constellation of male-inflicted injuries.

Conclusion: moral monitors and reform

At the end of *Secresy*, Murden and Sibella are dead and there is plenty of blame to go around, despite the original reviewers' exclusive focus on the errors of 'secrecy.'[51] Caroline blames Murden's death on 'an ungoverned passion – virtuous in its object, but vicious in its excess!' (357). That is, she blames him for allowing a romantic fantasy to grow into a dangerous, ungovernable passion. She blames Clement's behaviour not on Clement himself, but on Valmont, for not giving him 'one lesson of independence of mind' (350). And she blames Valmont, herself, and Sibella for Sibella's tragic death. Valmont's secrets, she says, were the first steps 'to the errors of Clement and Sibella' (336). Next she blames Sibella for her departure from 'strict truth and sincerity' in making her 'rash engagement' with Clement. And she blames herself for thinking more secrecy could 'repair the inability of reason' (336) rather than attempting yet more reason. Caroline's failure to save Sibella can be read as Fenwick's lack of faith in the ability of female friendship to rescue women from patriarchal oppression. As Ranita Chatterjee observes, Caroline fails 'not only to constitute the dominant emotional relationship in Sibella's life but also to protect her from the cruelty of men.'[52] Sibella, in contrast, places all the blame on herself: 'My uncle's secrets could have done me but a temporary harm, it was mine own secrets destroyed me – Oh that fatal contract' (358). Sibella's own words – nearly the last words in the novel – redirect blame from multiple men onto herself for departing from 'truth and sincerity' by keeping her relationship with Clement a secret. Although Sibella is correct that the violation of her integrity was a form of self-injury, her idealization of Clement remains intact, as she absorbs all the blame for her fatal condition.

It is striking that neither Caroline nor Sibella blames Clement at the end, and no one thinks to charge Lord Filmar with any responsibility; and it is telling that those characters who escape stated blame at the end are the libertines. The patriarchs, with their tyrannical desire for 'unexamined obedience' (349) and their mania for total control, get what they deserve when their sons grow into men who lack wisdom and moral knowledge. Men of feeling who lose their way when pursuing romantic fantasies are to blame for letting their erotic imaginations dominate their reason. And young women who lose their minds when they lose their lovers are to blame, not for their sexual transgressions, but for compromising their integrity.

The libertines escape blame because the novel targets them for reform rather than condemnation. With the old patriarchs beyond redemption and women unable to establish the relationships necessary to support one another, the only hope for change lies in convincing elite young men to alter how they think about women and what they want from them.[53] To do this, they need a moral monitor – a woman of parts who can teach them to attend to women's desires and to see women in a new way. Although Sibella asks Caroline to befriend Clement, and Caroline successfully counsels the hapless minor character Mr Davenport, Caroline's most important impact is on the unlikely figure of Lord Filmar – the young man foolish and entitled enough to abduct Sibella in hope of attaining a wife who is passive, docile, and rich.[54] He enters the novel as a quintessential young libertine and future patriarch; he exits it completely transformed. After leaving Sibella with Caroline and witnessing her psychological collapse, he flees the city in tears of remorse for his role in Sibella's tragedy; but he flees with a newfound appreciation for, and friendship with, Caroline. While Sibella was giving birth to the stillborn child, Filmar waited in the library, 'canvassing over all the exquisite concern [he] had in producing such misery to this injured Sibella' (347). He realizes that had he not swooped in to abduct her, she would have been returned to Caroline who could have shielded her from the emotional shock that killed her. 'In such a moment, who could palliate? Not I, indeed! I did not conceal from Miss Ashburn an atom of the truth: and she talked like an angel, for she not only told me that I should amend but taught me how to amend' (347). Although Caroline was unable to help Murden recover from his love-madness, she is able to act as monitor to Lord Filmar in this moment of self-realization and remorse. When he confesses his guilt, rather than chastise him for his ill-usage of Sibella and blame him for his share in her demise, Caroline urges reformation and shows him the way. Having recognized his role in Sibella's tragedy and now counting Caroline as a friend, he has perhaps experienced a transformation in how he sees women. From viewing women only as objects for his sexual gratification or financial gain, he now understands women to be worthy moral beings whose feelings and ideas should be respected.

Filmar's transformation gives him a privileged place in the novel: he narrates the reunion of Sibella and Clement and catalogues her final descent into madness; he is left money by Sibella to settle his debts; and he receives the letter from Caroline that closes the novel in which Caroline narrates Sibella's and Murden's deaths and describes Valmont's remorse. By having Caroline send Filmar the final letter, it is as if Fenwick puts the story into his hands. And by having the story in his hands, he – and the male readers he stands for – has everything he needs to reform and everything he requires to keep him from repeating the errors and injuries of the previous generation. Structurally, by being the final recipient, he replaces Valmont, who receives the first and the penultimate letters. Filmar can thus be understood as a semi-hopeful manifestation of the new man – one without the weakness of the man of feeling, one who accepts responsibility for having injured women, and one who takes a woman as his moral monitor. As the model male reader who is reformed by Sibella's story, Filmar has learned to both feel for women and to listen to their reasoning. His reform – but more importantly the reform of the privileged young libertines he represents – emerges as the only way to end the psychic injuries that cause female madness.

Ultimately, Caroline cannot save Sibella from the compound injuries of men – a failure that indicates a level of despair mirrored by the conclusion of *The Victim of Prejudice* and suggested by the fragmentary pieces of *Wrongs of Woman*. In *Secresy*, despair comes from male power that is manifested by patriarchal control of women's upbringing, women's internalization of damaging romantic fantasies, and libertine predations. Such power cannot be overcome by female friendship, as even the most rational, capable, and independent of women cannot effect a rescue. Even when the rational woman aligns herself with the man of feeling, it is to no avail, as men are either too powerful to defeat or too feeble to matter. For this reason, Fenwick turns to the only remaining option – the reform of the young libertine, a man not weakened by sensibility who has not yet hardened into an old patriarch. In the post-Revolutionary environment, when all hope of legal or political improvement had been extinguished, Fenwick clings to the possibility that the woman writer, acting as moral monitor to young, privileged men, may yet be able to affect change. By revising the story of the love-mad maid and delineating the mental collapse and tragic death of a glorious young woman, Fenwick hopes to reform her male reader through making him weep.

Notes

1 Eliza Fenwick, *Secresy; or, The Ruin on the Rock*, ed. Isobel Grundy (Peterborough: Broadview Press, 1994). All references are to this edition. *Secresy*'s title page bore the attribution: by 'a woman.' Fenwick later published educational works for children and ran schools in Barbados and North America. See Lissa Paul, *Eliza Fenwick: Early Modern Feminist* (Newark: University of Delaware Press, 2019).

2 Sophie is the young woman Rousseau introduces to be Émile's wife. Rousseau's ideas on female education are elaborated in Book V. See *Émile; or On Education*, trans. Allan Bloom (1763; New York: Basic Books, 1979).

3 Isobel Grundy, 'Introduction' in *Secresy*, 25–6.

4 Although it has received little critical attention compared to other more frequently discussed novels of the period, *Secresy* has nonetheless been read through a variety of interpretive contexts. For Gothic interpretations, see Sue Chaplin, *Law, Sensibility, and the Sublime in Eighteenth-Century Women's Fiction* (London: Routledge, 2016) and Ellen Malenas Ledoux, 'Defiant Damsels: Gothic Space and Female Agency in *Emmeline*, the *Mysteries of Udolpho* and *Secresy*,' *Women's Writing* 18, no. 3 (2011), https://doi.org/10. 1080/09699082.2010.508889. For political readings that see the novel in a 'Jacobin' context, see Miriam Wallace, *Revolutionary Subjects in the English 'Jacobin' Novel, 1790–1805* (Lewisburg: Bucknell University Press, 2009); Nicola Watson, *Revolution and the Form of the British Novel, 1790–1825: Intercepted Letters, Interrupted Seductions* (Oxford: Oxford University Press, 1994); Sarah Emsley, 'Radical Marriage,' *Eighteenth-Century Fiction* 11, no. 4 (July 1999), doi:10.1353/ecf.1999.0053; and Chaplin. Scholars interested the novel's complex use of genre include Jonathan Sadow, 'Moral and Generic Corruption in Eliza Fenwick's *Secresy*' in *Didactic Novels and British Women's Writing, 1790–1820*, ed. Hilary Havens (New York: Routledge, 2017) and Julia M. Wright, '"I am Ill-Fitted": Conflicts of Genre in Eliza Fenwick's *Secresy*' in *Romanticism, History, and the Possibility of Genre: Re-forming Literature 1789–1837*, eds Tilottama Rajan and Julia M. Wright (Cambridge: Cambridge University Press, 1998). A post-colonial perspective is taken by Malinda Snow, 'Habits of Empire and Domination in Eliza Fenwick's *Secresy*,' *Eighteenth-Century Fiction* 14, no. 2 (January 2002), https://doi.org/10.1353/ ecf.2002.0016, while Sapphic readings are offered by Ranita Chatterjee, 'Sapphic Subjectivity and Gothic Desires in Eliza Fenwick's *Secresy*,' *Gothic Studies* 6, no. 1 (May 2004), https://doi.org/10.7227/GS.6.1.5 and Susan Lanser, 'Second-Sex Economics: Race, Rescue, and the Heroine's Plot,' *The Eighteenth Century* 61, no. 2 (January 2020), https://doi.org/10.1353/ecy.2020.0016.

5 Chaplin, *Law, Sensibility, and the Sublime*, 114.

6 Patricia Cove is the only scholar to have offered a sustained interpretation of madness within *Secresy*, which she does through a Foucauldian reading in conjunction with an interpretation of Mary Wollstonecraft's *The Wrongs of Woman*. See '"The Walls of Her Prison": Madness, Gender, and Discursive

Of *madness and monitors*: Secresy 97

Agency in Eliza Fenwick's *Secresy* and Mary Wollstonecraft's *The Wrongs of Woman*,' *European Romantic Review* 23, no. 6 (December 2012), https://doi.org/10.1080/10509585.2012 .728828. Mercy Cannon also discusses Sibella's mental health, although it is not her focus. See 'Hygienic Motherhood: Domestic Medicine and Eliza Fenwick's Secresy,' *Eighteenth-Century Fiction* 20, no. 4 (Summer 2008), https://doi.org/10.3138/ecf.20.4.535.

7 Sibella's natural ability to reason has attracted considerable attention from scholars. See, for example, Chaplin, *Law, Sensibility, and the Sublime*, 118 and Cove, 'The Walls of her Prison,' 677.

8 For example, she is described by other characters as 'half-insane' (92), the 'wild girl of the castle' (205), and 'deranged in intellect' (207).

9 Watson, *Revolution and the Form of the British Novel*, 41. Chaplin, as well, notes Sibella's challenges to Valmont's authority. See *Law, Sensibility, and the Sublime*, 117.

10 Philip Martin, *Mad Women in Romantic Writing* (New York: St Martin's Press, 1987), 3.

11 See the section in my Introduction on 'Love-madness and the love-mad maid.'

12 Elaine Showalter, *The Female Malady: Women, Madness, and English Culture, 1830–1980* (London: Virago, 1985), 12–13.

13 Jennifer Radden has observed that fear and sadness without cause was one of the primary elements of melancholia. Jennifer Radden, *The Nature of Melancholy: From Aristotle to Kristeva* (Oxford: Oxford University Press, 2000), 10–12.

14 Chaplin, *Law, Sensibility, and the Sublime*, 118.

15 Richard Terry describes the romanticization of the Druidical past in literature of the period: 'The close linkage between melancholy and philosophizing is incarnated in a particular class of beings appearing perennially in mid-eighteenth-century poetry: The druids … reputedly lived in trees, or at least deep in forests, and were venerated both for their magical powers and their sagacity.' Richard Terry, 'Philosophical Melancholy' in *Melancholy Experience in Literature of the Long Eighteenth Century: Before Depression, 1660–1800*, Alan Ingram, Stuart Sim, Clark Lawlor, Richard Terry, John Baker, and Leigh Wetherall-Dickson (London: Palgrave Macmillan, 2011), 73.

16 Max Byrd, *Visits to Bedlam: Madness and Literature in the Eighteenth Century* (Columbia: University of South Carolina Press, 1974), 7.

17 Radden, *The Nature of Melancholy*, 15.

18 Anne Digby, *Madness, Morality, and Medicine: A Study of the York Retreat 1796–1914* (Cambridge: Cambridge University Press, 1985), 6.

19 Rousseau, *Émile*, 365.

20 Cannon, 'Hygienic Motherhood,' 552.

21 Watson, *Revolution and the Form of the British Novel*, 41.

22 Stephen Behrendt, 'Rousseau and British Romantic Women Writers' in *Jean-Jacques Rousseau and British Romanticism: Gender and Selfhood, Politics and Nation*, eds Russell Goulbourne and David Higgins (London: Bloomsbury, 2017), 14, ebook.

23 Cannon, 'Hygienic Motherhood,' 55.

98   *Women and madness in the early Romantic novel*

24 Stanley Jackson, *Melancholia and Depression: From Hippocratic Times to Modern Times* (New Haven: Yale University Press, 1986), 250.

25 As I discuss later in this chapter, Murden carries out a rescue of Sibella planned out by Caroline but loses Sibella to Lord Filmar when they stop at an inn. Filmar gives up the idea of marrying Sibella for her fortune when he sees she is pregnant.

26 Fenwick seems to be drawing here from traditions associated with portrayals of Ophelia. See Elaine Showalter, 'Representing Ophelia: Women, Madness, and the Responsibilities of Feminist Criticism' in *Shakespeare and the Question of Theory*, eds Patricia Parker and Geoffrey Hartman (New York and London: Methuen, 1985), 80–1. In modern terms, Sibella's confusion suggests a dissociative disorder coming from the shock of Clement's betrayal. See 'Dissociative Disorders,' *Diagnostic and Statistical Manual of Mental Disorders (DSM)*, 5th edn (Arlington: American Psychiatric Association, 2013), ebook.

27 There are many examples of medical writers linking women's tendency to suffer from hysteria to their essential physical weakness. See the section on 'Madness in the eighteenth century and early Romantic period' in my Introduction.

28 Michel Foucault, *Madness and Civilization: A History of Insanity in the Age of Reason*, trans. Richard Howard (1965; New York: Vintage Books, 1988), 89–90.

29 Roy Porter, 'Psychosomatic Disorders: Historical Perspectives,' in *Treatment of Functional Somatic Disorders*, eds Richard Mayou, Christopher Bass, and Michael Sharpe (Oxford: Oxford University Press, 1995), 36.

30 That Valmont represents patriarchal power has been observed by a number of scholars, but none have discussed the connection between that power and Sibella's afflictions in much detail. See Grundy, 'Introduction,' Wallace, *Revolutionary Subjects*, and Meghan Burke, 'Making Mother Obsolete: Eliza Fenwick's *Secresy* and the Masculine Appropriation of Maternity,' *Eighteenth-Century Fiction* 21, no. 3 (2009), https://doi.org/10.3138/ecf.21.3.357.

31 Grundy, 'Introduction,' 27.

32 Wallace, *Revolutionary Subjects*, 53.

33 Rousseau, *Émile*, 370.

34 Fenwick establishes the link between libertines and patriarchs through the clever use of the name 'Filmar,' which alludes to Sir Robert Filmer, author of *Patriarcha; or, the Natural Power of Kings* (1680). Chaplin describes Mr Valmont, with his Burkean ideologies, as 'absolutely Filmerian' in his assertion of his 'absolute authority' over wife and children (*Law, Sensibility, and the Sublime*, 111).

35 In a footnote to this letter, Grundy observes that 'Richardson's rakes in *Clarissa* also use the obsolete second person singular to indicate this "'zeal of friendship"' (*Secresy*, 98).

36 Jackson, *Melancholia and Depression*, 250.

37 G. E. Berrios, 'Of Mania: (from Bucknill and Tuke, 1858) Introduction,' *History of Psychiatry* 15, no. 1 (2004): 105, https://doi.org/10.1177/0957154X04041829.

Of madness and monitors: Secresy   99

38 Robert Whytt, *Observations On the Nature, Causes, And Cures of Those Disorders Which Have Been Commonly Called Nervous, Hypochondriac, Or Hysteric: to Which Are Prefixed Some Remarks On the Sympathy of the Nerves* (Edinburgh: T. Becket, P. Du Hondt, London, and J. Balfour, Edinburgh 1765), 115, HathiTrust.

39 Russell Noyes, Jr, 'The Transformation of Hypochondriasis in British Medicine, 1680–1830,' *Social History of Medicine* 24, no. 2 (2011): 292, https://doi.org/10.1093/shm/hkq052.

40 Mark Micale, *Approaching Hysteria: Disease and Its Interpretations* (Princeton: Princeton University Press, 1995), 19.

41 G. S. Rousseau, '"A Strange Pathology": Hysteria in the Early Modern World, 1500–1800' in *Hysteria Beyond Freud*, Sander Gilman, Helen King, Roy Porter, G. S. Rousseau, and Elaine Showalter (Berkeley: University of California Press, 1993), 67, ebook.

42 The Scottish physician John Brown (1735–1788) had a considerable impact on medicine in the last decade of the eighteenth century with the translation of his *The Elementa Medicinea* (1780) into English in 1787–1788. The primary factor in his system is excitability. John Brown, *The Elements of Medicine; or, A Translation of the Elementa Medicinae Brunonis* (London: J. Johnson, 1788), HathiTrust. Although outside factors could stimulate excitability, Brown's model emphasized predisposition. See Guenter Risse, 'The Brownian System of Medicine: Its Theoretical and Practical Implications,' *Clio Medica* 5 (1970): 45–6.

43 John Mullan, 'Hypochondria and Hysteria: Sensibility and the Physicians,' *The Eighteenth Century* 25, no. 2 (1984): 141, https://www-jstororg.libdata.lib.ua.edu/stable/41467321.

44 G. J. Barker-Benfield, 'Mary Wollstonecraft's Depression and Diagnosis,' *The Psychohistory Review* 13, no. 4 (1985): 25.

45 Cove, 'Walls of her Prison,' 678.

46 Grundy, 'Introduction,' 29.

47 Christopher Bundock points out the 'co-fatality' of this exchange and cleverly describes Murden's feelings for Sibella as a 'necromance.' 'The (inoperative) Epistolary Community in Eliza Fenwick's Secresy,' *European Romantic Review* 20, no. 5 (December 2009): 715–16, https://doi.org/10.1080/10509580903407894.

48 Fenwick's naming a character 'Richardson' prompts readers to think about *Clarissa*. The farmer himself may not have much to do with Samuel Richardson, but Sibella, like Clarissa, is betrayed while thinking she will escape from the oppressive environment of her house and instead finds herself in the power of an unscrupulous libertine.

49 Burke, 'Making Mother Obsolete,' 380.

50 In a statement quite applicable to Murden, Elaine Showalter observes that male hysteria 'has always been regarded as a shameful, "effeminate" disorder ... The male hysteric was assumed to be unmanly, womanish, or homosexual, as if the feminine component within masculinity were itself a symptom of disease.' Elaine Showalter, 'Hysteria, Feminism, and Gender' in *Hysteria Beyond Freud*, Sander Gilman, Helen King, Roy Porter, G. S. Rousseau, and Elaine Showalter, 289.

51 See, 'Secrecy: Or, the Ruin of the Rock,' *The Analytical Review: Or, History of Literature* 22, no. 1 (July 1795): 60–1, *British Periodicals*; 'Secresy; or, the Ruin on the Rock. In Three Volumes. By a Woman,' *English Review, or, An Abstract of English and Foreign Literature* 25 (June 1795), *British Periodicals*; and 'Secrecy; Or the Ruin of the Rock,' *Monthly Review, Or, Literary Journal, 1752–1825*, 18 (September 1795): 110, *British Periodicals*.

52 Chatterjee, 'Sapphic Subjectivity,' 49. In defence of Caroline, Meghan Burke argues that her '"failure" to save Sibella from doom is not … the result of her own fault, but caused by patriarchal forces that prevent her from exercising her intended duties' ('Making Mother Obsolete,' 383).

53 Chatterjee sees the conclusion very differently, arguing that despite its tragic outcome, the novel accomplishes the goal of validating a 'feminist, decidedly Wollstonecraftian, politics of education' as well as articulating a 'sapphic, erotics of subjectivity' ('Sapphic Subjectivity,' 55). Anne Close also downplays the tragic conclusion to argue that the novel supports 'powerful bonds between women that … eclipse the ambiguous promise of romantic love.' See Anne Close, 'Into the Public: The Sexual Heroine in Eliza Fenwick's *Secresy* and Mary Robinson's *The Natural Daughter*,' *Eighteenth-Century Fiction* 17, no. 1 (October 2004): 36, https://doi.org/10.1353/ecf.2004.0016. Lanser, 'Second-Sex Economics,' also sees value in the female bonds, despite the failed rescue.

54 The potential punishment suggests both the recklessness of his plan and his sense of entitlement, given that a man who abducted an heiress, whether he married her or not, could receive the death sentence. See Frank McLynn, *Crime and Punishment in Eighteenth-Century England* (New York: Routledge, 1989), 110.

3

Death by despair: fatal melancholia in *The Victim of Prejudice*

When Mary Raymond, the protagonist of Mary Hays' little-discussed second novel, *The Victim of Prejudice*, loses her lover, she does not lose her mind. Instead, she fights heroically for independence. But despite being brave, intelligent, and high-minded, Mary eventually succumbs to fatal melancholia, the victim not of prejudice, as the title suggests, but of male abuse. Mary's injuries at the hands of men range from the unintentional, to the selfish, to the premeditated. Each injury is closely connected to the others, forming a web of male power (benign, irresponsible, and malignant) that entraps Mary, making her physically and psychologically ill and preventing her from living a healthy and free life. Hays' stated aim for this novel is to delineate the harmful impact of society's fixation on female chastity, which she conveys through the title, the introductory 'Advertisement,' and the plot, in which Mary is the victim of a rape but is treated by society as a fallen woman. The story centres on the entrapments of male power that include, but are not limited to, a privileged man's ability to assault her with impunity and the lingering effects of Mary's status as the daughter of a prostitute brought up in ignorance of her origins.[1] With a strikingly modern approach to rape, and challenging both standard literary and medical accounts of female madness, Hays creates a story in which cumulative male injury causes a healthy, independent-minded woman's psychological disease and early death.[2] Hays joins Wollstonecraft and Fenwick in rejecting medical and sentimental models of female madness to expose psychological injury as one of the principal ways women suffer at the hands of men.[3]

Paradise and Paradise Lost

Most of *Victim of Prejudice* is written as a prison memoir in which Mary, incarcerated for debt, reflects on her life. Looking back, she is grateful to Mr Raymond, her guardian, for his affection and his progressive educational principles:

102   *Women and madness in the early Romantic novel*

> To the wisdom and kindness of my benefactor, who, with a contempt of vulgar prejudices, cherished notions somewhat singular respecting female accomplishments, I was indebted for a robust constitution, a cultivated understanding, and a vigorous intellect. I was early inured to habits of hardiness; to suffer, without shrinking, the changes and inclemencies of the seasons; to endure fatigue and occasional labour; to exercise my ingenuity and exert my faculties, arrange my thoughts and discipline my imagination. (5)[4]

Mary's constitution in childhood – both mental and physical – is central to Hays' critique of injurious male power, as well as to how she challenges standard medical and literary representations of female mental affliction. Like her friend, the radical philosopher William Godwin, Hays believed in the power of the environment and education to form individual character. In Gina Luria Walker's words, she 'embraced optimistic Enlightenment claims about the sensory basis of human thought that argued for the greater importance of environmental over inborn qualities.'[5] And like Mary Wollstonecraft, another friend, Hays was adamant that 'feminine' characteristics were the product of education. In keeping with this environmentalist understanding of gender, Hays casts Mary as strong and robust, rather than soft and delicate, and as intelligent and rational, instead of weak-minded and emotional. Mary is educated according to Enlightenment ideals of reason and independent thought, and thus she is not a victim of sensibility. Pure of heart, strong in mind and body, Mary comes to maturity entirely ignorant of the prejudices that govern society. In this way, she is very much a female Émile raised without Rousseau's debilitating ideas about women.[6] But this Émile-like education proves to be a double-edged sword. On the one hand, it makes her an extraordinary girl – confident, resourceful, courageous, and strong. On the other, it leaves her ignorant of societal rules and unable to comprehend, throughout much of her life, the workings of sexual stigma. Gradually, the injuries she experiences at the hands of men and the stress of learning about social prejudice the hard way destroy the beneficial aspects of her education. Her remarkable physical and mental strength gives way, leaving her subject to hysterical fits and a melancholia that saps her will to live.

Mary's paradise of childhood is lost in stages. Her world changes and her life goes off course with the arrival of William and Edmund Pelham, two privileged boys Mr Raymond takes in as students. Unconscious of differences of sex and status, 11-year-old Mary quickly finds she is superior to William in 'courage, in dexterity, and resource' as they wrestle, romp, and contend in 'various sports and feats of activity' (9). She also quickly excels him in their studies. The injuries Mary experiences, however, begin almost immediately upon the boys' arrival when she is introduced to both prejudice and sexuality. Presenting his sons to Mr Raymond, Mr Pelham

Fatal melancholia in The Victim of Prejudice 103

says: 'The family honour … ha[s] been preserved uncontaminated for many generations'; and he adds that it is 'his pride that it should descend unsullied to posterity' (9). In bringing his boys to be educated, Mr Pelham's first concern is to preserve them from lower-status women, lest their bloodline be polluted. This statement is a prelude to his questions about Mary and, later, to his objections to Mary becoming his son's wife. In response to Mr Pelham's inquiry whether Mary is his daughter, Mr Raymond responds that she is adopted, 'an unfortunate orphan, whom it is equally my duty and my delight to shelter from a world that will hardly be inclined to do her justice, and upon which she has few claims' (9). This description informs Mr Pelham that Mary has a low social status and no place in his sons' world.

Mr Raymond's tone prompts an emotional and physical reaction in Mary that stands as her first experience of an emotional wound that impacts her physically. Hays' description of Mary's reaction is in keeping with new medical ideas about emotional injury, ideas which, according to Stanley Jackson, made an 'affective disorder' possible.[7] Mary does not know her history and has no idea that she is at the bottom of a rigid socio-sexual hierarchy; and she cannot begin to comprehend Mr Pelham's comments about his 'uncontaminated' family line. Nonetheless, she has an overwhelming emotional response to what Mr Raymond says about her. 'Something' in Mr Raymond's tone thrills 'through [her] heart with a new and indescribable sensation' (9). She then bursts into tears, throws her arms around her adopted father, and sobs on his chest. Mary observes, 'for the first time in my life I had been sensible to an embarrassment, and a temporary feeling of depression and apprehension; a prelude, as it should seem, to those anxieties and sorrows which have since pursued me with unmitigated severity' (9). Mary intuits a problem with who she is, just from the tone of Mr Raymond's voice; and she perceives the ill-will Mr Pelham expresses. Hays suggests here, through Mary's experience, that melancholy is an affective response to a situation that can be intuited, but that may not be fully understood. The specifics of the description show Hays' interest in the psychological impact of prejudice on her character, and Hays' terms – 'embarrassment,' 'apprehension,' 'depression' – give Mary a psychological profile at age 11 that we would recognize today as anxiety and depression.

Mr Pelham's prejudice is the first step in Mary's loss of paradise and in the development of her melancholia. The second is her entry into Sir Peter's garden to steal some luscious grapes which she describes in retrospect as 'forbidden fruit.' In staging this scene, Hays effects a series of role revisions that both indemnify women from misogynistic charges going back to the Bible and that incriminate men for their emotional manipulations of women. Mary desires the tantalizing fruit, but has no interest in disobeying her guardian, who has forbidden her and William from entering Sir Peter's

104   *Women and madness in the early Romantic novel*

property. William, however, playing the role of Satan in *Paradise Lost*, manipulates Mary into disobeying her guardian and tasting the fruit.[8] While Mary resists temptation by averting her eyes and referring to her guardian's prohibition, William looks directly at the 'luscious bait' and insults her with a typical misogynistic comment, saying that she is 'timid and spiritless' like the rest of her 'weak sex' (12). And he manipulates her by expressing jealousy and anger that she would rather obey her guardian than please him: 'Your friendship for me is weak, since you will hazard nothing to oblige me' (12–13). Because she feels she must prove her love for William, Mary disobeys the father-figure and runs into the greenhouse to steal the grapes. This act of disobedience, however, is not, as it is in *Paradise Lost*, motivated by her own desire – be it for sex, power, knowledge, or even the fruit itself. Instead, like Milton's Adam who takes the fruit from Eve because he loves his wife more than he fears God, Mary steals the grapes because William doubts her love. Thus, in Hays' revision of the Fall, man is not the victim of woman's temptations and disobedience, but rather woman is the victim of man's emotional manipulations. It is man who transgresses for sensual pleasure here, as he will again in the novel (and again and again in real life). Up to this point, William has done nothing to injure Mary. But the scene, in reassigning blame for the Fall, identifies men as master manipulators and women as their victims.

The scene turns into a crisis when the loving, innocent Mary, by wanting to please one abusive man (boy), stumbles into the clutches of another. Although William and Sir Peter are not consciously working together, their injurious acts set up a framework for the structure of the trap Mary falls into as a young adult that will trigger her mental afflictions. Each man's wrong creates the opportunity for the next man's offense. Here, attempting to satisfy her would-be (child) lover, Mary falls into the hands of a 'tumultuous party of young men' (14) from which Sir Peter emerges to say, as he seizes her: 'Ah! My little lass … have we caught you in the fact? – Detection, upon my soul … a true daughter of Eve!' He startles when he becomes aware of the child's beauty and stares 'rudely' in her face, saying: 'By God! … a little beauty! A Hebe! a wood-nymph! I must and will have a kiss; and, d-n me! you shall be welcome to all the grapes in the green-house' (14). Sir Peter's delight in catching Mary is laced with sexual menace from the start, some of which comes from his belonging to a group of men, which highlights her sexual peril. Because Sir Peter has caught Mary pursuing his grapes, he believes she is a 'true daughter of Eve' – meaning sexually transgressive – and therefore an available sexual object, though still a child. Sir Peter's exclamation that she is a 'Hebe' – one of Hera's daughters who exemplifies youth – indicates he knows she is very young and, as Miriam Wallace observes, suggests that he sees her as just one of a series of 'interchangeable women' available for 'sexual predation and punishment.'[9] He is so struck by her beauty that he starts backward and stares when he sees her face, violating the rules of female modesty and gentlemanly behaviour by a gaze that reinforces his power over and objectification of her. When he says he wants a kiss, he is not bothered by either her age or her resistance. That he is willing to exchange the kiss for the grapes indicates the transactional nature of desires that will become more offensive and menacing over time. Taken as a whole, this restaging of the Fall shifts the blame from women to men in general who are shown to form a nexus of sexually motivated power that puts women and girls at risk.

Although Mary is able to break loose and run away, the garden scene prefigures Sir Peter's brutal rape of her when she is a young woman and establishes, early in the novel, the power of privileged men over unprivileged women and the risk such women run of sexual assault and corresponding mental distress. Mary responds with fear at the 'brutality of [his] manner,' and as she escapes, her hat falls, allowing her 'dishevelled hair [to stream] in wild disorder' (14). Mary injures herself escaping over a fence and returns home with an appearance consistent with that of a rape victim, 'clothes torn ... hands and arms bruised, scratched, and streaming with blood' (14). Mary is able to take refuge in the arms of her guardian this time, and this time she has not been sexually assaulted. But later, when Sir Peter does rape her, she will have nowhere to turn and no one to help her. Mary's vulnerability to Sir Peter increases as her guardian becomes weaker; and she is left easy prey after Mr Raymond dies. Hays thus shows through Mary's loss of childhood innocence how vulnerable women are to male predation, as all that stands between them and sexual assault is one male 'protector.'

The injuries of education

Mary is expelled from her paradise of childhood in her seventeenth year when Mr Raymond decides he must separate her from William because the young man's father will never support their marriage. And even if they were to marry against Mr Pelham's wishes, Mr Raymond is convinced William would eventually regret their union. Mr Raymond tells Mary he cannot bear to see her '"*contemned by the man she loves*"' should he permit the relationship to continue (32).[10] While Mr Raymond is perhaps correct, he and his educational principles are to blame for Mary's situation in that he allowed their attachment to flourish for years and, crucially, never explained to Mary anything about her background or the social prejudices she might encounter. Recalling his reasons for restricting her knowledge, Mary says: 'He knew not how to debauch the simplicity of my mind by acquainting me with the manners and maxims of the world' (25). Mary's enlightened and attentive father-figure has set out, with all the best intentions, to make his ward independent-minded, virtuous, and strong. Mary recalls him saying that he 'laboured to awaken, excite, and strengthen [her] mind' because 'an enlightened intellect is the highest of human endowments' (28). But, as Roxanne Eberle observes, Mr Raymond 'immerses her too thoroughly in an ideal and protected realm.'[11] He educates her to be free from prejudice, free from falsehood and injustice, and free from cowardice and all the other impurities that stain the human mind. But at the end of that education, he wonders if, by educating her for virtue, has he set her up for unhappiness in a sordid world. Mary reveres her guardian to the end, and so never thinks to question his decisions. Instead, writing her memoir from debtors' prison, she blames society for causing Mr Raymond such anxieties. However, readers can see that by attempting to preserve her mind from the taint of sexual knowledge and social prejudice, he ill prepares her for the truth about her own birth. And he fails to take into consideration that a woman's experience in society is profoundly different from that of a man.[12] In sum, he has set her up for injury by failing to prepare her intellectually and emotionally for the world as it is.

When Mr Raymond tells Mary she must leave her home to be separated from William, he causes her intellectual confusion and an emotional injury that manifests in what we might see as anxiety and depression, but that original readers would identify as hysteria and melancholia. Mary's distressed psychological state shows itself through the acute, physical responses that have come to plague her – in this instance, a 'convulsive tremor [shakes] her frame' (31). Such a convulsion would at the time have been understood as a symptom of hysteria, and Mary exhibits many more such symptoms later, after her rape. According to physician and medical writer Robert Whytt, 'violent affections of the mind, as terror, grief, anger, or disappointments, will sometimes so strongly affect the whole nervous system, as to bring on hysteric faintings, with convulsions [stemming from] the too great delicacy of the brain and nerves.'[13] Whereas Whytt suggests that women are predisposed to such afflictions by virtue of a more 'moveable' nervous system, Hays makes it clear that in each of Mary's hysterical episodes, the specific cause is male injury. In this instance, Mary's emotional distress is increased by her inability to understand why she and William must separate. Mr Raymond is concerned about a possible sexual relationship between Mary and William that will destroy her reputation, but he has educated her to know nothing about differences in status or the prohibition on female sexual activity. Mr Raymond's words only create anxiety in her because he is describing a peril she does not understand based on feelings she does not yet know she has.

Fatal melancholia in The Victim of Prejudice

Mary experiences an even stronger physical response from emotional shock when Mr Raymond informs her she cannot be William's wife. Mary recalls the moment: 'A shock of electricity appeared to rend my quivering nerves; my colour changed, my bosom palpitated, a faint sickness seemed for an instant to stop the current of my blood; the next moment it rushed impetuously through my veins, distended my heart, and dyed my face and neck with crimson' (32). Hays here follows a contemporary physiological understanding of the nervous system: an emotional shock travels around the body through the nerves, creating heart palpitations and swooning that are consistent with hysteria.[14] But Hays diverges from contemporary medical thinking in creating a heroine who is free from any predisposition to nervous disorders. Here, as elsewhere in the novel, while her response is felt in the body, it does not originate there. Rather, the response comes from the affective faculty which Mr Raymond has inadvertently injured by attempting to keep her mind pristine. After Mr Raymond stops speaking, Mary notes, 'a flood of ideas gushed upon [her] mind, novel, affecting, terrible, and bewildered [her] disordered senses' (32–3). Mary has no idea what Mr Raymond is talking about when he says William will become a 'man of the world,' and the only thing she comprehends is that she cannot marry him, which is something she had not previously considered. The result of the conversation is that Mary experiences a kind of mental haze in which her much-vaunted powers of mind seize up and she feels her principles becoming 'unhinged' and her passions 'thrown into disorder' (33). To describe how Mary experiences Mr Raymond's words, Hays uses terms that indicate Mary is temporarily cognitively impaired and highly emotionally distressed: confusion, suspension of reasoning, fear, and suspicion, unhinged principals, disorderly passions, conflict, contentious feelings, and fluctuating spirits. Contained within this list of symptoms are elements of madness in the form of hysteria and pronounced melancholia that will increasingly come to plague Mary's life.

Madness and the seduced maiden

While Mary is apart from William, living with Mr Raymond's friends the Nevilles, her guardian finally informs her about her mother's past. The story of Mary's mother, also named Mary, would have been a familiar one to Hays' readers, up to a certain point. A spoiled young lady with a typically fashionable education, Mary's mother is seduced into an illicit sexual relationship, cast off by her family, and abandoned by her lover. She then follows the standard path through prostitution to illness and death. This seduced maiden, however, does not go quietly. Rather, she responds to the

108   *Women and madness in the early Romantic novel*

stigma heaped upon her by seeking to inflict damage upon the society that cannot forgive her, becoming aggressive, vindictive, criminal, and, it would seem, mad. Her illness is not the delicate fading away of consumption but rather the raging infection of venereal disease, which she spreads with glee to the men who seek her services. Socially repudiated as an unmarried, sexually experienced woman, the first Mary intentionally turns her stigma into a weapon by spreading sexual contamination back into a society that has cast her out. The first Mary's story is thus a revision of the seduced-maiden narrative designed to make a didactic point about the injuries men and social stigma inflict on women.

Mr Raymond introduces Mary's mother's story from the perspective of a man who once loved her without return of affection. After five years spent out of the country, he returns to England to stumble upon the first Mary in a situation he calls a 'catastrophe full of horror' (59). The scene in the tavern in which he finds this Mary already tells her story – to a certain extent. The company she is in speaks to her promiscuousness; her tattered clothes and dishevelled hair indicate poverty, violence, and sexual abuse; and the ruffian into whose arms she has fainted suggests criminality. The first Mary, now a prostitute of the lowest kind, is accused of participating in a fight in which she has held the arm of a dying man while the other man, one with a 'fierce and gloomy aspect' stabbed him.[15] Mary's sexual guilt is magnified by being the object of competition between two criminal-seeming men and being held by yet a third.

When Mr Raymond encounters the first Mary in the tavern at the moment of the murder, she is in a state of temporary madness – seemingly the effect of alcohol and shock. Mr Raymond describes her eyes as 'wild and vacant,' but when they meet his, 'by degrees, their expression became more fixed and recollected' (60). The next morning, from her prison cell, she is able to write a coherent and powerful 'history' – essentially, a first-person fallen-woman narrative. Hays avoids sentiment in her account of the woman who falls into prostitution, and she endows the narrative with both a sociological and a psychological explanation of female criminality. Indeed, through the first Mary's 'history,' Hays 'anatomizes,' to use William Brewer's terms, the psychological condition of the fallen woman.[16] Mr Raymond's description of her as 'self abandoned' suggests she is to blame for her condition as a drunk, syphilitic prostitute caught up a bar-room brawl. However, in her narrative, she assesses her behaviour, accounts for her motivations, condemns her betrayers, and indicts society for stigmatizing her to such an extent that her only option was to continue on her path of vice and self-injury.

Once the story turns to Mary's mother's first-person narration, her psychological struggles come to the fore, and Hays lays out the connections between mental illness, education, male abuse, and social prejudice

Fatal melancholia in The Victim of Prejudice   109

that will be evident in Mary's story as well. It is not clear from the letter if the first Mary's sexual relationship had already begun in secret while Mr Raymond was attempting to court her, or if she was just at the stage of struggling with temptation. In either event, her lover's pressuring her to transgress caused an agitated state of mind and weakened her physical health. In telling such a story, Hays makes the point made by Mary Wollstonecraft in *A Vindication of the Rights of Woman* that women are only 'frail' because of their inadequate educations. Mary's mother writes that she rejected the man she should have accepted (Mr Raymond), and instead 'listened to the insidious flatteries of a being, raised by fashion and fortune to a rank seducing [her] vain imagination, in the splendour of which [her] weak judgement was dazzled and [her] virtue overpowered' (63). Mary's mother's mental frailty and inability to regulate her imagination comes from her poor (although fashionable) education. With a mind weak from her upbringing, she is 'dazzled' by her lover's status, and she experiences her time with him as a period of 'delirium,' a time of unreal delight akin to a feverish condition. Foucault makes use of identical terms when he describes 'unreason' as 'dazzlement,' writes of the 'complex of convictions and images which constitutes a delirium,' and links delirium to the passions that move from the mind into the body.[17] Mary's reason and sanity return when her lover abandons her (though she is pregnant) and throws her 'friendless and destitute upon the world, branded with infamy, and a wretched outcast from social life' (64). In Hays' revised fallen-woman narrative, desire – which is unregulated because of a bad education, turns into passion – which causes a 'delirium' that impedes cognitive ability and allows unreason free rein.

In contrast to the usual narrative of love-madness, the first Mary's reason returns, rather than flees, when she is abandoned, because the 'delirium' of pleasure that had impeded judgement dissipates. When Mary's mother regains her reason, she quickly comes to understand the role of social stigma in her situation. Her mind now sharpened by experience, she describes in her letter to Mr Raymond what amounts to a moment of social enlightenment: 'I perceived myself the victim of the injustice, of the prejudice, of society, which, by opposing to my return to virtue almost insuperable barriers, had plunged me into irremediable ruin' (66). The idea that society is to be blamed for stigmatizing women who transgress sexual rules is, of course, the main point of the novel. Hays lays this out in her 'Advertisement' where she explains her purpose is to delineate 'the mischiefs which have ensued' because of 'the too-great stress laid on the *reputation* for chastity in *woman*' (1). Mary's mother does not excuse her transgression, and she accepts responsibility for having been foolish, vain, and weak; although clearly Hays wants readers

110 *Women and madness in the early Romantic novel*

to see how her education has made her so. Moreover, Mary's mother represents her departure from her parents' house and her period of pleasure with her lover as occurring while she was in a state of temporary madness. The victim of a poor education, her passions easily overtook her reason, and she presents herself as a young woman whose rational mind was temporarily impaired, rather than as a person inherently weak because of her sex.

Stigma, however, prevents her reintegration into society, which causes Mary's mother to experience a new kind of mental affliction born from despair. But this despair, rather than make her melancholic, as it does much later for her daughter, creates a maniacal desire to inflict injuries on others.[18] This story of a woman whose madness and sexual desire are intertwined departs from contemporary accounts of nymphomania, a disease in which, as French medical writer M. D. T. de Bienville believed, the uterine nerves become inflamed by the erotic imagination.[19] In Hays' hands, however, the affliction that sends a woman out into the street seeking sex is not the pernicious interaction of the female body with a diseased imagination, but rather a different kind of illness – one caused by socially inflicted despair.[20] Mary's mother describes her emotional state as a prostitute: 'My mind became fiend-like, revelling in destruction, glorying in its shame … I became a monster, cruel, relentless, ferocious; and contaminated alike, with a deadly poison, the health and the principles of those unfortunate victims whom, with practised allurements, I entangled in my snares' (67).[21] Once a typical, poorly educated daughter of the aspirational lower gentry, the first Mary is now so altered by stigma that she has become a being who takes pleasure in inflicting harm on others. Her weapon of choice is her own contaminated body, through which she can spread both physical and moral disease to the population that condemns her. Mary's victims are, of course, men, and by infecting them and their families, she offers payback to all the other men who have injured her. The first Mary believes that men can never become as depraved as women because they are not subject to the same stigmatization. '*Despair* shuts not against him every avenue to repentance; *despair* drives him not from human sympathies; *despair* hurls him not from hope, from pity, from life's common charities, to plunge him into desperate, damned, guilt' (67). This despair the first Mary feels can be understood as a socially caused psychological condition that makes her want to harm others and that prevents her from living a healthy, productive life. Because the stigma placed on women's transgressive sexuality is totalizing, she cannot repent, have an emotional connection with another person, or imagine an alternative future. She can do nothing but fall into deeper and deeper levels of guilt, to the point that her desire for revenge becomes a maniacal compulsion.

Writing to Mr Raymond from her prison cell, Mary's mother reflects on the cause of her depravity. It is true that society inflicted a deep wound on her mind through stigma. But she specifically blames men for their selfish, almost routinely abusive sexual behaviour. She wants to warn the 'guileful seducer' and bid the 'thoughtless libertine' to 'stop, amidst his selfish gratifications, and reflect' (67). She would have the 'sordid voluptuary' consider that he takes his hour of his pleasure, an hour which quickly lapses into 'disgust and lassitude' at the price of considerable harm. Hays does not have the first Mary identify the injured party as young women, but rather has her discuss the problem through abstractions. The 'vain man, of civil refinements' fosters 'an evil, poisoning virtue at its source, diffusing through every rank its deadly venom, bursting the bounds of nature, blasting its endearments, destroying the promise of youth, the charm of domestic affections, and hurling its hapless victim into irremediable perdition' (67). She does get to the female victim, but prior to that, she complains that male desire harms every rank of society and destroys natural, domestic love. Mary's mother may be a victim of 'society,' but first and foremost, she is a representative victim of that 'vain man, of civil refinements' who destroys the domestic bonds of society through his selfish sexual abuse of women. This is the same man Hays points to in her 'Advertisement,' and it is the same man the protagonist Mary addresses, as we shall see, at the very end of her narrative.

In this revision of the fallen woman narrative, Hays does not let readers weep sympathetically over the spectacle of lovely, fallen virtue. Instead, writing in opposition to what Vivien Jones has described as the 'story of the penitent, suffering and redeemable prostitute,' which she terms a 'comforting myth,'[22] Hays places before the reader a vivid account of the mental disease caused by what society believes to be both routine and acceptable: men's sexual philandering and 'ruined' women's stigmatization. Here, she presents psychological destruction in an account designed to draw forth shock and horror rather than pity. When Mary's mother thinks about Mr Raymond as the man she should have married, her shame and despair become so great that she plunges into a self-harming maniacal fit. She throws her body on the dungeon floor, tears her hair and flesh with her nails, and groans, howls, and shrieks. Despite her words condemning men for their actions, her rage turns inward, and she falls into a state in which she could be an inhabitant of the asylum where Maria Venables in *Wrongs of Woman* is confined, a place where inmates howl and shriek in the dark.

Mary's mother is in this horrific condition all night, until the sight of her own blood, mixed with the relief of tears, recalls her 'from the verge of insanity' (68). She gains control of her mind by applying it to something that matters more to her than her guilt and shame: the future of her child. She therefore writes to Mr Raymond; and, as it was for Maria Venables,

112   *Women and madness in the early Romantic novel*

the process of writing for the benefit of a daughter proves therapeutic: 'I indulged in the mournful retrospect; I committed it to paper; while, as my thoughts were methodized, my spirit became serene' (68). Concerned that her daughter might meet a fate similar to her own, she urges Mr Raymond to shelter, educate, and strengthen the child (69). Tracing her own condition back to a poor education (of the sort Wollstonecraft criticizes in her second *Vindication*), the first Mary gives directions for her daughter to be raised as unlike herself as possible. Where she was weak, her daughter will be strong; where she was dependent, little Mary will be self-sufficient and self-respecting; where her mind was in bondage, the second Mary's will be free. What Mary's mother does not anticipate, however, is that no degree of education can remove her daughter from the perils that await her as a woman in a male-dominated society. Hays, like Wollstonecraft, knew that patriarchal power was a trap from which most women could not escape.[23]

Mary's hysteria

Mary describes her mother's letter as a 'fatal narrative' and remembers rushing out into a storm, which Hays uses to represent her character's distraught emotional and cognitive state. Over the course of the episode, Mary experiences physical problems that track with the symptomology of hysteria: a choking sensation in the throat, shortness of breath, a racing heart, fainting, and catatonic collapse. Among the medical writer Robert Whytt's list of hysterical symptoms were sensations of cold, trembling, depressed spirits, feelings of oppression, and suffocation.[24] Mary also hallucinates about her mother as a martyr to sexual stigmatization: 'I beheld her, in idea, abandoned to infamy, cast out of society, stained with blood, expiring on a scaffold, unpitied and unwept' (72). Hays adds delusions of a diseased imagination to other symptoms that impact Mary physically until finally, 'exhausted by the struggle of warring passions,' she sinks 'without motion on the turf' (72). This, the most acute episode Mary has experienced to date, is caused both by the overwhelming emotional pain of reading her mother's narrative and by the cognitive stress of suddenly being exposed to an assortment of social evils she does not yet understand. Although the episode stems from her mother's letter, her madness here is caused by the cumulative injuries of men, beginning with her mother's seduction and betrayal and extending through Mr Raymond's mistaken desire to maintain the purity of her mind through ignorance and secrecy.

With the assistance of Mrs Neville, Mary comes to understand the social reasons for her mother's stigmatization, and this knowledge strengthens her

Fatal melancholia in The Victim of Prejudice   113

resolve not to marry William. But William, using the language of political radicalism, argues strenuously against her, urging his desires to the point of emotionally wounding and insulting her by downplaying the reasons for her opposition. Expressing disbelief that Mary could suffer from his desires, he asks: 'And what is the dreaded, the chimerical evil, to avert which demands this expensive sacrifice?' And when Mary asks what will happen when she is no longer young and beautiful? William insists that her concerns are 'phantoms' that are 'fancifully arrayed' (77). Mary has just seen her mother as a phantom while in a delirious state that revealed her fear of violating social norms and ending up like her mother. William, however, ascribes Mary's fears to the imagination in order to delegitimize them when, in truth, Mary's imagination is processing her fears for her future through her agony about her mother's past. William also uses emotional manipulation and misogynistic tactics when, in response to Mary's objection to lying to his father, he says: 'You never loved me. Pride and fickleness have fortified your heart. It is vain to expect from a woman a stability for which sex and nature have incapacitated her!' (78). As in the grapes scene, William wields his words intentionally to wound her when he cannot get her to comply with his wishes. In this way, William uses Mary's feelings for him and her delicate mental state to gain power over her as he takes advantage of the 'dangerous tendency of romantic love' – in Miriam Wallace's words, to 'mask over relations of power between the sexes.'[25]

Although in a similar situation, Mary is distinct from Fenwick's Sibella in that she resists her lover's entreaties and refuses to sacrifice her honesty and self-respect for him. However, his selfish behaviour still takes its toll on her physical and mental health, much as Clement's does on Sibella's. Back at the Nevilles' house, and after Mary has been traumatized by reading her mother's story, William makes a passionate, wild, even frantic appeal that pushes her into another temporary state of madness that she describes in her memoir: 'Stunned, confounded, shocked, overborne, my senses grew bewildered: I sunk into a kind of stupor, and became unconscious to what was passing. I neither spoke nor wept; but, with a wild air, continued to gaze vacantly' (83). This is an affective and cognitive position similar to that of the love-mad maid. But whereas in the typical narrative the young woman loses mental focus because of a relatively simple story of loss from death or infidelity, Hays' story dwells on the harmful, selfish behaviour of privileged men who feel that their desires take precedence over anything the young woman might want. Hays thus refocuses the traditional love-mad woman's narrative onto the specifically damaging actions done by men. In Mary's case, William plays a considerable part in the series of emotional injuries that bring on her tragic end. Her mind already wounded by sudden knowledge of her mother's crime, Mary is so afflicted by William's excessive

114   *Women and madness in the early Romantic novel*

passionate outbursts and emotional attacks that her brain is forced to shut itself down for self-protection.

At this point, Mary's psychological condition is much more fragile than it had been earlier, when she experienced depressed spirits over the separation from William. She has moved from love-inspired melancholy to hysteria to a risk of mental impairment recognized by both Mrs Neville and William, who becomes 'apprehensive for [her] health and intellects' (83). This is her condition before the sexual assault, a condition caused not by feminine sensibility or female frailty, but by a series of injuries – some inadvertent, some not – beginning with her unknown biological father and extending to her much-loved adopted father and to the man she wishes she could marry. Mary thus emerges as a woman beset by injurious males, to whom only Mr Neville does no harm, although neither is he able to offer much assistance.

'A brutal violation' and post-traumatic response

Mary's rape, which she refers to as a 'brutal violation,' is the tragic apex of this story, and it serves as the culmination of a series of injuries inflicted on her by men. Going alone to London after Mr Raymond's death to seek employment through her guardian's connections, Mary is tricked by a woman she thinks is a new friend and ends up in Sir Peter's house. Sir Peter has made multiple appearances over the years as Mary has grown older, each time attempting forced physical contact and/or trying to convince her to become his mistress. Because she has consistently refused him, he uses his considerable financial and social power to imprison her in his mansion with the intention to weaken her resolve.[26] As she did with other parts of Mary's story, Hays 'anatomizes' the assault Mary experiences at the rake Sir Peter's mansion: she offers insights into Mary's weakened physical and mental state before the rape; describes, via Mary's memories, the act itself; records the perpetrator's self-justifications; and accounts for the aftermath in terms of Mary's psychological trauma and social stigmatization.[27] By covering Mary's experience as someone who is sexually assaulted and then struggles to remake her life, Hays crafts a new narrative of the sexually compromised woman, one in which the heroine is neither a seduced maiden nor a fallen woman, but rather an abused victim who suffers irreparable psychological damage from the combination of male power and social stigma.[28]

By the time Mary finds herself in Sir Peter's clutches, she is already in a debilitated mental state due to a series of losses – namely, the departure of both William and the Nevilles from England and Mr Raymond's death. In a destitute financial situation and with no friends to rely on, Mary is easy prey for Sir Peter, who locks her in a chamber to wear her out. Although frail

Fatal melancholia in The Victim of Prejudice

and physically ill after having refused to eat or sleep for eight days, Mary is able to leave her chamber by stealing the key from her intoxicated maid. As she attempts to find a way out of the house, Mary is 'distracted and perplexed' by Sir Peter's male guests, becoming disoriented by the shifting of the men, and moving back and forth as if trapped in a maze (116). Instead of finding a door onto the street, she ends up where the most danger awaits her – Sir Peter's private closet in his chamber. The fact that Mary is put into this situation by Sir Peter's guests suggests that other elite men are party to the inescapable situation in which she finds herself. Here, Hays seems to anticipate modern feminist ideas about male socialization and general male responsibility for sexual assault, what Larry May and Robert Strikwerda describe as 'distributive collective responsibility' in which 'each member of the group has a share in the responsibility for a harm such as rape.'[29] In each of her most threatening encounters with Sir Peter, he has been in the company of other men who occasionally intervene, but never fully protect her. Mary naturally thinks they will help again this time, but instead their movements force her into the maze, symbolically revealing that they have been accessories to her persecution the entire time.

By the time Mary backs herself into the 'small dressing-closet' in what turns out to be Sir Peter's private chamber, she is almost senseless with terror. It is central to Hays' portrayal of the rape that Mary is in a highly compromised cognitive and emotional state when Sir Peter enters the room, as her character must be unable to either consent or resist. Hays' depiction of the assault takes into account her society's understanding of rape, which legally rested on a woman's vigorous resistance.[30] As Miriam Wallace observes, 'Hays insists that terror, rage, and exhaustion might weaken a woman's physical capacity to resist effectively,' adding that Hays 'creates a heroine and an attack that are carefully worked to render the heroine resistant but plausibly overcome, and the attack fundamentally unerotic.'[31] Mary recalls she was too overwhelmed with emotion to shriek: 'I uttered only a deep groan, and sunk powerless on the floor; confounded, stunned, as it were, in a state of consternation, that, without depriving me of my faculties, seemed utterly to suspend them. From this unaccountable stupor, this lethargy of the senses, I was roused by the entrance of the vile Osborne' (116). The rape itself is conveyed in a broken and fragmented style that covers in an abbreviated form the elements of a whole scene.[32] Phrases are divided by hyphens, which indicate the overwhelming emotional impact of the assault and its memory, and the memory is cut off from the rest of the narrative by a line of asterisks.[33]

The way Mary records the rape in her memoir several years after the fact conveys the lasting emotional impact of a traumatic experience. 'Deaf to my remonstrances, to my supplications, – regardless of my tears, my rage, my

116   *Women and madness in the early Romantic novel*

despair, – his callous heart, his furious and uncontrollable vehemence, – oh! That I could conceal from myself, what, rendered desperate, I no longer care to hide from the world! – I suffered a brutal violation' (116–17). Mary is unable to stop his advances, as she had many times previously, by a rational rebuke to his sense of self as a gentleman. This time, her terror, combined with her mental exhaustion and physical weakness, makes a defence through reason impossible. Despite the broken style of the memory, Hays conveys a considerable amount of information about Mary's emotional resistance in that she chides, begs, weeps, rages, and expresses despair.[34] We learn that Sir Peter ignores Mary's emotional expressions because, as she tells us, his heart is hardened and his sexual desire is unbounded. Through Mary, Hays narrates a situation in which a woman objects to sexual intercourse using a variety of emotional expressions to convey her distress, but the man is too driven by his own sexual desire and lack of interest in female subjectivity and too protected by his feelings of impunity to care about what she wants or what she feels. Hays deviates from more well-known rape narratives such as *Clarissa* by leaving her heroine conscious during her assault.[35] By keeping Mary conscious, Hays risks the reader's suspicion of her complicity given that, in Simon Dickie's words, 'activity, passivity, speech, silence – all were open to lewd interpretation. All implied consent.'[36] But Hays challenges her culture's assumptions about rape by showing that all of the above – activity, passivity, speech, and silence – most definitely did not imply consent. Moreover, her attacker understands that she did not consent. Even though, as Dickie observes, 'in all sentimental and amatory fiction … the victim's complete unconsciousness worked to dispel any suspicion of complicity,'[37] Hays keeps Mary's mind alert because it is only through her character's consciousness that she can convey the full and lasting trauma of the experience.

Mary does not faint until after the rape; and later, when she sees Sir Peter again, she will faint repeatedly, as well as lapse into convulsions and show signs of mental derangement. Although we would understand these responses as evidence of post-traumatic-stress disorder, they would have been seen at the time as expressions of a dangerous hysteria. Since the development of medical writing in Ancient Greece, hysteria had been understood as a female condition prompted by a pernicious, inherent uterine condition. This association of hysteria with the female reproductive system, Ilza Veith explains, 'was in essence an expression of awareness of the malign effect of disordered sexual activity on emotional stability.'[38] As discussed in my Introduction, the disease was originally thought to be caused by a malignant uterus that moved around a woman's body; later, after dissections revealed the womb could not move, it was still understood to be able to exert its pernicious power in a variety of ways, whether through 'vapours,'

Fatal melancholia in The Victim of Prejudice   117

through its connection to the nervous system, or through internal bodily sympathy.[39] 'Somatic derangement' – such as Mary exhibits – was, as Mark Micale explains, key to physicians' ability to diagnose hysteria.[40] But what Hays describes is not a physical disease latent in all women because of the womb's ever-malicious influence. Rather, her somatic responses stem from a traumatic injury to the body and psyche. Hays thus revises a millennium of thinking about hysteria that connected it to a woman's malfunctioning body through linking the condition instead directly to sexual abuse – to a woman being forced into sexual intercourse through violence. In her hands, hysteria is still yoked to female sexuality, but it emerges because women's bodies and the patriarchal organization of society make them vulnerable to the sexual aggression of men.

When Mary recovers from the initial shock of her assault, she refuses the 'reparations' offered by Sir Peter and instead demands her liberty, insisting she will seek justice from the law. 'I ask no mercy; for, bowels of compassion, I know, to my cost, thou hast none: but liberty, the common *right* of a human being to whose charge no offence can be alleged ... I once more demand, which to refuse me be at thy peril' (118). The victim of a 'brutal violation,' Mary musters up the energy and courage to insist on her right to freedom, as if liberty for a woman were a natural right. In demanding her freedom, she is also asserting the right to control her body, a right he has taken from her, but only momentarily. It is a heroic, defiant moment for Mary, a moment that shows she maintains her strength of mind and still adheres to the ideas she was educated to revere. When he offers his reparation in the form of making her his richly rewarded mistress ('the uncontrolled mistress of my fortune as of my heart') Mary scornfully turns him down. And in response to his explanation that her reputation has been 'irretrievably injured' and that her 'honour and character' can never be restored, Mary says 'oh, 'tis false! 'tis base as barbarous' and declares: 'My spirit, superior to personal injury, rises above the sense of its wrongs, and utterly contemns you! I spurn the wealth you offer ... and will seek, by honest labour, the bread of independence' (118–19).[41] Mary offers heroic resistance here in chastising her rapist, rejecting his offers, and being able to summon up energy and a spirit of independence after a traumatic attack. Mary not only joins Sibella from Fenwick's *Secrecy* in earning the description of being a 'glorious girl,' she also makes women's ability to control their own bodies and to live autonomously into a political aspiration.

The problem, however, is that as a woman who has lost her virginity before marriage, Mary is considered impure, regardless of how that virginity was lost, and she lives in a society in which a woman's desire to control her own body and to live autonomously can only ever be aspirational. Moreover, patriarchal power ensures there is no legal redress

118   *Women and madness in the early Romantic novel*

for rape victims. It is a particularly poignant aspect of this story that, educated as she has been, apart from social regulations, Mary has to learn the social consequences of having been raped from her rapist when he says: 'What is called, in your sex, honour and character, can, I fear, never be restored to you; nor will any asservations or future watchfulness … obliterate the stain' (119).[42] In this way, Mary finds that her physical and psychic injuries will become a social wound that will never heal, one that will irreparably change her life by marking her with stigma. Mary is, of course, trapped in a society that values women considerably less than men, as seen through the failure to consider sexual assault as a crime worthy of true investigation.[43] Mary must learn from her rapist that she has no value to her society and that she is legally helpless: 'Who will credit the tale you mean to tell? What testimony or witnesses can you produce that will not make against you? Where are your resources … Who would support you against my wealth and influence? How would your delicacy shrink from the idea of becoming, in open court, the sport of ribaldry, the theme of obscene jesters?' (119). Sir Peter is unfortunately correct in everything he says, not just about how things will turn out for Mary, but also about the consequences in Hays' time for women who attempted prosecutions for rape. Anna Clark notes that in the eighteenth century, although rape was a crime punishable by death, most rapes of adult women were not prosecuted.[44] In court, Mary would have to describe the assault in detail; she would have to bear the obscene amusement of the spectators; and as an orphan, there would be no damages for the injury done to her.[45] As Clark explains, 'in the eyes of the law sexual assault was only significant when it involved the "property" of a man – a virginal daughter or a wife.'[46] Because she is an orphan, Mary is not the 'property' of any man, and so the courts would be hard-pressed to find her rape significant.[47]

In her description of the 'brutal violation' and its aftermath, Hays anticipates a great deal of modern feminist thought about sexual assault, including the slow legal change to conceptions of rape, how it functions as patriarchal control, how 'rape culture' makes men feel entitled to sex, and how the trauma of surviving rape impacts a woman's psyche. Importantly, in an age in which rape was still understood as a crime against a husband or father, Hays conveys to readers that this crime has been committed against Mary – against her body, but also against her psyche and sense of herself as an autonomous individual. Rebecca Whisnant observes that given the history of rape as a property crime against men, the modern feminist redefinition of rape as a crime against the woman is 'nothing short of revolutionary'[48] – so much more so, then, for Hays writing approximately 200 years before the modern feminist movement. Hays' emphasis on

Fatal melancholia in The Victim of Prejudice

Mary's experience and her insistence on bodily autonomy is in keeping with what Simon Dickie has identified as a slow change to legal concepts that recognized rape not as a property crime, but as a crime against the woman herself.[49] Hays understands that the trauma of Mary's rape is connected to the fact that, in treating her as an object, Sir Peter has violated her 'personhood' – a legal concept at the time not extended to women. Carolyn Shafer and Marilyn Frye consider that consent – which Mary clearly did not give to Sir Peter – is based on the idea that one's personhood is a domain over which one has control.[50] In committing the rape, Sir Peter presents the reader with a 'maze of humiliations' in which he uses her body for his own ends – ends, as Shafer and Frye explain, that are contrary to the goal of maintaining 'bodily integrity and health.'[51] Quite simply, he violates her personhood, as Hays demonstrates, by conveying to her that she is not a person, but rather a sexual object.[52] Sir Peter represents the rape as an excess of sexual desire brought about by intoxication and Mary's persistent refusal of him; but Hays allows readers to see that he degrades her as an autonomous individual in order to establish the power over her he had previously sought by other means.[53]

Although Mary is able to summon up sufficient mental and emotional strength to defy Sir Peter, she quickly succumbs to the psychological trauma of the rape, manifested by a blend of physical and mental afflictions. After leaving Sir Peter's house, she wanders the streets, her disoriented mental state, disordered hair and attire, 'unsettled and frenzied' eyes, and uncertain path working symbolically to suggest she is now both a fallen woman and a woman who has lost her mind (121). Sandra Sherman observes that 'Mary's fall, her loss of reputation and economic security, reified in her pointless urban walking, signifies an absence from normative modes entitling women to deference.'[54] Sherman is correct that Mary's pointless movements in the city represent the sexual fall, loss of reputation, and lack of economic security that destroy her entitlement to deference as a genteel woman. Mary's wild eyes at this point, as she wanders the streets, suggest a state of madness brought on by the trauma of her sexual assault and her social dislocation.[55] Hays draws on stereotypical images that link women's sexual license to madness, as she does with the portrayal of Mary's mother. But in this case, she severs the causal link by having already made it clear that Mary's 'fallen' sexual state and disordered mind have been caused by a traumatic injury inflicted on her by a man whose position in the patriarchal system makes him untouchable.

While wandering the streets, Mary is coincidentally found by William, who takes her to an inn. There, she finds solace in his affectionate presence, but soon she lapses into a dangerous illness brought on by psychological suffering. Mary experiences three weeks of a 'blank in [her] existence,' with a mental state considerably different than when she suffered from episodes of depression and anxiety prior to the sexual assault. This episode, although it occurs in conjunction with a feverish condition, is the closest Mary has come to madness as a state of complete unreason. In the midst of the three blank weeks, Mary is harassed by 'intervals of reflection, dark and dreadful, imaginary terrors, broken recollections, strange phantoms, wild and wandering thoughts' (123). These sorts of unwanted, frightening, and sporadic mental incursions were used in literature to describe madness for much of the eighteenth century. Michael DePorte observes that 'the association of imagination with insanity in the Restoration and eighteenth century is nowhere more striking than in the frequent use by psychologists of the dream as an analogue to madness.'[56] From a more modern perspective, Mary's mental state during these weeks can be understood as triggered by her traumatic experience of sexual assault. The *DSM-5* lists 'recurrent distressing dreams in which the content and/or affect of the dream are related to the traumatic event(s)' as one of the symptoms of traumatic psychological distress.[57]

During the worst part of this mad period, Mary sees images of her mother as a loose woman, a drunken prostitute, and a condemned criminal. Whether or not these are dreams or hallucinations, they operate as a window into Mary's unconscious mind under duress – a duress so great that Hays uses the term 'disorder' to describe Mary's mental state as she struggles to recall her 'wandering reason' when the 'terrific visions' depart (123). Hays' use of the dream to give access to Mary's unconscious mind puts her in step with what Jennifer Ford has identified as a preoccupation with dreaming in the 1790s, a time when 'interest in the forces and features of psychic life began to increase, and a concept of the "unconscious" mind began to emerge.'[58] Eleanor Ty argues that through this dream, 'it is as if Mary subconsciously desires to be linked with her mother and her disgrace,' but Vivien Jones is more persuasive when she stresses the 'powerful dynamic of revulsion which is also present, a representation of the terrible inevitability of the mother's corruption.'[59] The strain of how Mary feels about her mother and what she understands about her own situation emerges through this window into her unconscious mind, in which Mary associates her mother's sexual transgressions and the violence of her mother's death with the trauma of her own rape.

The dream, or vision, Mary has of her mother tells the story of the fallen woman as a Gothic narrative in which a woman's sexual pleasure, already viewed by society as criminal, inevitably leads to actual legal crime. The dream embedded in Mary's unconscious mind seems to contradict Hays' social critique by conveying highly conventional ideas that portray women's pursuit of sexual pleasure as both aberrant and criminal.

Fatal melancholia in The Victim of Prejudice 121

> One moment, methought I beheld her in the arms of her seducer, revelling in licentious pleasure; the next, I saw her haggard, intoxicated, self-abandoned, joining in the midnight riot; and, in an instant, as the fantastic scene shifted, covered with blood, accused of murder, shrieking in horrible despair, dragged to the scaffold ... Then, all pallid and ghastly, with clasped hands, streaming eyes, and agonizing earnestness, she seemed to urge me to take example from her fate. (123)

Mary imagines her mother through a narrative in which one immoral act leads to another. The first step is sexual pleasure, represented as licentious; the next is drunken whoredom followed by sanguinary criminality; the final step is execution. Mary's mother appears to her as a ghost, as if communicating from beyond the grave and begging her not to repeat the same story. Mary has already been solicited by Sir Peter to become his mistress; and she is about to receive the same offer from William, who, as she will discover when her mind clears, has just married a wealthy woman he does not love. The apparition of Mary's mother serves as a conventional reminder that any willing sacrifice of virtue is but the first step on a path to criminality and horrific punishment. Mary then imagines her mother's appalling death and her own efforts to give her mother comfort and to receive love from her: 'I rushed forward to clasp my hapless parent in a last embrace. I beheld the convulsive pangs, the gaspings, the struggles, the distortions of death' (123). Mary's dream illustrates the horror she feels at her mother's fate, her own sense of helplessness and loss, and her fear of the inter-connectedness of her fate with her mother's. It also exposes Mary's own feeling of loss of the mother's love, as well as her failure at not being able to save her mother.

Within these fevered dreams, Mary exposes the conventional opinion that her mother is in some way is responsible for her fate, since Mary's unconscious mind sees her mother as self-injuring through taking an immoral and lewd pleasure in her sexual relationship with her lover. And she sees her mother in the next phase of her decline as responsible for the damage done to body, mind, and spirit. The words 'self-abandoned' and 'joining' indicate that she has made a choice to become intoxicated, to participate in drunken revels, and to lose all self-control at midnight. These are choices that have led her to the scaffold, as if enjoying sex and pursuing sex outside of marriage are crimes that must be punished by death. A great deal of Mary's psychic pain comes from the fact that her mother actually is guilty – for leaving her parents, for embracing the life of a prostitute, for spreading contagion, and for being an accessory to murder. Hays perhaps emphasizes a conventional account of the culpability of female desire to show that regardless of whether a woman is self-injuring in her sexual experience or the innocent victim of an abusive man, society views all pre-marital sexual intercourse as the same.[60]

122 *Women and madness in the early Romantic novel*

When Mary recovers, William tells her he has recently married and tries to convince her to become his mistress. She refuses, however, saying: '*it is virtue only that I love better than William Pelham*' (127). The period after Mary recovers from her illness and leaves William marks the beginning of a long struggle for independence in which, as a result of repeated setbacks, she moves steadily toward fatal melancholia and her tragic conclusion. When Mary cannot pay her debts, she is taken to the sheriff's house where Sir Peter comes to see her, in another indication of his ubiquitous power. By having Mary collapse into a hysterical fit, or in our terms a post-traumatic response, Hays shows how profoundly Mary has been impacted by the rape. Such 'pathological reactions to traumatic events' were first reported in psychiatric literature in the late nineteenth century, which makes Hays' understanding of Mary's response 100 years ahead of its time.[61] This is Mary's first interaction with Sir Peter since she fled his house, and at first sight, she utters a 'fearful shriek,' falls at his feet in convulsions, and remains unconscious for a considerable amount of time (148). When she awakens, she reports: 'My eyes, wildly turning, sought, on every side, the terrific vision that had appeared as the chimera of a distempered brain, and before which life and sense had fled. I uttered a thousand incoherent interrogations, to which no answer was returned' (148). Mary's hysterical fit, which consists of the familiar symptoms of convulsions and fainting, transitions into a state of temporary madness.[62] Her wild eyes once again reveal mental affliction, indicating that she cannot make sense of what she sees nor distinguish between what is real and what is the fantastic invention of a tormented mind. When Sir Peter attempts to convince her to accept his assistance, her intense emotional response takes her again into the vicinity of madness as she entreats him to 'Begone!' and does so 'with frantic, vehemence, [her] senses disturbed with terror' (151). Mary's breakdowns in the presence of Sir Peter result from fear – fear coming from the traumatic memory of the rape and from the possibility that he might assault her again.

In recognizing that mental illness can come from a traumatic experience, Hays' thinking about such afflictions is more modern than that of many physicians at the forefront of medical thought at the time. Her perspective as a woman allows her to see what even the leading revisionist physicians of the day, such as Philippe Pinel, often did not: that hysteria was not caused by the female body. It could be caused by an injury to the body, and it could express itself through the body, but it was first and foremost a psychological affliction stemming from external injury. By evading reproductive and sexual explanations for women's mental disease, Hays insists that women, in their unharmed, natural state are not particularly prone to mental illness or sexual deviance. Women, Hays suggests, want to conform to societal expectations in that they seek love, marriage, and a sense of community. It is only because they are subject to male abuse that their minds give way to disease.

After experiencing an additional fear response that takes away her ability to speak and to control her bodily movements, Mary is finally able to confront Sir Peter and even to repudiate him when he offers her the 'compensation' of marriage.[63] Eventually he exits the novel, leaving Mary for the second time in debtor's prison which is yet another version of women's metaphorical confinement in male structures of power.[64] With no way to pay her debts and no friends to appeal to, Mary sinks deeply into melancholia, relying on her self-respect and clean conscience as the only consolation for her ruined body and mind. But at this point she can no longer resist the weight of the melancholy that has been dragging her down since Mr Pelham first appeared at her home, and her mental disease takes its toll: 'I sink beneath a torrent, whose resistless waves overwhelm alike in a common ruin the guiltless and the guilty' (168). She is in a deep depression and her mind is, as she says, broken as the novel moves out of its retrospective view and into the present tense. 'A deadly torpor steals over my faculties; principles loosen in my clouded mind; my heart, formed for tender sympathies ... withers in joyless, hopeless solitude; my beauty fades ... my confidence in humanity totters to its base; virtue appears to me an empty name; the current of life creeps slowly, wasted by inanity and clogged by disease' (168). Mary's self-anatomy here covers every aspect of her being. She is without energy or volition; her mind is clouded; her principles are weakened; her heart is withered; her beauty is lost; her social impulses are destroyed; and her are virtues gone. At this point, she prepares to die by suicide. She is not mad in the sense of not knowing the real from the unreal, but she is destroyed by the male-inflicted mental disease of melancholy, which creates the despair that prompts her to consider suicide.

'Idolatrous love' and marital madness

Somehow, Mary lives in this state of despair an additional two years. Hays seems to give the reader some hope when the Nevilles appear to rescue her from her cell: 'You are free! your sufferings are at an end!' says Mr Neville in this touching scene. A true Christian, he adds: 'Suffer not an ingenuous shame to overwhelm you. Who is free from error? Habitual depravity can never sink a soul like your's [sic]. Come, and share with us our prosperity; we will shelter you from a cruel, undistinguishing world: we will smooth, will assist, your return to virtue' (169). If this rescue had worked, if Mary had returned to health, then the treatment for the psychological injuries

124   *Women and madness in the early Romantic novel*

inflicted by patriarchal power would be Christian charity, familial love, and female friendship. With a strong, moral father-figure to shield her and a loving female friend/mother-figure to comfort her, Mary might have been restored to health, and she might have found her happy ending in a domestic retreat. But Hays does not choose this conclusion, and the poignant rescue is prelude to yet more tragedy. In the first place, Mary has exited prison in a state of 'premature old age ... [with] broken spirits and a shattered constitution' (170). She is now so debilitated in both body and mind that she cannot live the quiet life of domestic affection she has long desired. And second, as if that is not enough to eliminate the possibility of a happy ending, Hays has Mr Neville die from 'repeated colds' he contracts in a 'chill, humid autumn' (171). The death of Mr Neville, Mary's third father-figure, suggests that there are only two kinds of men: the strong who injure women, and the weak who cannot protect them.[65] Mr Neville's death also shows the impotence of Christian charity when faced with the strength of patriarchal power and social prejudice. Not only is there no Christian consolation for Mary in prison (her 'principles loosen in [her] clouded mind'), there is no power in Christian values to protect her when she is freed. And finally, Mrs Neville dies from melancholic disease soon after her husband's death, leaving two small children in addition to a now entirely bereft Mary.

The coda that concludes the novel, in which Mary is saved from debtors' prison only to lose Mr and Mrs Neville before dying herself, gives Hays the opportunity to include marriage in the litany of injuries women experience. Unlike Wollstonecraft, however, Hays does not critique the legal and financial injustices of marriage. Rather, she is interested in how women internalize the social pressure that encourages them to invest all their mental and emotional energy in their husbands. This type of woman – the soft, domestic type – is represented from the start as considerably weaker than Mary Raymond who is educated to think independently and to cultivate a healthy sense of self. And in terms of her mental health, Mrs Neville stands in stark contrast to Mary. Whereas Mary is from childhood bold, energetic, and healthful – that is, until she experiences a series of male-inflicted injuries – Mrs Neville is introduced as soft, delicate, and emotional. A woman of sensibility, her character is tinged with melancholy in a way that seems natural. But in making her so different from Mary, Hays suggests that delicacy and a proclivity to depressive disorders is not natural in women, but rather part of a feminine ideal that makes women dependent on men and restricts their intellectual and affective lives to the home. Mrs Neville is so emotionally tied to her husband that his death causes her to faint, lapse into a stupor, go mad, and then, after a brief conversation with Mary, die from melancholia, leaving her children to the care of relatives.

Fatal melancholia in The Victim of Prejudice   125

Hays reinforces the comparison between the domestic and the independent-minded woman through Mrs Neville's comments in an 'interval of sanity' (172). Through this comparison, Hays emphasizes that both the stereotypically feminine, domestic woman and the woman who attempts to live independently are prone to mental afflictions, although one lives in accordance with social expectations and the other attempts to evade them. Near death, Mrs Neville says 'You, my beloved Mary ... will not long survive your friends: over your stronger mind, *injustice* has triumphed, and consigned you to an early grave; while I sink, a feeble victim to *excessive* and therefore blameworthy, tenderness' (172). Mrs Neville goes on to explain that she loved Mr Neville with an 'enthusiasm' and an 'idolatrous devotion' that stemmed from her 'excess of ... sensibility.'[66]

The consequences of this devotion were that every absence, gesture, inadvertent word would injure her soul, and every accident, even the change of seasons, would alarm her. Her devotion extended to constant anxiety about losing his love. She stifles these concerns with the 'severest discipline,' explaining:

> lest they should wound the peace of him for whom alone I breathed – to promote whose happiness seemed to be the only *end* of my existence ... I had no individual existence; my very being was absorbed in that of my husband ... I was the slave, and am at length become the victim, of my tenderness. LOVE was the vital spark that animated my frame, that sustained my being; it is extinguished, and *I follow to the tomb its object.* (172)

Mary makes no mention of fever or lingering illness, and so the cause of Mrs Neville's death seems to be the 'insanity' that overtakes her the moment her husband expires. With 'agonies of her spirit' and experiencing an 'unequal conflict' to which her 'feeble frame' yields (172), Mrs Neville dies. In her description of her feelings for her husband, Mrs Neville herself conveys the idea that the excess of love she felt for her husband was a type of madness. She is monomaniacally focused on his every word and move; she is plagued by constant anxiety that saps her health; she has no independent sense of self; and once he dies, she has no further reason to live. Her feelings resemble the delusional romantic love of both Mr Murden and Sibella in Fenwick's *Secresy*, characters who agree that with the decease of the beloved (or the cessation of the beloved's love), one ought to 'die also.'[67] Such romantic love, leading, as it does, to melancholic madness, leaves no room for the sort of female friendships that might be able to help women avoid the injuries inflicted by patriarchal systems of power.

126   *Women and madness in the early Romantic novel*

Conclusion: lest I have lived in vain

Hays brings Mary's narrative up to the time of her death, ending, one assumes, moments before she expires. She gives the cause of death as 'the disorder which has gradually wasted my strength and sapped the powers of life' (174). As she has already noted, she never recovered from the years of imprisonment, even when cared for by the Nevilles. What exactly her 'disorder' might be is not clarified, although her ailment seems to be an affliction of the spirit that impacts her physical health. As she notes before narrating the death of the Nevilles, 'disappointment, confinement, unwholesome air, mental anguish, had combined to exhaust and ravage my frame ... the body survived, but the spirit was fled' (171). It had been Mary's spirit that sustained her through her injuries, sufferings, and trauma; but her final imprisonment breaks her spirit and her will to survive. Christian charity cannot heal her psychic wounds; neither can domestic happiness or female companionship.

As in *Secresy* and most of the fragments that conclude *The Wrongs of Woman*, *The Victim of Prejudice* ends on a bleak, pessimistic note.[68] Like *Secresy*, *Victim* actively destroys the possibility of escape through the female solidarity and shared motherhood offered in Wollstonecraft's only optimistic concluding fragment. And like *Secresy*, but possibly more surprisingly given Mary Hays' track record as a feminist thinker, the only way forward presented by the novel is to convince men to change their ways. Hays thus adopts the same strategy as Fenwick, which is to demonstrate, through writing a tragedy about a glorious girl who is psychologically destroyed by male power, how men abuse women. Pointing toward this strategy, Hays gives Mary the following words near the novel's end:

> *I have lived in vain!* Unless the story of my sorrows should kindle in the heart of man, in behalf of my oppressed sex, the sacred claims of humanity and justice. From the fate of my wretched mother ... let him learn, that, while the slave of sensuality ... he pours, by *his conduct*, contempt upon chastity, in vain will he impose on *woman* barbarous penalties, or seek to multiply restrictions; his seductions and example, yet more powerful, will defeat his precepts, of which *hypocrisy*, not virtue, is the genuine fruit. (174)

Hays begins Mary's assessment of her tragedy not by blaming society, but by blaming 'man.' All her sorrows, all her suffering will have been in vain if her story cannot reach into the 'heart of man' and convince him to change his ways. And although Mary begins her memoir writing to a future prisoner of her cell, she ends it by directing the moral of the story to the male reader. The words 'him,' 'he,' and 'his' indicate exactly who needs to change and why. The story is not a warning to women who might

Fatal melancholia in The Victim of Prejudice   127

be seduced, and it is not, in the end, a lamentation about the injustice of punishing victims of either seduction or sexual assault. Rather, it is a strategic argument that uses emotion to impact the privileged men who monopolize power. Hays tells men that they oppress women and that they violate humanity and justice when they behave as slaves to their sexual desires. And as slaves of their desires, they show contempt for the chastity they pretend to revere. They put restrictions and penalties on women that are ineffectual and, through their seductions and sexual assaults, they show their hypocrisy. In this passage, Hays identifies men as the originators of social rules about chastity: 'His seductions and example ... will defeat his precepts.' Hays sees that men such as Edward Moore, author of the *Fables for the Female Sex*, as well as other authors of conduct materials for women, are the ones who make the rules for women's moral conduct; yet men undermine their own rules by being the slaves of their sexual desires. Hays' lesson, then, given at the conclusion of this wrenching story, is not to female readers or to mankind (which would include women), but rather to men alone. Women will never overcome the prejudices of society and will never be free from oppression and the risk of madness until men practise what they preach to women. And so the men who run the country must stop seducing and raping women such as Mary and her mother. If they do not, then the 'toil of the visionary projector' (175) – the work of Hays herself – will have all been in vain.

Notes

1 A number of scholars have been interested in the relationship between Mary's story and her mother's 'fallen' woman narrative. See Vivien Jones, 'Placing Jemima: Women Writers of the 1790s and the Eighteenth-Century Prostitution Narrative,' *Women's Writing* 4, no. 2 (1997), https://doi.org/10.1080/09699089700200011; Toni Bowers, *Representing Resistance: British Seduction Stories, 1660–1800* (London: Blackwell, 2005); Katherine Binhammer, *The Seduction Narrative in Britain, 1747–1800* (Cambridge: Cambridge University Press, 2009); and Roxanne Eberle, *Chastity and Transgression in Women's Writing, 1792–1897: Interrupting the Harlot's Progress* (Basingstoke: Palgrave, 2002).
2 Despite the centrality of rape to this novel, few scholars have looked closely at how Hays represents the psychological impact of this trauma, or at how Mary struggles with what we would call 'mental health.' The primary exception is Miriam Wallace, who argues that Hays uses Mary's sexual assault to 'clarify the systemic and continuing traumatic construction of feminine subjects as suffering victims rather than full political and civic subjects.' See Miriam Wallace, *Revolutionary Subjects in the English 'Jacobin' Novel, 1790–1805* (Lewisburg: Bucknell University Press, 2009), 124. Margaret Kathryn Sloan covers Mary's

128 *Women and madness in the early Romantic novel*

episodes of madness, but she interprets them as part of a largely beneficial process through which Mary learns from her mother's narrative. Margaret Kathryn Sloan, 'Mothers, Marys, and Reforming "The Rising Generation": Mary Wollstonecraft and Mary Hays' in *Mentoring in Eighteenth-Century British Literature and Culture*, ed. Anthony Lee (London: Routledge, 2009), 238.

3 Several scholars have discussed Hays' critique of patriarchal society in this novel. See Marilyn Brooks, 'Mary Hays' *The Victim of Prejudice*: Chastity Renegotiated,' *Women's Writing* 15, no. 1 (May 2008), https://doi-org.libdata. lib.ua.edu/10.1080/09699080701871401; Wallace, *Revolutionary Subjects*; Ada Sharpe and Eleanor Ty, 'Mary Hays and the Didactic Novel in the 1790s' in *Didactic Novels and British Women's Writing, 1790–1820*, ed. Hilary Havens (New York: Routledge, 2017); Sandra Sherman, 'The Feminization of "Reason" in Hays' *The Victim of Prejudice*,' *The Centennial Review* 41, no. 1 (1997), www.jstor.org/stable/23737012; and Mark Zunac, '"The Dear-Bought Lessons of Experience": Mary Hays' *The Victim of Prejudice* and the Empiricist Revision of Burke's *Reflections*,' *Papers on Language and Literature: A Journal for Scholars and Critics of Language and Literature* 48, no. 1 (2012), bit. ly/3WVvnhq.

4 Mary Hays, *The Victim of Prejudice*, ed. Eleanor Ty (1799; Peterborough: Broadview Press, 1998). All references are to this edition.

5 Gina Luria Walker, *Mary Hays, (1759–1843): The Growth of a Woman's Mind* (Aldershot: Ashgate Press, 2006), 11.

6 Although Hays never mentions or alludes to Rousseau, Mary's education in many aspects resembles Émile's. She is isolated from society in a rural retreat and brought up without knowledge of society's 'prejudices.'

7 Jackson writes: 'With emotion increasingly recognized as a distinct and separate faculty of the mind, it became conceivable that some mental disorders might reflect a disturbance in that faculty alone. An 'affective disorder' was now possible.' Stanley Jackson, 'The Use of the Passions in Psychological Healing,' *Journal of the History of Medicine and Allied Sciences* 45, no. 2 (1990): 170, www.jstor. org/stable/24633133.

8 As Eberle observes, William is 'serpent-like' and 'undeniably the "Adam" to Mary's 'Eve'" (*Harlot's Progress*, 82). Wallace, in contrast, sees Sir Peter as 'serpent-like' (*Revolutionary Subjects*, 133). I would argue that both Eberle and Wallace are right, suggesting that Hays positions Man himself as the serpent that betrays Woman through various types of manipulation.

9 Wallace, *Revolutionary Subjects*, 134.

10 Mr Raymond leaves open the possibility that William might prove himself not 'a man of the world' by finding a profession through which he could support himself and Mary.

11 Eberle, *Harlot's Progress*, 81.

12 Gina Luria Walker makes the point that Hays herself was frequently disappointed in enlightened men's blindness to gender (*Growth of a Woman's Mind*, 1).

13 Robert Whytt, *Observations On the Nature, Causes, And Cures of Those Disorders Which Have Been Commonly Called Nervous, Hypochondriac, Or*

Fatal melancholia in The Victim of Prejudice 129

Hysteric: to Which Are Prefixed Some Remarks On the Sympathy of the Nerves (Edinburgh: T. Becket, and P. Du Hondt, London, and J. Balfour, Edinburgh, 1765), 235, HathiTrust.

14 G. S. Rousseau explains that 'by the mid-eighteenth century, the "nervous system" had become entrenched, in medical theory as well as diagnosis, and in anatomy and physiology as well.' G. S. Rousseau, '"A Strange Pathology": Hysteria in the Early Modern World, 1500–1800' in *Hysteria Beyond Freud*, by Sander Gilman, Helen King, Roy Porter, G. S. Rousseau, and Elaine Showalter (Berkeley: University of California Press, 1993), 206, note 184, ebook.

15 The first Mary is subsequently executed for having been an accessory to a murder.

16 William Brewer, *The Mental Anatomies of William Godwin and Mary Shelley* (Cranbury: Associated University Presses, 2001), 15. Brewer uses this term to discuss Hays' first novel, *Memoirs of Emma Courtney*.

17 Michael Foucault, *Madness and Civilization: A History of Insanity in the Age of Reason*, trans. Richard Howard (1965; New York: Vintage Books, 1988), 91, 96, 108.

18 As Eleanor Ty succinctly, although relatively harshly, puts it: 'the mother is presented as an object of male desire at first, and then, after her seduction, she becomes a madwoman and whore.' Eleanor Ty, 'The Imprisoned Female Body in Mary Hays' *The Victim of Prejudice*' in *Women, Revolution, and the Novels of the 1790s*, ed. Linda Lang-Peralta (Lansing: Michigan State University Press, 1999), 139.

19 See G. S. Rousseau on de Bienville's version of nymphomania. 'The Invention of Nymphomania' in *Perilous Enlightenment: Pre-and Postmodern Discourses; Sexual, Historical*, ed. G. S. Rousseau (Manchester: Manchester University Press, 1991), 56.

20 Even Philippe Pinel, who is credited with expanding the understanding of experiential and environmental causes of mental disease, emphasized the mutually interacting influence of bodily pathology and the sexual imagination in nymphomania. Ilza Veith gives a particularly striking example from Pinel's *Nosographie Philosophique* (1798) of a young woman's progress from a lascivious private imagination, through the abandonment of modesty, to indiscriminate sexual advances, to complete mania. See Ilza Veith, *Hysteria: The History of a Disease* (Chicago: University of Chicago Press, 1965), 179–80.

21 The similarity of the narrative of criminality to both Frankenstein's creature and Jemima from *Wrongs of Woman* is worth noting.

22 Jones, 'Placing Jemima,' 204.

23 Sandra Sherman sees this point from a different angle, focusing on gender as an imprisoning condition rather than male power as an imprisoning agent. See Sandra Sherman, 'The Law, Confinement, and Disruptive Excess in Hays' *The Victim of Prejudice*,' *1650–1850, Ideas, Aesthetics, and Inquiries in the Early Modern Era* 6 (2001), 137, https://repository.lsu.edu/sixteenfifty/vol6/iss1/7.

24 Whytt, *Observations*, 231–2. As Veith points out, these were manifestations that had been considered typical throughout the ages (*Hysteria*, 1).

130 *Women and madness in the early Romantic novel*

25 Wallace adds that 'romantic love between men and women ... is aligned here explicitly with domination and rape along the continuum of violations Mary suffers' (*Revolutionary Subjects*, 135).

26 Sir Peter's threats and actions leading up to the rape, in Susan Purdie and Sarah Oliver's words, 'describe the kind of patriarchal dominance and proprietorship that urge the rake to take sexual possession of a woman, in spite of her resistance.' Susan Purdie and Sarah Oliver, 'William Frend and Mary Hays: Victims of Prejudice,' *Women's Writing* 17, no. 1 (May 2010): 102, https://doi.org/10.1080/09699080903533304.

27 According to the *OED*, 'trauma' as a term denoting a physical wound was used in the late seventeenth century, but it was not until the late nineteenth that it was introduced into the psychological vocabulary. In this chapter, I use the term anachronistically to convey Hays' prescient understanding of the way sexual assault makes a deep and lasting impression on the psyche.

28 As Erin Johns observes, Hays' novel 'offers a complex, psychological portrait of the rape victim.' Erin Johns, 'Raping Prejudice: Mary Hays' *The Victim of Prejudice*, Gender, and Rape' in *Literary and Poetic Representations of Work and Labour in Europe and Asia during the Romantic Era: Charting a Motif across Boundaries of Culture, Place, and Time*, ed. Christopher Clason and Robert Anderson (New York: Edwin Mellen Press, 2010), 154.

29 Larry May and Robert Strikwerda, 'Men in Groups: Collective Responsibility for Rape,' *Hypatia* 9, no. 2 (April 1994): 145, www.jstor.org/stable/3810174.

30 Simon Dickie explains that 'a successful plaintiff had to prove that she had vigorously and vocally resisted her attacker.' Simon Dickie, *Cruelty and Laughter: Forgotten Comic Literature and the Unsentimental Eighteenth Century* (Chicago: University of Chicago Press, 2011), 193.

31 Wallace, *Revolutionary Subjects*, 140.

32 The typography is one of many points that beg a comparison with *Clarissa*.

33 Katherine Binhammer reads the dashes and asterisks as indicative of the 'muteness' she believes is characteristic of melodrama. She accepts that the 'textual muteness' also conveys trauma, but explains that the trauma 'is not so much the assault on Mary's body but what follows it: society's denial of justice and its brutal economic victimization' (*The Seduction Narrative*, 155). Mutism was for centuries understood as a symptom of hysteria, and so I would argue that Hays is using the typographical symbols of muteness to convey the lasting impact of the trauma of the physical rape (not of the subsequent social ostracization).

34 Wallace writes that Mary's language 'breaks down' when she attempts to describe the rape (*Revolutionary Subjects*, 138). But I think, on the contrary, that Hays gives Mary the ability to convey quite a bit of information as she recalls this traumatic experience.

35 As a number of scholars have observed, Hays uses this novel to revise how the rape and its aftermath were presented in *Clarissa*. See Eleanor Ty, 'Introduction,' to *The Victim of Prejudice*, xxxvi; Walker, *Growth*, 183; and Wallace, *Revolutionary Subjects*, 137, who calls Mary Raymond an 'anti-Clarissa.'

Fatal melancholia in The Victim of Prejudice   131

36 Dickie, *Cruelty and Laughter*, 247.

37 Dickie, *Cruelty and Laughter*, 208.

38 Veith, *Hysteria*, 2.

39 In his discussion of Robert Whytt's understanding of nervous disorders, Foucault writes: 'Diseases of the nerves are essentially disorders of sympathy; they presuppose a state of general vigilance in the nervous system which makes each organ susceptible of entering into sympathy with any other.' Hysteria, Foucault concludes, is the most sympathetic disease of all: 'is not the womb, with the brain, the organ that maintains most sympathy with the whole organism?' (*Madness and Civilization*, 153).

40 Mark Micale, *Approaching Hysteria: Disease and Its Interpretations* (Princeton: Princeton University Press, 1995), 111.

41 Mary's refusal to admit she has lost her honour through the rape is in stark contrast to Clarissa's response.

42 In her exploration of eighteenth-century rape cases, Anna Clark found that 'many women who had been sexually assaulted believed the law protected them,' but that the idea of protection under the law was deceptive. Anna Clark, *Women's Silence, Men's Violence: Sexual Assault In England, 1770–1845* (London: Pandora Books, 1987), 46.

43 Jean Hampton observes that 'what is striking … [about the] history of crimes against women is that they were not perceived as wrong until quite recently, and that the failure of people to understand them as wrong was intimately connected to a view of women as lower, inferior, lesser in value.' Jean Hampton, 'Defining Wrong and Defining Rape' in *A Most Detestable Crime: New Philosophical Essays on Rape*, ed. Keith Burgess-Jackson (Oxford: Oxford University Press, 1999), 134.

44 Clark, *Sexual Assault in England*, 50.

45 Clark explains that 'male judges, counsels, juries, and spectators were obsessed with the explicit sexual details of rape … In part, this curiosity stemmed from crude prurience; rape victims sometimes faced laughter from the galleries when they attempted to testify and transcripts of rape trials were sold as titillating literature' (*Sexual Assault in England*, 54).

46 Clark, *Sexual Assault in England*, 46–7.

47 According to Clark, there were only two ways for a rape prosecution to go forward. Either there had to be evidence and a witness to establish that the victim fought off her attacker, or a husband or father had to prosecute for loss of property in the woman's chastity (*Sexual Assault in England*, 47).

48 Rebecca Whisnant, 'Feminist Perspectives on Rape,' *The Stanford Encyclopedia of Philosophy* (Fall 2021), ed, Edward N. Zalta, no pagination, https://plato. stanford.edu/archives/fall2021/entries/feminism-rape.

49 Dickie, *Cruelty and Laughter*, 190.

50 Carolyn M. Shafer and Marilyn Frye, 'Rape and Respect,' in *Feminism and Philosophy*, eds Mary Vetterling-Braggin, Frederick A. Elliston, and Jane English (Totowa: Littlefield, Adams, & Co., 1978), 336.

51 Shafer and Frye, 'Rape and Respect,' 341.

132 *Women and madness in the early Romantic novel*

52 Shafer and Frye elaborate on this point: 'The person raping her sees her through a perceptual schema which presents her and anything she does as something associated or connected with sexual intercourse—with his penetration and ejaculation. The rape reveals to her his sexual perception of her; it gives her a picture of herself as a being within someone's domain and not as a being which has domain' ('Rape and Respect,' 341).

53 Hampton observes that the rapist's message is '"as a woman, you are the kind of human being who is subject to the mastery of people of my kind." Rape confirms that women are "for" men: to be used, dominated, treated as objects' ('Defining Wrong,' 135).

54 Sherman, 'The Law, Confinement, and Disruptive Excess,' 153.

55 Sander Gilman discusses the importance of eyes in the long iconography of madness. See Sander Gilman, *Seeing the Insane* (New York: J. Wiley; Brunner/Maze, 1982), 127.

56 Michael DePorte, *Nightmares and Hobbyhorses: Swift, Sterne, and Augustan Ideas of Madness* (San Marino: Huntington Library, 1974), 25.

57 Unsurprisingly, sexual assault is, according to the *DSM-5*, an event that can produce a trauma- or stressor-related disorder. 'Trauma- and Stressor-Related Disorders,' *Diagnostic and Statistical Manual of Mental Disorders*, 5th edn (Arlington: American Psychiatric Association, 2013), ebook.

58 Jennifer Ford, *Coleridge on Dreaming: Romanticism, Dreams, and the Medical Imagination* (Cambridge: Cambridge University Press, 1998), 14.

59 Ty, 'Introduction' to *Victim of Prejudice*, xxiii. Jones, 'Placing Jemima,' 213.

60 Hays also cannot, given the attacks she suffered after the publication of *Memoirs of Emma Courtney*, allow her novel to even appear to support consensual unmarried sex.

61 Edna B. Foa and David S. Riggs, 'Posttraumatic Stress Disorder following Assault: Theoretical Considerations and Empirical Findings,' *Current Directions in Psychological Science* 4, no. 2 (April 1995): 61, bit.ly/42rwoia.

62 A modern understanding of mental illness might see Mary's response in terms of a somatic symptom disorder, which can manifest in neurological phenomena that lack a pathological diagnosis. The *DSM*-4 explains that the symptoms of conversion disorder 'typically do not conform to known anatomical pathways and physiological mechanisms, but instead follow the individual's conceptualization of a condition' (*DSM*-4 'Conversion Disorder,' 492). The symptoms of conversion disorder (now called functional disorder) not only reflect Mary's post-traumatic response to seeing Sir Peter, they also cover many traditional aspects of hysteria.

63 Frances Ferguson explains that marriage assumed consent. If a woman is raped and then marries her attacker, then the problem is not her lack of consent, but rather the timing of the marriage. See Frances Ferguson, 'Rape and the Rise of the Novel,' *Representations* 20 (Fall 1987): 92, https://doi.org/10.2307/2928503. Mary, however, rejects this reasoning when she refuses to marry her rapist.

64 See Sandra Sherman, who writes that 'the text depicts [the] legal process [to] be ... in alliance with patriarchal practice, illuminating dark sexual undercurrents

Fatal melancholia in The Victim of Prejudice   133

absent from standard legal discourse' ('The Law, Confinement, and Disruptive Excess,' 159).

65 The second father-figure is the old servant James who rescues her from debtors' prison the first time and takes her to a rented farm in their old neighbour-hood. He dies shortly after Mary's reputation is ruined by Sir Peter's gossiping servants.

66 Mrs Neville's feelings about her husband mirror those expressed by the domestic dove in 'The Sparrow and the Dove'—the entry right before 'The Female Seducers' in the popular *Fables for the Female Sex*, from which Hays selected an extract for the novel's title page. 'The Sparrow and the Dove' extols the virtues and joys of a marriage much like the one Mrs Neville describes. See Edward Moore and Henry Brooke, *Fables for the Female Sex* (1744; London: Minerva Press, 1795) Fable XIV, 68–89, ECCO.

67 Eliza Fenwick, *Secresy; or, The Ruin on the Rock*, ed. Isobel Grundy (Peterborough: Broadview Press, 1994), 256.

68 Sharpe and Ty emphasize the bleakness, circularity, and didacticism of *Victim*, arguing that its 'motif of confinement' is intended to instruct the reader not through delight, but rather through discomfort ('Mary Hays and the Didactic Novel,' 102).

4

Misplaced passions, erroneous associations, and remorse: madness reconsidered in *Belinda*

Although Belinda and her friends Lady Anne and Mr Percival are paragons of reason and self-control, Edgeworth's novel about a young woman's entrance into society overflows with addiction and irrationality.[1] Belinda's love-interest, Clarence Hervey, almost drowns to win a bet and thinks he can train his own wife; her suitor, Mr Vincent, is a gambling addict; Mr Vincent's servant, Juba, almost dies from fear of witchcraft; Belinda's host, Lord Delacour, is an alcoholic who must be carried upstairs to bed; her rival for Clarence's affections, Virginia St Pierre, is in love with a figment of her imagination; and her friend, Lady Delacour, suffers from mania, melancholia, paranoia, opium addiction, hypochondria, delusions, and Methodism. These last two characters, Virginia and Lady Delacour, are not merely irrational – they suffer, at times, from madness. As these two characters show, Edgeworth is as interested as Wollstonecraft, Fenwick, and Hays in female madness; but she approaches the topic with a considerably different outlook on sentimental literature and social politics.

Like Wollstonecraft, Fenwick, and Hays, Edgeworth rejects medical models that blame women's madness on gendered physical causes, such as weak nerves or the malicious influence of the womb. And like her more radical contemporaries, she shifts the blame for women's mental afflictions away from the body and onto abusive men – but only to a limited extent. Overall, Edgeworth's response to her contemporaries' positions on women's madness is mixed. On the one hand, through Lady Delacour, Edgeworth revises their narratives of patriarchal victimization by rejecting avenues of male power as the cause of women's mental afflictions. On the other, through Virginia St Pierre, she echoes and intensifies their concerns about the injuries caused by Rousseau's gendered educational ideas. But even while she sharply critiques Rousseau, she undercuts the severity of the damage inflicted by his methods through a playful approach to genre at the end of the novel.

Through her complex approach to mental affliction in *Belinda*, Edgeworth moves the narrative of female madness toward a less gendered, more

Madness reconsidered in Belinda

psychologically detailed model that focuses on false associations, misplaced passions, and remorse, rather than on the injuries men and patriarchal structures of power inflict on women. With this revised causality for women's madness, Edgeworth introduces a new, more optimistic prognosis. If female madness is a form of psychic injury brought about by a tight grid of male control and abuse, as her more radical contemporaries maintained, then there could be only two remedies: a utopian escape into an all-female community or the eventual reformation of men. Edgeworth, however, with her different understanding of the cause of female madness and her more egalitarian position on gender politics, sees a third way. Through a novel in which women are given the power to help one another, unregulated passions are managed, false associations are corrected, and the wounds of remorse are healed. The result is a treatment plan that shows how the heart, the head, and the body can be harmonized to create a balanced and happy life.

Misplaced passions, erroneous associations, and madness

Virginia's real name – Rachel Hartley – offers an important clue into the workings of madness in this novel. With this allusion to the mid-century philosopher David Hartley, Edgeworth signals her rejection of physiological explanations for madness and her embrace of psychological ones.[2] Specifically, the allusion to Hartley suggests that her model explains madness as a combination of mistaken thinking, unbalanced passions, and emotional damage. At the time Edgeworth was writing *Belinda*, Lockean thinking about madness had become freshly influential through Joseph Priestley's abridgement of David Hartley's 1749 *Observations on Man*, entitled *Hartley's Theory of the Human Mind, on the Principle of the Association of Ideas*, which was published in a second edition in 1790. Louis Charland has pointed out that Locke's description of madness is affective as well as cognitive, and Hartley picks up on the affective aspects of Locke's doctrine of the association of ideas in his own account of how the passions become imbalanced. At the century's end, when Priestley edited and republished Hartley's work, Charland notes that 'the passions assumed a central role as both causes and characteristic signs and symptoms of madness.'[3] The Scottish physician Alexander Crichton's work on the passions, his influential *Inquiry into the Nature and Origin of Mental Derangement* (1798), offers additional insights into how imbalanced passions – understood as 'emotional states of mind' according to Kathleen Grange – can result in madness.[4]

Edgeworth makes use of the capaciousness of Hartley's understanding of madness when her characters make wrong judgements, display

136 *Women and madness in the early Romantic novel*

uncontrolled emotions, showcase fallacious memories, and engage in incoherent conversations, all potentially combining in various ways and to different degrees.[5] She also shares Hartley's belief, and that of other medical writers, that madness could be partial and temporary.[6] Hartley observed that some elements of madness occur in people of sound minds, for certain amounts of time. In others, he wrote, 'it is impossible to fix precise limits, and to determine where soundness of mind ends, and madness begins.'[7] Lady Delacour, the prime example of Hartleyan madness in this novel, is not entirely mad, but is so only in bits and pieces, sometimes appearing more mad than at other times. Her behaviour consists of wrong judgements, violent emotions, and at times incoherent accounts of events. The same could be said of Virginia, although her suffering is more subdued and less performative than Lady Delacour's. For both, it is difficult to determine where sanity ends and insanity begins.

Hartley offers a model through which to understand not just the madness of Lady Delacour and Virginia, but also their cure. The mental health of both characters is compromised by fallacious associations of ideas that are stirred by disordered and disruptive passions. In Lady Delacour's case, she believes she has been afflicted with a fatal disease because her husband killed a would-be lover in a duel. And Virginia associates her emergent erotic desires with a picture of a man she saw as a girl and with the romances she reads as a young woman. For both, these associations become ingrained as habits. Whereas Lady Delacour is aware of the associations her mind makes, Virginia is not – her connections are forged and reinforced at a more unconscious level. The cure for both characters involves correcting these wrong associations by healing the disordered passions; or, in Virginia's case, shifting her association of love and desire from the portrait of the man to the man in the portrait, when he appears at the novel's conclusion.[8]

But righting wrong associations is not the only, or even the most effective, cure Hartley offers, particularly when considering Lady Delacour. He also presents a 'model of psychological development,' to use Richard Allen's description, made up of six classes of intellectual pleasures and pains.[9] According to Allen, the elements of imagination, ambition, self-interest, sympathy, theopathy, and the moral sense form a prism that make up Hartley's conception of the psyche. When the novel opens, Lady Delacour is pursuing what Hartley called 'gross self-interest' – that is, her emotions reside at the unhealthy end of the prism as she attempts to maximize pleasure and minimize pain through satisfying 'sensation, imagination, and ambition.'[10] She will not be healed until she moves to the other end of the prism to pursue 'refined self-interest,' which consists of the pleasures of sympathy, theopathy, and the moral sense. In her movement from mental illness to mental health, Lady Delacour shifts from one side of the prism to the other, exchanging the pleasures of imagination, ambition, and self-interest for sympathy and inter-personal relationships. Lady Delacour's development of sympathy requires that her attention, in Allen's words, be 'directed toward other persons, other selves.'[11] When that sympathy acts to assist the wellbeing of others, particularly of Belinda and Clarence Hervey, it 'manifests itself as benevolence.'[12] That benevolence is both the moral sense and the indication of psychic health.[13]

Lady Delacour's condition of imbalanced passions can also be understood through the work of Alexander Crichton, whose acclaimed *Inquiry into the Nature and Origin of Mental Derangement* had a significant impact on the thinking of Philippe Pinel, known for developing the moral management technique in France.[14] Crichton understood the passions to be feelings that accompany the desire for pleasure and the avoidance of pain. He believed that desires and aversions were naturally 'attended with painful and powerful feelings' that would often 'destroy all the operations of cool reason, and ... throw the human frame into the most violent agitation and disorder.'[15] Crichton's basic passions, each of which have modifications, are joy, grief and sorrow, fear, anger, and love. According to Crichton, 'moderate and continued joy, mirth, and gaity' is beneficial to health. What he refers to as 'the serene and milder joys' give rise to 'much tranquillity and content of mind' and are of 'great advantage in the cure of chronic complaints.'[16] However, some modifications of joy, such as those based on hope, can lay 'the foundation for the greatest uneasiness and mental injury.' Such is the case with vanity and pride, which cause such 'shocks to the mental fabric of men as seldom fail to reduce it to a state of total ruin.'[17] Further, pride and vanity 'may give birth to two very opposite kinds of insanity': to mania when excitement occasions 'an impetuous and permanent delirium,' and to melancholy, when these passions are blasted and 'terminate in despair.'[18] Lady Delacour, in her pursuit of attention and acclaim, seeks joy through the unhealthy satisfactions of pride and vanity. Her gaiety in public is often excessive, which causes both her physical and mental health to suffer. She also experiences considerable melancholy, as is expected according to Crichton's model, not only because her pride and vanity cause her excessive joy to collapse when frustrated, but also because she hides a debilitating sadness. Crichton identifies the painful emotions as grief and sorrow, labelling those focused on a past event for which one is responsible as repentance, contrition, and remorse, which he describes as the 'most intolerable' of all painful feeling.[19] He observes that 'when grief or sorrow continue permanent for a great length of time, they occasion much disorder, both in mind and body, from which the disease called melancholy originates,' which can result in delirium.[20] Such is the case with Lady Delacour, who suffers from a prolonged, intolerable remorse that causes

138 *Women and madness in the early Romantic novel*

her to suffer from melancholy and eventually believe she has seen an omen of her own death.

Edgeworth had originally planned for Lady Delacour to die from cancer of the breast.[21] But instead of having her character die from a real disease, she allows her to recover from an imagined one, as well as from the mental disease that threatens her happiness and her physical health. Lady Delacour's cure is orchestrated by Belinda, who applies the methods of moral management associated with the Retreat at York and the work of Philippe Pinel.[22] In using the word 'moral,' Pinel's intention was, in Kathleen Grange's words, to describe 'the emotional factors in mental experience,' given that he, like many of his contemporaries, believed that the cause of madness was strong emotions and that the cure would result in the emotions being rebalanced.[23] From early in the novel, Belinda shows that she is the only person who can help Lady Delacour balance her passions through applying self-control and reason to her life.[24] Like Pinel and the therapists at the Retreat, Belinda is aware that the passions are the primary cause of Lady Delacour's fits of madness, and she applies this awareness to manage her friend's emotions, desires, and behaviour and to redirect her passions towards what Crichton called the tranquil and serene pleasures. As Vieda Skultans observes of moral management, 'The most important ingredient ... is the restoration of the attributes of humanity to the insane and with it the possibility of encouraging self-control and self-discipline.'[25] Using kindness, reason, and affection, as well as Lady Delacour's desire to win her esteem and maintain her friendship, Belinda – with the assistance of Dr X and Clarence Hervey – heals Lady Delacour by turning her away from self-destructive passions and towards the tranquil joy of love for her husband and daughter.

The madness of Lady Delacour

Belinda showcases Edgeworth's understanding that the burdens of emotional pain can compromise both the mental and physical health of individuals. For this reason, her most afflicted character is named Lady Delacour. 'Delacour' is routinely identified by scholars as a reference to corrupt French aristocracy through the translation 'of the court.' But the sound of Lady Delacour's name evokes the homophone in French, de la Coeur – of the heart.[26] Like the sound of Virginia's real last name, *Hart*ley, 'Delacour' points to the role of the emotions, or the passions, in these characters' afflictions. Emotions are at the root of Lady Delacour's mental disease and are essential to her cure which begins when she, because she loves Belinda, submits to her guidance. Under Belinda's care,

Madness reconsidered in Belinda 139

Lady Delacour embarks on a multi-step healing process that allows her to rebalance her passions by overcoming guilt, conquering despair, and accepting love of family as essential for happiness. Once this occurs, Lady Delacour is able to take more control of the plot, eventually facilitating Belinda's match with Clarence and orchestrating the concluding tableau. In this way, Edgeworth puts a healed passional system into the novel's most privileged position.

The narrator, Belinda, and Dr X all note that Lady Delacour alternates between high spirits and depression, between excessive, misdirected joy and a sorrow that manifests as melancholy. According to the narrator, 'abroad, and at home Lady Delacour was two different persons. Abroad she appeared all life, spirit, and good humour – at home, listless, fretful and melancholy' as she walks 'up and down the empty magnificent saloon, absorbed in thoughts of the most painful nature' (10). Dr X, with his clinician's eye, is not taken in by Lady Delacour's high spirits in public. In his first visit to the house, he observes: 'This gayety of Lady Delacour's does not seem to me that of a sound mind in a sound body' (104).[27] Indeed, Lady Delacour pursues pride and vanity, the lively and exhilarating modifications of the passion of joy, rather than its tranquil and serene manifestations.[28] This is a type of joy – the joy of acclaim and praise – that impacts the judgement and, in Crichton's estimation, can lead to mental and physical illness. At the other end of the emotional spectrum, painful feelings of grief and sorrow have pushed Lady Delacour into bouts of melancholy that are only interrupted by her pursuit of the joy of celebrity and attention. Thus the unhealthy vacillation between mania and melancholy that Dr X identifies has its root in a disturbance of the passions that Lady Delacour will shortly explain to Belinda.

Lady Delacour's passions are also disturbed by her certainty that she has a breast disease that is rapidly bringing her life to an end. It is not until much later that she agrees to submit to a medical examination and finds that her breast is not diseased at all. Given that a breast injury at the time was commonly considered to be a cause of cancer, and that the breast was injured in a duel when her pistol backfired, Lady Delacour has good reason to believe her breast is diseased.[29] Lady Delacour's fear, too, seems warranted given that, as Marjo Kaartinen explains, in the eighteenth century, 'breast cancer was a nightmarish, greatly feared disease' that seemed to 'kill with frightening certainty.'[30] Accordingly, she notes that anxiety and a fear of death were prominent emotions for women who suspected they had this disease, and that 'melancholy was a dominant passion' with the diagnosis.[31] Lady Delacour's anxiety about death is augmented by her desire to hide her condition and to avoid pity. Her approach to her depression and anxiety is to continue to live as gaily as possible in public, hide her distress, and

140   *Women and madness in the early Romantic novel*

relegate her treatment to a private boudoir where she receives the 'quack' who administers her treatment.

Lady Delacour understands that she has both a mental and a physical disease, and in her mind, the two are causally connected. To a great extent, Lady Delacour's wounds – both to her conscience and her body – are self-inflicted, but one did not cause the other, strictly speaking. Spurred by her desire for celebrity and attention, and desirous of impressing Harriot Freke, she crossed the sexual line to encourage Colonel Lawless' advances; and then, for the same reasons, she crossed the gender line to dress in men's clothing and engage in a duel with her rival Mrs Luttridge.[32] It is because she knows she is responsible for multiple linked wounds – for the wound that killed Lawless, the wound to her conscience, the wound to her family, and the wound to her body – that Lady Delacour is tormented into the affliction that manifests as melancholia. When she bares the 'hideous spectacle' of the breast to a horrified Belinda she says, 'Yes, pity me for what you have seen; and a thousand times more, for that which you cannot see – my mind is eaten away like my body, by incurable disease – inveterate remorse – remorse for a life of folly – of folly which has brought on me all the punishments of guilt' (30). She explains to Belinda: ' – The idea of that poor wretch, Lawless, whom I actually murdered, as much as if I had shot him, haunts me whenever I am alone – It is now between eight and nine years since he died – but it won't do – Conscience! conscience! Will be heard' (60). Lady Delacour has, thus, at the time the novel begins, been suffering for almost a decade from her secret guilt and the workings of her conscience. Although the connection is irrational, Lady Delacour believes her breast to be the outer manifestation of, and the punishment for, her life of folly, about which she feels a remorse that has destroyed her peace of mind. In Lady Delacour's thoughts, the most immediate link between the diseased breast and the diseased mind is her responsibility for the death of Lawless, the would-be lover that Lord Delacour killed in a duel. Indeed, right before her own duel with Mrs Luttridge in which her breast is injured, Lady Delacour thinks of Colonel Lawless and, as she says, has 'presentiments' and 'confused notions of poetic justice' (51). Even before her breast is impacted, Lady Delacour superstitiously connects her duel with the duel that killed Lawless, believing that she will get what she deserves for having caused an innocent man's death.

In the novel's first edition, there is little explanation of the quack's involvement in the breast's condition, and so Lady Delacour's conviction of its being diseased can be understood as delusionary or hypochondriacal, despite the fact that it looks 'hideous.' As David Thame notes, Alexander Crichton made the point that 'in the delirium of madness the body could not

Madness reconsidered in Belinda   141

distinguish the impressions of real objects from those of the imagination.'[33] And James Boswell, in his column 'The Hypochondriack,' emphasized the role of the imagination – and particularly thoughts about illness and impending doom – in the affliction he described.[34] At the time Edgeworth was writing *Belinda*, hypochondriasis was undergoing a shift to its more modern meaning of 'an excessive and persistent preoccupation with health, disease, and body, which is associated with a fear and suspicion that one is a victim of serious disease.'[35] The association with gastrointestinal distress, as well as the old connection to 'spleen,' had dropped out, leaving the psychological symptoms which, according to Russell Noyes, had become more prominent.[36] By the early nineteenth century, he observes, medical writers 'increasingly identified hypochondriasis as a mental disorder,' the symptoms of which were 'anxiety, passions of various kinds, loss or disappointment, long continued watching, intense application of mind, and an indolent or sedentary lifestyle.'[37] The psychological cause of Lady Delacour's conviction that she has a terminal breast disease, combined with her fears, apprehensions, and melancholy, suggests the latest understanding of hypochondriasis. Significantly, hypochondriasis had always been understood as a male condition, while hysteria was seen as its counterpart in women. The two conditions, however, did not correspond neatly, as the physical cause of hysteria was located in the uterus and its symptoms were played out through what we now understand as functional disorders rather than fears about illness and death.[38] That Lady Delacour's symptoms resemble hypochondriasis more than they do hysteria points to Edgeworth's efforts to establish a gender-neutral aetiology for Lady Delacour's madness by separating it from afflictions and causes traditionally associated with women.

Lady Delacour's disease and Lawless' death are linked through the idea of sexual and gender transgression, but the two have only an associative connection in Lady Delacour's life. Her linkage of Lawless' death to her breast affliction is an example of the false reasoning Locke used to explain madness. As Allen observes, 'Locke attributed "madness" that is "opposition to reason" to the accidental association of ideas, caused to adhere to each other by custom, habit, or personal trauma.' To a rational observer, Allen explains, there can be no evident connection between events, but the person's self will have been constructed through a long train of associations of ideas, reminders of painful impressions.[39] Allen continues, noting that 'Locke spoke of the "madness" that comes when a mind is in bondage to connections of ideas "wholly owing to Chance or Custom."' And, Allen notes that David Hartley, so often described as the 'father of association psychology,' was also aware that 'association alone would drive a person mad.'[40] Lady Delacour is unable to rid herself of this connection

142   *Women and madness in the early Romantic novel*

between Lawless and her breast disease, an association that later in the novel causes her to believe she sees Lawless' figure operating as a portent for her imminent demise the night before she submits to surgery for her supposed cancer.

If Lady Delacour indeed had cancer, there could be causal, reinforcing links between her thoughts and feelings and her physical state according to the medical thinking of the time. Even before Colonel Lawless' death, Lady Delacour feels responsible for having failed to nourish her two infants, which produces a sensation of guilt on top of her sorrow. These feelings are amplified by remorse over Lawless' death, which impacts her physical health. Kaartinen observes that eighteenth-century physicians believed that the negative passions could cause physical disease, and she quotes from the English medical writer William Falconer, who 'noted that it was understood that at least half of human diseases "originate from the influence of passions on the human system." Grief in particular was a great danger ... [that could] influence different parts of the body and lead to death through cancer.'[41] If Lady Delacour in fact had cancer, then extremes of emotion could make her condition worse.[42] The physical disease could also have an additional cause linked to Lady Delacour's infants, given that some medical experts at the time believed that not breastfeeding could cause dangerous blockages of curdled milk that might cause cancer.[43] Lady Delacour, then, could understand her disease as having two separate causes linked to gender failures or transgressions, making the cancer a moral pronouncement or a punishment for her behaviour.

It is important, however, that after leading readers to believe for most of the novel that Lady Delacour has cancer – and perhaps encouraging them to make associations of their own blaming her disorderly body, her troubled mind, or her moral failures – Edgeworth makes the breast disease disappear. In this way, Edgeworth pursues a tactic with the breast disease similar to her strategy with Lady Delacour's madness when she disassociates the cause of the affliction from anything physically inherent about the female body – apart from the existence of the breast itself. Her interest is thus not in the physical cause of the disease, or, as many scholars have claimed, in punishing Lady Delacour for her transgressions, but rather in the moral, or psychological, reasons why Lady Delacour thinks she has cancer.

The metaphorical and ideological aspects of Lady Delacour's breast injury have been much discussed.[44] But less time has been spent on its psychological aspects – that is, on the connections Lady Delacour makes between her breast, her remorse over her actions, and her emotional suffering. The loss of her two children is so painful that Lady Delacour can only sneak a mention of their deaths into the 'history' she tells Belinda. After describing how a power struggle and then her attempt to incite her

Madness reconsidered in Belinda 143

husband to jealousy poisoned her marriage, she mentions the loss of the children incidentally.

> I forgot to tell you, that I had three children during the first five years of my marriage. The first was a boy; he was born dead; and my lord and all his odious relations, laid the blame upon me, because I would not be kept prisoner half a year by an old mother of his ... My second child was a girl, but a poor, diminutive, sickly thing. —It was the fashion at this time for fine mothers to suckle their own children—so much the worse for the poor brats.—There was a prodigious rout made about the matter ... but after the novelty was over, I became heartily sick of the business; and at the end of about three months, my poor child was sick too—I don't like to think about it—it died. —If I had put it out to nurse, I should have been thought by my friends an unnatural mother—but I should have saved it's [*sic*] life. (39)

Although she scorns Lord Delacour's relations, she takes the deaths of both children to be her fault – the first, because she neglected the designated duties of a mother by refusing to stay at home while pregnant, and the second, because she carried out the designated duty of a mother by nursing, but by nursing badly. Although Lady Delacour certainly feels responsible for her children's deaths and is blamed by her husband's relations, her own words give the reader another way to understand what happened, apart from maternal failure. By having Lady Delacour mention 'fashion,' Edgeworth alludes to the influence of Rousseau who helped popularize maternal nursing with *Émile*. Ruth Perry notes that many treatises reinforced Rousseau's views by 'castigating women as selfish, callous, and unnatural who would not give themselves the trouble to nurse or waxing sentimental and voyeuristic at descriptions of lovely mothers suckling their infants.'[45] Edgeworth is highly critical of Rousseau in the Virginia section of the novel, and she certainly did not approve of his disdain for educated, sophisticated women. Lady Delacour's struggles with breastfeeding could be yet another way that Edgeworth critiques Rousseau's harmful impact on women's psyches.

In Lady Delacour's own mind, though, the breast bears the weight of multiple, linked traumatic meanings. At a conscious, although irrational, level, Lady Delacour believes that the wounding of her breast in a duel is payback for her role in Lawless' death in a duel. At a less conscious, or even a repressed level, she fixates on the breast as a site of disease to express her sorrow and guilt at having failed to nourish her two infants. Edgeworth expands these meanings by having Lady Delacour participate in the duel that injures her breast in order to impress Harriot Freke who, as her 'bosom friend,' fills the 'aching void' in her heart that opens up after the deaths of her two infants (40). Directing her affections toward Mrs Freke is an instance of misplaced passions: desperately in need of feeling love in order

144 *Women and madness in the early Romantic novel*

to distract herself from the sorrow and guilt of her children's death, and without the tenderness of her husband or support of family, Lady Delacour bestows her fondness on a person who encourages destructive forms of pleasure. Given Mrs Freke's attraction to Lady Delacour, the passion could be considered doubly misplaced according to the morality of the time as being a love more erotic than platonic.[46]

In the aftermath of her infants' deaths, Lady Delacour directs her passions ever more energetically away from her disastrous homelife and toward the celebrity of high society; but such a misdirection of her search for joy only causes more unhappiness. Lady Delacour is aware that she seeks pleasure through what she terms dissipation after the deaths of her two children, confessing to Belinda: 'I was intoxicated with the idle compliments of all my acquaintance, and I endeavoured to console myself for misery at home, by gayety abroad. Ambitious of pleasing universally, I became the worst of slaves—a slave to the world' (39). To dull her pain, Lady Delacour redirects her energies toward incessant socializing, but her gaiety in public is only a disguise, which she admits to Belinda when she confesses that in the mist of her dissipations, she had been 'constant prey to ennui.' She realizes that the 'want of domestic happiness could never be supplied by that public admiration of which she was so ambitious.' And Lady Delacour recognizes that the 'immoderate indulgence of her vanity had led her, by inevitable steps, into follies and imprudences which had ruined her health and destroyed her peace of mind' (63–4). Nonetheless, Lady Delacour is unwilling to give up her frantic lifestyle and declares to Belinda she will continue on her present course until she dies.

Although her emotional pain causes her to make the false association between her breast injury and Colonel Lawless' death, Lady Delacour's reason is relatively unimpaired until she is afflicted by an attack of paranoid jealousy over Belinda – what she will later describe as a 'paroxysm of madness' (306). The jealousy takes hold of Lady Delacour's mind when Belinda urges her to inform her husband about her breast disease and to tell him she plans to undergo a dangerous operation. When Belinda tells her she will not be involved in the surgery unless Lady Delacour reveals her plans to Lord Delacour, her jealousy rises to a frenzy. Lady Delacour rapidly puts together a number of discrete events, all of which add up in her mind to the fact that Belinda is plotting to marry Lord Delacour after her demise. Lady Delacour's false reasoning is based on an anxiety about love, spurred on by the imagination – an instance of rapid thinking and incorrect conclusions reminiscent of Locke's observation that 'mad men' are not without reason, but just reason incorrectly.[47] Now that she has regained her husband's attention, thanks to Belinda's efforts, she is terrified that he will reject her. Her language focuses on the revulsion she imagines he will feel about her diseased breast, and in arguing with Belinda about telling him, she uses the words 'disgust,' 'loathsome,' and 'horrid' (164). Just when she is on the verge of having him back, Belinda, in her opinion, is insisting that she do exactly what will push him away. In Lady Delacour's mind, the reason must be that Belinda's self-interest would be served by Lord Delacour's disgust, as she would then be able to position herself as the next Lady Delacour.

When Belinda later tells Lady Delacour that her Aunt Stanhope has conveyed rumours about her supposed scheme to marry Lord Delacour, her friend becomes extremely agitated and lapses once more into her mad logic. She utters broken sentences, clears her throat, energetically puts wafers onto notes, but does not speak clearly as she thinks rapidly to herself that she has been 'a dupe and an idiot' (185). And now, she thinks 'when the thing is to be concealed no longer, she comes to me with the face of simplicity, and, knowing my generous temper, throws herself on my mercy' (185). Lady Delacour then falls back in her chair with an 'hysteric laugh' (186), entering into a state in which her imagination and passion impede her ability to reason effectively and push her into temporary madness.[48] Lady Delacour's behaviour alarms Belinda, who notices a number of worrying signs that converge to give her the idea that Lady Delacour's 'intellects were suddenly disordered' (186). When Lady Delacour seems to threaten Belinda with a penknife, Belinda 'no longer [has] any doubt that this was insanity' (187). Although Belinda is alarmed, she sees this as a temporary fit, believing Lady Delacour will again revert to loving her when the passion has passed. However, when Lady Delacour admits that she has 'seen much in silence,' Belinda realizes she has suspected her secretly for some time. What that means is that this outburst is not a temporary fit of madness fuelled by passion, but rather a well-nurtured paranoia that Belinda takes as a betrayal. And such a violent passion, which at first Belinda thinks is temporary, she comes to see as something more habitual.[49]

The paroxysm of irrational jealousy that sends Belinda from the house is Lady Delacour's most violent and pronounced bout of madness, but she has other more quiet episodes of unreason that contribute to her overall mental instability. When she is not directing her passions toward the manic joys of dissipation, Lady Delacour uses both opium and Methodism to dull the pain of her sorrow and remorse.[50] When Belinda returns to Lady Delacour after her time with the Percivals, she finds her in a deep depression and in a condition of more pronounced and dangerous addiction to opium.[51] Lady Delacour says to Belinda, in response to her friend's encouraging words about her future, 'Is it not shocking to think … that in laudanum alone I find the means of supporting existence?' and she puts her hand to her head, 'as if partly conscious of the confusion of her own ideas' (247). Lady Delacour's Methodism is first brought up immediately after the

146   *Women and madness in the early Romantic novel*

revelation to Lord Delacour of her diseased breast, and it is mentioned in the context of her addiction to opium. After she says that only laudanum allows her to support her existence, she retires to her room with John Wesley's *Admonitions*.[52] The narrator explains that 'the early impressions that had been made on [Lady Delacour's] mind in her childhood, by a methodistical mother, recurred. Her understanding, weakened perhaps by disease, and never accustomed to reason, was incapable of distinguishing between truth and error; and her temper, naturally enthusiastic, hurried her from one extreme to the other—from thoughtless scepticism to visionary credulity' (247–8). Methodism in this novel is one of the several forms of irrationality from which Lady Delacour must be weaned if she is to regain her mental health.[53] She is susceptible to the mystical and scarcely intelligible beliefs (as Belinda sees them) for several reasons, all having to do with a compromised mind. Importantly, she never learned to reason correctly, and instead lets her mind follow her emotions from disbelief to belief in the supernatural. Her mind, never trained to moral reasoning, is weakened by disease and addiction, which lays her open to the false associations of childhood instilled by her 'methodistical mother' on an impressionable mind. Her temper is naturally enthusiastic, meaning driven by excitement and emotion, and it is a temper that never was schooled in the use of reason. Rather than having been trained in moral judgement, her mind was impressed, Lockean fashion, by the false associations of Methodism.

After her return, Belinda convinces Lady Delacour not to engage further with the quack who has been treating her and instead to use a qualified surgeon for her breast operation. At this point, under the combined influence of opium and Methodism, Lady Delacour is convinced she will die before the operation. On the night before the surgery, she says privately to Belinda, 'My dear friend ... my prophecy is accomplishing—I know I must die.' To which Belinda responds, 'Do not suffer a vain imagination thus to overpower your reason,' and Lady Delacour answers, 'It is no vain imagination—I must die' (280). Lady Delacour admits to Belinda she has seen a vision that has visited three times, and that she considers it a 'warning to prepare for death' (281). At this point, it appears that the new twist in Lady Delacour's madness is a diseased imagination that causes her to see visions. As she awaits a horrific operation that she may not survive, she believes the ghost of Lawless haunts her, and that he comes with a message that she will die – not in surgery or as a result of surgery, but before the surgery even occurs.

Lady Delacour's story is often interpreted as a critique of what Edgeworth viewed as an immoral lifestyle.[54] But Edgeworth, perhaps drawing on Crichton's approach to mental illness, is much more objective than that. According to Charland, Crichton firmly believed 'that the psychopathology of the passions should have nothing to do with ethics or other "moral" considerations.'[55] In Book III of the *Inquiry*, Crichton asserts that 'the passions are to be considered, in a medical point of view, as part of our constitution, which is to be examined with the eye of a natural historian, and the spirit and impartiality of a philosopher.' And he insists that 'whether passions be esteemed natural or unnatural, or moral or immoral affections' is irrelevant to their study.[56] This position of impartiality is applicable to Belinda, who treats Lady Delacour with compassion and understanding, but largely without moral judgements.[57]

Lady Delacour's cure

From the moment Belinda starts her attempt to cure Lady Delacour, she makes use of the methods of moral management.[58] She follows the approach Roy Porter describes in which moral management is 'directed to the mind and character of the sufferer, engaging his attention, gaining his respect, breaking his evil habits and associations.'[59] Belinda begins her therapeutic approach to Lady Delacour in the aftermath of her carriage accident, when Lady Delacour is begging for laudanum, which Belinda refuses to give her, as well as either screaming from pain or going into convulsions from repressing her screams. What Belinda wants is to break Lady Delacour's association of fear with a physician and get her to accept treatment for the ankle. Belinda uses the threat to depart and an appeal to Lady Delacour's emotions and her reason to control her: 'You see ... when I am gone your secret will inevitably be discovered, for without me Marriott will not have sufficient strength of mind to keep it' (119). Belinda follows William Tuke's system of manipulating the patient's fear and gratitude while appealing to what reason remains. Andrew Scull explains that because in the new system of moral management, madmen were not held to be completely lacking in reason, Tuke's system depended on appealing to what reason the patient had.[60] Moreover, moral management practitioners saw that a patient could be selectively mad on particular subjects without being in a condition of total mental derangement or being impervious to feelings of gratitude. Belinda understands that Lady Delacour is not without either reason or gratitude, and so she uses both to convince her friend to overcome her irrational resistance to physicians in order to get the benefits Belinda is holding out to her.

At the most important turning point in Lady Delacour's treatment, Belinda not only employs the methods of moral management to solve one of the key problems underlying her friend's mental disease, she also uses an approach resembling that of a modern psychologist.[61]

148 *Women and madness in the early Romantic novel*

Like a good psychologist, Belinda establishes a rapport between herself and Lady Delacour based on trust and an understanding that the patient's problems originate in emotional, not physiological, disturbance. Belinda uses an empirical approach that reveals the extent to which Lady Delacour's problems are multi-faceted and inseparable from her domestic relationships. Having spent months in the house observing and listening, Belinda knows that the emotional stress of domestic strife and misery is an important aspect of her friend's affliction. Accordingly, she understands that Lady Delacour's treatment must include the mending of her relationship with her husband. Belinda's earlier urging of Lady Delacour to reveal her diseased breast to her husband triggered the 'paroxysm of madness' (306) that was her paranoic fit. But Belinda has made considerable progress in her treatment of Lady Delacour, who is now willing to show Lord Delacour her breast once she is convinced that he loves her. When Lord and Lady Delacour exit the boudoir after her exposure of the breast, his face reveals all he feels about having finally discovered the truth about his wife's condition (246). Belinda has understood that Lady Delacour's behaviour stems from, as she says to her suffering friend, your 'despair of obtaining domestic happiness' (246). By getting husband and wife to admit their love for one another and, importantly, by establishing confidence between them, Belinda helps Lady Delacour see that the pursuit of happiness through domestic life is possible.[62]

Lady Delacour's case, however, is a complicated one. And even though she now welcomes and accepts the love of her husband and her daughter, Helena, and therefore no longer seeks distraction through the pleasures of pride and vanity, she is still deeply melancholic, addicted to opium, and haunted by guilt over her role in Colonel Lawless' death. When Lady Delacour, the day before her operation, seeks to delay it, Dr X and the surgeon are content with simple explanations: fear or caprice. Belinda, however, believes there is more to Lady Delacour's conviction that she will die the night before the operation.[63] In her description of Pinel's treatment methods, Dora Weiner writes that he 'believed that a doctor, and particularly a doctor concerned with mental illness, must first of all get to know his patients well. To do this, he must listen and observe.' And she continues, explaining that Pinel 'developed a method of systematic observation that helped him understand his patients' minds by studying their behaviour.'[64] Dr X's approach is merely to repeat that Lady Delacour is in no danger and take her pulse. Although an observant man, he is dedicated to the treatment of the body, and as the pulse indicates there is no fever, he discounts r delay as the caprice of a woman who, in his opinion, has always 'sted reason. Belinda, however, follows Pinel's methods by engaging , Delacour in conversation. In this way, she comes to know more of her thoughts and fears and is able to recognize that something might be happening exterior to Lady Delacour's mind. She believes Lady Delacour's description of her own experience (although not her interpretation of it), and as a result is able to facilitate the capture of Harriot Freke outside Lady Delacour's chamber, whom Lady Delacour had taken to be the ghost of Colonel Lawless and an omen of her own death.

Not only does the evidence of Harriot Freke act to dispel Lady Delacour's conviction that she saw a phantom, Belinda's approach allows her friend to come to a greater understanding of her own unconscious motivations and to adjust her thoughts and behaviour accordingly. Weiner explains that both Pinel and Crichton were able to perceive 'unconscious psychological meaning' in what appeared to be irrational behaviour. Their therapeutic strategy was to see if the patient's awareness of this meaning might allow him to 'realize its harmful consequences, and therefore change his ways.'[65] Following this methodology, Belinda helps Lady Delacour see that she is not capricious, delusional, or cowardly. She shows her friend that this instance of irrationality – this belief in a portent that she will die – comes from fear and guilt. Once Lady Delacour recognizes that emotions have caused her to behave in a way that damages her self-respect, she determines to impose more discipline upon herself in order to better control how fear affects her mind. When Lady Delacour reflects on her superstitious belief and determines to return to herself, a primary aspect of her motivation is her desire to gain Belinda's respect. Belinda thus uses one group of emotions – Lady Delacour's craving for respect as a person of strength and intelligence – against another – the fear and remorse that left her prey to her imagination and the machinations of Harriot Freke.

After finally submitting to an examination, when Lady Delacour discovers that her breast is not diseased at all and sees the relief on the faces of her husband and daughter, she is most of the way to recovery. Readers critical of what they see as the novel's affirmation of traditional ideas about gender argue that Lady Delacour's cure re-establishes her adherence to gender conformity, heteronormativity, and domesticity, which they see negatively.[66] It is important to consider, however, the novel's emphasis on the pursuit of happiness, which for Lady Delacour requires overcoming the mentally corroding influence of guilt and accepting the love of her family. Do to this, she must change her ways without completely altering her personality. Using a phrase that David Thame notes might serve as a 'motto for moral therapy,' Lady Delacour says: 'My actions, the whole course of my future life, shall show that I am not quite a brute. Even brutes are won by kindness' (287).[67] Her recovery is complete when Dr X cures her of her opium addiction and the mild and rational chaplain Mr Moreton is able to alleviate her guilt and free her from Methodism. Belinda herself is aware of

150   *Women and madness in the early Romantic novel*

her role in curing Lady Delacour. As the narrator observes, 'Nothing could be more delightful to Miss Portman than thus to feel herself the object at once of esteem, affection, and respect; to see that she had not only been the means of saving her friend's life, but that the influence she had obtained over her mind was likely to be so permanently beneficial to her family and herself' (293). What Belinda has understood is that Lady Delacour needed to experience the 'pleasures of domestic life' in order resist returning to her habits of dissipation which, Belinda knew, were born of 'a mixture of vanity and despair' (294–5). Although the body and mind must also be cured, Lady Delacour's problem all along has been an emotional disorder – an affliction of the heart. The narrator explains that her 'heart expanded with the sensations of friendship and gratitude, now that she was relieved from those fears by which she had long been oppressed' (288). Tormented by guilt, but also afraid of rejection from those she loved, she had pursued the distractions of vanity and admiration. When Lady Delacour, under Belinda's guidance, is able to adjust her passions, improvement in her mental health follows.

By the end of the novel, Lady Delacour has moved along the Hartleyian prism from the pursuit of the passions of gross self-interest to those focused on sympathy rather than on ambition. She has undergone a dispositional reform in which the pursuit, in Crichton's terms, of the lively and exhilarating pleasures of ambition and imaginative excess – with all their psychological pitfalls – have resolved into the pursuit of the tranquil and serene pleasures of familial love.[68] And her associations of pain have undergone a transformation as well. Whereas she previously connected pain with her home, family, and daughter, these are now her tranquil pleasures. Joy has healed her chronic complaints, and even her melancholy. Importantly, Lady Delacour's pleasures can now be directed toward increasing the happiness of others, which she does by focusing on the joys of sympathy and benevolence. Referring to Hartley, Richard Allen says 'it should be one's eventual goal to make this authentic form of sympathy one's spring of action.'[69] A healed Lady Delacour is a Lady Delacour full of authentic gratitude and active on behalf of her friends. In the last part of the novel, which is testament to the salutary power of friendship, Lady Delacour turns her attention to ensuring that Clarence and Belinda marry each other and not Virginia and Mr Vincent – terrible choices, not the least because these alternate spouses both suffer from the plague of unreason.

Clarence Hervey's Rousseauvian fancy

Virginia St Pierre emerges seemingly out of nowhere in this novel and threatens to upend the plot moving Belinda toward marriage with Clarence

Hervey, the man Lady Delacour and the readers know she loves. As others have observed, the seemingly extraneous subplot functions as a critique of Rousseauvian-inspired wife-training plans, such as that undertaken by Richard Lovell Edgeworth's friend Thomas Day.[70] And this critique is extended beyond Day in that, in Mitzi Myers' words, the 'abortive wife-training thematizes Edgeworth's ideological critique of contemporary fabrications of the feminine.'[71] Myers views the Virginia subplot through the lens of comedy, calling the relationship between Clarence and Virginia a 'sexual tease as well as a textual mystery.'[72] While the failure of the wife-training experiment allows both Virginia's and Clarence's marriage plots to resolve to their satisfaction, Edgeworth, like her more radical contemporaries, wants readers to see that the emulation of Rousseauvian educational ideas can inflict psychological harm on women. Edgeworth thus uses the Virginia section to show that texts such as Rousseau's *Émile*, Bernardin de Saint-Pierre's *Paul et Virginie*, and English conduct-books – which all sought to preserve women's 'natural' feminine sensibility, innocence, and simplicity – could degrade women's mental stability to the point of madness.

Edgeworth agrees with Wollstonecraft, Fenwick, and Hays on the topic of Rousseau, and her critique of his gendered educational ideas has a great deal in common with Fenwick's. However, Edgeworth offers considerably more psychological insight into how this sort of gendered education damages women's minds. In the Virginia subplot, she shows how male sexual fantasy is inseparable from Rousseauvian education, and she critiques these fantasies and that education for sapping women's intellectual and moral strength and for making them unable to know their own desires, make decisions, or otherwise operate like autonomous adults. Like the heroines of *Secrecy* and *Victim of Prejudice*, Virginia has been sequestered and miseducated by a man pursuing the fantasy of preserving his ward's delicate sensibility and purity of mind. This sequestered education has injured her by arresting her intellectual and emotional development and by causing her to foster a romantic imagination that encourages melancholy. Virginia's story, however, unlike the stories of Maria Venables, Sibella Valmont, and Mary Raymond, does not end in tragedy.[73] On the contrary, rather than succumbing to despair, this isolated, abused girl lives to marry the man she loves. Although Edgeworth agrees with Wollstonecraft, Hays, and particularly Fenwick about the psychologically detrimental impact of Rousseau's educational ideas and methods, she uses the Virginia plot to revise their narratives of harm. Countering Rousseauvian theory with practice, Edgeworth allows Clarence Hervey, her injurious patriarch/ libertine, to learn through experience the errors of his ways without making him responsible for a woman's tragic death. And she easily dispatches the injuries of both patriarchs and libertines to revise her contemporaries' ideas,

152 *Women and madness in the early Romantic novel*

determining that stories teach best not by making readers weep, but by making them laugh.

Virginia comes into view slowly, first by rumours and innuendo, as a young woman inseparable from a character in a different fiction. When Lady Delacour finds out her name, she says, 'Virginia St Pierre, a pretty romantic name,' calling the reader's attention, as Laura Kirkley observes, to the fact that Hervey's experiment was by this time a cliché.[74] Lady Delacour then refers to Virginia in conversation with Belinda as Clarence's 'mistress of the wood' (135), thereby linking her to an additional literary formula: to the child of nature, the young person whose natural purity has not been destroyed by the corruptions of society. Lady Delacour's light-hearted sense of the tiredness of the trope corresponds to Kirkley's comment that Edgeworth could 'presume widespread readerly knowledge of Williams' *Paul and Virginia*' – Helen Maria Williams' 1788 translation of Bernardin de Saint-Pierre's *Paul et Virginie*.[75] Readers later discover that Clarence Hervey, upon taking the girl into his care to train her to be his wife, has changed her name from Rachel Hartley to Virginia St Pierre. This renaming, in addition to signalling the importance of David Hartley's associationist psychological theories to the novel, also suggests that Clarence Hervey's Virginia, a supposed child of nature, is actually a male fantasy.

Edgeworth reinforces this point during the conversation at the portrait gallery in which a collection of characters view a painting of Virginia as Virginie. Sir Philip, Clarence's obnoxious friend, refers to the portrait as 'Clarence Hervey's fancy' (172). While Sir Philip, who knows Clarence keeps this girl sequestered, is implying that she is the object of Clarence's fancy, or his desire, his words also describe the kind of picture they are viewing – a picture that is imaginative, rather than realistically representative.[76] Although Sir Philip is only referring to Clarence's desire, Lady Delacour picks up on the idea that the piece is a product of Clarence's imagination as well as his desire (173). All the people in the conversation, including Belinda, take this young woman to be Clarence's mistress. But there's an uncertainty about her identity stemming from how her name connects to Bernardin's romance and to Clarence Hervey's life. Belinda sees that the 'figure is St Pierre's Virginia,' while Rochfort, another of Clarence's friends, jokes that she is 'Virginia St Pierre,' or 'Hervey's Virginia,' or even 'Virginia Hervey' (173). The scene, and the conversation around the portrait, introduce Virginia for what she is in this novel: the creation of not one, but three men's fancies as expressed through two other literary works. What Edgeworth is getting at is that the kind of woman Clarence thinks he wants before he learns otherwise is a fiction based on a fiction based on a fiction. As this part of the novel shows, the idea that any woman could be a 'Virginia' (or a Virginie or a Sophie) is pure fancy coming from the male erotic imagination.[77]

Edgeworth connects Clarence's erotic fantasy directly to Rousseau at the beginning of the chapter that details Virginia's history. Clarence has been in France just before the Revolution, and the narrator intimates that he is motivated by a disappointing affair with a woman in Paris. It is just at this moment that he reads *Émile* and, as a result: 'He was charmed with the picture of Sophia, when contrasted with the characters of women of the world, with women he had been disgusted; and he formed the romantic project of educating a wife for himself' (330). Edgeworth uses the adjective 'romantic' to describe Clarence's determination to find a young woman and bring her up to be his wife according to a description he has read in a book. This idea is 'romantic' in that it is an indulgence in the imagination that appeals to a fantastic, idealized, or otherwise unrealistic view of life. Clarence then goes in search of such a woman in England, but is unsuccessful until he runs into a beautiful girl living in isolation with her grandmother in the New Forest. Clarence's educational project – and the subsequent damage it inflicts on Virginia's psyche – is thus inseparable from Rousseau's belief that women's education should keep them free from societal contamination and preserve their supposedly natural qualities.[78]

Edgeworth makes it clear that Clarence's primary motivation is sexual, although he is not honest with himself about why he wants a wife uncontaminated by societal influence. Readers can see that Clarence is fascinated by Rachel from the moment he sees her in the woods tending her garden: 'The young girl did not appear to Clarence like any other young girl, that he had ever seen ... the blush of modesty overspread her cheeks, when she looked up at the stranger. In her large blue eyes, there was an expression of artless sensibility, with which Mr Hervey was so powerfully struck' (331). Clarence interprets the look in her eyes as 'artless sensibility' – the very opposite of the gaze of the sexually experienced Parisian women, and exactly what he has been looking for. He thinks he sees pure natural feeling, untouched by the corruptions of society. Edgeworth's descriptions show that what he is looking for is a sexual fantasy: 'Her simplicity, sensibility, and, perhaps more than he was aware, her beauty, had pleased and touched him extremely. The idea of attaching a perfectly pure, disinterested, unpractised heart, was delightful to his imagination: the cultivation of her understanding, he thought, would be an easy and a pleasing task: all difficulties vanished before his sanguine hopes' (335).

Clarence's desire for this girl, Edgeworth suggests, is heightened by the fact that Rachel has never seen another man. Thus, not only is she a physical virgin, she is also (so much the better for being made into 'Virginia') an emotional and mental one. Clarence's response to Virginia

154   *Women and madness in the early Romantic novel*

shows readers that the desire inculcated by Rousseau and further popular-ized by Bernardin's novel and by conduct materials consists of a partial lie about what the man is looking for. The 'innocence,' 'purity of mind,' and 'natural sensibility' he seeks are all ways of expressing the desirability of a childlike mental and emotional state in which the young woman's mind and feelings, as well as her body, are untouched by any other man. With a virgin mind, she can be moulded however he likes. And when she is made to love him, the fantasy is that he will be the first and only man to possess her body and make an impression on her heart and mind. It is a fantasy of total control over a woman, masquerading as a morally elevated, and even philosophical, desire for what is pure and natural.

For quite some time, Clarence is delighted by what he believes is Virginia's 'natural simplicity' and by her desire to please him. His mind is so clouded by both Rousseau's ideas and his own sexual desire that he inter-prets everything Virginia does as confirming the wisdom of his wife-training plan. In one of his most striking episodes of misunderstanding, when Virginia rejects a gift of diamonds, Clarence interprets Virginia's indiffer-ence to luxury as natural simplicity, rather than as a function of her limited education. 'Her indifference to objects of show and ornament appeared to him an indisputable proof of her magnanimity, and of the superiority of her unprejudiced mind.—What a difference, thought he, between this child of nature and the frivolous slaves of art!' (338). As Kirkley observes, Edgeworth rejects this 'coupling of female virtue with lack of knowledge' found in Bernardin and Rousseau.[79] The narrator explains why Clarence, a man of considerable intelligence and broad reading, fails to see that what he takes as natural purity of mind and simplicity of taste is merely the result of an isolated education: 'These reflections could not possibly have escaped a man of Clarence Hervey's abilities, had he not been engaged in a defence of a favourite system of education, or if his pupil had not been quite so handsome' (339).

Clarence is not just pleased by Virginia's beauty and her apparently 'unprejudiced mind,' he is also delighted by her obedience and docility. Whenever Virginia is asked what she wants, she defers to Clarence, hesitat-ing to express her own desires. For example, when Mrs Ormand, the woman caring for Virginia, explains that she could have pierced ears, she shrinks back, but then changes her tone, turns to Clarence and says, 'unless you wish it:—if you bid me, I will' (339). The narrator explains that 'Clarence was scarcely master of himself at this instant; and it was with the utmost difficulty, that he could reply to her with that dispassionate calmness, which became his situation and hers' (339). Intoxicated by his own desires and dedicated to an educational system that feeds those desires, Clarence continually misinterprets Virginia's ignorance and arrested development

Madness reconsidered in Belinda   155

as evidence of the natural taste and purity of his future wife, all the while hiding from himself the fundamentally sexual basis of his interest and the harm he is inflicting on her mind.

Although Clarence thinks he is behaving with generosity to Virginia, he is in fact acting according to a cluster of self-interested motives that are only partially successful. In this way, he behaves similarly to the guardians in *Victim of Prejudice* and, particularly, in *Secresy*. With a strategy reminiscent of Mr Valmont's he isolates his ward and deprives her of contact with anyone other than himself and an authorized companion. He does this to freeze her emotional and intellectual development, to keep her heart and her mind in a childlike state, and to reinforce his own control.[80] He believes the ideal wife is naturally docile and obedient, and so he limits her education and experience in order to squash any attempt at autonomy. And he makes sure she is so starved of love and companionship that she focuses her affections only on those he permits her to love. Like Mr Valmont's sequestration of Sibella, Clarence's endeavour is, as Siobhán Kilfeather observes, a blatant indulgence of his 'fantasies of power and sexuality.'[81] Clarence is considerably more successful than Mr Valmont in making his Sophie docile and ignorant, but less successful in directing her emotions toward her future spouse – in this case himself. Although, as the narrator observes, 'the affections of this innocent girl had no object but himself and Mrs Ormand' (340), Clarence has not counted on a few, crucial elements. To start, he is not the first man Virginia has ever seen: the honours of her virgin heart have already gone to a picture of a man she once saw. Moreover, the emotional engineering that is so essential a part of the plan has backfired. Virginia loves Mrs Ormand like a mother and Clarence more like a father – feeling for him only a ward's affection for her guardian.

The madness of Virginia St Pierre

Clarence leaves Virginia for some time after Mrs Ormand reminds him that it will be at least a year before she is old enough to marry. It is in this period of absence that he renews his acquaintance with Lady Delacour and meets Belinda. In leaving Virginia, he abandons her to a cloistered life with a woman of kind heart, but little sophistication. Alone with Mrs Ormand, Virginia's mental health takes a turn for the worse when she develops a passion for romances that compromises her sense of reality and warps her moral understanding. The narrator describes her situation and its impact on her mind: 'Without companions to interest her social affections, without real objects to occupy her senses and understanding, Virginia's mind was either perfectly indolent or exalted by romantic views and visionary ideas

156   *Women and madness in the early Romantic novel*

of happiness' (346). Commentators on this novel have described what Virginia reads as novels, but the fact that these are romances is essential to Edgeworth's delineation of Virginia's drift toward madness, as well as to Edgeworth's revision of her contemporaries' narratives of psychological harm. As the ultimate say-so regarding Virginia's education, Clarence has warned Mrs Ormand not to allow her to read '*common* novels,' but he 'made no objection to romances: these, he thought, breathed a spirit favourable to female virtue, exalted the respect for chastity, and inspired enthusiastic admiration of honour, generosity, truth, and all the noble qualities, which dignify human nature' (347). Clarence approves of romances because they offer an elevated picture of human virtues, including chastity for women (which he is quite concerned about), honour, generosity, and truth. But Virginia's education via romances is detrimental because it inculcates a false picture of society, of gender relations, and of virtues. Like Arabella in Charlotte Lennox's *The Female Quixote* (1752), Virginia immerses herself in a highly gendered world of elevated values in which the point of a woman's life is to maintain her chastity and secure the worship of men of the most noble qualities. Because Virginia is isolated, her immersion in romances makes her unable to tell the difference between what is real and what is not and causes her to embrace a moral code ill adapted to the modern era. But whereas Arabella gains considerable power from her absorption of romance lessons, in that she is capable of reasoning clearly according to the values of the romance world and holds herself and others to high moral standards, Virginia suffers psychologically from her miseducation. Like Lady Delacour, who is 'constant prey to ennui' when not stimulated by attention, Virginia falls 'prey to ennui' when her imagination is not stirred by romances (347). Moreover, she is tormented to the verge of madness by guilt over her desire for an imaginary romance lover and by her conviction that she is 'ungrateful' to Clarence Hervey.

With her birth name of 'Hartley,' it is appropriate that Virginia's mind has been formed by the small sampling of impressions to which she has been exposed and by the associations among them. David Thame argues persuasively that 'Virginia's story is offered as proof that madness ... is a rationally explicable phenomenon, the sure and certain result of ill-directed education and the creation of false or erroneous associations.'[82] David Hartley had established that 'every succeeding thought is the result either of some new impression, or of an association with the preceding.'[83] The only new impressions Virginia has to add to those of her childhood in the forest come from her steady diet of romances. Her mind is thus filled by the associations among the few elements to which she has been exposed: a picture of a man she once saw and the romance heroes of which she now reads. A new and crucial impression is made when she comes across Bernardin's novel in Mrs Ormand's room. This impression now adds the name 'Paul' and the awareness that sexual feelings are to be feared to her small assembly of ideas. Mrs Ormand tries to take the book from Virginia, but she will not give it up because of the new feelings the passage has awakened, and mimicking Virginie she tells Mrs Ormand she is not afraid of her, but rather of herself (347). The passage covers thoughts about Paul, which are troublingly erotic to Virginie. When Virginie leaves the 'dangerous shades' and goes to her mother 'to seek protection from herself,' she is unable to mention the name of 'Paul' and merely weeps on her mother's bosom (347).[84] Virginia learns from this passage what her attitude should be towards the feelings the passage has aroused. She throws her arms around Mrs Ormand and lays her head on her bosom 'as if she wished to realize the illusions, and to be the Virginia of whom she had been reading' (348). Hartley's ideas of association are, of course built on Locke's, and Louis Charland explains that central to Locke's discussion of madness is the belief that ideas become 'cemented' together as a result of a disordered affective process.[85] Virginia's isolation has caused her to attach her affections to the first man she ever saw, the man in the picture. The subsequent linkage of this man with the character Paul and the heroes of romances can be understood as a muddled association of ideas that develops out of the disordered affective state caused by her isolation. The feelings Virginia develops from reading romances become 'cemented' to the name 'Paul,' which, as Virginia knows because of her renaming, is the man these secret feelings are supposed to be attached to. But she is deeply conflicted because, at the same time, Mrs Ormand is constantly insinuating that these feelings are and should be directed toward Clarence Hervey.

Unfortunately, Mrs Ormand is also a reader of romances, as well as an adherent to the Rousseau-inspired conduct-book ideas about women that Clarence thinks he believes in. Mrs Ormand encourages Virginia's feeling of being in love but insists she must be in love with Clarence because he is the man she is to marry, and Mrs Ormand approves of what she understands to be Virginia's 'modesty' in her embarrassment about her feelings. Mrs Ormand listens to Virginia, but she interprets everything her charge tries to explain according to the playbook Clarence has given her. When Virginia says, 'how could you possibly know *all* my thoughts and feelings? I never told them to you; for, indeed, I have only confused ideas, floating in my imagination, from the books I have been reading. I do not distinctly know my own feelings' (348), Mrs Ormand interprets her comments according to the rules of conduct modesty, which prohibit young women from an awareness of their own sexual feelings lest they lose the 'innocence' that makes them so sexually alluring to men. Mrs Ormand, with her insinuations and manipulations, fails to realize that she is talking of one kind of

158 *Women and madness in the early Romantic novel*

love, and Virginia of another. The confusion is perhaps inevitable, given that the guardian and the lover in this novel are the same man, unlike in *Secresy* in which all the guardian can do is live out his Rousseauvian erotic fantasy vicariously through his illegitimate son and niece.

After Mrs Ormand disregards Clarence's orders and tells Virginia he is educating her to be his wife, Virginia has a nightmare that reveals she suffers from anxiety and a confusion over the proper direction of the passions – passions she has learned from Bernardin's Virginie she should repress and fear. Virginia is tormented by an awareness that she should, but does not, love her guardian and that she should not, but does, love another man. That young women must be both unaware and ashamed of their erotic desire is central to the paradoxical version of femininity conveyed by Rousseau, Bernardin, and writers of conduct materials.[86] Virginia's dream illustrates the psychic stress experienced by young women when they are expected to direct passions they are not supposed to know they have toward a figure they may not love. Writing at a time when, in Jennifer Ford's words, the 'concept of the "unconscious" mind began to emerge,' Edgeworth is able to use the dream to show psychological distress.[87] In her dream, Virginia's unconscious mind blends her life at the cottage with the exotic landscape of *Paul et Virginie* and mixes this setting with the courtship and chivalry of romances. She dreams of a figure that 'seemed a real living person' who kneels to her at Virginie's fountain and offers to kiss her hand. At the end of the dream the figure from the fountain, whom she calls 'Paul,' dressed as a white knight, defeats Mr Hervey, dressed as a black knight. In an inversion of Lady Delacour's dream of a mysterious figure prophesying her own death, Virginia dreams of the death of the mysterious figure. As the black knight lies 'weltering in his blood' he says to her, 'Perfidious *ungrateful* Virginia! you are the cause of my death' (355). When Virginia tells Mrs Ormand about her dream, the older woman cannot see what is obvious: that Virginia does not love Mr Hervey; that she does not wish to marry him; that her romantic investment is in the figure she terms 'Paul'; that she is emotionally distressed by the expectation that she should love Mr Hervey; and that her isolation and her education through romances is injuring her mind.

Edgeworth uses the dream to show Virginia's true desires, but also to convey the disruptions of her psyche. Readers familiar with Priestley's edition of *Hartley's Theory of the Human Mind* would know that 'there are many useful hints relating to the strength of our passions deducible from [dreams].'[88] Virginia's dream conveys so much anxiety about disappointing Mr Hervey that she feels she will inflict an injury on him by not wanting to marry him. As it is for Lady Delacour, a large part of Virginia's mental disturbance is caused by guilt. By loving someone else, Virginia feels she has been unfaithful, duplicitous, and ungrateful to Clarence. Because her moral understanding has been entirely shaped by romances, Virginia's feeling of being 'perfidious' conveys a sense of being unworthy of the benefits she has received. Thus Virginia's dream reveals the extent of her emotional stress as her sense of the obligation to love Clarence conflicts with her inability to do so.

After the dream, Virginia's unhappiness deepens to the extent that Clarence becomes aware of the change in her behaviour toward him and realizes that he may be inflicting harm upon her. Now reserved and timid, she will not meet his eye, trembles when he approaches, and bursts into tears if he is grave or fails to take notice of her. She has 'fits of melancholy and exertion' (356) that Clarence thinks might indicate a desire to see the wider world, but that in fact suggest the mood disruption of melancholy and mania. And, as Kirkley observes, Virginia's lack of curiosity signals her 'emotional immaturity and intellectual impoverishment.'[89] It would be easy to blame Virginia for her lack of interest in anything other than romances and pleasing Clarence, but her diminished mental state is a result of her confinement. Clarence understands something of the detrimental impact his actions have had on her, but he does not fully comprehend the way he has stunted her intellectual, emotional, and moral development. In Clarence's mind, she is a girl of 'melancholy temperament, who has a great deal of natural sensibility, whose affections have all been concentrated, who has lived in solitude, whose imagination has dwelled, for a length of time, upon a certain set of ideas, who has but the one object of hope' (357).

The narcissism of the beginning of Clarence's experiment extends to his realization that it might end in disaster. Now that he has met Belinda and is not as interested in Virginia, he fears what might happen if he does not marry his young ward. 'In such a mind, and in such circumstances, passion may rise to a paroxysm of despair' (357). Hervey's account of Virginia's delicate mental state conveys a great deal of truth, although it is also subject to misinterpretation based on his belief that Virginia's emotional life must be focused on himself. It is not clear how melancholy she is by nature, or how extensive her 'natural' sensibility might be, but it is certain that he has put her into a solitary state in which her affections have been concentrated and in which her imagination has dwelled for some time on one set of ideas. Believing himself to be the individual upon whom all her affections are directed, Clarence thinks that, should he abandon her, she would be seriously harmed if her rising passions were to trigger a violent emotional attack. Although Clarence is incorrect in his interpretation of Virginia's feelings for him, he is not wrong about the harm his project has inflicted on her. He has, as he said, 'taken her out of a situation, in which she might have spent her life usefully and happily' (357) and attempted to mould her

160   *Women and madness in the early Romantic novel*

according to his own pleasure. As a result, the once contented girl living a simple life in the forest is now a young woman whose sequestration by her guardian has injured her mental and physical health.

Virginia's plot is tied up after her father, Mr Hartley, is located, but not before she experiences an emotional shock that makes Clarence believe she might actually go mad. Clarence had commissioned a portrait of Virginia as Bernardin's Virginie in an attempt to locate the man he discovered had been looking for her.[90] Lady Delacour then has a large portrait of 'Paul' painted, based on the image of the picture Rachel fell in love with in the forest. In the chapter entitled 'Denouement,' Virginia's confused feelings and fragile mental state are thrown into crisis when Lady Delacour has the painting delivered to the house of Mrs Margaret Delacour, where Virginia and her newly found father are staying. When Lady Delacour unveils the object she has had delivered, 'a companion for your Virginia' (425), Virginia shrieks and falls senseless on the floor because the man in Lady Delacour's portrait is the man she is in love with – the man she calls 'Paul' whom she once saw in a picture as a girl in the New Forest. When Virginia recovers, she is left alone with Clarence, but the hysterical fit is not yet over. She is 'seized with an universal tremor,' and she attempts to speak, but 'could not articulate'; then she bursts into tears that finally relieve her (426). According to David Hartley, 'Violent Fits of Passion' that would 'so transport Persons … [fell] within the Limits of the Distemper called Madness.'[91] Indeed, Virginia's attempt to explain her response to the picture shows how close she is to insanity as a result of the injuries Clarence has inflicted on her.

When Clarence urges Virginia to speak the truth to him, her responses are muddled, not only because of her anxiety about being thought ungrateful and her efforts to hide her desire for 'Paul,' but also because she now has difficulty distinguishing between what is real and what is imaginary. In an introductory essay on Hartley's theories, Joseph Priestley wrote that in cases of madness, 'very vivid ideas actually [impose] upon the mind, so that they are mistaken for realities, as in dreams and reveries.'[92] In response to the direct question: why did you shriek at the sight of the picture? Virginia responds with what is the truth to her: that the man in the picture has knelt to her and kissed her hand, which means that Clarence will call her '*perfidious, ungrateful Virginia*' (427). When Clarence asks her where she met this man, she shows her confusion by responding 'what man?' (427). Clarence has to point to the picture for her to recollect, and then she explains she saw him in the forest, at her neighbour Mrs Smith's house. As Clarence continues to try to understand Virginia's relationship with a man he believes she knows, her confusion and her muddled mental state hint at a deeper madness than that suggested by her hysterical collapse. She says to him: 'Indeed I am quite bewildered … I know not what I feel,'

Madness reconsidered in Belinda   161

and then finally explains that the man kissed her hand in a dream and that she had only seen him in a picture (428–9). While Virginia may naturally be a person of strong feelings, this inability to understand and to control her emotions can be traced to Hervey's Rousseauvian desire to keep her in a childlike state. But, as the Virginia subplot demonstrates, a woman with a child's mind and experiences can undergo considerable psychic distress when faced with the pressures and expectations of adulthood.

Clarence's questions push Virginia to the verge of madness, as she is forced to admit that she is in love with the picture of a man she has never seen in person. As he probes for answers, looking for a logical explanation, Virginia experiences considerable mental stress, becoming bewildered and looking around wildly. She then confesses in a flood of description that suggests her grasp on the difference between what she has imagined or dreamt and what she has experienced is tenuous at best. When Virginia finally admits she has never seen the 'original' of the picture Lady Delacour has presented – that is, never seen the actual man – she says, 'And I wish to Heaven I had never, never seen that fatal picture! The image haunts me day and night. When I read of heroes in the day, that figure rises to my view, instead of yours. When I go to sleep at night I see it, instead of yours, in my dreams; it speaks to me, it kneels to me.' Clarence observes her carefully while she speaks, and he marks the 'wild animation of her eyes [and] the sudden changes of her countenance' while he recollects her 'her father's insanity' (429). Feeling horror and pity, Clarence pulls Virginia back from the edge of madness by speaking gently to her and by assuring her she is not ungrateful, which is her greatest fear and deepest torment. Clarence finally seems to understand what his wife-training has done to her when he recognizes that 'her imagination, exalted by solitude and romance, embodied and became enamoured of a phantom' (430).

Conclusion: the demystification of patriarchal power

But Virginia does not go mad, and she does not, like Sibella Valmont and Mary Raymond before her, die of male-inflicted injuries. Instead, she is able to retreat back into the safety and protection of a patriarchal system. With the arrival of Mr Hartley, now of sound mind, the mentally and emotionally fragile Virginia is returned to her father's care. When Mr Hartley introduces her to Captain Sunderland, the man in the portrait, he says, 'give me leave to introduce to you a friend, to whom I owe more obligations than to any man living, except to Mr Hervey' (435).[93] Mr Hartley owes a debt to Captain Sunderland because he saved his life in a slave revolt.[94] And, presumably, Mr Hartley owes a great obligation to Mr Hervey because he helped him find Rachel. In what is a quintessential patriarchal move, Mr Hartley seeks to bestow his daughter on his chosen lover, conceiving of her as owing her hand first to Clarence and then to Captain Sunderland for services rendered to himself. With Virginia able to marry the literal man of her dreams, thanks to her father, the conclusion of her subplot seems to reinforce the goodness of patriarchal power structures.

But despite Mr Hartley's handing Virginia to a suitor desired by both father and daughter, patriarchal power is undermined in *Belinda*'s conclusion, as in fact it has been all along. When Lady Delacour places Virginia and Captain Sunderland kneeling at Mr Hartley's feet in the 'tableau' at the conclusion, she is showing that obedience to patriarchal wishes is an artificial construct. By this point, the resolution of Virginia's story has already been cast as the stuff of fairy tales. Not only is Virginia identified as the missing Rachel through a mole and by her resemblance to her dead mother – in keeping with old romance and fairy-tale formulations – Lady Delacour has several times referred to these genres in describing the resolution of Virginia's plot. Thus, in the only part of the novel in which patriarchy appears to be both competent and benign, male power is shown to be a romance – that is, it is shown to be fantastical and unrealistic. In other parts of the novel, the power of men is undermined by their irrationality, such as Lord Delacour's alcoholism and Mr Hartley's bouts of insanity. Far from either supporting patriarchal control, as some critics would have it, or expressing a sense of overwhelming doom at patriarchy's power, the novel, in Mitzi Myers' words, engages in an 'aesthetics of play that demystifies paternal authority.'[95] All sense of the abuse of male power in *Belinda* is wiped away by the collapse of the wife-training plan, by the weaknesses of fathers and guardians, and by the playful approach to genre at the end.[96] Kilfeather writes that although Edgeworth's use of fairy-tale motifs 'softens the story,' Edgeworth's conclusion still unmasks the 'dangerous abusiveness of [the wife-training] scheme,' which is certainly the case.[97] But Edgeworth uses romance and fairy-tale motifs to undermine Rousseau's influence and demystify his ideas. Moreover, although *Belinda* expresses serious concern about the influence of Rousseau's ideas about gender, her use of romance motifs at the denouement, her characters' repeated references to genres of fiction (fairy-tales, romances, novels), and Lady Delacour's theatrical tableau and concluding mocking rhyme show that men – including Rousseau – pose no threat worrisome enough to be taken seriously.

The reason why Edgeworth avoids blaming patriarchal power overmuch owes a great deal to her optimism about education and her egalitarian position on gender.[98] Under the influence of Rousseau, Clarence sequesters a young woman for sexual reasons, allows her to be miseducated, risks her reputation, causes her to devote herself to romantic fantasies, makes her want to please him, and pushes her to the brink of madness. He then does what no young libertine in *Wrongs, Secresy, or Victim* did before him: he takes responsibility for his actions and admits he was wrong. After the full revelation of Virginia's feelings for Captain Sunderland (aka 'Paul'), Clarence says, 'but I blame nobody, I have no right to blame any one so much as myself. Nothing could be more absurd than my scheme of educating a woman in solitude, to make her fit for society' (432). Clarence gets credit for self-reflection and for accepting blame, but Edgeworth still seems to let him off the hook relatively easily, rewarding him through marriage to Belinda, rather than punishing him for attempting to train his own wife.[99] As Kilfeather notes, it is remarkable that 'Hervey remains attractive and sympathetic in spite of this appalling project.'[100] This is the case, I would argue, because more than anyone else in the novel, Clarence Hervey learns from his own mistakes and from the good counsel of others. Clarence goes wrong because, in his youthful exuberance, he mistakes the ideas in Rousseau's *Émile* for truth. He has read one enticing book, thought it was true, and has determined to follow its precepts to happiness. But in his life, as he gains experience, he discovers Rousseau is entirely wrong about women. Through experience and reflection, through making the right kinds of friends and giving up the wrong, he discovers the pleasure of egalitarian relationships with intelligent, sophisticated women. Clarence has undergone a transformation à la David Hartley: he has accumulated new associations and new habits that have indicated where his happiness lies. And Maria Edgeworth has defeated Jean-Jacques Rousseau.

Although Clarence acts as patriarch through his guardianship of Virginia, his role is similar to that of the libertines and privileged young men in *Secresy* and *Victim of Prejudice*. Motivated by sensual desires, he has inflicted harm on a young woman with no external checks on his behaviour. In the end, he resembles Lord Filmar in that he stands in for the reform the author expects of her male readers. Indeed, although there is no parallel character in *Victim of Prejudice* – no abusive libertine who is given the grace of reform – Hays, like Fenwick, hoped her novel would encourage men to change their ways. But Edgeworth has a different strategy for the reform she, Fenwick, and Hays wish to see. Edgeworth does not want her male readers to have an emotional transformation. That is, she does not think that making them weep over the tragic story of a once-glorious young woman whose mind is broken will lead to improvement. Rather, she wants them, like Clarence Hervey, to experience an intellectual education – to think about what they really want in a wife. Edgeworth accepts that the fantasy of the docile girl with the virgin mind, heart, and body is enticing for some men. But she also believes that when presented with alternatives, such as those she depicts in this novel – the alternatives of Lady Delacour,

164   *Women and madness in the early Romantic novel*

Lady Anne Percival, and Belinda – male readers will learn that their future happiness depends on equality, not on subservience, and that what they want is not a child in a woman's body, but an intelligent, emotionally balanced domestic partner.

Belinda is linked to *Wrongs of Woman*, *Secresy*, and *The Victim of Prejudice* through the psychological harm inflicted on Virginia by a Rousseauvian education, as well as through the novel's overall focus on women's madness. But in contrast to these novels by authors much more frequently termed 'feminist,' novels that end in victimization and despair, *Belinda*'s suffering characters are granted a happy ending. The difference comes down to Edgeworth's alternative understanding of society, of the power dynamic between men and women, and of relationships among women themselves. Rather than see a society in which men destroy women's minds through their patriarchal power and libertine ways, Edgeworth believes men and women can be partners in the project of helping one another live healthy, happy lives. And rather than express despair over women's inability to come to one another's aid, Edgeworth gives women the power to understand mental disease and to help one another heal their injured minds. Ultimately, *Belinda* offers optimism through an idea of healing that is built on her faith in people's ability to redirect their passions and to learn new, better ideas. As the novel shows, when people, under the influence of wrong associations, seek self-interested pleasures – or when they pursue the joys of ambition and acclaim to an excess – they can fall ill, as well as inflict injuries on others. But Edgeworth is confident that they can improve and that those they harm can be healed. Regardless of their gender, those with injured minds and those who injure other minds can be cured by learning through social interaction, good influences, and reflection that their happiness lies in balancing their passions and righting their wrong associations. In Edgeworth's vision of society, women are the key to this process. As Mitzi Myers has written, in *Belinda*, 'Edgeworth grants women reason, wit, worldly wisdom, command of language, conversational skills, sociability, and the power to change [themselves] and others.'[101] This makes Edgeworth, then, as much (or more) of a feminist than those writers who, in a time of political disappointment, inflicted cases of fatal melancholia on their victimized protagonists.

Notes

1 Despite the centrality of irrationality and madness to *Belinda*, neither has attracted much attention from scholars. Two primary exceptions are Marie McAllister, 'Ungovernable Propensities: Belinda and the Idea of Addiction,'

The Age of Johnson 23 (2015), www.proquest.com/scholarly-journals/ungo
vernable-propensities-belinda-idea-addiction/docview/1771787728/se-2; and
David Thame 'Madness and Therapy in Maria Edgeworth's *Belinda*: Deceived
by Appearances,' *British Journal for Eighteenth-Century Studies* 26 (2003),
https://doi.org/10.1111/j.1754-0208.2003.tb00272.x. See also Hilary Teynor
Donatini, 'Moral and Medical Diagnosis in Maria Edgeworth's *Belinda*,' *The
Eighteenth-Century Novel* 9 (2011).

2 David Thame connects Edgeworth's views on madness to those of William
Pargeter's in *Observations on Maniacal Disorders* (1792). Among other factors,
Pargeter blames fashionable life and Methodism, both of which apply to Lady
Delacour, for mental disease. See 'Madness and Therapy,' 273–4. James K.
Chandler, in linking Edgeworth to the Lunar Society, argues for Erasmus
Darwin's influence on the medical and psychological aspects of *Belinda*. See
'Edgeworth and the Lunar Enlightenment,' *Eighteenth-Century Studies* 45,
no. 1 (2011): 93, https://doi.org/10.1353/ecs.2011.0053.

3 Louis Charland, 'Science and Morals in the Affective Psychopathology of
Philippe Pinel,' *History of Psychiatry* 21, no. 1 (2010): 38, https://doi.org/10.1
177/0957154X09338334.

4 Although 'passions' applied to a wide variety of states and feelings, Grange
believes the term is useful because 'moral and medical discussions of the
passions and affections were concerned with what we would call emotional
disease.' Kathleen Grange, 'Pinel and Eighteenth-Century Psychiatry,' *Bulletin
of the History of Medicine* 34, no. 5 (1961), 445–6.

5 In Hartley's words, as published by Priestley: 'Mad persons differ from others
in that they judge wrong of past or future facts of a common nature; that their
affections and actions are violent and different from, or even opposite to, those
of others upon like occasions, and such as are contrary to their true happiness;
that their memory is fallacious, and their discourse incoherent; and that they
lose, in great measure, that consciousness which accompanies our thoughts and
actions, and by which we connect ourselves with ourselves from time to time.'
Joseph Priestley, *Hartley's theory of the human mind, on the principle of the
association of ideas; with essays relating to the subject of it*, 2nd edn (London:
J. Johnson, 1790), 224, ECCO.

6 See G. E. Berrios, 'David Hartley's Views on Madness,' *History of Psychiatry*
26, no. 1 (2015): 105, https://doi.org/10.1177/0957154X14562300.

7 Priestley, *Hartley*, 224.

8 Thame brings readers' attention to the third volume of *Practical Education*,
in which Edgeworth writes that wrong associations cannot be addressed by
reason but must be replaced by correct associations ('Madness and Therapy,'
287, note 55).

9 Richard Allen, *David Hartley on Human Nature* (Albany: State University of
New York Press, 1999), 8.

10 Allen, *David Hartley*, 284.

11 Allen, *David Hartley*, 285.

12 Allen, *David Hartley*, 285.

166 *Women and madness in the early Romantic novel*

13 Hartley includes 'theopathy' in his list of beneficial pleasures. Edgeworth glances toward 'theopathy' when Lady Delacour talks with the chaplain, Mr Moreton, in her recovery phase. But the Edgeworths were never known for their religiosity.

14 Louis Charland, 'Alexander Crichton on the Psychopathology of the Passions,' *History of Psychiatry* 19, no. 3 (208): 276, https://doi.org/10.1177/0957154X0 7078703.

15 Alexander Crichton, *An Inquiry Into the Nature And Origin of Mental Derangement: Comprehending a Concise System of the Physiology and Pathology of the Human Mind and a History of the Passions And Their Effects*, vol. III (London: T. Cadell, junior and W. Davies, 1798), 112, HathiTrust.

16 Crichton, *Inquiry*, vol. III, 160–1.

17 Crichton, *Inquiry*, vol. III, 165–6.

18 Crichton, *Inquiry*, vol. III, 169.

19 Crichton, *Inquiry*, vol. III, 176.

20 Crichton, *Inquiry*, vol. III, 184–5.

21 Maria Edgeworth, *Belinda*, ed. Linda Bree (1801; Oxford: Oxford World's Classics, 2020). See Appendix 1. All references are to this edition.

22 The Retreat at York, founded by William Tuke and the Society of Quakers, opened in 1796 and gave humane treatment in the form of 'moral therapy' to its patients. Allan Ingram and Stuart Sim observe that it is 'difficult to overstate the significance of The Retreat.' Allan Ingram and Stuart Sim, 'Introduction: Depression Before Depression,' in *Melancholy Experience in Literature of the Long Eighteenth Century: Before Depression, 1660–1800*, ed. Allan Ingram and Stuart Sim (London: Palgrave, 2011), 16.

23 Grange, 'Pinel,' 443.

24 It is likely that Edgeworth had access to information about moral therapy, despite the fact that Samuel Tuke's *A Description of the Retreat* (1813) and the translation of Pinel's *Traité médicophilosophique sur l'aliénation mentale ou la manie* were both published after the completion of *Belinda*. Pinel had published some articles in French in the late 1790s and his *Traité* was published in 1800. Edgeworth read French fluently and was in close contact with French-speaking intellectuals on the Continent. And the Retreat would have been in operation for several years before she wrote *Belinda*.

25 Vieda Skultans, *English Madness: Ideas on Insanity, 1580–1890* (London: Routledge & Kegan Paul, 1979), 62.

26 Only a few scholars consider both meanings of 'Delacour.' Laura Kirkley, for example, uses the name's link to the 'court' to discuss Edgeworth's engagement with French ideas and Lady Delacour's understanding of the importance of love. Kirkley also connects the name to 'courtesan,' suggesting a knowledge of love, sex, and the condition of being a 'fallen' woman. Laura Kirkley, 'Translating Rousseauism: Transformations of Bernardin de Saint-Pierre's *Paul et Virginia* in the Works of Helen Maria Williams and Maria Edgeworth' in *Women Readers in Europe: Readers, Writers, Solonnieres, 1750–1900*, eds Hilary Brown and Gillian Dow (London: Routledge, 2011), 105. Siobhán Kilfeather also

Madness reconsidered in Belinda 167

considers both meanings, emphasizing that 'Lady Delacour is both worldly and emotional.' Siobhán Kilfeather, 'Introductory Note' in *Belinda. The Pickering Masters The Novels and Selected Works Of Maria Edgeworth*, vol. 2 (2003; New York: Routledge, 2016), 368, ebook.

27 Dr X alludes to the opening lines of Locke's *Some Thoughts Concerning Education* (1693).

28 Crichton, *Inquiry*, vol. III, 165–9.

29 See Marjo Kaartinen, *Breast Cancer in the Eighteenth Century* (London: Routledge, 2016), 17.

30 Kaartinen, *Breast Cancer*, ix.

31 Kaartinen, *Breast Cancer*, 90.

32 Scholars disagree considerably about whether Harriot Freke's role in the novel is liberatory or reactionary or neither. For a sampling of interpretations, see Elizabeth Kowaleski-Wallace, *Their Fathers' Daughters: Hannah More, Maria Edgeworth, and Patriarchal Complicity* (New York: Oxford University Press, 1991), chapter 4; Lisa Moore, *Dangerous Intimacies: Toward a Sapphic History of the British Novel* (Durham, NC: Duke University Press, 1997), chapter 3; Claudia Johnson, *Equivocal Beings: Politics, Gender, and Sentimentality in the 1790s: Wollstonecraft, Radcliffe, Burney, Austen* (Chicago: University of Chicago Press, 1995), introduction; Jason Farr, *Novel Bodies: Disability and Sexuality in Eighteenth-Century British Literature* (Lewisburg: Bucknell University Press, 2019), chapter 4; and my own *The Female Philosopher and her Afterlives: Mary Wollstonecraft, The British Novel, and the Transformations of Feminism, 1796–1811* (Basingstoke: Palgrave, 2017), chapter 5.

33 Thame, 'Madness and Therapy,' 276. He quotes from Crichton's *Inquiry*, vol. II, 149.

34 James Boswell, *Boswell's Column. Being his Seventy Contributions to The London Magazine under the pseudonym The Hypochondriack from 1777 to 1783*, ed. Margery Bailey (London: William Kimber, 1951), 44–5.

35 Vladan Starcevic, 'Clinical Features and Diagnosis of Hypochondriasis' in *Hypochondriasis: Modern Perspectives on an Ancient Malady*, eds Vladan Starcevic and Don R. Lipsitt (Oxford: Oxford University Press, 2001), 21.

36 Russell Noyes, Jr, 'The Transformation of Hypochondriasis in British Medicine, 1680–1830,' *Social History of Medicine* 24, no. 2 (2011): 284, https://doi.org/10.1093/shm/hkq052.

37 Noyes, 'Transformation of Hypochondriasis,' 286.

38 Functional disorder, previously known as conversion disorder, is a condition in which impediments in motor or sensory function cannot be explained through physical models. Common examples include blindness, paralysis, non-epileptic seizures, difficulty swallowing or walking, and involuntary muscle contractions. Symptoms 'typically begin with some stressor, trauma, or psychological distress that manifests itself as a physical deficit' and there is 'no underlying physical cause for the symptom (s).' Shahid Ali, Shagufta Jabeen, Rebecca J. Pate, Marwah Shahid, Sandhya Chinala, Milankumar Nathani, and Rida Shah,

'Conversion Disorder – Mind versus Body: A Review,' *Innovations in Clinical Neuroscience* 12, nos 5–6 (May-June 2015): 27, bit.ly/3OX1lba.

39 Allen, *David Hartley*, 21.

40 Allen, *David Hartley*, 24.

41 William Falconer, *A Dissertation on the Influence of the Passions upon Disorders of the Body* (London: C. Dilly and J. Phillips 1788), xiii. Quoted in Kaartinen, *Breast Cancer*, 18.

42 See Kaartinen, *Breast Cancer*, 26.

43 Kaartinen, *Breast Cancer*, 15. Kaartinen references John Burrows, who blamed women who did not breastfeed for their own diseases, including cancer. John Burrows, *A New Practical Essay on Cancers*, (London: J. Barker, G. Kearsly, and T. Axtell. 1783), 41–2. Quoted in Kaartinen, *Breast Cancer*, 16.

44 See, for example: Ula Klein, 'Bosom Friends and the Sapphic Breasts of *Belinda*,' *ABO: Interactive Journal for Women in the Arts* 3, no. 2 (2013), http://dx.doi.org/10.5038/2157–7129.3.2.1; Katherine Montwieler, 'Reading Disease: The Corrupting Performance of Edgeworth's *Belinda*,' *Women's Writing* 12, no. 3 (2005), https://doi.org/10.1080/09699080500200268; and Ruth Perry, 'Colonizing the Breast: Sexuality and Maternity in Eighteenth-Century England,' *Journal of the History of Sexuality* 2, no. 2 (Oct. 1991), www.jstor.org/stable/3704034.

45 Perry, 'Colonizing the Breast,' 217.

46 There are a number of influential sapphic readings of Lady Delacour's relationship with Harriot Freke. See, for example, Lisa Moore, *Dangerous Intimacies*, chapter 3; Ula Klein, 'Bosom Friends'; and Jason Farr, *Novel Bodies*, chapter 4.

47 The complete quote is: 'For they do not appear to me to have lost the faculty of Reasoning: But having joined together some Ideas very wrongly, they mistake them for Truths; and they err as Men do that argue right from wrong Principles. For by the violence of their Imaginations, having taken their Fancies for Realities, they make right deductions from them.' John Locke, *An Essay Concerning Human Understanding*, 5th edn (London: Awnsham and John Churchill, 1706), 93, ECCO.

48 The convergence of imagination and passion into madness was described by the medical writer Thomas Arnold. See his *Observations on the nature, kinds, causes and prevention of insanity, lunacy or madness*, vol. i (Leicester: G. Ireland for G. Robinson and T. Cadwell, 1782), 108, ECCO.

49 According to Hartley, such instances of violent passions should be considered 'temporary madness' (Priestley, *Hartley*, 233). Should these violent passions become habitual, then the madness would be considered permanent.

50 Kaartinen has found that opium was commonly prescribed for breast cancer, not only to dull the pain, but also to soften the tumour (*Breast Cancer*, 37).

51 Richard Hunter and Ida Macalpine observe that 'in the eighteenth century the laity as well as the profession used opium freely for all kinds of conditions and diseases in various preparations.' Richard Hunter and Ida Macalpine, *Three Hundred Years of Psychiatry 1535–1860: A History Presented in Selected*

Madness reconsidered in Belinda 169

English Texts (London: Oxford University Press, 1963), 395. Citing William Pargeter's *Observations on Maniacal Disorders* (1792), Thame notes that medical writers were aware that opium could 'hasten mental collapse' when taken in large doses ('Madness and Therapy,' 276).

52 Siobhán Kilfeather identifies this book as *The works of the Rev. John Wesley, M.A. Late Fellow of Lincoln-College*, Oxford, 1783 (Kilfeather, end notes to *Belinda*, 397, note 111).

53 Edgeworth's anti-Methodism was not unusual for the time. See Brett C McInelly, '"I had rather be obscure. But I dare not": Women and Methodism in the Eighteenth Century' in *Everyday Revolutions: Eighteenth-Century Women Transforming Public and Private*, eds Diane E. Boyd and Marta Kvande (Cranbury: Rosemont Publishing, 2008), 146.

54 For example, Hilary Teynor Donatini writes that Lady Delacour's story offers a 'cautionary tale against what Edgeworth views as selfish and immoral behaviour' ('Moral and Medical Diagnosis,' 269).

55 Charland, 'Crichton,' 277.

56 Crichton, *Inquiry*, 98.

57 Impartiality is an important aspect of the novel's interest in the scientific method. See Chandler, 'Edgeworth and the Lunar Enlightenment' and Nicole Wright, 'Opening the Phosphoric "Envelope": Scientific Appraisal, Domestic Spectacle, and (Un) "Reasonable Creatures" in Edgeworth's *Belinda*, *Eighteenth-Century Fiction* 24, no. (Spring 2012), https://doi.org/10.3138/ecf.24.3.509.

58 Thame also sees Belinda as a therapist practising moral management therapy, and Donatini notes that 'Belinda's role in Lady Delacour's domestic reform resembles that of a doctor diagnosing and treating a patient' ('Moral and Medical Diagnosis,' 248). She does not, however, connect Belinda to moral therapy, as does Thame.

59 Roy Porter, *Madmen: A Social History of Madhouses, Mad-Doctors, and Lunatics* (Rpt *Mind Forg'd Manacles*, 1987; Stroud, Gloucestershire: Tempus Publishing, 2004), 209.

60 Andrew Scull, 'Moral Treatment Reconsidered: Some Sociological Comments on an Episode in the History of British Psychiatry' in *Madhouses, Mad-Doctors, and Madmen: The Social History of Psychiatry in the Victorian Era*, ed. Andrew Scull (Philadelphia: University of Pennsylvania Press, 1981), 110.

61 Thame also comments on the key role of moral management in this episode, but he overlooks the importance of how Belinda guides Lady Delacour's passions in this and in other scenes ('Madness and Therapy,' 280).

62 There is little agreement among scholars about how to interpret domesticity in this novel. Opinions vary from condemning Edgeworth for her support of domesticity to defending her. On the condemnation side, see Kowaleski-Wallace, *Their Fathers' Daughters*; Susan Greenfield, '"Abroad and at Home": Sexual Ambiguity, Miscegenation, and Colonial Boundaries in Edgeworth's *Belinda*,' *PMLA* 112, no. 2 (1997), https://doi.org/10.2307/463091; and Jordana Rosenberg, 'The Bosom of the Bourgeoisie: Edgeworth's *Belinda*,' *ELH* 70, no. 2 (2003), https://doi.org/doi:10.1353/elh.2003.0022. Defenders

170   *Women and madness in the early Romantic novel*

include Caroline Gonda, *Reading Daughters' Fictions, 1709–1834: Novels and Society from Manley to Edgeworth* (Cambridge: Cambridge University Press), 1996; Mitzi Myers, "'My Art Belongs to Daddy?'" Thomas Day, Maria Edgeworth, and the Pre-Texts of *Belinda*: Women Writers and Patriarchal Authority' in *Revising Women: Eighteenth-Century "Women's Fiction" and Social Engagement*, ed. Paula Backscheider (Baltimore: Johns Hopkins University Press, 2000); and Nicholas Mason, 'Class, Gender, and Domesticity in Maria Edgeworth's *Belinda*,' *Eighteenth-Century Novel* 1 (2001): 271.

63 That Lady Delacour would be fearful should not surprise readers, either then or now. Kaartinen describes the process of conducting a mastectomy: 'Surgeons had two methods available in treating cancer: cautery and surgery. Cautery basically meant burning, and was performed with hot irons; burning with medications was often called caustic remedy as well. Surgery was carried out with knives, scalpels and other such instruments. In the treatment of cancer, both methods were in use in the removal of tumours and whole breasts' (Kaartinen, *Breast Cancer*, 39). Such operations were performed without anaesthesia.

64 Dora Weiner, 'Mind and Body in the Clinic: Philippe Pinel, Alexander Crichton, Dominique Esquirol, and the Birth of Psychiatry' in *The Languages of Psyche: Mind and Body in Enlightenment Thought*, ed. G. S. Rousseau (Berkeley: University of California Press, 1990), 333 and 336, ebook.

65 Weiner, 'Mind and Body,' 337.

66 For example, Susan Greenfield writes: 'The cure constructs her as a domestic woman, whose internal femininity proves her fitness to serve the interior space of the home' ('"Abroad and at Home,"' 218).

67 I agree with Thame that this moment is not 'just a gender transformation in which Lady Delacour learns domesticity.' He views it as a moment in which women are 'endowed with a powerful and valuable interiority' that applies to men as well as women ('Madness and Therapy,' 282).

68 Patricia Matthew makes the insightful point that the presence of Helena at the conclusion signals a departure from novels in which the child dies, or the mother dies and the child lives. Patricia Matthew, 'Corporeal Lessons and Genre Shifts in Maria Edgeworth's *Belinda*,' *Nineteenth-Century Gender Studies* 4, no. 1 (2008), parag. 20, https://www.ncgsjournal.com/issue41/matthew.html. The establishment of a healthy mother–daughter relationship is thus another way that Edgeworth revises her contemporaries' narratives of psychological harm. In so doing, she expresses much more optimism about women's ability to find happiness and control their lives.

69 Allen, *David Hartley*, 293.

70 Thomas Day, author of the popular children's book *Sandford and Merton* (1783–1789), was a disciple of Rousseau and a friend of Edgeworth's father. Inspired by Rousseau's approach to female education, Day secured two orphaned girls and took them to France so they would be influenced by no one other than himself. His plan was to select one of them for his wife. See Mitzi Myers, '"Daddy,"' 123. Laura Kirkley builds on Myers' discussion of

Madness reconsidered in Belinda 171

Edgeworth's use of the Virginia subplot to critique Rousseau's ideas about women. See 'Translating Rousseauism.'

71 Myers, '"Daddy,"' 110.

72 Myers, '"Daddy,"' 110.

73 I acknowledge that Maria Venables' story in *Wrongs of Woman* does not necessarily end in tragedy, given that the most developed concluding fragment offers her a reprieve. However, Maria's suicidal state—even while pregnant—in several of the fragments cannot be disregarded.

74 Kirkley, 'Translating Rousseauism,' 110.

75 Kirkley 'Translating Rousseauism,' 83.

76 Linda Bree, in her notes to the Oxford edition of *Belinda*, makes the point that Edgeworth is playing with the multiple meanings of 'fancy,' including that of an imaginative artwork (*Belinda*, 486, note 172).

77 Readers will recall that Sophie is the name of the young woman Rousseau invents to be Émile's wife. Her upbringing and education are described in Book V.

78 Andrew McCann writes that 'Edgeworth is clearly attacking aspects of the pedagogical schemes inspired by Rousseau's theories of nature … in order to criticize not only the denial of autonomy to women and the enforcement of their seclusion in private space, but also the effacement of their actual natures.' Andrew McCann, 'Conjugal Love and the Enlightenment Subject: The Colonial Context of Non-identity in Maria Edgeworth's *Belinda*,' *NOVEL: A Forum on Fiction* 30, no. 1 (1996): 72, https://doi.org/10.2307/1345847.

79 Kirkley, 'Translating Rousseauism,' 111.

80 In this way, as Kilfeather notes, 'Edgeworth satirizes the notion that an ideal woman is formed in ignorance of the world' ('Introductory Note,' xxvii).

81 Kilfeather, 'Introductory Note,' xxxiii–xxxiv.

82 Thame, 'Madness and Therapy,' 282.

83 Priestley, *Hartley*, 217.

84 Kilfeather makes the intriguing observation that this passage is not from Williams' translation of Bernardin's *Paul et Virginie*. She speculates that it is Edgeworth's own translation from the original 1787 French edition ('Introductory Note,' xliv). Kilfeather's speculation is plausible given Edgeworth's facility with French. Edgeworth's translation (if it is hers) is smoother, more lyrical, and more natural than Williams', and it eliminates exoticism while accentuating Virginia's erotic feelings.

85 Louis Charland, 'John Locke on Madness: Redressing the Intellectualist Bias,' *History of Psychiatry* 25, no. 2 (2014): 145, https://doi.org/10.1177/09571 54X13518719.

86 For an in-depth discussion of the contradictions of modesty in the eighteenth century, see Ruth Bernard Yeazell, *Fictions of Modesty: Women and Courtship in the English Novel* (Chicago: University of Chicago Press, 1991).

87 Jennifer Ford, *Coleridge on Dreaming: Romanticism, Dreams, and the Medical Imagination* (Cambridge: Cambridge University Press, 1998), 14.

88 Priestley, *Hartley*, 223.

172 *Women and madness in the early Romantic novel*

89 Kirkley, 'Translating Rousseauism,' 111.
90 Mr Hartley had denied his marriage to Rachel's mother and abandoned them both. After living sometime in the West Indies, he returns to England in search of Rachel, but soon has a mental breakdown. Clarence comes to discover that there is a man looking for a girl who might be Virginia, and so has her portrait painted in the hope of locating him. Edgeworth introduces the possibility that Virginia may have an hereditary tendency toward madness through her father's condition; however, Mr Hartley's mental afflictions could also be understood as stemming from guilt and the suggestion of moral sickness so often associated with the West Indies in British literary works.
91 Priestley, *Hartley*, 223.
92 Priestley, *Hartley*, xviii–xix.
93 Captain Sunderland, whom Lady Delacour has painted as 'Paul,' is the man in the picture Rachel saw as a girl in the New Forest. Lady Delacour has figured out the connection and has had the portrait painted to test her theory and to test Virginia.
94 There are a number of compelling readings of the Virginia episode in the context of race, slavery, and colonialism. See McCann, 'Conjugal Love' and Greenfield, '"Abroad and at Home."' Kilfeather refers to Virginia as 'Clarence's colony, a virgin territory on which he plans to inscribe his meaning' ('Introductory Note,' xxxiii).
95 Myers, '"Daddy,"' 110.
96 Even Mr Percival, who is in general a good influence on both Belinda and Clarence, is a weak guardian of his ward, Mr Vincent. Mr Percival does not know that Mr Vincent is a gambling addict and deeply in debt.
97 Kilfeather, 'Introductory Note,' xi.
98 I make this argument in 'The Extraordinary Ordinary Belinda: Maria Edgeworth's Female Philosopher,' *Eighteenth-Century Fiction* 19, no. 4 (Summer 2007), https://doi.org/10.1353/ecf.2007.0027.
99 James Chandler makes a similar observation, although he has a different explanation, finding that 'Edgeworth's patience with the experiment shows the degree of her ongoing sympathy for Rousseau's critique of modern society' (Chandler, 'Lunar Enlightenment,' 102). Rather than feeling sympathy for Rousseau, I would argue that Edgeworth dismantles his gendered educational ideas to encourage readers not to take his fantasies quite so seriously.
100 Kilfeather, 'Introductory Note,' xi.
101 Myers, '"Daddy,"' 126.

5

The impossibility of love-madness:
The Father and Daughter

At age 16, Amelia Alderson (later, Opie) went in search of a love-mad maid, but she came home disappointed. In an autobiographical fragment published after her death, Opie dwells on her encounters with mentally afflicted people, beginning with her fear of two mad women in her neighbourhood when still in her nurse's arms.[1] She explains how she frequently visited the local 'bedlam' as a child to converse with the inmates from outside the gate. In one anecdote, she describes how she would stand at the window of an acquaintance's house across the street from the Norwich asylum and listen to a woman singing who supposedly had been crossed in love. Several years later, in the company of two male friends, Amelia entered the 'bedlam' in search of romantic characters, intent on finding a particular love-mad maid – a friend's servant just arrived who had gone mad after losing her lover. Going through the corridors, Amelia saw a different woman who looked promising, primarily because of the long dark hair that fell in 'picturesque confusion' around her shoulders. But this woman was too exhausted to talk, so Amelia was unable to have the sentimental encounter she was hoping for.[2] Opie describes how she passed right by the love-mad maid she was specifically seeking, and was only able to locate her after following the attendant's directions.[3] Opie makes it clear that this woman was not at all what she expected. She was unrecognizable as a love-mad maid, presumably because she lacked the requisite beauty and delicacy, but also because she failed to behave as expected. There was no plaintive song, no passive allure, no enticing mental vacancy. Instead, the woman was hostile and aggressive, and she let out a 'screaming' laugh that sent Amelia running terrified through the corridors of the asylum in search of her friends.[4] Opie's tone in recounting this experience in the 'bedlam' is bemused and worldly-wise. Quoting from *A Midsummer Night's Dream*, Opie says they were disappointed to find 'no "eye in a fine phrensy rolling," no interesting expression of sentimental woe, sufficient to raise its victims above the lowly walk of life in which they had always moved.'[5] She and her friends were looking for romantic victims of sensibility – people who

174   *Women and madness in the early Romantic novel*

loved too much and whose passion manifested in alluring, picturesque ways. What they found were nondescript individuals who lacked gentility, shuffled about, and had no affecting stories to tell. And they certainly did not find any love-mad maids who resembled those they had seen on the page, in prints, or on the stage. They went looking for the romance of madness, but what they found was its mundane reality.

Although she did not find a love-mad maid in the Norwich asylum, Opie offers one to her readers in her popular 'moral tale,' *The Father and Daughter*.[6] However, this character is far from the stereotypical sentimental figure Opie had once hoped to find. Opie's protagonist, Agnes Fitzhenry, experiences bouts of madness, but her affliction is caused by a lost father not by a lost lover.[7] And this mad woman is the perpetrator of an injurious act, rather than the victim of abuse or abandonment. Agnes is driven to episodes of madness herself because she caused her father to go mad when she ran away with her lover. David Thame observes that the tale challenges the conventions of love-madness, emphasizing that the 'introversion of the love-mad maiden is replaced by an active public role.'[8] But Opie does more than just challenge conventions by making the love-mad woman active in the public arena – she entirely upends both the standard formula of love-madness and her older contemporaries' revisions to that formula. In addition to making her love-mad maid largely responsible for her own afflictions, Opie positions Agnes' psychological crisis as the catalyst for her development into an autonomous, financially independent woman.

In some ways, rather than seeming like a challenge to models of love-madness, *The Father and Daughter* reads like a fallen-woman narrative that reinforces the status quo of a patriarchal society deeply invested in controlling the sexual activity of women. Indeed, Susan Staves makes this tale the prime example of the seduced-maiden story, a formula she argues expresses nostalgia for 'an idealized older form of the family undisturbed by the free exercise of the wills of the inferior members,' namely, of daughters.[9] Other scholars have concurred in seeing this tale as supportive of patriarchal families, in part because Agnes is harshly punished for making her own decision about her erotic life, and because the conclusion recommends that women yet 'innocent' should 'tremble with horror' rather than listen to the 'voice of the seducer' (156).[10] However, although the final paragraphs clearly warn women away from sexual transgression, that does not mean the story as a whole supports patriarchal control, as other scholars have, in fact, argued.[11] But neither does it mean that the tale critiques the avenues of male power that Wollstonecraft, Fenwick, and Hays have shown to be injurious to women.[12] Instead, Opie follows a different path. On the one hand, like her slightly older contemporaries, when she rewrites the love-mad maid's story she rejects misogynistic, physiological models of female madness in

Love-madness: The Father and Daughter 175

favour of psychogenic explanations. But on the other hand, in telling a new tale of love-madness, Opie avoids blaming women's mental afflictions on male actions. Indeed, Opie severs the connections between male avenues of control and female madness that so interested Wollstonecraft, Fenwick, and Hays. Whereas Edgeworth, in revising the narratives of female victimization, explores male responsibility in order to demystify men's power, Opie entirely rejects the idea that patriarchal control could be the cause of women's mental afflictions. In her story of love-madness, all the patterns of injury recognized by her contemporaries as responsible for causing female madness are reversed or eliminated. And while it might seem as if all these reversals and eliminations of her contemporaries' positions amount to a support, or at least a defence, of male power, this is not the case. Rather, Opie's revision of the story of the love-mad maid discloses the pathetic weakness of patriarchal power in its various manifestations and demonstrates the mental strength and moral courage of women.

The father's madness

The most important reversal in *The Father and Daughter* is that a man – the father – is in the position of the love-mad maid. Like the stereotypical female figure, Agnes' father loses his mind when he loses his beloved. This madness, however, is not occasioned by the loss of his wife, who dies when Agnes is very young. Rather, after his wife's death, Mr Fitzhenry resolves 'to form no second connection' for Agnes' sake (63). Like a young woman who loves too much, Mr Fitzhenry lives only for his beloved – in this case, his beloved is the daughter for whom he is unwilling to remarry and displace her from the primary spot in his affections.[13] When his beloved deserts him for another (as does the lover of the love-mad maid), he loses his mind.[14] And like the love-mad maid, Mr Fitzhenry demonstrates the sincerity of his all-consuming love, as well as his underlying psychological fragility, by being unable to bear the pain of her desertion.[15] He goes mad rather than have to live with the knowledge that the person he adored abandoned him for someone she loved more.[16]

In her version of love-madness, Opie positions the father as the innocent victim of his daughter's betrayal, rather than make the daughter the victim of her father's mercenary machinations, as is the case of the young mad women in both *The Man of Feeling* and *Wrongs of Woman*. Patriarchs, as represented by Mr Fitzhenry, are neither powerful nor abusive in this tale, but are rather fragile and impotent. The narrator explains that upon hearing of his daughter's flight with her lover, Mr Fitzhenry sits for hours 'absorbed in a sort of dumb anguish.' He then exclaims against her

176 *Women and madness in the early Romantic novel*

ingratitude, weeps tears of tenderness, and imagines how he will forgive her when she returns, married and repentant. Rather than go in search of the runaways, he resorts to his imagination, finding solace in picturing the scene of forgiveness. He wishes to care for her rather than punish her for her disobedience, and although she is the offender, he casts her as the sufferer in need of her father's consoling love: 'Poor girl! ... how miserable she will be when she comes to reflect! and how she will long for my forgiveness! and, O yes! I am sure I shall long as ardently to forgive her!' Then he imagines folding his arms around Agnes, 'whom he pictured to himself confessing her marriage to him, and upon her knees imploring his pardon' (72). If Mr Fitzhenry were to have his daughter back in the way that he imagines, on her knees begging for forgiveness, then the novel would be demonstrating the benignity of patriarchal power. But she does not come back, and so rather than fold her in his fatherly arms and forgive her, he goes mad. As Roxanne Eberle observes, Fitzhenry proves to be weaker than Agnes in that he responds to her 'ruin' not 'with his daughter's fortitude, but with madness.'[17]

Like the classic love-mad maid, Mr Fitzhenry is emotionally fragile before he loses his mind and is overly dependent on his beloved as his primary affective connection. When his beloved daughter leaves him, he is so devastated that he neglects his business and goes bankrupt while waiting for her to return. Because he has nothing to live for but love, he lapses into depression when his beloved abandons him. But when he learns that she has not just deserted but betrayed him as well – when he learns that she is living with Clifford as his mistress – he instantly goes mad. As the narrator says, 'this was the death-stroke to his reason' (92). Bankrupt and with no one to care for him, Mr Fitzhenry is put into the local madhouse that he himself had founded in his prosperous, charitable days. His madness manifesting in delusion, mania, and melancholia, Mr Fitzhenry thinks of nothing but Agnes, most of the time believing she is dead regardless of what anyone else might say, but at other times complaining of her ingratitude. In the asylum, the narrator explains, 'so complete was the overthrow his reason had received, that he knew no one, and took no notice of those whom friendship or curiosity led to his cell' (93). Thus, Mr Fitzhenry, in his single-minded fixation on his daughter, cannot recognize the people he has known all his life, and neither can he register the existence of anyone other than the dead Agnes he keeps in his mind. He swings between mania and melancholia, sometimes running wild with frenzy at the very idea of his daughter, other times lapsing into a deep depression over her loss. Rather than admit that she ran away and betrayed him and that she lives as a man's mistress, he thinks she is dead, which suggests his madness is a form of emotional protection through cognitive breakdown.

Love-madness: The Father and Daughter 177

The novel opens with Agnes making her way on foot back to her father's house with her child at her breast. After a narrative backtrack that brings the plot to where it began, Agnes encounters a mysterious figure in the woods that, after many pages, is revealed to be her father, now a madman having escaped from his keepers. Although the long scene culminates in the sentimental melodrama of Agnes' recognition of her father, Opie avoids making Mr Fitzhenry a sentimental figure when he first appears as a madman. Instead, she keeps the focus on Agnes' perceptions as she makes her way through the forest anticipating her father's forgiveness. Indeed, Opie rejects all sentimental portrayals of madness in this extended scene in order to convey the madman's lack of human reason and alienation from society and to emphasize the fear and horror that the madman provokes. The madman first seems to Agnes to be something between a human and an animal, but once she realizes the creature is a man, she is terrified by his behaviour. Her responses, however, are highly changeable, and thinking he might be a poor wanderer like herself, she determines to meet him; but then he looks hastily around, takes alarm, and runs off. She is forced to recognize based on his behaviour that he is not a poor wanderer like herself – not someone she can find community with in the midst of the forest – but some other kind of being that shuns society. He then appears to Agnes to be a criminal, and therefore someone whom she cannot sympathize with but must instead fear: 'But what can express the horror of Agnes when she again heard the clanking of the chain ... 'Sure he must be a felon ... O! my poor boy! perhaps we shall both be murdered!' (89). After another mile she finds the stranger now seated quietly on the ground, at which point she finally realizes that this being is neither an animal, nor a fellow wanderer, nor an escaped felon, but rather a madman. Agnes is able to determine that the man is deranged when she sees him talking and laughing to himself – the introverted communication signalling a mental absorption so intense he cannot interact appropriately with the outside world. Pitying him, Agnes wishes to share her food, but she has another abrupt emotional shift when she hears the clanking of his chain, at which point her pity shifts once again into terror and horror.

Opie's representation of how the madman appears to Agnes and of Agnes' changing perceptions and feelings gives the reader considerable anxiety on the way to the shocking emotional apex of the story (still to come): that this creature (animal, felon, murderer, madman) is Agnes' own father. But the extended scene does more than just cause emotional dilation. Using Agnes and the being she does not yet know is her father, the scene eliminates sentiment in its exploration of how people see and what they feel about the insane. Agnes experiences a range of feelings about this being: concern for an animal; sympathy for a fellow outcast; terror at a felon;

178   *Women and madness in the early Romantic novel*

and, finally, pity for a person who has lost his rational faculties. In this way, Agnes' perceptions map the ways mental patients were understood before they were sentimentalized late in the century: as animals, outcasts, criminals, and people afflicted with an incurable illness. By moving Agnes through these various categories before exposing who the figure is, Opie shocks the readers and forces them to recognize the enormity of what Agnes has done to her father in depriving him of his reason and his humanity.[18]

The daughter has so injured the father that, in his terrifying madness, he attempts to kill his own grandchild. Before Agnes recognizes the madman as her father, he initiates conversation, addressing her as 'woman' and asking if she sees 'them.' When she says she does not, he jumps for joy and appears uninterested in her, but then the noise of his chains wakes Agnes' child who screams in fear and attracts his attention. He bids her take it away, says he does not like children, and then, as the child continues to scream, 'the angry agitation of the maniac increased. —"Strangle it! strangle it! he cried,—do it this moment, or—."'(91). The two actually struggle physically for a few moments, as the madman clenches his fist and seizes Agnes' left arm while she defends her child with the other. Just when she thinks the lunatic will kill her child, a burst of wind frightens him off, his violence at this moment checked only by the stimulus of a different passion, which is the fear of capture. Although he does not consciously recognize Agnes, Mr Fitzhenry's infanticidal madness is directly connected to the injury she has inflicted on him. The baby's crying pierces the bubble of his preoccupations, forces his attention, and makes him think of what his own child has done. When the madman returns a little later, the child is asleep, and he is calmer. Seemingly aware of what he has just tried to do, the lunatic tells Agnes he does not like children because 'if you trust them they will betray you.' He then tells her he had a daughter once who died, although they told him she 'ran away from me with a lover' which he knew was false because 'she was good, and would not have deserted the father who doted on her' (91). Although he does not know that this woman is Agnes, his agitation comes from the conflict in his mind between what he wants to believe and what he knows at some level to be true – that his daughter has grievously injured him through her betrayal.[19]

Opie does not intend the madman in the forest to consciously know the lady is his daughter or to be aware that he has attempted to kill his own grandson. She does, however, set the scene up to suggest that at some level he knows who she is and has unconscious reasons for wanting to kill the baby. As the 'pledge' of Agnes' sexual relationship with Clifford, the baby embodies her betrayal and is the incarnation of her crime. It represents her shame, and so to do violence to it is to attack the very sin itself, punish it, and make it disappear. The baby is also responsible for Agnes' transformation

Love-madness: The Father and Daughter 179

from a daughter into a mother, which Mr Fitzhenry resents because the child competes with him for her love and attention. Mr Fitzhenry's most cherished wish is the resurrection of the father–daughter love dyad, which the child blocks through serving as evidence that their exclusive relationship can never be reconstituted. Mr Fitzhenry seems to believe, at some submerged level, that if he were to get rid of the child, then he could have his devoted daughter back with no other object to care for but himself, and no reminder that things were ever any different between them.

Agnes only realizes her tremendous culpability in wounding her father by having run away with Clifford when she recognizes that the madman who tried to kill her child is her own father. At this point – the emotional climax of the tale –'a death-like sickness, an apprehension so horrible as to deprive her almost of sense took possession [her] soul' when, in 'dreadful confirmation of her fears, Agnes beheld her father!!!' (92). The narrator confirms Agnes' perception and emphasizes that she is responsible for the derangement of the figure who stands before her: 'It was indeed Fitzhenry, driven to madness by his daughter's desertion and disgrace.' The scene shifts into sentimental mode when Agnes realizes her 'insane companion' is her 'injured father, the victim probably of her guilt,' puts her child on the ground, and prostrates herself at his feet, crying, 'O God! my father!' (93). The scene becomes even more emotionally overwrought when the name 'father' prompts a deranged fit in which Fitzhenry starts and gazes at her 'with savage wildness,' while his whole frame convulses. Displaying the horrifying extent of his madness, he runs away and dashes himself on the ground in a frenzy. 'He raved, he tore his hair; he screamed, and uttered the most dreadful execrations and with his teeth shut and his hands clenched, he repeated the word father, and said the name was mockery to him' (93). When Agnes presents herself before him and calls him 'father' it is as if she does violence to him all over again. There can be no denying that her betrayal and sexual sin have inflicted such emotional pain on him that not only has he gone mad, he has been completely transformed. Where he was once a loving father and successful merchant, a leader in his community, he is now a 'wildman,' a raving lunatic running through the woods attempting infanticide and inflicting physical harm on himself.[20]

Mr Fitzhenry does not, however, spend the entire tale in this state of violent insanity, but rather often exhibits an emotionally affecting docility. After he is captured and subdued, he is taken back to the asylum where he is calmer, but does sometimes become agitated – particularly when provoked by the topic of his daughter. And while Agnes is satisfied with nothing other than a full recovery, he improves considerably with more modern, more humane treatment. When her father is released from the asylum, Agnes takes him to a specialist who uses modern methods resembling those of

180   *Women and madness in the early Romantic novel*

moral management.[21] Mr Fitzhenry emerges from six months of treatment fatter and physically more healthy, suggesting that the humane approach of moral management is superior to the methods of physical deprivation and corporeal control practised in traditional asylums. That said, the doctor is not able to return him to sanity.[22] Although he remains mad, Mr Fitzhenry comports himself with greater self-control and appears much more content being out of the asylum and with his family, under the direction of a 'moral' approach to his care. Mr Fitzhenry briefly regains his sanity right before he dies, maintaining cogency long enough to recognize and forgive Agnes; but since he dies immediately thereafter, it cannot be said that he ever recovers from the injury that his daughter has inflicted upon him.

The weakness of men

Mr Fitzhenry's descent into madness at his daughter's betrayal and disgrace is the most striking, but far from the only, example of the weakness of men in *The Father and Daughter*. The tale presents an assortment of male characters who represent various forms of patriarchal power in an array of ineffectiveness. As Joanne Tong observes, fathers in this tale all represent 'crucial segments of society' that include the military, the aristocracy, and the government.[23] The ineffective patriarchs include the prominent merchants of this provincial town (Mr Fitzhenry and Mr Seymour); the military (Clifford); the aristocracy (Clifford's father and Clifford as Lord Mountcarrol); and local government (the board of governors of the asylum). While Clifford and his father exert their power in such a way as to injure Agnes, their methods illustrate their weakness: both lie as a form of control, but these are feeble lies, easy to disprove (although no one tries), that showcase their cowardice and moral weakness. The other men in positions of power, such as Mr Seymour, the father of Agnes' friend Caroline, and the board of governors, are sentimental hypocrites, easily swayed from harshness to indulgence; and even the physician who treats Mr Fitzhenry can do little for him.

When first introduced, Mr Seymour seems to be a stern father intent on keeping fallen women and his unfallen daughters in their place. When Agnes returns to town, her plan is to appeal to Mr Seymour, one of the town's leading citizens, for permission to work as a servant in the asylum where her father is confined. When she goes to Mr Seymour's house, his response makes it seem as if he, the representative of the town's male elite, is controlling and unforgiving. He will not allow her to enter the house, and he keeps Caroline, his daughter, under tight control by 'seizing her arm,' pushing her back into the parlour, and commanding her to her stay where

Love-madness: The Father and Daughter 181

she is when she attempts to see her friend. He then takes an authoritative attitude by telling Agnes, who has come with a penitential attitude, to 'leave his house directly' and orders the doors closed on her (106). This appears to be a moment that confirms patriarchal control as tyrannical, severe, and powerful in that Mr Seymour physically restricts his adult daughter, forbids her to interact with her friend, and exercises complete authority over his house.

But despite his efforts, Mr Seymour turns out to be almost as weak as Mr Fitzhenry. He is, as Joanne Tong describes him, 'a well-meaning but finally inferior guardian of the community.'[24] To start, Agnes does not go meekly away when he orders her from his house but rather chastises him and attempts to win his favour by reminding him of the proper Christian response: 'But will you not allow ... shelter for one moment the wretched and the penitent' (106). Although Mr Fitzhenry refuses her request, he is immediately undermined by the servant, William, who refuses to carry out his orders and instead insubordinately tells Mr Seymour that if he wants the door shut on Agnes, he must do it himself, saying he, William, is not 'hard-hearted enough' (107). And Caroline, too, disobeys her father by slipping out and running after Agnes to give her 20 guineas with a note that reads, 'For my still dear Agnes—would I dare say more!' (108). The wilful disobedience of both servant and daughter undermines the father's authority in his own household and shows that patriarchal power, far from being strong enough to injure women's minds and ruin their lives, is weak and ineffectual. Moreover, although Mr Seymour thinks he is taking the moral high ground, the other three characters in the scene either implicitly or explicitly reproach him for his lack of Christian charity – a lack that translates into moral weakness. Whereas William wishes to show gratitude for Agnes' past goodness to him and Caroline offers charity and love regardless of what her friend has done, Mr Seymour shuts his door on her, unable to practise the Christian virtues demonstrated by his servant and daughter.

As it turns out, Mr Seymour is not the rigid, patriarchal authority he appears to be, but rather a more nuanced figure, a man who is weak and hypocritical, but also kind-hearted. The narrator characterizes Mr Seymour as a man of feeling who did not want to be severe toward Agnes and wished it had not been necessary. However, the narrator explains several factors that make him disregard his compassion. Primarily, he believes he must make an example of Agnes to his daughters, to forcibly show them that 'the loss of virtue must be to them the loss of friends' (109). Mr Seymour is also worried that the morally rigid mother of Caroline's fiancé could develop a prejudice against Caroline were he to let Agnes into the house, and call off the wedding. And, according to the narrator, Mr Seymour is ruled by anxieties about what the 'world' might say about him (109). Although the

182   *Women and madness in the early Romantic novel*

narrator intends to show Mr Seymour's softer side when he feels proud of Caroline for giving Agnes money, his response illustrates that he is a hypocrite and a coward. He does not chastise Caroline for disobeying him as an authoritative father would, but instead is pleased that his daughter has lived up to the virtues he wished he could have acted on himself. But he is too cowardly to show his daughter his pride or to allow it to become known publicly that his family has helped Agnes. Although Mr Seymour is unwilling to sully his own household with Agnes' presence or to allow his grown daughter to follow her conscience, he decides to help Agnes by recommending her scheme of working as a servant in the asylum to the other trustees, feeling 'pleased to have an opportunity of obliging her, without injuring himself' (109). Far from being a man with sufficient power to inflict harm on women, Mr Seymour, the second most prominent father in the story, cannot muster the fortitude to manage either his household or his anxieties and is too faint-hearted to even know, much less follow, the right course of action.

The other town fathers – the governors of the asylum – resemble Mr Seymour in that they wish to project power but are ruled by emotions they cannot control. Rather than represent an injurious avenue of power driving Agnes to madness, the town fathers are more or less putty in her hands when she appears before them to request access to her father. When confronted by Agnes, appearing before them as a sorrowful penitent, the members of the board are immediately impacted by their emotions and by a psycho-sexual response that reveals the attraction they feel for younger women who remind them of their daughters. When they look at Agnes, their first feeling is shock at how much she has fallen in status, as they see a young woman they once admired and whose father they envied for 'the possession of such a daughter' now before them in the humble garb of a servant.

> Every one present beheld with surprise, and with *stolen* looks of pity, the ravages which remorse and anguish had made in her form, and the striking change in her apparel; for every one had often followed with delight her graceful figure through the dance, and gazed with admiration on the tasteful varieties of her dress; every one had listened with pleasure to the winning sound of her voice, and envied Fitzhenry the possession of such a daughter. (110)

The typographical emphasis on '*stolen*' highlights the governors' hypocrisy and concern for others' opinions. Each town father wishes to hide his shock and dismay at Agnes' appearance – his concern that she is no longer the attractive, prosperous, charming young woman she once was. Through giving the reader access to their thoughts, the narrator shows the extent of their previous attraction to this young woman whom they identified as

Love-madness: The Father and Daughter 183

another man's daughter. They enjoyed watching her dance in her beautiful clothes; they admired her graceful figure; and they took pleasure in the sound of her voice. But now, they see from Agnes' body, body language, and clothes that she is not the woman she once was. Although they know that Agnes' sexual transgression drove her father mad, they are instantly moved to pity, in part because of their awareness of their own daughters' susceptibility to the machinations of seducers. Consequently they all, as if of one mind, drop their resolution to receive Agnes with severity. While the governors' instant pity for Agnes is certainly intended to signify their benevolence in an age of sensibility, their weakness is apparent in their waffling and in their being guided by feeling rather than principle. The fact that their feelings overwhelm their principles – regardless of whether those initial principles might have been unduly harsh – makes them as a body soft and morally pliable.

The town patriarchs respond to Agnes according to the sentimental script for men of feeling who encounter a seduced maiden or a love-mad maid. Thus, they pity Agnes as men of feeling do – for having been the victim of a libertine's seductions. They certainly do not think about the structures of power that permit and encourage libertines to 'ruin' women, but neither do they consider Agnes as an autonomous adult who made decisions injurious to her father and to herself. Instead, they merely see her as a once beautiful daughter brought low by seduction who merits charity rather than severity for her victimization. The novel clearly represents pity as preferable to the condemnation offered by the appropriately named Mrs Macfiendy, who says hateful things in public about Agnes, but it also suggests that the local patriarchs' melting attitude toward the fallen woman is not productive. And, the narrative suggests that their motivations come from the wrong place – from feeling, repressed desire, and paternal anxiety rather than from Christian principles of forgiveness. Lacking the courage to use their compassion as the basis for moral action and unable to harness or articulate Christian virtues, the members of the board go home with their hearts full of sympathy for Agnes but give short evasive answers to their families. Their response as a board and as individuals at home suggests the general ineffectiveness of the pity men of feeling offer to women brought low by seduction – an ineffectiveness inseparable from their desire to see such women as innocent, childlike victims.

Although the local patriarchs choose not to afford Agnes any agency in her seduction, they are right that a libertine has treated her poorly. Agnes' seducer, Clifford, has tricked her into being his mistress, and he has manipulated her into staying with him by making her believe her father has remarried. But he is liable to injury, as well, from her and from his own actions. Thus, even the libertine who is partially to blame for Agnes' and

184 *Women and madness in the early Romantic novel*

her father's madness is weak, as are the other men in this tale. Clifford first shows his ability to be injured by Agnes when, after she has confronted him about his deceptions, he fears that her feelings about him will change. Distressed that he has 'incurred the contempt of Agnes,' he realizes that she must soon 'cease to love the man whom she had once learned to despise' (131). When Clifford learns that Agnes has escaped in the night with the child into a storm, 'he [falls] into an agony amounting to phrensy,' then his senses fail him, and he collapses unconscious onto a sofa. When he recovers, it is to a 'sense of misery and unavailing remorse' (132). When Clifford realizes that his machinations have put Agnes in danger, his emotions are so overpowering as to cause a (male) hysterical episode. And like Agnes, his emotional wellbeing is thereafter compromised by remorse. Clifford ends up marrying a disagreeable woman for her money and becoming an alcoholic who hastens his own death through dissipation.

Whereas Opie's older contemporaries (Wollstonecraft, Fenwick, and Hays) present the libertine as a man who never pays for the injuries he inflicts on women, Opie's libertine lover suffers more than Agnes herself. The final part of the narrative, in which Clifford – now Lord Mountcarrol – passes through town during the funeral, is chaotic and highly unlikely, even for a tale little concerned with probability. At this point, Agnes' story is complete. Her father has regained his sanity long enough to recognize and forgive her before dying, and she has died as well. But Opie is presumably not satisfied with how she has left the villain of the tale and so she adds a coda designed to show the extent of the libertine's self-injuries. In this coda, Lord Mountcarrol discovers that Agnes was alive only to find that she is dead. Arriving in the town with a new (second) wife, Clifford is already in a state of mental unease, 'incapable of resting in one place for a minute together,' his remorse having unsettled his mind (155). When he learns from Mr Seymour that Agnes considered him a 'monster of inhumanity' for never having come in search of her, and that she 'dismissed him entirely from her remembrance,' Clifford is so overcome that he experiences a mental and emotional breakdown: 'he beat his breast, he rolled on the floor in frantic anguish, lamenting, in all the bitterness of fruitless regret, that Agnes died without knowing that he loved her, and without suspecting that while she was supposing him unnaturally forgetful of her and her child, he was struggling with illness caused by her desertion, and with a dejection of spirits which he had never, at times, been able to overcome' (155). Clifford the libertine is at this point subject to various mental illnesses as a result of his having tricked, betrayed, and seduced Agnes, and he is distraught to the point of a breakdown to learn that she never knew he loved her.

In contrast to Agnes, who is finally able to receive her father's blessing and who earns both social and (one assumes) heavenly forgiveness for her

Love-madness: The Father and Daughter 185

sins, Clifford has no such relief. The narrator says, he feels 'all the horrors of remorse, without the consolations of repentance' (136). Thus, when he dies, he dies without having expiated his sins. To quote Roxanne Eberle: 'The narrator promises even greater punishment in the afterlife since Clifford never fully acknowledges the horrendous moral wrongs he has committed.'[25] Moreover, he is tormented while alive by the extinction of his family line. Clifford's adoption of his and Agnes' son, Edward, raises the boy's status and gives him wealth, but it cannot make him the legitimate heir of an aristocratic title. After two years, Clifford is 'worn to the bone by the corroding consciousness that Agnes had died in the persuasion of his having brutally neglected her' (156). And, never having had any other children, he is 'almost frantic with regret that [Edward] was not legally his son' (156). The narrator offers little sympathy for Clifford, informing the reader that he was selfish to the end, attentive only to his own misery, and unaware of having inflicted misery on others. Thus, the libertine who ruins the young woman, and is generally exempt from punishment in stories about mad maidens and fallen women, is among the most emotionally tormented characters in Opie's tale.

The daughter's madness

The governors of the asylum deem Agnes a victim of seduction, but the narrator gives her considerable responsibility for her sexual transgressions, and Agnes blames herself for her father's madness. While it might seem as if Opie is blaming the victim, it could be argued that her intention is to de-victimize women as they are presented in sentimental literature and socially critical novels and give them agency and responsibility. With Agnes, this agency begins with how, exactly, she is manipulated by Clifford into eloping with him. Opie quotes from fellow novelist and playwright Elizabeth Inchbald's *Nature and Art* (1796), another fiction about a fallen woman, to explain the 'ingredients,' as she calls them, that go into Agnes' passion for Clifford, the most important of which is 'pride in the object.' Agnes respects Clifford's superior understanding and brilliant talents, esteems his apparent virtues, and finds him attractive, but most of all, she reveres his 'high birth and great expectations,' feeling flattered that such a man is interested in her – making 'pride in the object' the greatest 'excitement to love' (68). Moreover, the narrator explains that Agnes overestimates and takes pride in her ability to read character; thus, having esteemed Clifford, she cannot correct herself. Between her overconfidence, her attraction to Clifford, and her pride in being the object of his affections, Agnes is easily convinced to elope with her lover and leave her devoted father, who has declined to

186 *Women and madness in the early Romantic novel*

approve the match.[26] And when Clifford comes up with an excuse to go to London rather than Scotland, where they could be legally married, Agnes' pride and overconfidence prevent her from demanding to be returned to her father.[27] Thus, while Agnes is up against an accomplished seducer, she is also portrayed as responsible for the actions that drive her father mad and that cause her so much pain.

Although Agnes lives for some months with Clifford as his mistress, she does not fully understand the seriousness of her actions until she finds she is pregnant and realizes that Clifford will not marry her before the baby is born. The realization that she would 'in all probability be a mother before she became a wife' prompts her first bout of madness in which she 'rolled herself on the floor in a transport of frantic anguish, and implored Heaven in mercy to put an end to her existence' (75). The fit itself is not motivated by discovering that Clifford is lying to her (this is yet to come) but rather by the realization that she has betrayed and disappointed her father: 'O! my dear injured father!' she cries, 'I who was once your pride, am now your disgrace!' (75). Agnes' rolling shows that her emotional anguish at having injured her father is so acute as to necessitate the physical response of a fit, which original readers would have understood as hysteria. While being a man's mistress is certainly shameful, being pregnant with an illegitimate child is even more so as it gives visual, concrete evidence of what, without a pregnancy, is only imagined or supposed. The pregnancy is thus the material evidence of the destruction of her family and of her moral crime against her father, whom she realizes, now for the first time, has been injured by her actions. Her disgrace is his disgrace, and she is finally aware that her relationship with her father has been severed. From the point she knows she will deliver an illegitimate child to the end of the tale, Agnes stays in an emotional state in which any additional shock causes an hysterical fit. For example, when Clifford returns six months after the baby's birth, he tells her he has sworn to his own father never to marry Agnes without his consent, at which point Agnes' whole body 'trembles with agitation' and, recriminating herself for sacrificing her father for him, and chastising him for the oath, she falls into a 'long a deep swoon' (77). Although Shelley King and John Pierce describe Agnes as a 'model of sensibility,' there is no indication before she first realizes she will deliver the baby unmarried that she is prone to fits, swoons, or other nervous disorders or sensitivities.[28] However, she has put herself into a condition of extreme emotional stress brought on by remorse, anxiety, and fear that now makes her susceptible to hysterical fits and maniacal episodes.

Agnes' self-inflicted, overwrought emotional state and psychological fragility prompt an extensive hysterical attack when she goes to the theatre and overhears a conversation between an unnamed army officer and a

Love-madness: The Father and Daughter

187

nobleman sitting behind her. Through this eavesdropping, Agnes learns that Clifford is an accomplished seducer about to marry another woman for her money. She also learns that she is known by name to be Clifford's 'favourite mistress' and that the men know enough for one of them to opine that she 'deserved a better fate' (83). Further, Agnes discovers from the conversation that Clifford has fed her false information about her father's remarriage to prevent her from returning to her 'afflicted parent,' as one of the speakers describes him. As far as the supposed remarriage goes, Agnes hears the nobleman say it is more likely that Agnes' father is dead than that he is married again (83). Agnes sits quietly, although in distress, through the revelation that Clifford is engaged to someone else and that she is known to be his mistress, but at the very idea of her father's death, she has a loud and public breakdown: 'At the mention of this horrible probability, Agnes lost all self-command, and, screaming aloud, fell back on the knees of his astonished lordship, reiterating her cries with all the alarming helplessness of phrensy' (83). Agnes is then taken for a drunken prostitute, insulted by some theatre goers, and struck by the man in the next box while the nobleman and the officer behind attempt to assist her, unaware that she is Miss Fitzhenry. Agnes exclaims, 'O! God! my brain is on fire!' and then jumps over the seat and runs into the lobby, followed by her landlady, Mrs Askew, who cannot keep pace with Agnes' 'desperate speed' (83).[29] The screaming, falling back, and frenzy mark this as a maniacal episode (anticipating that of her father later in the forest) that continues with her frantic leaping over seats and running through the theatre with a brain 'on fire.' Agnes can control her behaviour until the topic of her father's possible death comes up, at which point she becomes emotionally overwhelmed. While she may not have lost cognitive awareness, she has in this instance lost emotional control and the ability to manage her behaviour appropriately in public.

Importantly, and in contrast to novels in which women are emotionally victimized by men, there are no injurious structures of patriarchal control in this novel. Clifford has lied to and manipulated Agnes, but he has largely acted on his own, with the exception of the man he has paid to deliver a false message about Mr Fitzhenry.[30] The nobleman at the theatre and his companion, the army officer, resemble the governors of the asylum in that their interactions with Agnes are another instance in this novel of the relative neutrality of men when it comes to injuring women. On the one hand, they are not colluding against her – they are not part of a web of male power responsible for her mental afflictions. On the other, they do nothing substantial to assist her. The nobleman knows her entire story, even to the details of Clifford's lies about her father, but has not been moved to intervene. And while the gentlemen show their gallantry by grabbing the

188 *Women and madness in the early Romantic novel*

man who has struck her and briefly supporting her when she falls on them, they are unable to help her any further. By the time the nobleman realizes who she is, she is already back with Clifford and Mrs Askew, the landlady. In an odd moment of indeterminacy for a tale with an omniscient third-person narration, the narrator wonders if the nobleman would have offered Agnes the 'protection of a friend' (84), or if she would have accepted; but nothing comes of this narrative uncertainty, presumably because male assistance is not part of Agnes' story. The nobleman, the embodiment of the male ruling class, is left suspended by indeterminacy. He is not part of the problem; but neither does he offer a solution. He is not the target of critique; but neither is he upheld as the foundation of society and the saviour of suffering women.

Like her breakdown in the theatre, Agnes' subsequent attacks of madness originate in guilt over the injuries she has inflicted on her father and her destruction of their parent–child relationship. One of these attacks stems from an anxiety about her child that overlaps with her agony about her father. At their exit from the forest, when the keepers take her father back into custody, Agnes experiences considerable emotional duress and a mental collapse. When she tells the keepers the madman is her father, they mock her, and one of them laughs at her 'wild anguish,' saying 'we shall have the daughter as well as the father soon, I see, for I do not believe there is a pin to choose between them' (95), suggesting maliciously that like her father, she is mad. Agnes loses consciousness as a result of this hysterical attack, and when she awakens, she looks around with 'renewed phrensy' for her child, who is sleeping on the ground, at which point she becomes convinced that she will be the destroyer of her child as well as of her father. Once again displaying the socially inappropriate behaviour of a maniacal state, she runs along the road with the child to the first cottage she comes to, sinks on her knees, and holds the child out to the woman of the house, asking her to save the boy, who is inert from cold. The boy recovers, but Agnes is still frantic, and her excessive emotions lead the cottagers, who are 'wholly unaccustomed' to such 'violent expressions and actions' to think she is insane, 'an idea which the pale cheek and wild look of Agnes strongly confirmed' (96). Agnes then bears out this suspicion by talking wildly of her father. After the wife attempts to console her by saying she recently lost her own father, but is comforted by knowing that she did her duty by him, the woman remarks: 'O! it must be a terrible thing to lose one's parents when one has not done one's duty to them' (97). Agnes then reaches the height of her insanity and grabs a kitchen knife with the intent to 'put an end to her existence' (97). When the wife takes the knife, Agnes' mania suddenly turns into hysterical catalepsy: 'her violence instantly changed into a sort of stupor; then throwing herself back on the bed on which she was sitting,

Love-madness: The Father and Daughter 189

she lay with her eyes fixed, and incapable of moving' (97). An appeal to maternal duty wakes Agnes from her stupor and seems to restore her sanity as she embraces the child, lies back on the bed, and falls asleep.

The narrator attributes Agnes' excess of emotion in this episode to her 'cultivated sensibility,' which would have been a familiar explanation to contemporary readers, despite the fact that there is little evidence elsewhere in the text that too much sensibility is the cause of Agnes' madness. As far as explanations for her madness go, Gary Kelly's reading has been influential. He argues that Opie's fictions are dominated by the female characters who feel 'remorse for incurring a debt,' and who repay their debt through the public performance of 'inner emotional distress' in the form of 'benevolence, "phrenzy," or even madness.'[31] I argue instead that Agnes' distress comes not from her inability to repay her father for his devotion, but rather from the injuries she has inflicted on him through her own actions. She feels a guilt so profound it destroys her emotional control, compromises her social behaviour, and makes her want to take her own life. Rather than a debt that can never be repaid, Agnes feels a sense of guilt that can only be relieved if the person she has injured – her father – forgives her. But Agnes has so damaged her father that he is no longer a person who can offer forgiveness because he is not in his right mind. Given that she seeks forgiveness, Agnes cannot be satisfied with a mild improvement in her father's behaviour or mood or with her own self-denying devotion to him. Instead, she continues to hope and expect that he will regain his sanity, which adds the stress of perpetually disappointed expectations to her unrelenting remorse. As Melina Esse observes, 'Agnes's greatest sorrow is that ... despite her loving care and attendance on him, [her father] does not recognize her and insists she is dead.'[32] Agnes can never make her pain go away because she can never make her father believe she still exists so that she might be forgiven. Instead, she determines to atone for her sins through hard labour and through publicly embracing a fallen station in life. But no amount of atonement or debasement can take away the guilt because, as long as her father remains mad, she cannot be forgiven. She is trapped, then, true to her name's origins as 'lamb of God,' in a situation of perpetual self-sacrifice because atonement must replace the forgiveness she cannot receive.

Agnes' need for her father to fully recover leads to a state of delusive monomania in which the only thing she can think about and the only thing she cares about is her father. This fixation affects her personal relationships, making her harsh to Fanny, her most devoted friend, and neglectful of her child. For example, when Agnes explains her plan to Fanny, that she will take her father into her own house and care for him, Fanny is worried about Agnes' wellbeing, but before she can express her concerns Agnes, in a manner 'overpoweringly severe,' tells her to 'be silent' and then 'angrily'

190   *Women and madness in the early Romantic novel*

leaves the room (138). And when Fanny expresses reservations about Mr Fitzhenry's improvement, Agnes replies cruelly: 'I tell you he will, he certainly will recover; and those are not my friends who doubt it,' leaving Fanny in tears (148). She speaks to Fanny in terms of 'when' her father recovers, makes plans to take him to London for more treatment, and 'every day fancied his symptoms of returning reason' while 'no one of her friends dared to contradict her' (150). Agnes' fixation on her father also brings on a brooding melancholy in which she fantasizes about her father rather than tends to her son. The narrator explains that, when Edward goes to play with the cottagers' children, Agnes is happier alone because she 'delighted to brood in uninterrupted silence over the soothing hope, the fond idea, that alone stimulated her to exertion, and procured her tranquillity' (128). In order to escape from the constant torture of her guilt, Agnes retreats into fantasies that, requiring all the energies of her mind and body, sap her physical and psychological strength and leave her uninterested in her child. Previously, Agnes lost emotional control and the ability to maintain socially appropriate behaviour when under extreme emotional duress. But now, and for the remainder of the tale, she lives in a compromised mental and emotional state marked by irrational hopes, a dereliction of duty to others, irritability, and mental distraction.

For two years, Agnes lives with her father, following the specialist's advice and expecting him to recover. One day, she gets what she has been living for: Mr Fitzhenry awakens to his senses and recognizes Agnes, at which point she falls on her knees and asks for his forgiveness. Her father answers, 'Thou art restored to me,—and God knows how heartily I forgive thee!' and he embraces her (150). Mr Fitzhenry wishes to converse with her, but Agnes 'pours out the hasty effusions of her joy' and is unaware that her father, 'overcome with affection, emotion, and, perhaps, sorrowful recollections, was struggling in vain for utterance' (150). Even at this point, at the very end of her story, Agnes is still to blame for how she behaves toward her father in that her selfish desire to express her feelings leaves him unable to speak. Mr Fitzhenry manages to bless her before falling back on his pillow and abruptly dying. The shock of having what she has lived for during the past five years suddenly snatched away is too much for Agnes who, as the narrator explains, when convinced her father is dead, falls into a 'state of stupefaction, from which she never recovered' (151). Like Opie herself, Agnes is buried in the same grave as her father. From a late eighteenth-century medical perspective, Agnes can be understood as being in a delicate physical and emotional state after so much strain and self-sacrifice. The shock, then, of recovering her father and then losing him, is too much for body and mind to bear, and so it kills her. Although Joanne Tong argues that Agnes 'successfully wills her own death' to spend eternity with her

Love-madness: The Father and Daughter   191

father because 'no physiological cause is given for [her] sudden collapse,' Agnes' death is explainable according to the period's understanding of the impact of an acute emotional crisis on the body.[33] Like Mary Raymond and Sibella Valmont, Agnes began life strong and vibrant, untouched by any inherent weakness that might give her a propensity for mental disease. And like Mary and Sibella, the events of her life wear away her emotional and physical resilience until she is killed by the shock of a profound emotional experience on a weakened physical and mental system. But in stark contrast to Mary and Sibella, Agnes is not destroyed by cumulative male injuries, but rather by a self-inflicted emotional wound.

The strength of women

Although the narrator's single comment in the cottager scene about Agnes' 'cultivated sensibility' and her fits of madness suggest she might be fragile, she is, in fact, quite psychologically robust. At the beginning of the tale, when the narrator describes Agnes and her father, there is no sign that she is particularly delicate, or even that she is a woman of sensibility. Rather, she is described as being lovely, gentle, and good-tempered, but also strong-minded and intelligent: 'Agnes united to extreme beauty of face and person every accomplishment that belongs to her own sex, and a great degree of that strength of mind and capacity for acquiring knowledge supposed to belong exclusively to the other' (65). In terms of what Agnes does – run away with an officer and not get married – the introduction sets her up as a person who should definitely have known better.[34] Once Agnes comes to realize the consequences of her actions – after the scene in the theatre and Clifford's admission of his engagement to another woman – she determines, quite resolutely, to leave him. Showing integrity and courage, she says to Clifford: 'think not, fallen as I am, that I will ever condescend to receive protection and support, either for myself or my child, from a man whom I know to be a consummate villain. You have made me criminal, but you have not obliterated my horror for crime, and my veneration for virtue—and, in the fulness of my contempt, I inform you, sir, that we shall meet no more' (85). This act of moral fortitude is Agnes' first step toward redemption. All in one moment, she accepts guilt, refuses to continue her illegitimate life, announces her independence, declares her desire to regain her self-respect, and separates from the man she now knows to be a liar and a fraud. As Roxanne Eberle observes, 'Agnes responds to her lover's betrayal by inaugurating a new identity as a proud if prodigal "fallen woman."'[35] She then, at night in a terrible storm, and with only a shawl wrapped around herself and her child, sets out to return to her father and,

192   *Women and madness in the early Romantic novel*

if possible, to receive his forgiveness (86). The strain of her guilt certainly causes her bouts of madness and her monomaniacal fixation on curing her father, but her psychological afflictions do not cancel out her fortitude and moral courage.

Agnes demonstrates this strength and courage through her ability to persevere in her penitential plan despite her crushing guilt and shame.[36] When Agnes awakens her first morning back in her home town to discover Fanny has made an elaborate breakfast, she refers to herself as the 'prodigal,' and like the prodigal son, she plans to work as a servant for her father (in the asylum) to make amends for her transgressions (105). As a servant, she will have access to him, be in a position to care for him, and be able debase herself in a way she feels is necessary for her penitence. She says to Fanny that she has been 'severely punished' for her crime and that she intends to live out the rest of her days in 'solitude and labour' (104). The punishment of her father's madness and her inability to receive forgiveness is not enough for Agnes, who feels she must suffer through isolation and labour that is degrading for one of her station.[37] Although Agnes does not end up working as a servant, she does take on low-level employment as a shawl maker, and later she produces crafts that the wealthy townspeople buy. Agnes' penance is dependent upon exposing herself to the execrations of society, to feeling herself despised, and to living through her labour. She says to Fanny that she 'should welcome insults as part of the expiation she meant to perform' (105). Later, when she refuses assistance from the governors of the asylum, she tells them she will work to support herself and her son, explaining that 'from the wretchedness into which my guilt has plunged me, nothing henceforward but industry shall relieve me' (112). That Agnes, a privileged young lady raised in comfort, is able to support herself and her child for many years through labour – and do it in the town where she was raised – is testament to her strength of character and her courage.

While Agnes' determination to work too much and too hard and to expose herself to condemnation could be seen as an exaggerated response to her transgression, or as a form of masochism, it is in fact a means to achieve her ends. In explaining to Fanny why she does not dress as a wealthy woman and why she insists on taking any kind of work available, she says: 'it would be presumption in any woman who has quitted the path of virtue to intrude herself, however high her rank might be, on the meanest of her acquaintance whose honour is spotless' (104). Agnes is aware that her sexual transgression has cast her out of her own class and thrust her down to a level below that of a respectable working-class woman. To present herself as if that were not the case would be to show people she thinks she is better than she is. The only way Agnes can expiate her sins, and the only

Love-madness: The Father and Daughter   193

way she can demonstrate her penitence to the community, is through this public debasement.[38] Agnes' determination to work for her support and to refuse all charity is a way to signal her virtue and the genuineness of her repentance. As she says to the governors of the asylum: 'I will not eat the bread of idleness, as well as of shame and affliction, and shall even rejoice in being obliged to labour for my support, and that of my child—happy, if, in fulfilling well the duties of a mother, I may make atonement for having violated those of a daughter' (112). While Agnes is represented as being authentic in her desires, her use of labour as a way to demonstrate penitence is successful in that the gentlemen realize, with admiration, that hers is an 'expiatory plan of life' (112); and while Agnes at first is met with reproach from friends and acquaintances (with the exception of Fanny and Caroline), eventually the majority of the community becomes convinced of her repentance and is won over by her ceaseless work and self-sacrifice for her father.[39]

Agnes' strategic self-presentation is most evident when she appeals to the board of governors for permission to work at the asylum in order to be close to her father. Agnes understands that to get what she wants from these men, she must impact them emotionally. As Melina Esse observes, Agnes is 'self-conscious [in her] use of sentimental conventions to further her own aim of obtaining forgiveness from her father.'[40] Rather than come right out and say that she would like to try to restore her father to reason through spending time with him, she manipulates her audience's emotional interest through her appearance and through the way she tells her story. As the narrator observes, she gives vent to tears and speaks to the men in a weak voice, 'however, as she proceeded, she gained courage, remembered it was in her interest to affect her auditors, and make them enter warmly into her feelings and designs' (110). Even in the midst of her crying, she remembers that she is performing before an audience with a specific goal in mind. Indeed, in Esse's words, 'she is not only a weeper but also an observer and an actor.'[41] She then tells her story concisely from the time of her leaving Clifford to her father 'being torn from her by the keepers' (111). Agnes here only tells part of her story – the part most likely to have an emotional impact on her audience – because this is the part of her greatest suffering. And it is the part that appeals most to the listeners' own positions as fathers of daughters. All that passes between her leaving Clifford and having her father torn from her in the forest is material bound to excite the pity of older men who are already kindly disposed from considering her as a once-beautiful victim of a seducer's machinations. When Agnes breaks into tears and cannot continue, the narrator observes, 'she had the satisfaction of seeing that the tears of her auditors kept pace with her own' (111). With her emotional outburst, Agnes proves to her audience her devotion to her father,

194   *Women and madness in the early Romantic novel*

which secures their pity and makes them weep for her suffering. When she has them on her side, she asks to work at the asylum and expresses complete contrition: 'I feel it my duty to be with him ... and, if there be any balm for a heart and conscience so wounded as mine, I must find it in devoting all my future days to alleviate, though I cannot cure, the misery I have occasioned' (111). Agnes does not get what she asked for from the town fathers – they will not permit her to debase herself by working as a servant – but she does get what she wants, which is access to her father. Thus, Agnes, despite the impact of remorse on her mental health – and despite her earlier hysterical fits – manages her appearance, controls her story, secures compassion, and gets more than what she originally wanted from the patriarchs who control the town.

Not only does Agnes exhibit intelligence, moral courage, and the ability to withstand social pressure, so too do Fanny and Caroline, the other young women in the tale.[42] Nowhere in this narrative are women controlled by men or injured by patriarchal power. Instead, they are able to think for themselves and act as independent moral agents.[43] When Agnes comes to her door, Fanny, the daughter of her former nurse, is delighted to see her and does not for a minute think about her friend's sexual transgression. Instead, she declares her devotion to Agnes: 'Indeed, my dear young lady, I love you as well as my mother did, and will do as much for you as she would have done' (103). Fanny thinks only of the assistance Agnes gave to her mother and herself in times of need and of Agnes' other charitable endeavours (103). Fanny passes the test of gratitude, and her loyalty and moral courage are subsequently demonstrated when she is ostracized and loses her pupils as a result of having taken Agnes into her house. She ends up having to close her school after having 'loudly raved against the illiberality which had robbed her of the society of all she held dear' and in her leisure time she inveighs against the cruelty of those who had driven Agnes from her house (127). Opie rewards Fanny for her loyalty and her courage by having a local tradesman fall in love with her, primarily because of her 'faithful attachment to Agnes,' and because he finds her quite beautiful in her 'virtuous indignation' (127). At no point does this new husband attempt to control Fanny or pressure her about her dishonoured friend.

While Fanny provides material support, friendship, and, for a while, a place to stay, Caroline is the driving force behind Agnes' eventual acceptance by society. As the 'moral voice of the novel' who outlines the 'moral middle ground,' to use Katherine Binhammer's words, Caroline demonstrates female strength by instructing her father, the community, and readers how to respond charitably to Agnes' sexual transgression.[44] When Caroline rushes to the door upon hearing Agnes' voice, she does so without

Love-madness: The Father and Daughter   195

a thought about the potential danger to her own reputation if, just days before her own wedding, she were to bring a fallen woman into her house. After Mr Seymour blocks her access to the door a second time, and after he turns Agnes away, Caroline runs after Agnes, takes her hand, provides her with money, and gives her a note assuring her of her love. Far from being controlled by her father, Caroline acts in direct disobedience to his wishes in order to follow her own conscience and offer love and support to her friend.

Caroline's status as the moral voice of the novel is highlighted by her difference from men like her father and the governors of the asylum – men who are moved by sentiment to pity Agnes, but who lack the underlying moral principles and courage that would propel them to public action. Because she is so secure in her moral principles, Caroline ends up schooling her father on how to stand up to public pressure. When Mr Seymour tells Caroline he will speak favourably about Agnes' behaviour to the governors, Caroline informs him that his plan will be insufficient. She tells him he must speak favourably of Agnes wherever he goes: 'Avow the change [her penitent behaviour] has made in your sentiments towards her; you must be her advocate' (117). When Mr Seymour expresses his concern about public opinion, Caroline responds with force, telling him that the 'world' will say what he wishes it to say: 'Believe me, my dear father, the world is in many instances like a spoiled child, who treats with contempt the foolish parent that indulges its caprices, but behaves with respect to those who, regardless of his clamours, give the law to him, instead of receive it' (117). Essentially, Caroline is telling her father that he must not be passive and let others dictate his beliefs to him; rather, he must show the world what he stands for and be a model for others to follow. When Mr Seymour says that Caroline speaks without experience, she disagrees. She says the world will deem him a 'just judge' if he acknowledges Agnes' enormous guilt but also dwells with 'equal justice on the deep sense she [Agnes] entertains of it, and on the excellence of her present intentions' (117). And even if the world thinks him lenient, the approval of his own conscience should be its own compensation. Caroline is instructing her father in this scene, which is an inversion of moral authority that could undermine the original readers' respect for her and prompt suspicions about Opie's political leanings. Opie manages that risk by confronting it directly when Mr Seymour, accepting Caroline is right, asks her what the 'world' would think about her schooling her father. Caroline's response is, 'when the world hears me trying to exalt my own wisdom by doubting my father's, I hope it will treat me with the severity I deserve' (117). Opie is able to put the daughter in the position of moral authority over the father by making her aware of the need to avoid 'exalting herself.' While Caroline does not behave as if she

196   *Women and madness in the early Romantic novel*

were superior to her father, she does make it clear that he needs to act with moral courage rather than with cowardice and hypocrisy.

Although Caroline leaves the town when she gets married, Opie keeps her as the moral voice of the tale through a letter she sends to Agnes along with money to help pay for Mr Fitzhenry's treatment. The letter, which accompanies the money, makes a statement about how society should view fallen women and serves to quite intentionally separate Opie from the positions of her former friends, Mary Wollstonecraft and William Godwin.[45] Without naming names, Caroline, speaking for Opie, criticizes radical thinkers for conveying to readers the idea that women who transgress sexually are pushed further into degradation by society's refusal to accept them.

> It is the *slang* of the present day, if I may be allowed this vulgar but forcible expression, to inveigh bitterly against society for excluding from its circle, with unrelenting rigour, the woman who has once transgressed the salutary laws of chastity; and some brilliant and persuasive, but, in my opinion, mistaken writers, of both sexes, have endeavoured to prove that many an amiable woman has been forever lost to virtue and the world, and become the victim of prostitution, merely because her first fault was treated with ill-judging and criminal severity. (139)

Opie here stands in opposition to those 'brilliant and persuasive' writers who have argued that society is to blame for pushing women who have made one misstep into prostitution. Not only does Opie disagree with these authors – her own friends and associates from a few years past – she argues that their positions are harmful:

> This assertion appears to me to be fraught with mischief, as it is calculated to deter the victim of seduction from penitence and amendment, by telling her that she would employ them in her favour in vain. And it is surely as false as it is dangerous. I know many instances; and it is fair to conclude that the experience of others is similar to mine, of women restored by perseverance in a life of expiatory amendment, to that rank in society which they had forfeited by one false step, while their fault has been forgotten in their exemplary conduct, as wives and mothers. (140)

The argument Opie makes through Caroline is that telling women who have transgressed sexually that they are forever ostracized actually prevents them from engaging in the necessary acts of penance that would allow them to return to society.[46] Caroline notes that such women cannot be expected to be welcomed back into society easily. As prodigals, they have to undergo a 'long and painful probation' and they must, for a time, live a life of 'self-denial, patience, fortitude, and industry' (140). But if they do – as indeed Agnes has done long before the conclusion of the tale – they should be considered rehabilitated. As Opie represents the situation via

Love-madness: The Father and Daughter   197

Caroline, the problem for the fallen woman is not societal prejudice at all, but rather the 'brilliant and persuasive' but 'mistaken' writers themselves who tell fallen women they are doomed from the start. Although Opie does not make this point, these writers join the Mrs Macfiendys of the world to prevent such women from attempting social recuperation. But in-between those who cannot forgive sexually transgressive women and writers who cannot forgive society are the 'candid and enlightened' who, like Caroline, her husband, and Agnes' supporters in the town, are able to judge for themselves and recognize genuine repentance when they see it. These people will forgive and will even forget when a woman reintegrates into society and continues to display her virtue through doing her duty as a wife and mother.

Conclusion: the impossibility of love-madness

The blaming of radical writers for the fallen woman's inability to reintegrate into society is just one of many inversions and revisions of her slightly older contemporaries' positions that Opie works into her short tale. As she carves out a position between condemning and condoning sexual transgression, she reverses the positions of father and daughter, making the daughter the father's guardian, which gives the daughter control over the father and makes her responsible for his safety and wellbeing. She gives women the power to emotionally injure men and drive them to madness. And she makes patriarchs weak and sentimental rather than powerful and heartless. Her libertine is only partly responsible for the protagonist's mental afflictions; and the libertine is more injured by the seduced maiden's abandonment of him than she is by his lies and manipulations. It might seem that Opie, in so extensively revising her contemporaries' fictions, does so in support of patriarchal power. But that is not the case. In Opie's tale, all the branches of patriarchal power are weak, while women of various socio-economic classes are strong, allowing women in her fictional world to outpace men in mental resilience, the ability to bear pain, and moral courage. Whereas Maria Edgeworth countered the narratives of victimization written by Wollstonecraft, Fenwick, and Hays with a novel expressing the equality of women and men, Opie does so by promoting women's superiority to men.

Opie enacts her revisions of the narrative strategies of Wollstonecraft, Fenwick, and Hays by writing a novel about love-madness in which there is no love-mad maid. And there is no love-mad maid in *The Father and Daughter* because in Opie's world she does not exist. For the love-mad maid to exist, Opie would have to believe in women's greater susceptibility to madness, either from natural or social causes. But women in her tale are not more prone to mental affliction than men for any reason, including

198 *Women and madness in the early Romantic novel*

being victimized by the collusion of guardianship, libertinism, and gendered education. They are not prone to such injuries because in her tale, there are no avenues of male power hidden within sentimental vignettes or exercised freely to the detriment of women's mental health. And women are not subject to the mental ravages of abandonment because romantic love lacks the power to make a woman lose her mind when she loses her lover. When a woman goes mad in Opie's tale, it is, as in Edgeworth's *Belinda*, from a far more serious cause – from the inescapable guilt of having done wrong herself. In this case, the guilt of paternal betrayal stands in *The Father and Daughter* as the only passion strong enough to undermine a woman's mind. This gives women strength rather than weakness, makes them autonomous instead of dependent, and positions them as agents and not as victims – all of which makes love-madness impossible.

Notes

1 As a very young child, Amelia was terrified of the two mad women, so her mother insisted that she greet and give charity to them. Mrs Alderson's method was in keeping with John Locke's recommendation in his influential *Some Thoughts Concerning Education* (1693) that parents cure phobias through encouraging children to interact with the object of their fear.
2 Cecilia Lucy Brightwell, *Memorials of the Life of Amelia Opie* (1854; New York: AMS Press, 1975), 16, HathiTrust.
3 David Thame, too, observes that Amelia is looking for a love-mad maiden, which he describes as a 'figure represented in a well-established literary and visual code which prescribed loose and disordered clothing, and long dishevelled hair often twisted with straw or flowers.' David Thame, 'Amelia Opie's Maniacs,' *Women's Writing* 7, no. 2 (2000): 310, https://www.tandfonline.com/doi/abs/10.1080/09699080000200104.
4 Brightwell, *Amelia Opie*, 16.
5 Brightwell, *Amelia Opie*, 16.
6 *The Father and Daughter* was Opie's second publication, but the first to which she put her name. Shelley King and John B. Pierce write that it was 'as much a cultural phenomenon as a simple work of literature. Passing through at least nine editions … in the first three decades of the nineteenth century.' Shelley King and John B. Pierce, 'Introduction' to *The Father And Daughter with Dangers of Coquetry* (1801; Peterborough: Broadview Press, 2003), 11. All references are to the Broadview Press edition of *The Father and Daughter*.
7 Although madness is crucial to the plot of *The Father and Daughter*, the topic has received little attention. Scholars generally mention Mr Fitzhenry's madness without looking at his condition in any detail. And when they cover Agnes, it is usually in terms of sentimental suffering rather than madness. In their Introduction to the novel, King and Pierce have a section in which they

Love-madness: The Father and Daughter   199

contextualize Mr Fitzhenry's madness in a useful way, but they discuss Agnes' condition primarily in terms of sentimental excess. Thame, in 'Amelia Opie's Maniacs,' views *The Father and Daughter* as a rejection of the tradition of love-madness, as do I, but spends little time discussing the tale.

8 Thame, 'Opie's Maniacs,' 312.

9 Susan Staves, 'British Seduced Maidens,' *Eighteenth-Century Studies* 14, no. 2 (1980–1981): 122, www.jstor.org/stable/2738330.

10 See Diane Long Hoeveler, 'Talking About Virtue: Paisiello's "Nina," Paër's "Agnese," and the Sentimental Ethos,' *Romantic Circles/Praxis. Romanticism and Opera* (2005), English Faculty Research and Publications, https://epub lications.marquette.edu/english_fac/110; and Nowell Marshall, *Romanticism, Gender, and Violence: Blake to George Sodini* (Lewisburg: Bucknell University Press, 2013), 155.

11 Several scholars have argued persuasively that the tale is politically radical in its critique of patriarchal power. See Katherine Binhammer, *The Seduction Narrative in Britain, 1747–1800* (Cambridge: Cambridge University Press, 2009), chapter 5; Roxanne Eberle, *Chastity and Transgression in Women's Writing, 1792–1897: Interrupting the Harlot's Progress* (Basingstoke: Palgrave, 2002), chapter 4; Meghan Burke Hattaway, 'Amelia Opie's Fiction: Contagious and Recuperative Texts,' *European Romantic Review* 24, no. 5 (2013), https://doi.org/10.1080/0509585.2013.828203; and Joanne Tong, 'The Return of the Prodigal Daughter: Finding the Family in Amelia Opie's Novels,' *Studies in the Novel* 36, no. 4 (Winter 2004), www.jstor.org.libdata.lib.ua.edu/stable/295 33647.

12 Binhammer sees *The Father and Daughter* as distinct from *Wrongs of Woman* and *The Victim of Prejudice* in its rejection of the 'double victimization' of women by evil seducers or rapists and then by an implacable society (*The Seduction Narrative*, 146). I agree that Opie rejects victimization, although where Binhammer reads emotional excess as politically purposeful melodrama, I read it as politically purposeful madness.

13 Tong also notes the multiple roles played by Agnes in Mr Fitzhenry's affective life, as well as the erotic overtones of his affection. She blames his madness not on Agnes' betrayal, but rather on his own 'immoderate devotion' to a woman positioned as 'both natural daughter and surrogate wife to her father' ('Prodigal Daughter,' 469).

14 In an interesting approach, Nowell Marshall maintains that Mr Fitzhenry's madness—which he describes as melancholia—is caused by both Agnes' and Mr Fitzhenry's gender failures (*Romanticism, Gender, and Violence*, 153).

15 Eberle argues that Opie acknowledges Agnes' culpability, but that she highlights 'Fitzhenry's vanity and Clifford's treachery' in a 'battle over Agnes's "heart"' that is motivated in part by 'masculine delight in ownership and class pride' (*Harlot's Progress*, 95).

16 The temptation to read this tale biographically is quite strong. As is generally noted in scholarship on Opie, she had an unusually close relationship with her own father, who also did not remarry after his wife's death.

200   *Women and madness in the early Romantic novel*

17 Eberle, *Harlot's Progress*, 98.

18 Eleanor Ty doesn't discuss Mr Fitzhenry's loss of humanity, but she does observe the lack of sentiment in this mad scene and connects it, rightly I think, to Lear's raging against the elements. Eleanor Ty, *Empowering the Feminine: The Narratives of Mary Robinson, Jane West, and Amelia Opie, 1796–1812* (Toronto: University of Toronto Press, 1998), 138.

19 Mr Fitzhenry's condition appears to be maniacal madness. The celebrated physician and medical author William Cullen described the condition in a frequently reprinted textbook: 'There is sometimes a false perception or imagination of things present that are not … The false judgment … very often turns upon one single subject: but more commonly the mind rambles from one subject to another, with an equally false judgment concerning the most part of them; and as at the same time there is commonly a false association, this increases the confusion of ideas, and therefore the false judgments.' Cullen adds that 'maniacal persons are in general very irascible; but what more particularly produces their angry emotions is, that their false judgments lead to some action which is always pushed with impetuosity and violence; when this is interrupted or restrained, they break out into violent anger and furious violence against every person near them, and upon every thing that stands in the way of their impetuous will.' William Cullen, *First lines of the practice of physic*, vol. 4 (Edinburgh and London: C. Elliot, 1788), 144–5, ECCO.

20 Sander Gilman traces the 'wildman' as an image of madness back to the Middle Ages. Sander Gilman, *Seeing the Insane* (New York: John Wiley and Sons, 1982), 2.

21 King and Pierce note that Opie might have known of the Retreat at York through her ties to the Gurney family, who were prominent Quakers of Norwich ('Introduction,' 28).

22 It is possible that Mr Fitzhenry is afflicted by dementia, which at the time would have been known as 'dotage.' David Hartley includes 'the dotage of old persons,' which he understands as a physical affliction of the brain caused by old age, in his section on 'Imperfections in the Rational Faculty.' He writes: 'The dotage of old persons is oftentimes something more than a mere decay of memory. For they mistake things present for others, and their discourse is often foreign to the objects that are presented to them.' David Hartley, *Observations on Man, his Frame, his Duty, and his Expectations* (London: S. Richardson, 1749), 392, ECCO.

23 She argues that these fathers illustrate Opie's 'misgivings about the commitment of local leaders to a progressive national agenda' (Tong, 'Prodigal Daughter,' 471).

24 Tong, 'Prodigal Daughter,' 473.

25 Eberle, *Harlot's Progress*, 104.

26 The narrative represents Mr Fitzhenry's rejection of the match as reasonable, given that Clifford is an army officer and cannot offer his daughter a settled, secure life and that Clifford's own father does not approve.

27 Characters in late eighteenth-century novels often head to Scotland to be married because Scotland still followed the old laws in which, as Lisa O'Connell explains,

Love-madness: The Father and Daughter 201

'marriages were sealed simply by an exchange of vows undertaken before two witnesses.' Lisa O'Connell, 'Dislocating Literature: The Novel and the Gretna Green Romance, 1770–1850,' *NOVEL: A Forum on Fiction* 35, no. 1 (2001): 8, https://doi.org/10.2307/1346041. Prior to the Clandestine Marriage Bill of 1753, a woman would have been considered married in England if she and the man had bound themselves together through a verbal promise. See Eve Tavor Bannet, 'The Marriage Act of 1753: "A Most Cruel Law for the Fair Sex,"' *Eighteenth-Century Studies* 30, no. 3 (1997): 233–4, https://doi.org/doi:10.1353/ecs.1997.0008.

28 King and Pierce, 'Introduction,' 14.

29 Mrs Askew's name suggests her moral laxity at allowing a mistress to board at her house.

30 This is another point of disagreement with King and Pierce, who describe Clifford as a 'formidable opponent' who is able to 'turn the virtues of sensibility against their owner.' And they describe Agnes as 'more victimized than vicious, the prey of more hardened vice and the unequal advantages the unprincipled Clifford possesses' ('Introduction,' 14–15).

31 Gary Kelly, 'Discharging Debts: The Moral Economy of Amelia Opie's Fiction,' *The Wordsworth Circle* 11, no. 4 (1980): 199, www-jstor-org.libdata.lib.ua.edu/stable/24040631.

32 Melina Esse, 'Performing Sentiment; or, How to Do Things with Tears,' *Women and Music: A Journal of Gender and Culture* 14 (2010): 13, doi:10.1353/wam.2010https://doi.org/10.1353/wam.2010.0002.0002.

33 Tong, 'Prodigal Daughter,' 471.

34 King and Pierce write that Agnes attempts to 'define herself in individualist terms first through the error of choosing to elope with Clifford, and later in her attempt to control and shape the treatment of her father's madness' ('Introductory Note,' 21). It is doubtful Opie's original readers would have seen Agnes' decision to elope with Clifford and abandon her father in a positive light as an act of self-definition. I do, however, agree that after deciding to leave Clifford, Agnes exerts considerable control over her own life and that of her father.

35 Eberle, *Harlot's Progress*, 97.

36 Eberle makes a similar observation when she writes: 'Agnes's willingness "to think, to decide, and to act" radically transforms Opie's conventional narrative of seduced innocence. Even as Agnes assumes the predictable role of repentant wanderer returning to the familial home … Opie's heroine deliberately scripts her tale to have the greatest possible effect upon her father and community' (*Harlot's Progress*, 97).

37 According to Gary Kelly, Opie's tales all centre on 'this "passion," in the Christian sense: "the sufferings of a martyr."' Gary Kelly, *English Fiction of the Romantic Period 1789–1830* (London: Routledge, 1989), 85.

38 Staves' historical discussion of seduction helps us understand Agnes' need to perform penance. Staves writes that in the eighteenth century, 'seduced maidens were guilty of fornication, a crime punishable in the ecclesiastical courts' ('British

202 *Women and madness in the early Romantic novel*

Seduced Maidens,' 122). Staves explains that earlier in the century, churchwardens were able to exact public performances of penance; but such practices were in disuse by the time Opie wrote her tale. Agnes can be understood as subjecting herself to the ecclesiastical discipline that no longer existed.

39 Eberle argues that 'Opie's avowed purpose is not to dissect Agnes' fall from grace but to trace her reintegration into the community' (*Harlot's Progress*, 92). While it is the case that the tale does not dwell on Agnes' transgression, I argue (echoing Kelly) that its focus is not reintegration, but rather the psychological suffering Agnes inflicts on herself.

40 Esse, 'Performing Sentiment,' 11–12.

41 Esse, 'Performing Sentiment,' 12. Esse makes the point that regardless of her mental or emotional state, the sentimental heroine is frequently able to use her suffering strategically.

42 Tong also sees the tale as supportive of female strength and solidarity, which flourishes 'in the absence of male patriarchs and providers' ('Prodigal Daughter,' 473).

43 Eberle understands the strength of women in this tale to be an implicit criticism of men: 'Opie launches her subtle critique of masculine privilege by endowing most of her female characters with superior virtues' (*Harlot's Progress*, 99).

44 Binhammer, *The Seduction Narrative*, 166.

45 For a discussion of Opie's relationship with Wollstonecraft and Godwin, see chapter 4 of my *The Female Philosopher and her Afterlives* (Basingstoke: Palgrave, 2017).

46 Staves offers implicit support for Caroline's point by noting that 'the benevolent founders of the Magdalen Asylum had by 1786 admitted 2,415 repentant prostitutes to their institution and returned 1,571 to decent places in society' ('British Seduced Maidens,' 134). Caroline (or Opie, rather) is not talking about prostitutes, but basically makes the same argument about the possibility of social reintegration.

Coda: *Wide Sargasso Sea* – the erasure of love-madness and the mad woman's revenge

Charlotte Brontë's Bertha is a woman who may have been driven mad by her husband's actions, but the reader must look beneath the surface of Rochester's account to come to that conclusion. Taken at face value (meaning according to what Rochester says), Bertha's madness is inevitable: she is the mad daughter of a mad mother, a woman whose deranged mental state is inseparable from an inheritance of maternal insanity, miscegenation, and promiscuity. And taken at face value, Rochester is the victim, having been sold a false bill of goods in Jamaica, he is forever yoked to a deranged, polluted wife. Jean Rhys' Rochester (who is never named) comes to believe the same thing, but the woman he names 'Bertha' and confines in a small room at the top of his house has a long backstory as well as a subjective presence that Brontë's Bertha lacks. This backstory changes the maniacal Bertha of *Jane Eyre* into a woman whose madness is not caused by inheritance, but rather by her complex history and by her abusive husband – the very man who, in Brontë's story, claims to be the victim whose life has been ruined by his marriage to a woman who is both morally repugnant and mentally deranged.

In its portrayal of Antoinette Cosway, the woman who becomes 'Bertha,' Rhys' *Wide Sargasso Sea* has more in common with *Wrongs of Woman*, *Secresy*, and *Victim of Prejudice* than it does with *Jane Eyre* itself. Like these early Romantic-period novels, *Wide Sargasso Sea* reimagines the love-mad maid to expose the forms of patriarchal control and abuse that inflict psychological damage on women. Rhys identifies the same avenues of male power, the same sexual dynamics, and the same outcome for her heroine as Wollstonecraft, Fenwick, and Hays did before her. Failed male guardianship, unjust marriage laws, and libertine male behaviour all work together in *Wide Sargasso Sea* to drive a sympathetic young heroine to madness while the male perpetrator hides behind a flimsy screen of medical science. The lovely, sensitive Antoinette suffers considerably from her husband's flagrant infidelity and the loss of his love, but these are not the factors that lead to her madness. And while she might on the surface look

204   *Women and madness in the early Romantic novel*

like a love-mad maid – as do Maria Venables, Sibella Valmont, and Mary Raymond – like them, Antoinette does not lose her mind because she loses her man. Rather, she is driven mad by her husband's purposeful actions and by his determination that she is mad, which compounds the psychological damage she has already suffered from a traumatic past that includes her mother's own male-inflicted injuries. Like the feminist authors of the early Romantic period, Rhys gives the mad woman both a backstory and a subjectivity to which the reader has access. This backstory, which combines the inner monologues of both Rochester and the woman he calls 'Bertha,' inculpates not only the unnamed husband himself, but also the very avenues of patriarchal control identified and exposed by Rhys' predecessors over a century and a half before. Abusive male power replaces lost love as the cause of women's madness.

In *Wide Sargasso Sea*, the impact of failed male guardianship on women's mental health begins with emancipation itself, when the British government 'frees' the enslaved population of Jamaica and changes the socio-economic system of the island. With no governmental plans to ease the transition, the sudden abolition of slavery creates an environment in which the heroine Antoinette, her mother, and her incapacitated younger brother are, as her mother says, 'marooned' on their estate (16).[1] In a more personal act of male failure, Antoinette's libertine father has abandoned the family by drinking himself to death, leaving his beautiful, fragile, foreign-born wife and young children alone in sea of animosity. This state of being abandoned and at risk impacts the mental health of Antoinette and her mother, Annette, both of whom suffer from anxiety. As Antoinette says shortly after the story opens, 'My father, visitors, horses, feeling safe in bed—all belonged to the past' (15). With no one to help her, particularly after she learns her son's condition is incurable, Annette suffers from depression as well as anxiety, growing 'thin and silent,' refusing to leave the house, and pacing on the terrace overlooking the sea (17). The mother's depression has its impact on the daughter's mental health: she feels unloved and insecure, which sets the stage for her later unhealthy emotional dependency on the unnamed man who becomes her husband.

As is suggested in *Jane Eyre*, 'Bertha's' mother was indeed mad, but her madness, like the eventual affliction of her daughter, is caused by male failure and male abuse. And she too has a backstory that undermines pseudo-medical accounts of madness as a form of inherent moral failure. The pampered daughter of a Martinique slave owner, Annette knows only how to use her beauty to survive, and so she finds a new man to marry named Mr Mason, who becomes Antoinette's stepfather. By failing as a caretaker of both his wife and stepchildren, this man indirectly causes Annette to go mad. Mr Mason's literary lineage is that of the male guardian who, through his weaknesses, inadvertently injures the woman he is supposed to care for. He is a newcomer to Jamaica, and a well-meaning man, but he has typical male failings – namely, he is paternalistic and refuses to take women's concerns seriously. Crucially, Mr Mason doesn't give credence to Annette's growing anxieties about the family's safety at the estate, Coulibri. When Annette attempts to explain that their new prosperity puts them at risk from the restive Black population, he uses the recognizable male tactic of blaming her concerns on her imagination and her emotional volatility – 'always one extreme or another' (29) – rather than accepting that she might know more about the environment in which they live than he. The overconfident Mr Mason also disregards Antoinette's wise Aunt Cora who agrees that they should leave the house at Coulibri. There is an attack, and because Mr Mason has refused to listen to the women and take any precautions, the house is burned down, and Antoinette's disabled brother Pierre is killed.

The burning of Coulibri is the determining trauma of the novel, leading to Annette's madness and creating an emotional loss that colours the rest of Antoinette's experiences. As a result of the events that play out after the fire, Antoinette is left with neither mother nor father and little sense of security. The trauma of the fire and Pierre's death sets Annette against her husband, whom she blames for the disaster, and it plunges her into an episode of madness. In imitation of the parrot that falls burning to its death in the Coulibri fire, she screams '*Qui est là?*' and threatens to kill her husband. All these screams and threats ring 'loud and terrible' to the terrified Antoinette who lies at her aunt's house recovering from an injury and lengthy illness incurred at the time of the fire (42). Antoinette's mother, emotionally remote before, is now permanently lost to her as a result of the decisions Mr Mason makes in the face of her madness. And Annette's reputation as a madwoman in a society that already dislikes her for her Martinique origins and her beauty leaves Antoinette open to social ridicule and ostracization.

Mr Mason, already responsible, if not for the destruction of Coulibri then certainly for the death of Pierre, again demonstrates failed guardianship in his approach to Annette's mental and emotional state after the disaster. He quickly abandons his wife, whom he had previously adored, unable to bear her madness and the blame she places on him for Pierre's death. He buys a house, puts Annette in it, hires a man and a woman to tend to her, and then leaves the island. Annette is 'marooned' once again, and now, as a woman whose husband has determined she is mad, is more vulnerable than before. Annette's fate, explained by her former slave and servant Christophine, is particularly horrible. In an argument with Antoinette's husband, Christophine explains exactly how Annette came to lose her mind, and it is not what Antoinette's husband thinks: 'They drive her to it. When she lose her son she lose herself for a while and they

206   *Women and madness in the early Romantic novel*

shut her away. They tell her she is mad, they act like she is mad … But no kind word, no friends, and her husban' he go off, he leave her' (142–3). From Christophine's perspective, Annette's madness would have been a temporary response to trauma and grief, had it not been for Mr Mason's poor decisions. Rather than engage with her, rather than give her access to people who love her, rather than let her be free, Mr Mason locks her away and runs away. His dereliction of duty as his wife's guardian then leaves her prey to the unscrupulous people he hired to care for her. They will not allow Christophine or Antoinette to visit, keep her perpetually drunk, and sexually abuse her. Mr Mason's failure as his wife's guardian is so extensive, and its consequences so tragic for Annette, that Christophine remarks 'Ah there is no God' (143) when she finishes her account, despite keeping a picture of the Holy Family in her room (28). In a signal betrayal stemming from cowardice, Mr Mason leaves his wife to go mad from grief, isolation, and sexual abuse.

Mr Mason's son Richard is a weaker version of his father and lacks even a trace of good intentions. After his father's death, he inherits the guardianship of Antoinette, his stepsister, and proceeds according to his own self-interests. The novel does not go into why Richard is responsible for Antoinette, rather than her Aunt Cora, but presumably this is an automatic patriarchal arrangement. Disregarding Christophine's and Aunt Cora's objections, Richard carries through with his father's plan to marry Antoinette to a stranger from England. Like his father, he refuses to listen to women. Aunt Cora, elderly and ill, attempts to argue with him over the lack of legal protection afforded Antoinette in the marriage arrangements: 'It's disgraceful … It's shameful. You are handing over everything the child owns to a perfect stranger. Your father would never have allowed it. She should be protected, legally. A settlement can be arranged and it should be arranged. That was his intention' (104). Calling her an 'old fool' and telling her to 'shut up,' Richard exercises his prerogative as a man and the legal right patriarchal society has given him to make decisions for his young stepsister. The women know that he is eager to get rid of his responsibility for Antoinette, and so he passes her and her £30,000 fortune on to a stranger. Antoinette's husband is well aware of how he and Richard have taken advantage of his new bride. As he and Antoinette ride up to the house at Grandbois where they will honeymoon, he thinks about the financial transaction that made her his wife: 'The thirty thousand pounds have been paid to me without question or condition. No provision made for her (that must be seen to)' (63). The passive construction and parenthetical reference to the future show how little he cares about his wife's welfare now that he has sufficient money never to be a 'disgrace' to his father or the older brother he so resents. Antoinette has been passed from one selfish, callous man to another

Wide Sargasso Sea *and the mad woman's revenge*   207

and as a result is left without a penny of her own, completely dependent on a mercenary stranger, and prey to the injustices of English marital law.

The reason why Richard is so anxious to be quickly rid of Antoinette is that he is afraid that word of her mother's reputation as a mad, lascivious woman will reach the intended groom. Word of her reputation does reach the husband, but only after he has spent some time with Antoinette at her remote mountain house Granbois, which she inherited from her mother. Although the two were strangers when they married and Antoinette very fearful for her future, he succeeds in making her love him quite quickly after their first night together. Their happiness, however, is destroyed when the husband becomes convinced, via insidious letters from a man calling himself Daniel Cosway, that his new bride is tainted. According to Daniel, who claims to be the son of Antoinette's father, Antoinette is already just like her mother – polluted by madness, lasciviousness, and miscegenation. The husband had promised Antoinette 'peace, happiness, safety' (72) in response to her anxiety about marrying a stranger, but he violates his vow by returning her affection with revulsion and even hatred. The man, Daniel, tells him: 'Lies. Her mother was so. They say she worse than her mother, and she hardly more than a child. Must be you deaf you don't hear people laughing when you marry her' (114). One of the husband's primary concerns is his own reputation – what people think about him. And he is governed in his behaviour by the anxiety that he has been made a fool, that the whole community knows his wife is tainted. His pride is injured because he feels he has been bought and he thinks: 'They bought me, *me* with your paltry money. You helped them to do it. You deceived me, betrayed me, and you'll do worse if you get the chance' (154). Hating Antoinette for what he has decided was her role in the scam, he makes her into the scapegoat of his own insecurity.

His anxieties now fuelled by Daniel's insinuations, the husband is convinced that she must be controlled, lest she bring even more disgrace upon him. The pathway for him is the madness that he decides she has inherited from her mother. At a time in the narrative in which there is nothing wrong with Antoinette, apart from her heartbreak over losing her husband's love, the husband tells Christophine he will take her to the Spanish Town doctors and consult with them and Richard, to 'follow their advice' because 'she is not well.' At this point, Christophine spits on the floor: 'You want her money but you don't want her. It is in your mind to pretend she is mad. I know it. The doctors say what you tell them to say. That man Richard he say what you want him to say—glad and willing to, I know. She will be like her mother. You do that for money?' (145). The husband's plan is clearly visible to Christophine, and he is somewhat disturbed by the accusation that hits so close to home. If his wife is 'not well,' which no one will contest given her mother's reputation and her husband's legal power, he will be free to do with her as he likes, with no questions asked. Christophine's words reveal the stark truth, not just about the husband, but also about the avenues of male power that will allow him to drive his wife mad through abuse. The guardianship he assumes from Richard, British property laws, and the medical system are all avenues of power he can manipulate in order to keep Antoinette's money but be rid of her.

The husband's moral weakness is evident in how he makes up his mind about Antoinette the moment he reads Daniel's first letter. He immediately becomes cold, where he previously had been affectionate; and he loses interest in sex, where he previously had been consumed by desire. When Antoinette attempts to explain her mother's condition, he doesn't want to listen and patronizingly insists that she go to bed. But even when she perseveres and explains her entire past – the reasons for her mother's mental condition, their isolation at Coulibri, the trauma of the destruction of the house and her brother's death, and her witnessing her mother's abuse – he does not care. At the end of her narrative, Antoinette realizes that her story has had no impact on her husband: 'I have said all I want to say. I have tried to make you understand. But nothing has changed' (122). She is right. The husband's selfishness and insecurity cause his image of her to be irrevocably altered by his communications with Daniel: she is impure; she is like her mother, but even worse; and he has been made a fool. No degree of explanation can change how he feels about her.

It is at this point that the husband first calls Antoinette 'Bertha,' which he does to gain control of her through changing her identity. She has just laughed at realizing her story has had no impact on him, to which he replies: 'Don't laugh like that Bertha.' In a fight for her very sense of self, she responds, 'My name is not Bertha; why do you call me Bertha?' (122). They continue to struggle over her name until she gives up. The husband never explains his renaming of his wife and just says that he likes the name and that he thinks of her as Bertha. The renaming, however, comes immediately after she tells the story about her mother, whose name is the basis for her own – from Annette, the mother, to Antoinette, the daughter. The name change is no doubt an attempt to separate her from what he sees as the pollution of her mother's madness and promiscuity – never mind the carefully detailed psychological history of abandonment and abuse that led her to mental illness. But the husband does not just separate Antoinette from her mother with this name change. He also separates her from everything that makes her who she is. As Antoinette, she has a history separate from him, people who love her and are loyal to her, and a remarkable place that is her home.

As 'Bertha,' she has none of this, only a husband who owns all her property and has her under his complete control.

The husband acts intentionally to destroy Antoinette psychologically and to set her up anew as 'Bertha.' His first step is to inflict a terrible emotional wound on her when he has sex with Amélie, a servant girl who may or may not be Antoinette's half-sister. In his mind, this is an act of revenge for Antoinette's having used a potion obtained from Christophine to win back his love. He claims the potion was not necessary, that he desired her that night, before having drunk the tainted wine. It may be that his desire for her returned, the result of renaming her 'Bertha,' but the consequence of the potion is to make him violently desire her, and then hate her. As he watches her sleep, he draws a sheet over her as if he 'covered a dead girl,' suggesting she is now dead to him because she drugged him. This symbolic act frees him to pursue the desire he has been harbouring for the servant Amélie, whom he describes at the beginning of his narrative as a 'lovely little creature but sly, spiteful, malignant perhaps' (59). The day after he awakens from the potion and draws the sheet up to hide Antoinette and symbolically mark her as dead, he has sex with Amélie in the room next to Antoinette's so that she will hear everything. This sexual betrayal, an intentional act of revenge, effectively turns Antoinette into Bertha, although her actual descent into madness comes only after he has imprisoned her in the attic in England. When Antoinette emerges from her room later that day, she is drunk and physically transformed for the moment into what she will look like many years later in the attic at Thornfield, in *Jane Eyre*. The husband notes he was 'too shocked to speak' and that her 'hair hung uncombed and dull into her eyes which were inflamed and staring, her face was very flushed and looked swollen. Her feet were bare' (133). When he calls her Bertha again, she says: 'Bertha is not my name. You are trying to make me into someone else, calling me by another name. I know, that's obeah too' (133). Antoinette's reference to 'obeah,' the occult religious practice of the West Indies, suggests she understands that his ultimate aim is to take away her identity completely. It is this destruction of her sense of self, not the loss of her husband's love, that eventually drives her mad.

Christophine, the voice of clear-eyed truth in this novel, is well aware that the husband intends to inflict psychological harm on Antoinette. She lays out a simple story of selfishness and greed in which he marries her for her money, takes everything she has, and then attempts to 'break her up' (139). The husband admits privately that what Christophine says is true. He has understood the depth of Antoinette's love for him and its erotic base, which he has fostered and enjoyed before his communication with Daniel. But then, having decided she is polluted and to blame for what he views as a con, he attacks her exactly at her point of vulnerability, which is her love

210   *Women and madness in the early Romantic novel*

for him. Christophine observes that the potion she has given Antoinette has not helped her regain the husband's love because the husband does not love her at all. She says to him: 'But you don't love. All you want is to break her up. And it help you break her up' (139). Christophine's words contest his own claims about having desired Antoinette again before taking the potion. It seems as if the concoction backfires because he does not want to love her, but rather to hurt her, to inflict emotional damage on her, or even to cause a mental breakdown. What he wants, Christophine says, is to take her money, take her love, and destroy her in return.

Through Christophine, Rhys explains women's madness as an emotional and social condition, rather than how the husband understands it, as an inherent moral flaw. Christophine understands that life is more difficult for women, that, as she says, 'woman must have spunks to live in this wicked world' (92). Without 'spunks' women will experience emotional crises and will need love and care to recover. But as Christophine knows, and as this novel shows, men control women but fail to care for them and instead make decisions that push then into madness. During their argument, the husband uses Annette's madness to justify everything he has done to Antoinette. But Christophine answers, in defence of Annette, that 'they drive her to it,' and explains the chain of traumatic events that Antoinette has already delineated. Christophine says she knew in advance that the husband would not care properly for Antoinette, that, as a 'hard' man, he would not help her in times of trouble. 'I tell her so. I warn her. I say this is not a man who will help you when he sees you break up' (142). What Antoinette needs at this moment, as her mother did after the fire and Pierre's death, is love and care from a man able to feel for a woman's emotional suffering and to respond with tenderness and support. Christophine's point is that Antoinette, like her mother before her, is experiencing an emotional crisis from which she could recover if she were treated well. Her explanations are to no avail, however, as she is right about the husband being a 'hard' man about to repeat the errors of the past and drive his wife to madness.

Despite having been told Annette's story twice, the husband persists in understanding female madness as an inherent moral flaw passed down from mother to daughter. With absolutely no evidence, he decides that Antoinette is exactly like her mother – both mad and lewd – and that he is the victim of his wife's sexually expressed derangement. At a time when Antoinette is emotionally devastated from his actions and drinking heavily from the rum he orders be given to her, he self-pityingly contemplates his life as the husband of a 'drunken, lying lunatic.' And then he thinks about the sexual promiscuity he imagines a part of her character: 'She'd loosen her black hair, and laugh and coax and flatter (a mad girl. She'll not care who she's loving). She'll moan and cry and give herself as no sane woman would—or could. *Or could*' (149). The husband's image of Antoinette reads like a version of nymphomania in which a woman's enjoyment of sex and seeking of multiple partners marks her as insane. What the husband is doing, in effect, is blaming Antoinette for enjoying sex more than a proper woman should and marking her as insane because he has decided she responds to sex as no sane woman could. What he conveniently forgets is that he has taught her to enjoy sex and that her erotic response to him comes from the deep love he has awakened in her. But he uses her natural sensuality and her cultural difference against her by determining that her distance from sexual propriety means she is both mad and lascivious.

The husband does not just decide Antoinette *is* mad, he determines that she *must* be mad so that he can blame her for his victimization and be rid of her. His determination of her madness, however, is clearly contradicted by his own account of her mental clarity when they leave Grandbois. As they prepare to ride away, and immediately after the husband has been ruminating on her supposed madness – 'blank lovely eyes. Mad eyes. A mad girl' – she calmly explains to him why a little boy is crying. The husband's response is anger, hatred of the place and people, and a resolute determination that his wife is mad. In a particularly chilling sequence as they ride away from the house down the mountain, he imagines how his wife will join the legions of the insane who can be recognized by their 'white faces, dazed eyes, aimless gestures, high-pitched laughter.' And in a gesture to the future at Thornfield, he thinks of her as the mad woman in the attic: 'She's one of them. I too can wait—for the day when she is only a memory to be avoided, locked away, and like all memories a legend. Or a lie ...' (156). The husband eventually is able to make Antoinette into 'Bertha,' but not until he has completely broken her up by taking away her identity, her property, her home, her sense of security, her freedom, and everything and everyone she loves; and not until he has drained her of her humanity, her individuality, and her psychological depth by making her one of 'them' – one of an endless train of dehumanized lunatics who scream, laugh, and harbour intensely violent desires.

Although her husband has withdrawn his love and betrayed her, Antoinette is not mad when she leaves Grandbois, and neither is she mad when she arrives at Thornfield. In the final section of the narrative, she recalls how when she first arrived, she thought there must be a reason for her confinement, that it would only last a short time, and that she would be able to reason with her husband when he came. But, she notes 'he never came' (161). Locked in a room at the top of a chilly mansion, seeing no one but a single taciturn woman, far from her island home and the people she knows and loves, Antoinette begins to lose track of time and place and self. While Grace Poole sleeps, she is able to free herself to walk through the

212 *Women and madness in the early Romantic novel*

house as the spectre that haunts *Jane Eyre*. In Rhys' reimagining of the con-flagration that destroys Rochester's home, the idea of setting the house on fire comes to Antoinette in a dream in which she is aided by Christophine, and in which the burning of Thornfield becomes the second iteration of the burning of Coulibri, complete with parrot asking '*Qui est là*?' In the dream, the man who hates Antoinette (Rochester) follows her in the fire, calling 'Bertha,' which of course is not her name. And the dream ends with a scream, that readers know is 'Bertha' – really Antoinette reprising the parrot's fate – falling to her death from the top of Thornfield Hall. But she is not mad when she arrives, as she was not mad when she left Grandbois, or during her period of emotional distress over her husband, and as her mother was not originally mad before her. The plunging of 'Bertha' from the flaming rooftop is indeed the result of generational madness; but it is the generational madness that comes from generations of male abuse.

The great irony, of course, for which *Wide Sargasso Sea* is famous, is that the novel makes the husband – Mr Rochester himself – largely responsible for driving the woman he calls Bertha mad. Within *Jane Eyre*, Rochester's responsibility, however, is accessible only through considerable interpretive excavation. At the surface level, Brontë elevated and romanticized male power and patriarchal control. However, in pushing the damage inflicted on women by men into the substratum of the novel, Brontë left consider-able room for feminist interpretations of women's madness. Rochester's injuries in the fire themselves suggest that the loss of sight and the use of one hand is an authorial chastisement of a male protagonist who too readily abused his power. Rhys joins Brontë in making his vision and his home the price the husband pays for all he has taken away from the woman he calls 'Bertha.' In Rhys' novel, right before the husband kicks Christophine out of Grandbois, the place his wife loves that he now owns, he says, 'And do you think I wanted all this? I would give my life to undo it. I would give my eyes never to have seen this abominable place.' Christophine laughs and replies: 'And that's the first damn word of truth you speak. You choose what you give, eh? Then you choose. You meddle in something and perhaps you don't know what it is' (146). She then mutters in a language that the husband cannot identify, suggesting to the reader that she is using her obeah powers to make a curse. What the reader knows, but the husband does not, is that he, Mr Rochester, will indeed lose his eyes in a fire that will destroy his home. The symbolic punishment that Brontë inflicts on him through losing his sight and a hand takes away his overbearing masculine power and makes him dependent on his second wife, Jane, who heals him through the love and care he denies his first wife in Rhys' story, after he intentionally 'breaks her up.' Both authors allow the mad woman some degree of agency in the end, but only Rhys offers her well-justified revenge and joins the early

Romantic-period women writers in identifying webs of male abuse, rather than inherent fragility and lost love, as the cause of women's madness.

Note

1 Jean Rhys, *Wide Sargasso Sea* (1966; New York: WW Norton, 1982). All references are to this edition.

Select bibliography

Definitions

'Conversion Disorder.' *Diagnostic and Statistical Manual of Mental Disorders*, 4th edn. American Psychiatric Association, 2000, ebook.

'Dissociative Disorders.' *Diagnostic and Statistical Manual of Mental Disorders*, 5th edn. American Psychiatric Association, 2013, ebook.

'Trauma- and Stressor-Related Disorders.' *Diagnostic and Statistical Manual of Mental Disorders*, 5th edn. American Psychiatric Association, 2013, ebook.

'affliction, n.' *OED* Online. March 2023. Oxford University Press. www-oed-com. libdata.lib.ua.edu/view/Entry/3461?redirectedFrom=affliction.

'frantic, adj. and n.' *OED* Online. March 2023. Oxford University Press. www-oed-com.libdata.lib.ua.edu/view/Entry/74248?rskey=EVfjWX&result=1.

'mad, adj.' *OED* Online. March 2023. Oxford University Press. www-oed-com.libd ata.lib.ua.edu/view/Entry/112000?rskey=YX1ulc&result=5&isAdvanced=false.

'madness, n.' *OED* Online. March 2023. Oxford University Press. www-oed-com. libdata.lib.ua.edu/view/Entry/112066?redirectedFrom=madness.

'psychology, n.' *OED* Online. March 2023. Oxford University Press. www-oed-com.libdata.lib.ua.edu/view/Entry/153907?redirectedFrom=psychology.

'trauma, n.' *OED* Online. March 2023. Oxford University Press. www-oed-com. libdata.lib.ua.edu/view/Entry/205242?redirectedFrom=trauma.

Books and journals

Ali, Shahid, Shagufta Jabeen, Rebecca J. Pate, Marwah Shahid, Sandhya Chinala, Milankumar Nathani, and Rida Shah, 'Conversion Disorder – Mind versus Body: A Review.' *Innovations in Clinical Neuroscience* 12, nos 5–6 (May–June 2015): 27–33, bit.ly/3OX1lba.

Allen, Richard. *David Hartley on Human Nature*. Albany: State University of New York Press, 1999.

Andrews, Jonathan and Andrew Scull. *Undertaker of the Mind: John Monro and Mad-Doctoring in Eighteenth-Century England*. Berkeley: University of California Press, 2001.

Arnold, Thomas. *Observations on the nature, kinds, causes and prevention of insanity, lunacy or madness*, vol. 1. Leicester: G. Ireland for G. Robinson and T. Cadwell, 1782. ECCO.

Select bibliography 215

'Auld Robin Gray.' National Library of Scotland. Last accessed 11 October, 2022. https://digital.nls.uk/publications-by-scottish-clubs/archive/78395475.

Bailey, Margery. 'Introduction.' In *Boswell's Column. Being his Seventy Contributions to The London Magazine under the pseudonym The Hypochondriack from 1777 to 1783*, edited by Margery Bailey. London: William Kimber, 1951.

Bannet, Eve Tavor. 'The Marriage Act of 1753: "A Most Cruel Law for the Fair Sex."' *Eighteenth-Century Studies* 30, no. 3 (1997): 233–54, https://doi.org/doi:10.1353/ecs.1997.0008.

Barker-Benfield, G. J. 'Mary Wollstonecraft's Depression and Diagnosis.' *The Psychohistory Review* 13, no. 4 (1985): 15–31.

Battie, William. *A treatise on madness*. London: J. Whiston, and B. White, in Fleet-Street, 1758. ECCO.

Behrendt, Stephen. 'Rousseau and British Romantic Women Writers.' In *Jean-Jacques Rousseau and British Romanticism: Gender and Selfhood, Politics and Nation*, edited by Russell Goulbourne and David Higgins, 11–32. London: Bloomsbury, 2017, ebook.

Bending, Stephen. 'Melancholy Amusements: Women, Gardens, and the Depression of Spirits.' *Studies in the Literary Imagination* 44, no. 2 (2011): 41–62, https://doi-org.libdata.lib.ua.edu/10.1353/sli.2011.0013.

Berrios, G. E. 'Dementia during the Seventeenth and Eighteenth Centuries: A Conceptual History.' *Psychological Medicine* 17 (1987): 829–37.

Berrios, G. E. 'Of Mania: (from Bucknill and Tuke, 1858) Introduction.' *History of Psychiatry* 15, no. 1 (2004): 105–24, https://doi.org/10.1177/0957154X04041829.

Berrios, G. E. 'David Hartley's Views on Madness.' *History of Psychiatry* 26, no. 1 (2015): 105–116, https://doi.org/10.1177/0957154X14562300.

Binhammer, Katherine. *The Seduction Narrative in Britain, 1747–1800*. Cambridge: Cambridge University Press, 2009.

Blackmore, Richard. *A Treatise of the Spleen and Vapours: or, Hypocondriacal and Hysterical Affections. With three discourses on the nature and cure of the cholick, melancholy, and palsies. Never before Published*. London: J. Pemberton, 1725. ECCO.

Boswell, James. *Boswell's Column. Being his Seventy Contributions to The London Magazine under the pseudonym The Hypochondriack from 1777 to 1783*, edited by Margery Bailey. London: William Kimber, 1951.

Bowers, Toni. *Representing Resistance: British Seduction Stories, 1660–1800*. London: Blackwell, 2005.

Brewer, William. *The Mental Anatomies of William Godwin and Mary Shelley*. Cranbury: Associated University Presses, 2001.

Brightwell, Cecilia Lucy. *Memorials of the Life of Amelia Opie*. New York: AMS Press, 1975 [rpt 1854], HathiTrust.

Brooks, Marilyn. 'Mary Hays' *The Victim of Prejudice*: Chastity Renegotiated.' *Women's Writing* 15, no. 1 (2008): 13–31, https://doi-org.libdata.lib.ua.edu/10.1080/09699080701871401.

Brown, John. *The Elements of Medicine; or, A translation of the Elementa Medicinae Brunonis*. London: J. Johnson, 1788. HathiTrust.

Bundock, Christopher. 'The (inoperative) Epistolary Community in Eliza Fenwick's *Secresy*.' *European Romantic Review* 20, no. 5 (December 2009): 709–20, https://doi.org/10.1080/10509580903407894.

216 *Select bibliography*

Burke, Meghan. 'Making Mother Obsolete: Eliza Fenwick's *Secresy* and the Masculine Appropriation of Maternity.' *Eighteenth-Century Fiction* 21, no. 3 (Spring 2009): 357–84, https://doi.org/10.3138/ecf.21.3.357.

Burrows, John. *A New Practical Essay on Cancers*. London: J. Barker, G. Kearsly, and T. Axtell, 1783. ECCO.

Butler, Marilyn. 'Introduction.' In *The Works of Mary Wollstonecraft*, edited by Janet Todd and Marilyn Butler, 7–28. London: Pickering and Chatto, 1989.

Butler, Melissa A. 'Eighteenth-Century Critics of Rousseau's Views on Women.' In *Rousseau et la Critique/Rousseau and Criticism*, edited by Lorraine Clark and Guy LaFrance. Ottawa: North American Association for the Study of Jean-Jacques Rousseau, Pensee libre No. 5, 1995, http://rousseauassociation.org/wp-content/uploads/2020/07/PL5-Butler.pdf.

Busfield, Joan. 'The Female Malady? Men, Women and Madness in Nineteenth-Century Britain.' *Sociology* 28, vol. 1 (1994): 259–77, www.jstor.org/stable/428 55327.

Byrd, Max. *Visits to Bedlam: Madness and Literature in the Eighteenth Century*. Columbia: University of South Carolina Press, 1974.

Cafarelli, Annette Wheeler. 'Rousseau and British Romanticism: Women and the Legacy of Male Radicalism.' In *Cultural Interactions in the Romantic Age: Critical Essays in Comparative Literature*, edited by Gregory Maertz, 125–55. Albany: State University of New York, 1998.

Cannon, Mercy. 'Hygienic Motherhood: Domestic Medicine and Eliza Fenwick's *Secresy*.' *Eighteenth-Century Fiction* 20, no. 4 (Summer 2008): 535–61, https://doi.org/10.3138/ecf.20.4.535.

Chandler, James K. 'Edgeworth and the Lunar Enlightenment.' *Eighteenth-Century Studies* 45, no. 1 (2011): 87–104, https://doi.org/10.1353/ecs.2011.0053.

Chaplin, Sue. *Law, Sensibility and the Sublime in Eighteenth-Century Women's Fiction*. London: Routledge, 2016.

Charland, Louis. 'Alexander Crichton on the Psychopathology of the Passions.' *History of Psychiatry* 19, no. 3 (2008): 275–96, https://doi.org/10.1177/0957 154X07078703.

Charland, Louis. 'Science and Morals in the Affective Psychopathology of Philippe Pinel.' *History of Psychiatry* 21, no. 1 (2010): 38–53, https://doi.org/10.1177/0957154X09338334.

Charland, Louis. 'John Locke on Madness: Redressing the Intellectualist Bias.' *History of Psychiatry* 25, no. 2 (2014): 137–53, https://doi.org/10.1177/0957 154X13518719.

Chatterjee, Ranita. 'Sapphic Subjectivity and Gothic Desires in Eliza Fenwick's *Secresy*.' *Gothic Studies* 6, no. 1 (May 2004): 45–56, https://doi.org/10.7227/GS.6.1.5.

Clark, Anna. *Women's Silence, Men's Violence: Sexual Assault In England, 1770–1845*. London: Pandora Books, 1987.

Close, Anne. 'Into the Public: The Sexual Heroine in Eliza Fenwick's *Secresy* and Mary Robinson's *The Natural Daughter*.' *Eighteenth-Century Fiction* 17, no. 1 (October 2004): 35–52, https://doi.org/10.1353/ecf.2 004.0016.

Conger, Syndy. *Mary Wollstonecraft and the Language of Sensibility*. Rutherford, NJ and London: Fairleigh Dickinson University Press, 1994.

Select bibliography

Cooper, Christine. 'Reading the Politics of Abortion: Mary Wollstonecraft Revisited.' *Eighteenth-Century Fiction* 14, no. 4 (2000): 735–82, https://doi.org/10.1353/ecf.2004.0057.

Cove, Patricia. '"The Walls of Her Prison": Madness, Gender, and Discursive Agency in Eliza Fenwick's *Secresy* and Mary Wollstonecraft's *The Wrongs of Woman*. *European Romantic Review* 23, no. 6 (December 2012): 671–87, https://doi.org/10.1080/10509585. 2012.728828.

Craciun, Adriana. *Fatal Women of Romanticism*. Cambridge: Cambridge University Press, 2002.

Crichton, Alexander. *An Inquiry Into the Nature And Origin of Mental Derangement: Comprehending a Concise System of the Physiology and Pathology of the Human Mind. And a History of the Passions And Their Effects*. London: T. Cadell, junior and W. Davies, 1798. HathiTrust.

Cullen, William. *First lines of the practice of physic*, vol. 4. Edinburgh and London: C. Elliot, 1788. ECCO.

Darcy, Jane. *Melancholy and Literary Biography, 1640–1816*. Basingstoke: Palgrave Macmillan, 2013.

De Bienville, M. D. T., M.D. *Nymphomania, or, a dissertation concerning the furor uterinus*, translated by Edward Sloane Wilmot, M.D. London: J. Bew, 1775. ECCO.

DePorte, Michael. *Nightmares and Hobbyhorses: Swift, Sterne, and Augustan Ideas of Madness*. San Marino: Huntington Library, 1974.

Dickie, Simon. *Cruelty and Laughter: Forgotten Comic Literature and the Unsentimental Eighteenth Century*. Chicago: University of Chicago Press, 2011.

Digby, Anne. *Madness, Morality, and Medicine: A Study of the York Retreat 1796–1914*. Cambridge: Cambridge University Press, 1985.

Dolan, Elizabeth. 'British Romantic Melancholia: Charlotte Smith's *Elegiac Sonnets*, Medical Discourse and the Problem of Sensibility.' *Journal of European Studies* 33, no. 3/4 (2003): 237–53, https://doi.org/10.1177/004 7244103040416.

Donatini, Hilary Teynor. 'Moral and Medical Diagnosis in Maria Edgeworth's *Belinda*.' *The Eighteenth-Century Novel* 9 (2011): 247–69.

Eberle, Roxanne. *Chastity and Transgression in Women's Writing, 1792–1897: Interrupting the Harlot's Progress*. Basingstoke, Palgrave, 2002.

Edgeworth, Maria. *Belinda*, edited by Linda Bree. Oxford: Oxford World's Classics, 2020 [1801].

Emsley, Sarah. 'Radical Marriage.' *Eighteenth-Century Fiction* 11, no. 4 (1999): 477–98, doi:10.1353/ecf.1999.0053.

Esse, Melina. 'Performing Sentiment; or, How to Do Things with Tears.' *Women and Music: A Journal of Gender and Culture* 14, (2010): 1–21, https://doi.org/10.1353/wam.2010.0002.

Falconer, William. *A Dissertation on the Influence of the Passions upon Disorders of the Body*. London: C. Dilly and J. Phillips, 1788. ECCO.

Farr, Jason. *Novel Bodies: Disability and Sexuality in Eighteenth-Century British Literature*. Lewisburg: Bucknell University Press, 2019.

Faubert, Michelle. 'A Gendered Affliction: Women, Writing, Madness.' In *Cultural Constructions of Madness in Eighteenth-Century Writing: Representing the Insane*, by Allan Ingram, 136–69. Basingstoke: Palgrave, 2005.

Faubert, Michelle. 'The Fictional Suicides of Mary Wollstonecraft.' *Literature Compass* 12, no. 12 (December 2015): 652–59, https://doi.org/10.1111/lic3.12282.

Faubert, Michelle, editor. 'Suicidal Romanticism: Origins and Influences,' special issue, *Studies in the Literary Imagination*, vol. 51, no. 1 (Spring 2018), https://doi.org/10.1353/sli.2018.0000.

Fenwick, Eliza. *Secresy; or, The Ruin on the Rock*, edited by Isobel Grundy. Peterborough: Broadview Press, 1994 [1795].

Ferguson, Frances. 'Rape and the Rise of the Novel.' *Representations* 20 (Fall 1987): 88–112, https://doi.org/10.2307/2928503.

Ferguson, Frances. 'Jean-Jacques Rousseau, *Émile* and Britain.' In *Jean-Jacques Rousseau and British Romanticism Gender and Selfhood, Politics and Nation*, edited by Russell Goulbourne and David Higgins, 187–208. London: Bloomsbury, 2017, ebook.

Foa, Edna B. and David S. Riggs. 'Posttraumatic Stress Disorder following Assault: Theoretical Considerations and Empirical Findings.' *Current Directions in Psychological Science* 4, no. 2 (April 1995): 61–5, bit.ly/42rwoia.

Ford, Jennifer. *Coleridge on Dreaming: Romanticism, Dreams, and the Medical Imagination*. Cambridge: Cambridge University Press, 1998.

Foucault, Michel. *Madness and Civilization: A History of Insanity in the Age of Reason*, translated by Richard Howard. New York: Vintage Books, 1988 [1965].

Foyster, Elizabeth. 'At the Limits of Liberty: Married Women and Confinement in Eighteenth-Century England.' *Continuity and Change* 17, no. 1 (January 2002): 39–62, https://doi.org/10.1017/S0268416002004058.

Gilbert, Sandra and Susan Gubar, *The Madwoman in the Attic: The Woman Writer and the Nineteenth-Century Literary Imagination*. New Haven: Yale University Press, 1979.

Gilman, Sander. *Seeing the Insane*. New York: J. Wiley; Brunner/Mazel Publishers, 1982.

Grange, Kathleen. 'Pinel and Eighteenth-Century Psychiatry.' *Bulletin of the History of Medicine* 34, no. 5 (1961): 442–53, www.jstor.org/stable/44446818.

Greenfield, Susan. '"Abroad and at Home": Sexual Ambiguity, Miscegenation, and Colonial Boundaries in Edgeworth's *Belinda*.' *PMLA* 112, no. 2 (1997): 214–28, https://doi.org/10.2307/463091.

Greentree, Shane. 'Writing against Sophie: Mary Hays's *Female Biography* as Enlightenment Feminist Critique of Jean-Jacques Rousseau's *Émile*.' *Eighteenth-Century Life* 41, no. 2 (April 2017): 73–88, https://doi.org/10.1215/00982601–3841384.

Gonda, Caroline. *Reading Daughters' Fictions, 1709–1834: Novels and Society from Manley to Edgeworth*. Cambridge: Cambridge University Press, 1996.

Grundy, Isobel. 'Introduction.' In *Secresy; or, The Ruin on the Rock*, edited by Isobel Grundy, 7–30. Peterborough: Broadview Press.

Hampton, Jean. 'Defining Wrong and Defining Rape.' In *A Most Detestable Crime: New Philosophical Essays on Rape*, edited by Keith Burgess-Jackson, 118–56. Oxford: Oxford University Press, 1999.

Hartley, David. *Observations on Man, his Frame, his Duty, and his Expectations*. London: S. Richardson, 1749. ECCO.

Select bibliography 219

Hattaway, Meghan Burke. 'Amelia Opie's Fiction: Contagious and Recuperative Texts.' *European Romantic Review* 24, no. 5 (2013): 555–77, https://doi.org/10. 1080/10509585.2013.828203.

Hays, Mary. *The Victim of Prejudice*, edited by Eleanor Ty. Peterborough, Ontario: Broadview Press, 1998 [1799].

Hoeveler, Diane Long. 'Reading the Wound: Wollstonecraft's *Wrongs of Woman, or Maria* and Trauma Theory.' *Studies in the Novel* 31, no. 4 (1999): 387–408, www.jstor.org/stable/29533355.

Hoeveler, Diane Long. 'Talking About Virtue: Paisiello's "Nina," Paër's "Agnese," and the Sentimental Ethos.' *Romantic Circles/Praxis. Romanticism and Opera*, edited by Gillian D'Arcy Wood, (2005): No pagination. English Faculty Research and Publications, https://epublications.marquette.edu/engl ish_fac/110.

Hunter, Richard and Ida Macalpine. *Three Hundred Years of Psychiatry 1535–1860: A History Presented in Selected English Texts*. London: Oxford University Press, 1963.

Ingram, Allan and Stuart Sim. 'Introduction: Depression Before Depression.' In *Melancholy Experience in Literature of the Long Eighteenth Century: Before Depression, 1660–1800*, edited by Allan Ingram and Stuart Sim, 1–24. London: Palgrave, 2011.

Ingram, Allan and Stuart Sim, editors. *Melancholy Experience in Literature of the Long Eighteenth Century: Before Depression, 1660–1800*. London: Palgrave, 2011.

Jackson, Stanley. *Melancholia and Depression: From Hippocratic Times to Modern Times*. New Haven: Yale University Press, 1986.

Jackson, Stanley. 'The Use of the Passions in Psychological Healing.' *Journal of the History of Medicine and Allied Sciences* 45, no. 2 (1990): 150–75, www.jstor. org/stable/24633133.

Jacobus, Mary. *Reading Woman: Essays in Feminist Criticism*. New York: Columbia University Press, 1986.

James, Robert. *A medicinal dictionary; including physic, surgery, anatomy, chymistry, and botany. In all their branches relative to medicine. Together with a history of drugs; ... With copper plates*. Vol. 2. London: T. Osborne, 1743–45. ECCO

Johns, Erin. 'Raping Prejudice: Mary Hays's *The Victim of Prejudice*, Gender, and Rape.' In *Literary and Poetic Representations of Work and Labor in Europe and Asia during the Romantic Era: Charting a Motif across Boundaries of Culture, Place, and Time*, edited by Christopher Clason and Robert Anderson, 137–55. New York: Edwin Mellen Press, 2010.

Johnson, Claudia. *Equivocal Beings: Politics, Gender, and Sentimentality in the 1790s: Wollstonecraft, Radcliffe, Burney, Austen*. Chicago: University of Chicago Press, 1995.

Johnson, Samuel. *A Dictionary of the English Language*, Vol 2. London: W. Strahan, for J. and P. Knaptor & etc., 1755. ECCO.

Johnson, Samuel. *The History of Rasselas, Prince of Abissinia*, edited by Thomas Keymer. Oxford: Oxford World's Classics, 2009 [1759]).

Jones, Vivien. '"The Tyranny of the Passions": Feminism and Heterosexuality in the Fiction of Wollstonecraft and Hays.' *Political Gender: Texts and Contexts* (1994): 173–88.

Jones, Vivien. 'Placing Jemima: Women Writers of the 1790s and the Eighteenth-Century Prostitution Narrative.' *Women's Writing* 4, no. 2 (1997): 201–20, https://doi.org/10.1080/09699089700200011.

Kaartinen, Marjo. *Breast Cancer in the Eighteenth Century*. London: Routledge, 2016.

Kelly, Gary. 'Discharging Debts: The Moral Economy of Amelia Opie's Fiction.' *The Wordsworth Circle* 11, no. 4 (1980): 198–203, www-jstor-org.libdata.lib.ua.edu/stable/24040631.

Kelly, Gary. *English Fiction of the Romantic Period 1789–1830*. London: Routledge, 1989.

Kelly, Gary. 'Introduction.' In *Mary and the Wrongs of Woman*, edited by Gary Kelly, ix–xxxi. Oxford: Oxford World's Classics, 2009.

Kilfeather, Siobhán. 'Introductory Note.' In *The Pickering Masters: The Novels and Selected Works Of Maria Edgeworth*, Vol 2, *Belinda*, edited by Siobhán Kilfeather, vii–xlv. New York: Routledge, 2016. [2003], ebook.

King, Shelley and John B. Pierce. 'Introduction.' In *The Father And Daughter with Dangers of Coquetry*, edited by Shelley King and John B. Pierce, 11–51. Peterborough: Broadview Press, 2003.

Kirkley, Laura. 'Translating Rousseauism: Transformations of Bernardin de Saint-Pierre's *Paul et Virginie* in the Works of Helen Maria Williams and Maria Edgeworth.' In *Women Readers in Europe: Readers, Writers, Solonnieres, 1750–1900*, edited by Hilary Brown and Gillian Dow, 93–118. London: Routledge, 2011.

Kirkley, Laura. 'Jean-Jacques Rousseau.' In *Mary Wollstonecraft in Context*, edited by Nancy E. Johnson and Paul Keen, 155–63. Cambridge: Cambridge University Press, 2020, ebook.

Klein, Ula. 'Bosom Friends and the Sapphic Breasts of *Belinda*.' *ABO: Interactive Journal for Women in the Arts* 3, no. 2. (2013), http://dx.doi.org/10.5038/2157-7129.3.2.1

Komisaruk, Adam. 'The Privatization of Pleasure: "Crim. Con." in Wollstonecraft's *Maria*.' *Law and Literature* 16, no. 1 (2004): 33–63, https://doi.org/10.1525/lal.2004.16.1.33.

Kowaleski-Wallace, Elizabeth. *Their Fathers' Daughters: Hannah More, Maria Edgeworth, and Patriarchal Complicity*. New York: Oxford University Press, 1991.

Kromm, Jane. 'Olivia Furiosa: Maniacal Women from Richardson to Wollstonecraft.' *Eighteenth-Century Fiction* 16, no. 3 (April 2004): 343–72, https://doi.org/10.1353/ecf.2004.0020.

Lanser, Susan. *Fictions of Authority: Women Writers and Narrative Voice*. Ithaca: Cornell University Press, 1992.

Lanser, Susan. 'Second-Sex Economics: Race, Rescue, and the Heroine's Plot.' *The Eighteenth Century* 61, no. 2 (January 2020): 227–44, https://doi.org/10.1353/ecy.2020.0016.

Lawlor, Clark. 'Fashionable Melancholy.' In *Melancholy Experience in Literature of the Long Eighteenth Century: Before Depression, 1660–1800*, edited by Allan Ingram and Stuart Sim, 25–53. London: Palgrave, 2011.

Ledoux, Ellen Malenas. 'Defiant Damsels: Gothic Space and Female Agency in *Emmeline, The Mysteries of Udolpho* and *Secrecy*.' *Women's Writing* 18, no. 3 (2011): 331–47, https://doi.org/10.1080/09699082.2010.508889.

Select bibliography

Locke, John. *An Essay Concerning Human Understanding*, 5th edn. London: Awnsham and John Churchill, 1706 [1689]. ECCO.

Locke, John. *Some Thoughts Concerning Education*. London: J. and R. Tonson, 1779 [1693]. ECCO.

Logan, Peter Melville. *Nerves and Narratives: A Cultural History of Hysteria in Nineteenth-Century British Prose*. Berkeley: University of California Press, 1997.

Mackenzie, Henry. *The Man of Feeling*. London: J. M. Dent, 1893 [1771]. HathiTrust.

Marshall, Nowell. *Romanticism, Gender, and Violence: Blake to George Sodini*. Lewisburg: Bucknell University Press, 2013.

Martin, Philip. *Mad Women in Romantic Writing*. New York: St Martin's Press, 1987.

Mason, Nicholas. 'Class, Gender, and Domesticity in Maria Edgeworth's *Belinda*.' *Eighteenth-Century Novel* 1 (2001): 271–85.

Matthew, Patricia. 'Corporeal Lessons and Genre Shifts in Maria Edgeworth's *Belinda*.' *Nineteenth-Century Gender Studies* 4, no. 1 (2008): no pagination. https://www.ncgsjournal.com/issue41/matthew.html.

Matthews, S. Leigh. '(Un)Confinements: The Madness of Motherhood in *Wrongs of Woman*.' In *Mary Wollstonecraft and Mary Shelley: Writing Lives*, edited by Helen M. Buss, D. L. Macdonald, and Anne McWhir, 85–97. Waterloo, Ontario: Wilfrid Laurier University Press, 2001.

Maurer, Shawn Lisa. 'The Female (As) Reader: Sex, Sensibility, and the Maternal in Wollstonecraft's Fictions.' *Essays in Literature* 19, no. 1 (1992): 34–54.

May, Larry and Robert Strikwerda. 'Men in Groups: Collective Responsibility for Rape.' *Hypatia* 9, no. 2 (Spring 1994): 134–51, www.jstor.org/stable/3810174.

Mayo, Robert. 'The Contemporaneity of the Lyrical Ballads,' *PMLA* 69, no. 3 (June 1954): 486–522, https://doi.org/10.2307/460070.

McAllister, Marie. 'Ungovernable Propensities: *Belinda* and the Idea of Addiction.' *The Age of Johnson* 23 (2015): 301–31.

McCann, Andrew. 'Conjugal Love and the Enlightenment Subject: The Colonial Context of Non-identity in Maria Edgeworth's *Belinda*.' *NOVEL: A Forum on Fiction* 30, no.1 (1996): 56–77, https://doi.org/10.2307/1345847.

McInelly, Brett C. '"I had rather be obscure. But I dare not": Women and Methodism in the Eighteenth Century.' *Everyday Revolutions: Eighteenth-Century Women Transforming Public and Private*, edited by Diane E. Boyd and Marta Kvande, 135–58. Cranbury, NJ: Rosemont Publishing, 2008.

McLynn, Frank. *Crime and Punishment in Eighteenth-Century England*. New York: Routledge, 1989.

Meek, Heather. 'Motherhood, Hysteria, and the Eighteenth-Century Woman Writer.' In *The Secrets of Generation: Reproduction in the Long Eighteenth Century*, edited by Raymond Stephanson and Darren N. Wagner, 238–57. Toronto: University of Toronto Press, 2015.

Meek, Heather. 'Medical Discourse, Women's Writing, and the "Perplexing Form" of Eighteenth-Century Hysteria.' *Early Modern Women: An Interdisciplinary Journal* 11, no. 1 (2016): 177–86, www.jstor.org/stable/26431447.

Mellor, Anne K. 'Righting the *Wrongs of Woman*: Mary Wollstonecraft's *Maria*.' *Nineteenth-Century Contexts* 19, no. 4 (1996): 413–24, https://doi.org/10.1080/08905499608583434.

222 *Select bibliography*

Micale, Mark. *Approaching Hysteria: Disease and Its Interpretations*. Princeton: Princeton University Press, 1995.

Micale, Mark. 'Hysteria and its Historiography: A Review of Past and Present Writings (I).' *History of Science* 27 (1989): 223–61, https://doi.org/10.1177/0073 27538902700301.

Mitchell, Juliet. *Women, the Longest Revolution: Essays on Feminism, Literature, and Psychoanalysis*. London: Virago, 1984.

Montwieler, Katherine. 'Reading Disease: The Corrupting Performance of Edgeworth's *Belinda*.' *Women's Writing* 12, no. 3 (2005): 347–368, doi:10.1080/09699080500200268.

Moore, Edward and Henry Brooke. 'The Sparrow and the Dove' (Fable XIV). In *Fables for the Female Sex*, 68–89. London: Minerva Press, 1795 [1744]. ECCO.

Moore, Lisa. *Dangerous Intimacies: Toward a Sapphic History of the British Novel*. Durham: Duke University Press, 1997.

Mullan, John. 'Hypochondria and Hysteria: Sensibility and the Physicians.' *The Eighteenth Century* 25, no. 2 (1984): 141–74, www-jstororg.libdata.lib.ua.edu/stable/41467321.

Myers, Mitzi. '"My Art Belongs to Daddy?" Thomas Day, Maria Edgeworth, and the Pre-Texts of *Belinda*: Women Writers and Patriarchal Authority.' In *Revising Women: Eighteenth-Century "Women's Fiction" and Social Engagement*, edited by Paula Backscheider, 105–49. Baltimore: Johns Hopkins University Press, 2000.

Noyes, Russell Jr. 'The Transformation of Hypochondriasis in British Medicine, 1680–1830.' *Social History of Medicine* 24, no. 2 (2011): 281–98, https://doi.org/10.1093/shm/hkq052.

O'Connell, Lisa. 'Dislocating Literature: The Novel and the Gretna Green Romance, 1770–1850.' *NOVEL: A Forum on Fiction*, 35, no. 1 (2001): 5–23, https://doi.org/10.2307/1346041.

Opie, Amelia. *The Father and Daughter*. In *The Father And Daughter with Dangers of Coquetry*, edited by Shelley King and John B. Pierce. Peterborough: Broadview Press, 2003 [1801].

O'Quinn, Daniel. 'Trembling: Wollstonecraft, Godwin, and the Resistance to Literature.' *ELH* 64, no. 3 (Fall 1997): 761–788, www.jstor.org/stable/30030239.

Paul, Lissa. *Eliza Fenwick: Early Modern Feminist*. Newark: University of Delaware Press, 2019.

Perry, Ruth. 'Colonizing the Breast: Sexuality and Maternity in Eighteenth-Century England.' *Journal of the History of Sexuality* 2, no. 2 (1991): 204–34, www.jstor.org/stable/3704034.

Poovey, Mary. 'Mary Wollstonecraft: The Gender of Genres in Late Eighteenth-Century England.' *NOVEL: A Forum on Fiction* 15, no. 2 (1982): 111–26, https://doi.org/10.2307/1345219.

Poovey, Mary. *The Proper Lady and the Woman Writer: Ideology as Style in the Works of Mary Wollstonecraft, Mary Shelley, and Jane Austen*. Chicago: University of Chicago Press, 1984.

Porter, Roy. 'Was There a Moral Therapy in Eighteenth Century Psychiatry?' *Annual of the Swedish History of Science Society* 81 (1981): 12–26.

Porter, Roy. 'Psychosomatic Disorders: Historical Perspectives.' In *Treatment of Functional Somatic Disorders*, edited by Richard Mayou, Christopher Bass, and Michael Sharpe, 17–41. Oxford: Oxford University Press, 1995.

Select bibliography

Porter, Roy. *Madmen: A Social History of Madhouses, Mad-Doctors, and Lunatics.* Reprint of *Mind-Forg'd Manacles* [1987]. Stroud, Gloucestershire: Tempus Publishing, 2004.

Priestley, Joseph. *Hartley's theory of the human mind, on the principle of the association of ideas; with essays relating to the subject of it,* 2nd edn. London: J. Johnson, 1790. ECCO.

Purdie, Susan and Sarah Oliver. 'William Frend and Mary Hays: Victims of Prejudice.' *Women's Writing* 17, no. 1 (May 2010): 93–110, https://doi.org/10.1080/09699080903533304.

Radden, Jennifer. *The Nature of Melancholy: From Aristotle to Kristeva.* Oxford: Oxford University Press, 2000.

Rhys, Jean. *Wide Sargasso Sea.* New York: WW Norton, 1982 [1966].

Richardson, Alan. *British Romanticism and the Science of the Mind.* Cambridge: Cambridge University Press, 2001.

Risse, Guenter. 'The Brownian System of Medicine: Its Theoretical and Practical Implications.' *Clio Medica* 5 (1970): 45–51.

Rosen, George. *Madness in Society: Chapters in the Historical Sociology of Mental Illness.* Chicago: University of Chicago Press, 1968.

Rosenberg, Jordana. 'The Bosom of the Bourgeoisie: Edgeworth's *Belinda*.' *ELH* 70, no. 2 (2003): 575–96, https://doi.org/doi:10.1353/elh.2003.0022.

Rousseau, G. S. 'Nerves, Spirits, and Fibres: Towards Defining the Origins of Sensibility.' In *Studies in the Eighteenth Century III: Papers Presented at the Third David Nichol Smith Memorial Seminar, Canberra 1973,* edited by R. F. Brissenden and J. C. Eade, 137–57. Toronto: The University of Toronto Press, 1976, ebook.

Rousseau, G. S. 'The Invention of Nymphomania.' In *Perilous Enlightenment: Pre-and Postmodern Discourses; Sexual, Historical,* edited by G. S. Rousseau, 44–64. Manchester: Manchester University Press, 1991.

Rousseau, G. S. '"A Strange Pathology': Hysteria in the Early Modern World, 1500–1800.' In *Hysteria Beyond Freud,* by Sander Gilman, Helen King, Roy Porter, G. S. Rousseau, and Elaine Showalter, 91–221. Berkeley: University of California Press, 1993, ebook.

Rousseau, G. S. 'Depression's Forgotten Genealogy: Notes Toward a History of Depression.' *History of Psychology,* xi (2000): 71–106, https://doi.org/10.1177/0957154X0001104104.

Rousseau, G. S. 'Psychology.' In *The Ferment of Knowledge: Studies in the Historiography of Eighteenth-Century Science,* edited by George Rousseau and Roy Porter, 144–210. Cambridge: Cambridge University Press, 2010.

Rousseau, Jean-Jacques. *Émile; or On Education,* translated by Allan Bloom. New York: Basic Books, 1979 [1762].

Rousseau, Jean-Jacques. *Julie; or, The New Heloise,* translated by Philip Stewart and Jean Vaché. Lebanon, NH: Dartmouth College Press, 1997 [1761]).

Sadow, Jonathan. 'Moral and Generic Corruption in Eliza Fenwick's *Secresy*.' In *Didactic Novels and British Women's Writing, 1790–1820,* edited by Hilary Havens, 74–89. New York: Routledge, 2017.

Scull, Andrew. 'Moral Treatment Reconsidered: Some Sociological Comments on an Episode in the History of British Psychiatry.' In *Madhouses, Mad-Doctors, and Madmen: The Social History of Psychiatry in the Victorian Era,* edited by Andrew Scull, 105–18. Philadelphia: University of Pennsylvania Press, 1981.

224 *Select bibliography*

Scull, Andrew. *The Most Solitary of Afflictions: Madness and Society in Britain 1700–1900*. New Haven: Yale University Press, 1993.

'Secrecy: Or, the Ruin of the Rock.' ART. XXVII. *The Analytical Review: Or, History of Literature* 22, no. 1 (July 1795): 60–61, www.proquest.com/histori cal-periodicals/art-xxvii-secrecy-ruin-rock/docview/8045796/se-2.

'Secrecy; Or, the Ruin on the Rock. In Three Volumes. By a Woman.' ART. XXXII. *English Review, Or, an Abstract of English and Foreign Literature, 1783–1795* 25 (June 1795): 473, https://www.proquest.com/historical-periodicals/art-xxxii-secrecy-ruin-on-rock-three-volumes/docview/6515969/se-2.

'Secrecy; Or the Ruin of the Rock.' E. Art. 58. *Monthly Review, Or, Literary Journal*, 1752–1825 18 (September 1795): 110, www.proquest.com/historical-periodicals/art-58-secrecy-ruin-rock/docview/4793797/se-2.

Shafer, Carolyn M. and Marilyn Frye. 'Rape and Respect.' In *Feminism and Philosophy*, edited by Mary Vetterling-Braggin, Frederick A. Elliston, and Jane English, 333–46. Totowa, NJ: Littlefield, Adams, & Co., 1978.

Sharpe, Ada and Eleanor Ty. 'Mary Hays and the Didactic Novel in the 1790s.' In *Didactic Novels and British Women's Writing, 1790–1820*, edited by Hilary Havens, 90–105. New York: Routledge, 2017.

Sherman, Sandra. 'The Feminization of "Reason" in Hays's *The Victim of Prejudice*.' *The Centennial Review* 41, no. 1 (1997): 143–72, www-jstor-org.libdata.lib.ua.edu/stable/23737012.

Sherman, Sandra. 'The Law, Confinement, and Disruptive Excess in Hays' *The Victim of Prejudice*.' *1650–1850, Ideas, Aesthetics, and Inquiries in the Early Modern Era* 6 (2001): 131–61.

Showalter, Elaine. *The Female Malady: Women, Madness, and English Culture, 1830–1980*. London: Virago, 1985.

Showalter, Elaine. 'Representing Ophelia: Women, Madness, and the Responsibilities of Feminist Criticism.' In *Shakespeare and the Question of Theory*, edited by Patricia Parker and Geoffrey Hartman, 77–94. New York and London: Methuen, 1985.

Showalter, Elaine. 'Hysteria, Feminism, and Gender.' In *Hysteria Beyond Freud*, by Sander Gilman, Helen King, Roy Porter, G. S. Rousseau, and Elaine Showalter, 286–336. Berkeley: University of California Press, 1993, ebook.

Showalter, Elaine. 'On Hysterical Narrative,' *Narrative* 1, no. 1 (1993): 24–35, www.jstor.org/stable/20106990.

Sim, Stuart. 'Despair, Melancholy and the Novel.' In *Melancholy Experience in Literature of the Long Eighteenth Century: Before Depression, 1660–1800*, edited by Allan Ingram and Stuart Sim, 114–41. London: Palgrave, 2011.

Skultans, Vieda. *English Madness: Ideas on Insanity, 1580–1890*. London: Routledge & Kegan Paul, 1979.

Sloan, Margaret Kathryn. 'Mothers, Marys, and Reforming "The Rising Generation": Mary Wollstonecraft and Mary Hays.' In *Mentoring in Eighteenth-Century British Literature and Culture*, edited by Anthony Lee, 225–43. London: Routledge, 2009.

Small, Helen. *Love's Madness: Medicine, the Novel, and Female Insanity, 1800–1865*. Oxford: Clarendon Press, 1998.

Snow, Malinda, 'Habits of Empire and Domination in Eliza Fenwick's *Secresy*.' *Eighteenth-Century Fiction* 14, no. 2 (January 2002): 159–75, https://doi.org/10.1353/ecf.2002.0016.

Select bibliography

Starcevic, Vladan. 'Clinical Features and Diagnosis of Hypochondriasis.' In *Hypochondriasis: Modern Perspectives on an Ancient Malady*, edited by Vladan Starcevic and Don R. Lipsitt, 21–60. Oxford: Oxford University Press, 2001.

Staves, Susan. 'British Seduced Maidens.' *Eighteenth-Century Studies* 14, no. 2 (1980–81): 109–34, www.jstor.org/stable/2738330.

Sterne, Lawrence. *A Sentimental Journey Through France and Italy by Mr York*. In *A Sentimental Journey and other Writings*, edited by Ian Jack and Tim Parnell. Oxford: Oxford World's Classics, 2008 [1768].

Suzuki, Akihito. 'Dualism and the Transformation of Psychiatric Language in the Seventeenth and Eighteenth Centuries.' *History of Science*, xxxiii (1995): 417–47, https://doi.org/10.1177/007327539503004.

Temple, Kathryn. 'Heart of Agitation: Mary Wollstonecraft, Emotion, and Legal Subjectivity.' *The Eighteenth Century* 58, no. 3 (2017): 371–82, https://doi.org/10.1353/ecy.2017.0031.

Terry, Richard, editor. 'Depression in the Enlightenment.' Special issue, *Studies in the Literary Imagination*, vol. 44, nos 1 & 2 (Spring/Fall 2011).

Terry, Richard. 'Philosophical Melancholy.' In *Melancholy Experience in Literature of the Long Eighteenth Century: Before Depression, 1660–1800*, edited by Alan Ingram and Stuart Sim, 54–82. London: Palgrave Macmillan, 2011.

Thame, David. 'Amelia Opie's Maniacs,' *Women's Writing* 7, no. 2 (2000): 309–26.

Thame, David. 'Madness and Therapy in Maria Edgeworth's *Belinda*: Deceived by Appearances.' *British Journal for Eighteenth-Century Studies* 26 (2003): 271–88.

Todd, Janet, editor. *The Collected Letters of Mary Wollstonecraft*. London: Penguin, 2003.

Tong, Joanne. 'The Return of the Prodigal Daughter: Finding the Family in Amelia Opie's Novels.' *Studies in the Novel* 36, no. 4 (Winter 2004): 465–83, www.jstor.org.libdata.lib.ua.edu/stable/29533647.

Trouille, Mary. *Sexual Politics in the Enlightenment: Women Writers Read Rousseau*. Albany: SUNY Press, 1997.

Ty, Eleanor. *Empowering the Feminine: Narratives of Mary Robinson, Jane West, and Amelia Opie, 1796–1812*. Toronto: University of Toronto Press, 1998.

Ty, Eleanor. 'Introduction.' In *The Victim of Prejudice*, edited by Eleanor Ty, vii–xxxix. Peterborough: Broadview Press, 1998.

Ty, Eleanor. *Unsex'd revolutionaries: Five Women Novelists of the 1790s*. Toronto: University of Toronto Press, 1993.

Ty, Eleanor. 'The Imprisoned Female Body in Mary Hays's *The Victim of Prejudice*.' In *Women, Revolution, and the Novels of the 1790s*, edited by Linda Lang-Peralta, 133–53. Lansing: Michigan State University Press, 1999.

Veith, Ilza. *Hysteria: The History of a Disease*. Chicago: University of Chicago Press, 1965.

Vickers, Neil. 'Coleridge and the Idea of "Psychological Criticism."' *British Journal for Eighteenth-Century Studies* 30 (2007): 261–78, https://doi.org/10.1111/j.1754-0208.2007.tb00336.x.

Walker, Gina Luria. *Mary Hays, (1759–1843): The Growth of a Woman's Mind*. Aldershot: Ashgate Press, 2006.

Wallace, Miriam. *Revolutionary Subjects in the English "Jacobin' Novel," 1790–1805*. Lewisburg: Bucknell University Press, 2009.

Watson, Nicola. *Revolution and the Form of the British Novel, 1790–1825: Intercepted Letters, Interrupted Seductions.* Oxford: Oxford University Press, 1994.

Weiner, Dora. 'Mind and Body in the Clinic: Philippe Pinel, Alexander Crichton, Dominique Esquirol, and the Birth of Psychiatry.' In *The Languages of Psyche: Mind and Body in Enlightenment Thought*, edited by G. S. Rousseau, 331–402. Berkeley: University of California Press, 1990, ebook.

Weiss, Deborah. 'Suffering, Sentiment, and Civilization: Pain and Politics in Mary Wollstonecraft's *Short Residence.' Studies in Romanticism* 45, no. 2 (Summer 2006): 199–221, https://doi.org/10.2307/25602044.

Weiss, Deborah. 'The Extraordinary Ordinary Belinda: Maria Edgeworth's Female Philosopher.' *Eighteenth-Century Fiction* 19, no. 4 (Summer 2007): 441–462, https://doi.org/10.1353/ecf.2007.0027.

Weiss, Deborah. *The Female Philosopher and her Afterlives: Mary Wollstonecraft, The British Novel, and the Transformations of Feminism, 1796–1811.* Basingstoke: Palgrave, 2017.

Whisnant, Rebecca, 'Feminist Perspectives on Rape.' *The Stanford Encyclopedia of Philosophy* (Fall 2021), edited by Edward N. Zalta. https://plato.stanford.edu/archives/fall2021/entries/feminism-rape/.

Whitehead, James. *Madness and the Romantic Poet: A Critical History.* Oxford: Oxford University Press, 2017.

Whytt, Robert. *Observations On the Nature, Causes, And Cures of Those Disorders Which Have Been Commonly Called Nervous, Hypochondriac, Or Hysteric: to Which Are Prefixed Some Remarks On the Sympathy of the Nerves.* Edinburgh: T. Becket, and P. Du Hondt, London, and J. Balfour, Edinburgh, 1765. HathiTrust.

Wollstonecraft, Mary. *Maria; Or, The Wrongs of Woman.* In *Mary and The Wrongs of Woman*, edited by Gary Kelly. Oxford: Oxford World's Classics, 2009 [1798].

Wollstonecraft, Mary. *The Vindications: The Rights of Men and The Rights of Woman*, edited by D. L. Macdonald and Kathleen Scherf. Peterborough: Broadview Press, 1997 [1792].

Wright, Julia M. '"I am Ill-Fitted": Conflicts of Genre in Eliza Fenwick's *Secresy.'* In *Romanticism, History, and the Possibility of Genre: Re-forming Literature 1789–1837*, edited by Tilottama Rajan and Julia M. Wright, 149–75. Cambridge: Cambridge University Press, 1998.

Wright, Nicole. 'Opening the Phosphoric "Envelope": Scientific Appraisal, Domestic Spectacle, and (Un) "Reasonable Creatures" in Edgeworth's *Belinda. Eighteenth-Century Fiction* 24, no. 3 (Spring 2012): 509–36, https://doi.org/10.3138/ecf.24.3.509.

Yeazell, Ruth Bernard. *Fictions of Modesty: Women and Courtship in the English Novel.* Chicago: University of Chicago Press, 1991.

Zunac, Mark. '"The Dear-Bought Lessons of Experience": Mary Hays's *The Victim of Prejudice* and the Empiricist Revision of Burke's *Reflections.' Papers on Language and Literature: A Journal for Scholars and Critics of Language and Literature* 48, no. 1 (2012): 70–100, bit.ly/3WVvnhq.

Index

addiction 134, 145–6, 149, 164n.1
Allen, Richard 136–7, 141, 150
anxiety 6, 8, 16, 17, 43, 67n.8, 79–80, 87, 103, 106, 120, 125, 139, 144, 158, 160, 181–2, 186, 188, 204–5, 207
Arnold, Thomas 14, 17, 37n.80, 168n.48

Barker-Benfield G. J. 42, 88
Battie, William 12, 34n.43
Behrendt, Stephen 79
Bernardin de Saint-Pierre, Jacques-Henri: *Paul et Virginie* 151–2, 157–8, 166n.26
Berrios, G. E. 33n.33, 87
Bienville, M. D. T. de 20, 38n.101, 110, 129n.19
Binhammer, Katherine 127n.1, 130n.33, 194, 199nn.11–12
Blood, George 67n.4, 67n.8
Bossier de Sauvages de Lacroix, François 37n.82
Boswell, James: *Boswell's Column, 'The Hypochondriack'* 17, 36n.79, 47–8, 69n.28, 141
Brewer, William 70n.49, 108, 129n.16
Brontë, Charlotte: *Jane Eyre* 1, 203, 212
Brown, John 99n.42
Bundock, Christopher 99n.47
Burke, Edmund 98n.34, 128n.3
Burke, Meghan 91, 100n.52
Burney, Frances 30n.1
Burrows, John 168n.43

Busfield, Joan 38n.102
Butler, Marilyn 56, 68n.13, 71n.68
Byrd, Max 77

Cafarelli, Annette Wheeler 31n.7, 56, 70n.45
Cannon, Mercy 79, 80, 96n.6
Chandler, James K. 165n.2, 169n.57, 172n.99
Chaplin, Sue 74, 77, 96n.4, 97n.7, 97n.9, 98n.34
Charland, Louis 13, 59, 135, 146, 157
Chatterjee, Ranita 93, 96n.4, 100nn.52–3
Cheyne, George 12, 49
Choderlos de Laclos, Pierre 82
Clark, Anna 118, 131n.42, 131n.45, 131n.47
Coke, Mary Campbell Coke, Viscountess 51
Conger, Syndy 67n.3, 71n.71
Cooper, Christine 67n.11, 72n.72
Cove, Patricia 66n.2, 88, 96n.6, 97n.7
Cowper, William 20, 57
Craciun, Adriana 33n.31
Crichton, Alexander 7, 14, 135, 137–41, 146–7, 149, 150
Cullen, William 12, 14, 19, 36n.66, 37n.82, 200n.19

Dacre, Charlotte 39n.104
Darcy, Jane 36n.76, 36n.79, 43, 67n.6, 68n.18
Darwin, Erasmus, 165n.2
Day, Thomas 151, 170n.70

Index

DePorte, Michael 39n.111, 70n.56, 120

depression 6, 9, 15–17, 32n.13, 33n.31, 36n.79, 43, 45, 47–8, 51–2, 54, 103, 106, 112, 114, 120, 123–4, 139, 145, 176, 204

despair 5, 41, 46, 59, 65, 79, 91, 95, 115–16, 121, 123, 139, 148, 150–1, 164
  cause of mental affliction 22, 24, 29, 38n.93, 110–11, 137, 159
  faced with male power 29, 65, 95, 116

Dickie, Simon 116, 119, 130n.30

Digby, Anne 77

Dolan, Elizabeth 45

Donatini, Hilary Taylor 165n.1, 169n.54, 169n.58

Eberle, Roxanne 106, 127n.1, 128n.8, 176, 185, 191, 199n.15, 201n.36, 202n.39, 202n.43

Edgeworth, Maria 1, 3, 134, 164
  and Bernardin de Saint-Pierre 152, 154, 166n.24, 26
  Practical Education 165n.8

Edgeworth, Maria: *Belinda* 1–2, 4, 27–8
  Belinda and Lady Delacour's recovery 27, 138–40, 144–50, 165n.8, 166n.13, 166n.24, 169n.58, 169n.61
    and rationality 134
  Clarence Hervey 153, 163
    erotic fantasy of innocence 153–4, 158, 161, 162
    and Rousseauvian education 134, 151–4, 157, 159–61, 164
  female friendship 143–4, 164
  Lady Delacour's cancer 138–45, 168n.43, 168n.50, 170n.63
  Lady Delacour's mental afflictions 139–43, 150
    addiction 134, 145–6, 49, 164n.1, 168nn.50–1
    fear of illness and death 139–41
    hypochondriasis 134, 140–1
    mania 134, 137, 139, 144–5

melancholia 134, 137–41, 148, 150
  Methodism 27, 134, 145–6
  and patriarchy 134–5, 151, 161–4
  psychologized theory of madness 3, 27, 134–9, 150, 158, 168n.49
    false associations 3, 13, 27, 135–6, 141, 146–7, 150, 156, 164, 165n.8
    misplaced passions 3, 27, 38n.93, 135–6, 139, 143–5, 165n.4
    remorse 3, 135–8, 141–4
    See also Crichton, Alexander; Darwin, Erasmus; Hartley, David; Locke, John
  Rousseauvian education, opposition to 28, 134, 143, 151, 153–5, 158, 161–3, 171n.80, 172n.99
  Virginia St Pierre 152, 155–7
    imaginary romance lover 134, 156–8, 160, 162
    mental afflictions 156–60
    and *Paul et Virginie* 157–8
    romantic imagination 155–6, 158, 160

Edgeworth, Richard Lovell 151, 170n.70

Emsley, Sarah 96n.4

enthusiasm 59, 78, 85, 90, 125, 146, 156
  See also Methodism; passions

Esse, Melina 21, 39n.115, 189, 193, 202n.41

Falconer, William 142

Farr, Jason 167n.32, 168n.46

Faubert, Michelle 40n.120, 72n.72

female friendship 26–8, 65–6, 93–4, 95, 100n.53, 124–5, 138, 150, 194, 202n.42

Fenwick, Eliza 2, 95

Fenwick, Eliza: *Secresy; or, The Ruin on the Rock* 2, 73, 126, 151, 155
  female independence 75–6, 79
  female integrity 75–80, 93–4
  female reason 74–6, 78, 93, 97n.7

Index

love-madness 26, 73–4, 76, 78, 81–2,
  86–8, 92–3, 113
Murden 75, 81, 85–6, 89
  libertine or man of feeling 87–9,
    91
  madness, 26, 73, 87–93
  patriarchal and libertine abuse 73,
    80–7, 94–5
  Rousseauvian education 4, 26, 73–4,
    77–80, 82, 85–6, 93
  Sibella 77, 80
    mental afflictions 73, 76–7, 80–2,
      113–14
    sexuality 78–80, 86, 91–2
  Valmont and patriarchal power 82–6,
    98n.30
Ferguson, Frances 132n.63
Filmer, Sir Robert 98n.34
Ford, Jennifer 120, 158
Fordyce, James 4, 31n.7
Foucault, Michel 11, 14, 35n.63, 59,
  66n.2
  on female physiology 13, 19,
    131n.39
  on madness 11, 13, 15, 82, 96n.6,
    109
Foyster, Elizabeth 44–5, 50–1

gender 129n.23, 199n.14
  crossdressing 140–2
  egalitarian politics of 135, 149,
    162
  neutral models of mental afflictions
    27, 29, 81, 141, 164
  See also Rousseauvian education of
    women
gender, female 9–10, 63, 68n.13, 156,
  170n.67
  all-female communities 71n.71,
    135
  childbirth and motherhood 10, 61,
    65–6, 71n.71
  fallacies of weakness 1–4, 7, 13,
    18–19, 26, 37n.89, 42, 61, 73,
    80–1, 91, 98n.27
  medical ideologies and 9, 12, 17, 19,
    25, 87, 134

gender, male 81, 128n.12
  gendered power dynamics 1–2, 29,
    50
  potential for reformation 27, 52,
    94–5, 135, 163
  socialization 114–15
Gilbert, Sandra, and Susan Gubar 7–9
Gilman, Sander 132n.55, 200n.20
Godwin, William 30n.2, 43, 67n.10,
  70n.49, 102, 196, 202n.45
Gonda, Caroline 169n.62
gothic, the 46, 59, 83, 96n.4, 120
Grange, Kathleen 11, 135, 138, 165n.4
Greenfield, Susan 169n.62, 170n.66,
  172n.94
Gregory, John 4, 14, 31n.7
Grundy, Isobel 73, 83, 90, 98n.30,
  98n.35
guardianship 2, 24–6, 29, 79, 101,
  104–7, 114, 155, 158, 162–3,
  172n.96, 197–8, 203–6
  enlightened, benevolent guardians
    26, 102–3, 106
  and patriarchal power 1, 25–6,
    59–60, 74–6, 79, 82–4, 103,
    155, 160, 163, 198, 208
  weakness and failure 162, 172n.96,
    181, 204–6

Hartley, David 7, 135–7, 141, 150,
  158, 166n.13, 200n.22
  associationist psychology 136, 141,
    152, 156–7, 163
  on madness 135–6, 141, 160,
    165n.5, 168n.49
Havens, Hilary 96n.4, 128n.3
Hays, Mary 1, 101–2, 117, 126, 117,
  151
  Memoirs of Emma Courtney 79,
    129n.16, 132n.60
  and Wollstonecraft 2, 101, 102, 109,
    124, 126
Hays, Mary: *The Victim of Prejudice* 2,
  26–7, 101, 103–4, 155
  education and miseducation 4,
    101–3, 105–6, 108–13, 151
  love-madness revised 113–14

Hays, Mary: *The Victim of Prejudice* (*cont.*)

male power 26–7, 101, 104
  psychological injury 101, 113–14
  social status 102, 106, 122–3
Mary's mental afflictions 27, 101, 119–23
  emotional shock 5, 18, 21, 61, 82, 88, 94, 107, 160
  hysteria 106–7, 112–13, 122
  and male injury 106, 108, 116–19
  melancholia 101, 103, 106–7, 113
  no predisposition 107, 122
Mary's mother's mental afflictions, 107–10, 112, 114, 129n.18
rape 114–19
sexuality:
  chastity as social fixation 101, 109, 127
  social-sexual hierarchy 103, 106, 108
  stigma 110, 112–13, 114
  teaching men 126
Haywood, Eliza 39n.104
Hoeveler, Diane Long 46, 71n.67, 199n.10
Hippocrates, 17
Hunter, Richard, and Ida McAlpine 168n.51
hypochondria 5, 6, 12, 17–18, 85, 134, 141
  modern sense of 5, 6, 17, 36n.79, 141
hypochondriasis 15, 17, 27, 37n.80, 42, 87–8, 141
  as male form of hysteria 17, 88, 141
hysteria 2, 3, 5–6, 8–9, 17–19, 27, 37n.81, 42, 50, 62, 69n.33, 81, 107, 116–17, 130nn.33–4
  female fragility 3, 13, 17–20, 34n.47, 37n.89, 61, 73, 98n.27, 99n.50
  childbirth and motherhood 8, 17, 61, 62, 71n.65
  fatality 26, 73, 81, 90
  Freud and 37n.82, 98n.27
  hypochondriasis 6, 17–19, 42, 87, 141

male hysteria 88, 92–3, 99n.50, 184
medical definitions of 18, 37n.82, 62, 65, 73, 116, 141
  genital theories 17–19, 116–17, 38n.97, 141
  melancholy and 6, 18, 36n.70, 106, 107, 114
  as nervous condition 12, 18, 34n.47, 37n.89, 42, 81, 107
  psychological affliction caused by injury 50–1, 69n.33, 106, 115, 117, 122, 132n.62
  sexuality 19–20, 116
  symptomology 18, 197, 112, 141
    catalepsy, fainting, convulsions 106, 107, 116–17, 188
    hysteric fits 13, 15, 18, 51, 86, 88, 92, 102, 160, 122, 186, 188, 194
    mental derangement 116, 145
  See also love-madness; nervous afflictions; nymphomania; spleen; vapours

imagination 11, 37n.80, 43, 48, 67n.9, 75, 102, 120, 136–7, 205
  and madness 15, 46, 48, 59, 87, 90–1, 112–13, 120, 125, 141, 145–6, 149, 168n.48, 200n.19
  uncontrolled 48, 59, 87–8, 109
  wrong reasoning and 11, 144
imagination, romantic 25–8, 41, 90, 134, 151, 153, 156–7, 159, 161, 176
  avenue of male control 28, 49, 53–65, 66, 113
  pleasure vs. independence 56, 65
imagination, sexual 20, 38n.101, 94, 152–3
  bodily pathology and 3, 110, 129n.20
  female erotic imagination 54–5, 57, 100n.53, 136, 157–8, 171n.84
  male erotic imagination 4, 57–8, 73–4, 76, 94, 152–4
Imlay, Gilbert 42, 43, 67n.7, 71n.70

Inchbald, Elizabeth 185
Ingram, Allan, and Stuart Sim 16,
    166n.22

Jackson, Stanley 11, 34n.38, 36n.69,
    80, 87, 103, 128n.7
Jacobus, Mary 8
James, Robert 13, 19, 38n.93
Johns, Erin 130n.28
Johnson, Claudia 71n.71, 167n.32
Johnson, Joseph 70n.49
Johnson, Samuel 5, 11, 31n.10, 36n.79,
    68n.25
  imagination and madness 48

Kaartinen, Marjo 139, 142, 168n.43,
    168n.50, 170n.63
Kelly, Gary 61, 70n.45, 189, 201n.37,
    202n.39
Kilfeather, Siobhán 155, 162–3,
    166n.26, 169n.52, 171n.80,
    171n.84, 172n.94
King, Shelley, and John Pierce 188,
    198nn.6–7, 200n.21, 201n.30,
    201n.34
Kirkley, Laura 31n.5, 152, 154, 159,
    166n.26, 170n.70
Komisaruk, Adam 69n.42, 71n.64
Kowaleski-Wallace, Elizabeth 167n.32,
    169n.62
Kristeva, Julia 8
Kromm, Jane 55, 71n.61

Lanser, Susan 71n.71, 96n.4, 100n.53
law 52, 62–4, 208
  avenue of patriarchal power 42,
    44–5, 52–3, 62–4, 117–18
  incarceration of wives 44–5, 64
  rape 116–19, 132nn.52–3
  women as perpetual minors 53
  women as property 63, 118–19
  See also guardianship
  crim. con. 51, 62–3, 66n.1
  marital law 52–3, 200n.27, 203,
    207
    divorce 71n.68
    husbands' legal power 25, 62

women's limited recourse 117–18,
    131n.42–8
Lawlor, Clark 36n.79
Ledoux, Ellen Malenas 96n.4
Lennox, Charlotte 38n.103, 156
libertinism 2, 23, 26, 81, 86, 94, 95,
    98n.34, 99n.48, 104, 111, 116,
    151, 163–4, 183–4, 204
  avenue of male control 1, 3, 41, 49,
    73–4, 86, 185
  and female mental affliction 26,
    27, 82, 85–8, 95, 203
  libertine men of feeling 24, 87, 94,
    184
  libertine self-injury 184–5, 197
  libertines reformed 26, 89, 94–5,
    163, 184
Locke, John 13, 167n.27, 198n.1
  cognitive error and madness
    11, 13, 59, 141, 144, 146,
    168n.47
  disordered affective states 13, 135
  influence of 59, 135, 157
love-madness 3, 9, 26–30, 39n.108,
    41–3, 58–60, 74, 76–7, 81, 95,
    109, 173–4, 198n.3
  archetype, myth, or icon 24, 30,
    40n.119
  etiology:
    abandonment 20–1, 58, 198
    death of beloved 20–2
    erotic betrayal 20, 24–5
    female susceptibility 75, 198
    patriarchal oppression 1, 2, 21–3,
      25, 57, 60, 73–4, 82, 86, 93,
      175–6
    socially-sanctioned abuse 3,
      21–2
  literary love-madness 2, 20, 22–4,
    39nn.104–8, 76
    the figure of Ophelia 39n.108,
      40n.120, 98n.26
    pathos obscures male injury 21–2,
      24, 25, 42
    sentimental versions 21–2, 24, 25,
      27, 29, 57–8, 60–1, 81, 73, 173,
      183

232   *Index*

love-madness (*cont.*)
  love-madness revised 24–30, 57, 174,
    197–8
    insistence on female reason 74,
      109
    patriarchal power exposed 25,
      41–2, 57–61, 73, 95, 175, 203–4
    rejection of female fragility and
      instability 57, 73–5, 77
    rejection of gendered view of mind
      25, 42, 73
    reversal of previous formulas 175,
      197
    male love-madness 26–9, 73, 90–4,
      197
  symptomology:
    affective blankness 58, 78
    cognitive dislocation 21, 58
    erasure of self 24, 78
    fatality 21, 28, 41, 73, 78, 82,
      86–7, 90–3
    hysteria 81, 86
    mania 20, 39n.104, 59–61, 125
    melancholia 20, 21, 73, 76–7, 70,
      80
    mental distraction 21, 78, 173
    passivity 20, 30, 57, 76, 78, 113
    violence 30, 39n.104, 60
    voyeur-spectators 21–2, 24, 59–60,
      76

Mackenzie, Henry: *The Man of Feeling*
  20, 22–4, 39n.114, 57, 60–1,
  175
Mandeville, Bernard 16
mania 3, 5, 15, 27, 33n.31, 39n.104,
  58, 59–60, 85, 97, 110–11, 134,
  137, 159, 176, 186–8, 200n.19,
  203
  deforms all concepts and ideas 15,
    87
  excess imagination and passion 58,
    87
  excitement and wildness 36n.69, 87,
    137, 178
  frenzy 87, 91, 119, 144, 176, 179,
    187–8

hysterical mania 20, 186, 188
  fury, wildness, rage 5, 15, 58, 87,
    70n.51, 87
  laughter 60, 87
  violence 58, 87, 110
melancholic mania 20, 46, 68n.19,
  139, 192
  mental vacancy 20
  passivity 20, 60
  sorrow 20, 46
monomania 125, 189, 192
uncontrollable imagination and
  thoughts 15, 58, 87
marriage 42, 56, 59–61, 65, 80, 105,
  123, 125, 143, 150, 163, 176,
  200n.27
  avenue of male control 1, 21, 52–3,
    60, 84
  confinement 47, 51, 57, 64
  destroys wife's autonomy,
    happiness, and mental health 41,
    45, 49, 54, 63, 84
  husbands' legal power 45, 51–2,
    62–5, 66n.1, 124, 203, 206
  marital cruelty and abuse 50–2,
    62, 172n.90
  separation and divorce 52, 63–4,
    71n.68
  erotic love outside marriage 78–9,
    86
  stigma and extramarital sex 117,
    121
  patriarchal marriage 25–6, 124,
    133n.66
  wife-training 151, 154, 161–2
Martin, Philip 21, 33n.31, 39n.114,
  40n.119, 58, 76
Marshall, Nowell 199n.14
Mason, Nicholas 169n.62
Matthew, Patricia 170n.68
Matthews, S. Leigh 70n.58
May, Larry, and Robert Strikwerda
  115
Mayo, Robert 39n.106
McAllister, Marie 164n.1
McCann, Andrew 171n.78, 172n.94
McInelly, Brett C. 169n.53

Index

233

medical profession, misogyny of 18
women's mental afflictions 1–3, 24,
13, 33n.31, 44, 62, 102
women incarcerated in mental
institutions 44
See also hysteria; hypochondriasis;
mania; melancholia
medical terminology modern, 5–9
functional (conversion) disorders 6,
32n.12, 132n.62, 141
mental illness 1, 6, 8, 12, 15, 17, 27,
38n.102, 62, 71n.65, 73, 108,
122, 132n.62, 136, 146, 148,
184, 208
paranoia 134, 144–5, 148
psychiatry 6, 13–14, 35n.56, 122
the unconscious mind 120, 136, 149,
158, 178
Meek, Heather 8, 18, 49, 69n.33,
71n.65
melancholia 2–3, 5, 15–16, 25,
36nn.70–2, 41, 43, 53–5, 58,
73, 80, 97n.15, 102, 137, 190,
199n.14
etiology 5, 12, 25, 137, 148
affective response to injury 27, 42,
103
emotional shock 92
entrapment in male power systems
48, 54, 56, 101, 103
romantic imagination 28, 57, 78,
114, 125, 151
hypochondria and 6, 17–18
hysteria and 6, 15, 17, 26, 37n.89,
106–7
mania and 6, 15–16, 46, 85, 134,
139, 159, 176
melancholic sensibility and genius 16,
36n.74, 36n.76, 45, 54, 68n.19,
69n.37, 76–7, 159
symptomology 36n.69
delirium 137
despair 110
disproportionate reflection,
delusion 15, 16, 43, 135
fatality 5, 26, 82, 90, 101, 122,
124, 164

indolence, listlessness, torpor 43,
46, 52, 139
lowness of spirits 43
sadness and fear 15–16, 20, 80,
97n.13, 139–40
suicidal ideation 41, 43, 123, 138
Mellor, Anne K. 66n.2
men of feeling 20–3, 95, 181, 183
libertine men of feeling 24, 87, 89
and madness 91, 94
susceptibility to mental and physical
afflictions 88
sentimental pleasure of pity, 58, 60
mental afflictions, forms of:
affective disorders 5, 11, 13, 87, 103,
107, 113, 128n.7, 135, 157,
176, 199n.13
blankness 52, 58, 81, 113,
119–20
disrupted emotional balance 4, 59,
117
physical effects of shock 103,
106–7, 116–117
cognitive disorders 5, 11, 20, 46, 53,
58, 112, 115, 135
delirium 88, 109, 113, 137, 140
dislocation 58, 82, 119
madness of cognitive affliction 11,
13, 176
stupor 113, 115, 124, 188–9
dementia (dotage) 12, 53, 200n.22
disordered motor control 4–5,
32n.12, 186
catalepsy 188
fainting and swoons 5, 13, 18, 81,
88, 91–2, 106, 108, 112, 116,
122, 124, 186
palpitations 18, 88, 107
paralysis 5, 8, 17, 32n.12, 82
trembling 42, 112, 159, 186
passions disorders of 11, 13, 59
mental afflictions, etiological theories
of:
moral failure and 91, 142, 204
physiological model 10, 34n.38
aberrant female body 3, 7, 17, 19,
29, 116–17, 142

mental afflictions, etiological theories of: (*cont.*)
  physiological model (*cont.*)
    disordered nervous system 7, 11–13, 16–19, 25, 33n.33, 34n.47, 36n.70, 37n.91, 42–3, 49–51, 61, 81–2, 85, 88, 106–7, 117, 129n.14, 131n.39, 186
    somatic effects 12–13, 17, 19, 34n.38, 34n.40, 35n.64, 41, 117, 132n.62
   predispositional 7, 34n.38, 88, 99n.42, 107
   sociological model 42, 65, 119, 130n.33
    patriarchal oppression 1–2, 21–3, 25, 27, 41, 45, 50, 57, 59, 60–2, 85–6, 93, 104, 175–6
mental afflictions, remedies for:
  curing phobias 198n.1
  healing disordered passions 136–8, 150, 164
  healing hysteria 17–18
  reformation of men 27, 52, 87, 94–5, 135, 163
  righting wrong associations 27, 135–6, 146–7, 163–4, 165n.8
  women helping one another 3, 66, 125, 135, 138, 148–9, 164
  writing 49, 69n.30
  See also moral management
mental afflictions, women's:
  etiology revised:
    emotional response to circumstances 3, 5, 7, 43, 47, 77, 103, 106
    male-inflicted injuries 1–3, 5, 23, 25, 41, 44–5, 50, 59, 66, 81, 101, 106, 117–19, 134–5, 175
    mistaken associations, passions, and remorse 3, 27, 29, 80, 135, 160
  the figure of Ophelia 39n.108, 40n.120, 98n.26

traditional etiologies:
  dysfunctional reproductive system 3, 17–20, 37n.82, 116, 38n.101, 110, 116, 133, 141
  female debility and disorder 1, 3, 7, 12–13, 29, 33n.32, 37n.81, 38n.93, 41, 61, 117, 122, 142
  nervous predisposition 7, 12, 82, 99n.42, 106
  tenuous sanity 59
mental institutions 35nn.56–8
  Bedlam (Bethlehem) Hospital 15, 22, 36n.67, 39n.111, 39n.114, 57, 59
  Wollstonecraft's visit to 70n.49
  mansions of despair, 46, 51
  in Opie's *The Father and Daughter* 173–4, 176, 179–80, 182, 185, 187, 192–5
  Opie's visit to local 'bedlam' 173–174
  physical deprivation and restraint 14, 180
  Pinel's Salpêtrière and Bicêtre 14
  Tuke's Retreat at York 14, 166n.22, 200n.21
  in Wollstonecraft's *Wrongs of Women* 44, 46–7, 51, 53–5, 58–9, 63–5
  wrongful confinement of women 44–6, 63
  See also moral management
Methodism 146, 169n.53
  and mental affliction 27, 134, 145–6, 149, 165n.2
Micale, Mark 17–20, 37n.82, 38n.97, 88, 117
Milton, John: *Paradise Lost* 101, 103–4
misogyny 9, 82, 84–5, 103, 104, 113
  biblical authority for 103
  doctors and medical authors 174
Montwieler, Katherine 168n.44
Moore, Edward, and Henry Brooke 127, 133n.66
Moore, Lisa 168n.46
moral management 14–15, 27, 35n.63, 137–8, 147, 169n.58, 179–80

Index

Mullan, John 37n.91, 49, 61, 88
Myers Mitzi, 151, 162, 164, 169n.62,
    170n.70

nervous afflictions (nerves) 7, 10–12,
    18, 33n.33, 34n.40, 44–5, 50,
    82, 85, 106, 129n.14, 131n.39
  and female reproductive system
    17–19, 110, 116–17, 134
  and female weakness and delicacy
    12–13, 18–19, 34n.47, 37n.89,
    61, 81, 88, 134
    susceptibility of genteel women 12,
      49–50
  sensibility and 'finer' nerves 16,
    37n.91, 49–51, 88
  triggers:
    excessive passions 13, 82, 106–7
    excitement and trauma 12–13, 25,
      51, 88, 106
    mental harassment 51
nymphomania 19–20, 38n.101, 110,
    211
  erotic imagination and bodily
    pathology 110, 129n.20
  pathologizing female desire 211
  furor uterinus 19

O'Connell, Lisa 200n.27
Opie, Amelia 1, 3, 28–9, 199n.16
  encounters with the mentally afflicted
    173
  Wollstonecraft and Godwin 30n.2,
    196
Opie, Amelia: *The Father and Daughter*
    28–9
  Agnes's madness 174, 185
    cognitive breakdown 187, 190
    emotional shock and death 190–1
    guilt over betrayal of father 186–7,
      189, 192
    hysteria and mania 186–8, 194,
      200n.19
    patriarchal response to 183–4
    responsible for her own
      afflictions 174, 176, 186, 190–1,
      200n.22

  suicidal ideation 188, 189–90
  Agnes's mental strength and moral
    courage 175, 191–2, 194,
    201n.34
    determination to cure father 192–3
    psychologically robust at first 191
    self-presentation 193–4
    willingness to labour 192
  Clifford's libertinism 182–3, 185,
    201n.30
  Fanny and Caroline, moral agents
    194–6
  Mr Fitzhenry's madness 175–6,
    188–90, 198n.7, 199n.11,
    199n.14, 200n.22
    Agnes's betrayal 178–9
    cognitive breakdown 176
    love-madness 28–9, 173–5
    moral management 180, 200n.21
    weakness of patriarchal power
      175–7, 180–2
  Opie rejects theories of mental
    affliction:
    double victimization 197, 199n.12
    patriarchal etiology 175, 187,
      197–8
    physiological models 28, 174–5,
      197
    sentimental models 177–8
  sensibility 186, 189, 191
  sexual transgression and penitence
    196–7, 201n.38
    Magdalen asylum 202n.46
O'Quinn, Daniel 69n.38

Pargeter, William 165n.2, 168n.51
passions 59, 147, 165n.4
  both cause and symptom of madness
    135, 137–8
  disorders of the passions 11, 59, 107,
    112, 136–7, 139, 141, 144–5
  misplaced passions 3, 27, 135–6,
    150, 158
  negative passions 13, 137–8, 142,
    150
  toxic to reason 59, 110
dreams and 158–9

Index

passions (*cont.*)
  female susceptibility to 13, 38n.93
  moderation and rebalancing 137,
    139, 150, 164, 169n.61
  unwholesome and dangerous 59,
    70n.56, 138, 159
  violent passions temporary madness
    168n.49
patriarchy 5, 23, 41–2, 98n.30, 128n.3,
  184, 197, 212
  anti-patriarchal views 27, 57,
    199n.11
  control of women 48, 61, 74, 83, 85,
    93–4, 100n.52, 104, 112, 162,
    164, 203–4
    destroys desire for autonomy 42,
      57
    drives women mad 1, 5, 8–9, 21–3,
      25, 27, 29, 44–5, 57, 59–60,
      73–4, 82, 86, 93, 175–6
    fear of female sexual independence
      85, 174
    socially-sanctioned abuse 3, 62,
      84, 117–19, 130n.26
    love and marriage 56–7, 74, 83–5
  patriarchal power demystified 161–2,
    176, 187
  weak, ineffective patriarchs 29, 175,
    180–3, 194
Perry, Ruth 143, 168n.44
Pinel, Philippe 11, 14, 37n.82, 122,
  129n.20, 137, 138, 148–9,
  166n.24
Poovey, Mary 67n.3, 69n.40, 71n.67
Porter, Roy 12, 14, 31n.9, 35n.56,
  36n.65, 44, 59, 82, 147
Purdie, Susan, and Sarah Oliver 130n.26

Radden, Jennifer 16, 34n.38, 35n.64,
  36n.72, 45, 68n.19, 69n.37, 77,
  97n.13
rape 27, 105, 114–19, 131n.45,
  132nn.52–3, 132n.63
  as a property crime 118–19
  rarely prosecuted 118, 131n.42,
    131n.47
  stigma 101, 118, 131n.41

trauma 101, 106, 115–16, 119,
  120, 122, 127n.2, 130nn.33–5,
  132n.57
  in *The Victim of Prejudice* 114–19
Rhys, Jean, *Wide Sargasso Sea*:
  Antoinette's (Bertha's) madness:
    damaged by abuse 203–8
    destruction of self 209
    not inherited 204, 207, 210–11
    supposed sexual promiscuity 210
    Brontë's *Jane Eyre* and 203–4,
      209, 212
  patriarchal power 203–8
  Wollstonecraft, Fenwick, Hays 203–4
Richardson, Alan 48
Richardson, Samuel 85, 98n.35, 99n.48
Risse, Guenter 88n.42
Rosenberg, Jordana 169n.62
Rousseau, G. S. 6, 7, 12, 18, 32n.13,
  34n.39, 34n.43, 34n.47, 37n.89,
  39n.104, 88, 129n.14
Rousseau, Jean-Jacques, 3–4
  Émile; or, On Education 27,
    30nn.3–4, 73, 79, 83, 85,
    90, 96n.2, 128n.6, 151, 163,
    171n.77
  Julie: ou, La Nouvelle Héloïse 4, 41,
    49, 55–7, 69n.41, 70n.45, 78–9,
    90
Rousseauvian education of women 1,
  26, 31n.5, 128n.6, 134, 143,
  151, 157, 164, 171n.78
  training women to please men 4,
    31n.7, 77, 79, 83–4
  female passivity 26, 28
  female sensibility, ignorance, and
    innocence 151, 154, 161
  male sexual fantasy 28, 79–80,
    151, 153–4, 158, 161–3
  social and intellectual isolation 26,
    28, 73–4, 82, 128n.6, 153
  wife-training 83–4, 151, 153,
    170n.70
  critique of 26, 28, 151, 86, 153
  Edgeworth 162–3, 170n.70,
    171nn.76–8, 171n.80, 171n.84,
    172n.99

Wollstonecraft 30nn.3–4, 31n.5, 56–7, 70n.45
See also Bernardin de Saint-Pierre, Jacques-Henri; Day, Thomas; Fordyce, James; imagination, romantic; Gregory, John
Rush, Benjamin 14

Sadow, Jonathan 96n.4
Saint-Pierre. *See* Bernadin de Saint-Pierre
sapphic readings 96n.4, 100n.53, 168n.44, 168n.46
Scott, Sir Walter 39n.104
Scull, Andrew 11, 14–15, 35n.63, 44, 147
sensibility 3, 16, 67n.3, 68n.18, 77, 88, 95, 102, 175, 183, 201n.30
    excess of 37n.91, 125, 189
    feminine 3, 37n.91, 50, 73, 79, 92, 114, 124, 151, 153–4, 159, 186, 191
    impact on readers 23, 54
    literature of 49, 61
        anesthetizes and injures women 25–6, 42, 45, 48, 54, 57, 61
        and romantic imagination 25–6, 42, 45, 48, 54, 175
        Rousseau's *Julie: ou, La Nouvelle Hélöise* 55–8
    and melancholy 16, 36n.76 45, 49–50, 61, 77, 88, 124
sentimentalism 1, 39n.115, 52, 177, 179, 195
    and female madness 2, 26–7, 29, 81, 101, 173–4, 193, 198n.7
    sentimental literature 3, 20, 22–4, 39n.105, 39n.108, 39n.115, 49, 55–6, 60, 92, 116, 141, 185
    avenue of male control 25, 27, 30, 41–2, 45, 63, 134, 180, 183
    sentimental suffering 22, 57, 60, 88, 198n.7, 202n.41
    viewing the mad 57–8, 173, 178
    sympathy 36n.76, 39n.115
    weak and sentimental patriarchs 181–3, 193–5

sexuality, female 8, 17, 20, 28, 38n.101, 39n.108, 50, 69n.41, 76, 78, 91–2, 103, 106–8, 114, 116, 174
    desire 19, 21, 124, 129n.29, 157
    male constructions of 8, 20, 116
        chastity a male invention 127
        female pursuit of pleasure aberrant 120–1
        over-sexualization 2, 4, 105, 182
        passivity 4, 28, 78, 116
        Rousseau and 102, 151, 154, 162
        taint of sexual knowledge 106
        women as desirable children 4, 28
    sexual agency and autonomy 51, 56, 63–4, 71n.67, 78–9
    patriarchal fear of 85
    sexual license:
        and madness 78, 119, 122, 185, 210
        promiscuity and guilt 108–9
        transgressive sexuality, 94, 104, 110, 120, 140–1, 174, 183, 196–7, 211
    social stigma 102, 108, 110, 121, 114, 179, 192, 194
        'fallen' or 'ruined' women 108, 110–12, 119, 121–2, 127n.1, 182–3, 185
        prostitution, illness, death 107–8
    socio-sexual hierarchy 103
sexuality, male:
    assault and abuse 10, 27, 105, 108, 111, 114–16, 120, 130n.25, 132n.57, 206, 209. *See also* rape
    predation 21, 49, 71n.71, 104–5, 127
    desire 116, 153–5, 157
    objectification of women 28, 60, 86, 95, 105, 119, 130n.26, 132n.52
    sexual fantasy 28, 151, 153, 155, 182
    See also libertinism
Shafer, Carolyn, and Marilyn Frye 119, 132n.52, 132n.64
Shakespeare, William 39n.108, 40n.120, 98n.26, 173, 200n.18

Sharpe, Ada, and Eleanor Ty 128n.3,
133n.68
Shelley, Mary 129n.20
Sherman, Sandra 119, 129n.23
Showalter, Elaine 8–9, 38n.102, 76,
98n.26, 99n.50
Skultans, Vieda 14, 15, 36n.70, 138
Sloan, Margaret Kathryn 127n.2
Small, Helen 7–9, 20, 29, 33n.29,
33n.31, 39n.108, 40n.120,
57–9
Snow, Malinda 96n.4
spleen, the 12, 15–18, 36n.70, 44, 141
Staves, Susan 20, 174, 201n.38,
202n.46
Sterne, Laurence: *Sentimental Journey*
40n.118, 60
'Mad Maria' 20, 23–4, 57, 59, 76
Yorick's sentimental tears 23
sublime, the 16, 77, 80
suicide 41–3, 64, 65–6, 71n.70, 72n.72,
123, 171n.73
Suzuki, Akihito 7, 13–14, 33n.32
Sydenham, Thomas 37n.82, 88
sympathy 16, 36n.76, 39n.115, 55,
60, 76, 89, 110, 123, 131n.38,
136–7, 150, 203
and reader engagement 76, 111

Temple, Kathryn 64
Terry, Richard 97n.15
Thame, David 140–1, 149, 156,
165nn.1–2, 165n.8, 168n.51,
169.58, 169n.61, 170n.67, 174,
198n.3, 198n.7
Tong, Joanne 180, 181, 190, 199n.11,
199n.13, 200n.23, 202n.42
Trouille, Mary 30n.4
Tuke, Samuel 166n.24
Tuke, William 14, 147, 166n.22
See also moral management
Ty, Eleanor 120, 129n.18, 130n.35,
133n.68, 200n.18

vapours, the 12, 15, 17, 18, 44, 116
Veith, Ilza 116, 129n.20, 129n.24
Vickers, Neil 7

Walker, Gina Luria 102, 128n.12,
130n.35
Wallace, Miriam 83, 96n.4, 104–5,
113, 115, 127n.2, 128n.8,
130n.25, 130nn.34–5
Watson, Nicola 30n.4, 75, 79
Weiner, Dora 35n.59
Wesley, John 146, 169n.52
West Indies, the:
British colonialism 172n.90, 203,
205
obeah 209
slavery 172n.94, 204
Whisnant, Rebecca 118
Whitehead, James 36n.74
Whytt, Robert 12–13, 18, 82, 88, 106,
112, 131n.39
Williams, Helen Maria 152, 166n.26,
171n.84
Willis, Thomas 15, 18, 37n.82
Wollstonecraft, Mary 2, 43, 45, 95,
70n.49, 101–2, 109, 151
on injustices of marriage 124
*Letters Written During a Short
Residence* 46, 68n.12
and Mackenzie 57
and Rousseau 4, 30n.4, 31n.5, 151
sensibility of 67n.3, 68n.18
sentimental literature and male
power 25–6, 42, 45, 55–8
*A Vindication of the Rights of
Woman* 2, 4, 42, 44, 50, 109,
171n.73
Wollstonecraft's own mental health
42–3, 45, 67n.7, 71n.70
Wollstonecraft, Mary: *The Wrongs of
Women; or, Maria* 1, 4, 25–6,
41–66, 126, 199n.12
Maria in the madhouse 41, 57–61
horror and fear of madness 46,
58–9
mental imprisonment 45
metaphor for repression 42, 44,
47
and romantic fantasies 49
Maria's melancholia 41, 45–6, 51,
54–5

patriarchal power and women's
  mental afflictions 25, 42, 44, 47,
    53, 61–2, 175
  creating fragility 57, 61
  eroticizing mentally afflicted
    women 58
  law 25, 42, 44–5, 51–3, 62–4, 118,
    131n.42, 203, 207–8
  medicine 1, 3, 42, 45–53, 57, 208
  repressions of marriage 25, 41–2,
    45, 47, 49–53, 61

resisting the madhouse 47–9, 71n.66
romantic imagination 55–6, 65
  dangers of 25–6, 42, 45, 48, 53–5
seriousness of female feeling 43, 64
  the right to act accordingly 62–3
sexual liberation, 62–3, 71n.67
suicidal ideation 41, 72n.72

Yeazell, Ruth Bernard 171n.86

www.ingramcontent.com/pod-product-compliance
Ingram Content Group UK Ltd.
Pitfield, Milton Keynes, MK11 3LW, UK
UKHW021448160125
4146UKWH00007B/304